arts & architecture

The Entenza Years

arts & architecture

The Entenza Years

Edited by Barbara Goldstein/Essay by Esther McCoy

The MIT Press, Cambridge, Massachusetts, and London, England

DEDICATED TO THE MEMORY OF JOHN ENTENZA AND ESTHER MCCOY

Dust jacket: collection of original covers includes Ray Eames,
   April 1942; Hans Hofmann, November 1949, February 1956;
   Herbert Matter, April 1942, January 1946, June 1946,
   September 1946; Fred Usher, June 1949; Alvin Lustig, June
   1948; Charles Kratka, August 1949, September 1956; Meek,
   October, 1948; Rex Goode, July 1959.

The publication of this book was made possible by support from
   the Visual Arts Program, California Arts Council, a state
   agency;the Design Arts Program, National Endowment for the
   Arts, a federal agency; the Graham Foundation for Advanced
   Studies in the Fine Arts; Cesar Pelli and Diana Balmori.

This book contains pages reproduced from the original
   Arts & Architecture magazine, spanning the years 1943
   through 1959.

Photograph of John Entenza and Charles Eames on page 7,
   courtesy of The Eames Office. Photograph of John Entenza on
   page 9 and photograph of R. Buckminster Fuller and John
   Entenza on page 10, courtesy of the Graham Foundation.
   Photograph of Esther McCoy on page13, courtesy of Deborah
   Sussman and Paul Prezja.

Editor:
   Barbara Goldstein
Editorial Assistant:
   Noel Millea
Art Director:
   Lorraine Wild
Designer:
   Robin Cottle

Introduction, newly typeset articles and continuation pages
   set in Bodoni, City and Metro by Ad Compositors,
   Los Angeles, California.
Printed by Columbia Lithograph, Inc., Santa Fe Springs, California.
Copyright © 1990 by Massachusetts Institute of Technology

Library of Congress Cataloging-in-Publication Data
Arts & Architecture, The Entenza Years, edited by Barbara
Goldstein: essay by Esther McCoy.
      p. cm.
      ISBN 0-262-07131-2
   1. Arts, Modern - 20th century. 2. Modernism (Art) I. Entenza,
   John, 1903-1984. II. Goldstein, Barbara. III. McCoy, Esther. IV.
   Arts & Architecture.
NX456.5.M64A7 1990
700'.9'04--dc20   90-5855 CIP

Acknowledgments

MANY PEOPLE CONTRIBUTED to the creation of this book, first and foremost John Entenza
and Esther McCoy to whom it is dedicated. My contact with Entenza was brief, but
intense, confined to a few visits during his convalescence and retirement in La Jolla.
Despite his impaired speech, we managed to strike up a friendly dialogue, and I learned
to know his judgment, taste and wit. I spent many enjoyable hours with Esther McCoy
discussing, among other subjects, Arts & Architecture and John Entenza. She acted as
my conscience and energy-source throughout the project until her death late last year.

The staff of ARTS + ARCHITECTURE magazine in the 1980s—Laurie Garris,
Leslie Clagett, Bruno Giberti, and Dan Moyer—were involved in the early development
of this project. David Travers, publisher of ARTS & ARCHITECTURE from 1962-67,
graciously granted me the right to reproduce pages of the magazine here. John Entenza's
friends, colleagues and contemporaries: June Wayne, Felix Candela, Craig Ellwood,
Edward Frank, Julius Shulman, Judith Wachsmann, Carter Manny, Cesar Pelli,
Marvin Rand, Deborah Sussman and Paul Prezja all contributed to my thinking about
this book. Ed Killingsworth and Elaine K. Sewell Jones were particularly generous with
their time, and both loaned me old issues of ARTS & ARCHITECTURE for reproduction,
as did Allen Jutzi of the Huntington Library. The Architecture Foundation of Los
Angeles and Astro Artz shepherded grants for this book through the California Arts
Council and the National Endowment for the Arts, respectively. May Babitz helped me
to locate old copies of the magazine. Lorraine Wild was instrumental in assisting with the
graphic organization, and Robin Cottle contributed long, patient hours to its final
design. Noel Millea aided in the organization and research; and my husband, John
Pastier, encouraged me to complete what often seemed like an endless project. To these,
and many others who helped along the way, I offer my thanks.

BARBARA GOLDSTEIN

Chronology/Contents

THE '30S AND '40S WERE A PERIOD OF GREAT leavening in California architecture. They were years when high ideals and optimism dictated a change from the living patterns that came before. There was a sincere belief in the goodness of technology, and a faith that design could solve many of society's problems. And John Dymock Entenza was at the heart of this movement.

Entenza published and edited *Arts & Architecture* magazine from 1938 until 1962 . During those years, his efforts changed public perception of California architecture and design, and influenced the shape of architecture worldwide. Within the pages of *Arts & Architecture* he championed the cause of modernism in architecture and the other arts, and perfected a genre of magazine which many have emulated since.

This book examines that era through the pages of the magazine, selecting articles from the period 1943-59, when Entenza's presence was most evident. It presents a slice of modern culture, and describes America's last "moral" era, a time, according to Esther McCoy, when "people stood together," or shared a common belief in the correctness of their actions.

Although the Case Study House program is the best-remembered aspect of *Arts & Architecture* magazine, the cultural climate which produced that program was of enormous significance. This book centers on the articles which surrounded that program, illuminating the intellectual ambience of the era. It celebrates the years when the magazine's contents were most inspiring, and demonstrates the complexion of the time through articles published before and during the Case Study House program.

Arts & Architecture magazine was inclusive rather than focused on a single subject. It encompassed all aspects of contemporary culture, from architecture and design to music and theatre. An individual issue was likely to contain a lengthy column on modern music, a review of a current art gallery exhibition, an article on pottery, jewelry or textiles as well as new ideas on architecture. John Entenza believed in the importance of integrating the arts, and his magazine stimulated the practical development of that idea.

The magazine also had a strong social agenda. Like so many intellectuals of his time, John Entenza was socially-motivated, and he used the magazine to express his ideals both in his own voice, and through the words of others. His editorial column, "Notes in Passing" discussed political conditions far more frequently than design issues, and the magazine contained articles examining on race relations, human rights, and child care. Many of these articles, like Dalton Trumbo's 1943 "Minorities and the Screen," and Jules Langsner's 1951 McCarthy Era "Art Summoned Before the Inquisition," have great resonance today.

John Entenza didn't come early to architecture. Born in 1903 in Michigan, he was the son of a Scottish mining heiress and a Spanish attorney involved in veterans' and migrant workers' issues.

He studied liberal arts at Tulane University and the University of Virginia in Charlottesville. After preparatory training for the diplomatic service with the Department of Labor in Washington, D.C., his career path changed, and he moved to California.

From 1932-36, Entenza worked in an MGM experimental film production unit, under Paul Bern and Irving Pitchel. The unit folded during the Depression and, soon after, Entenza's passion for in architecture was sparked. Always interested in the design of boats, he began to develop a fascination with modern architecture when his father's partner commissioned, then rejected, a house design by Harwell Hamilton Harris. Entenza commissioned Harris to build him a house in 1937, and later, through his father's partner, he began working as an editor of *California Arts & Architecture* magazine, a rather staid provincial publication focusing on local residential architecture and gardening. Within two years, Entenza had purchased the magazine and begun redirecting it.

John Entenza's friends describe him as a very moral man with a strong work ethic, the result of a "good Presbyterian upbringing." He was dignified and immaculate, usually dressed in a dark suit and polished shoes. At the same time, he enjoyed his comfort, and being surrounded by friends. He seldom arrived at the office before noon, had a caustic wit, and loved gossip. A lifelong bachelor, he lived for many years with his adopted son, Kenneth, a homeless teenager who had been living on the beach when Entenza met him during the Depression.

In 1938, when Entenza began working at *California Arts & Architecture*, the magazine had been in existence for 27 years, beginning as the *Pacific Builder*, and evolving from a trade magazine to a genteel regional publisher of homes, gardens and theatre reviews. As Entenza became involved, the magazine rapidly transformed further. By 1939, it was beginning to publish a substantial amount of modern architecture and, by 1943, he had completely overhauled the magazine, dropping "California" from the name, and building an advisory team that included Dorothy Liebes, Gregory Ain, Sumner Spalding, Grace Clements, Peter Yates, Richard Neutra. Southern California proved fertile ground for this effort, attracting people interested in the movie industry and European intellectuals fleeing Hitler. The new *Arts & Architecture*, a large format, slim publication designed by Alvin Lustig, was to have worldwide influence.

The early years were stirring, tumultuous, writ against the backdrop of America preparing for war, anticipating dramatic changes in lifestyle, and facing severe material shortages. Entenza

Charles Eames and John Entenza

viewed these changes from a positive perspective and transformed them into a quest for postwar housing design. In 1943, the magazine featured a precursor to the Case Study House program, a competition for the design of a small, modern, worker's-family house, sponsored by twenty-two materials manufacturers and entitled "Design for Postwar Living." Hundreds of submissions were received, and the magazine immediately published the three winners—architects Saarinen and Lundquist, Pei and Duhart, and Soriano—and continued to publish other schemes for the remainder of the year. In 1944, *Arts & Architecture* followed this competition with a long, inventive discussion of prefabricated housing by R. Buckminster Fuller, Eero Saarinen, Herbert Matter and Charles Eames.

Producing a magazine is a collaborative effort and, to succeed, an editor requires both a vision and antennae for ideas which enhance and illustrate it. A great believer in talent, Entenza surrounded himself with the most creative artistic and design minds of the era, and published their work. He encouraged designers to express new ideas through the magazine, and as a result, *Arts & Architecture* was among the first magazines in America to present the work of Hans Hofmann, Craig Ellwood, Margaret DePatta, George Nakashima, Bernard Rosenthal, Charles Eames, Konrad Wachsmann, and others. He drew talented writers, graphic designers and photographers to the magazine, although he seldom paid for their efforts. Intensely loyal, he published work by his most admired artists and architects frequently.

The population of contributors changed as Entenza discovered new ideas and as differences developed with old contributors. A highly opinionated and autocratic individual, his fervor sometimes cost him friends. During the 1940s, Charles Eames was a big influence on Entenza, contributing articles, and introducing ideas. The Eames House, a 1949 Case Study, remains

John Entenza

R. Buckminster Fuller & John Entenza

Ray Eames
Cover of Arts & Architecture,
January, 1944

the most celebrated house in the program. However, the friendship between Eames and Entenza deteriorated in the early 1950s after the Plyformed Wood Company, a joint business venture to produce molded plywood splints and airplane components for the war effort, ended in a law suit.

     Arts & Architecture built its reputation as a showcase for new talent. When architects travelled to Los Angeles from the East Coast or Europe, they visited Entenza. When young designers felt they had produced something significant, they sent it to *Arts & Architecture*. Ed Killingsworth recalls visiting the magazine office and seeing Entenza's desk "piled high with goodies"—the work of architects and designers from around the world hoping to be published in its pages. The magazine was the first to publish many well-known architects from A. Quincy Jones and Harry Seidler to Paul Rudolph and Ray Kappe. Because of its reputation, both nationally and internationally, publication in *Arts & Architecture* usually led to far broader recognition.

     Beginning in January 1945, the Case Study House program promoted an aesthetically rigorous vision of postwar housing. The program, characterized by its allegiance to social and aesthetic ideals, was noteworthy for the youth and enthusiasm of its practitioners. These included, among others, Charles Eames, Richard Neutra, Craig Ellwood, Ralph Rapson and Pierre Koenig. The Case Study House program also improved the health of the magazine. Based on actual construction and a commitment to the innovative use of new and existing materials, the program attracted advertisers who vied for participation. It was a formula which benefitted everyone involved: the clients received new products at a discount, the architects had an opportunity to experiment with new materials, and the advertisers received initial exposure as thousands visited the houses, and residual publicity in the form of republication in other national and international magazine. Nevertheless, the magazine never proved to be profitable, partly because Entenza

Herbert Matter
Cover of Arts & Architecture,
April, 1945

Frank Brother's advertisement
published in April, 1958

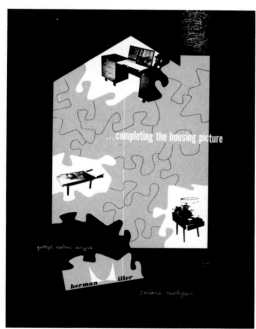

George Nelson,
Herman Miller advertisement
published in November, 1947

was as selective about the advertisers as he was about the editorial content.

Along with the Case Study Houses came the need to outfit their interiors, affording a showcase for contemporary art and furnishings. Edward Frank of Frank Brothers, a furniture showroom known for its commitment to modern European, Scandanavian and American design, consulted with the architects on their choice of furniture. Manufacturers, including Architectural Pottery, Knoll, Herman Miller, and Van Keppel-Green, received support and exposure in the process.

In parallel with the Case Studies, which offered primarily a single-family perspective, Entenza continued to publish ideas about mass-produced housing, including articles on housing tracts by Gregory Ain, Anshen and Allen, and Smith Jones and Contini, and prefabricated housing by Walter Gropius and Konrad Wachsmann. In retrospect, these articles were more prescient than the Case Studies about the future shape of housing production in America.

As the postwar years evolved into a building boom, the magazine published a greater proportion of built architecture, often by young architects. Many were in their late 20s when their designs were built and published. At the same time, *Arts & Architecture* continued its commitment to publishing long, critical articles on other aspects of culture, and explored in laymen's terms the underlying issues in visual art and music. During this period, Dore Ashton and Jules Langsner wrote regularly about contemporary art. Peter Yates, a foremost proponent of modern music, wrote lucidly about the structure of new musical forms. Frequently Entenza introduced important voices from outside

California—an interview with Hans Hofmann, a critical article by Sybil Moholy-Nagy, a discussion of art theory by Gyorgy Kepes.

In 1950, when Esther McCoy began writing for *Arts & Architecture*, the magazine assumed further depth. McCoy, who also wrote for *The Los Angeles Times Home Magazine*, already had a deep commitment to California modernism. She had written the catalogue notes on Schindler for the Roots of California Architecture show, and travelled regularly to Mexico to study its contemporary architecture. Her first major article for *Arts & Architecture* was on the architecture of Mexico. She continued to write frequently, sometimes signed, sometimes unsigned, on historic topics such as the Bradbury Building and Irving Gill, and contemporary subjects ranging from Felix Candela to contemporary Mexican and Italian architecture. McCoy and Entenza formed a powerful team: her taut writing complemented the modernism of the magazine, and Entenza trusted her eye and her judgment.

As the '50s moved into the '60s, the contents of *Arts & Architecture* became increasingly international in scope. At the same time, it seemed to lose much of its originality and edge. The cause of international modernism had been taken on by many other magazines, and much of the work published in the pages of *Arts & Architecture* assumed a familiar tone. The most interesting architectural works it published continued to be experimental, from Peter Blake's pinwheel house to Paul Rudolph's lyrical designs. In 1960, John Entenza accepted the Directorship of the Graham Foundation for Advanced Study in the Fine Arts in Chicago, where he continued to act as a lightening rod for new talent until his retirement in 1971. In 1962, he sold *Arts & Architecture* to David Travers. He died in La Jolla, California, where he had gone to retire, in April, 1984.

Epilogue

ARTS & ARCHITECTURE WAS TAKEN OVER by David Travers in 1962, John Entenza having found it burdensome to edit the magazine from Chicago. Travers continued to publish articles on art and architectural theory and design, and to introduce the work of young American and foreign architects. Notable among these were Hans Hollein, Frank Gehry, Richard Meier, Ettore Sottsass, Frei Otto, James Polshek and B.V. Doshi.

Travers enlarged the Case Study House program to include multi-family projects, —one built in 1964, one unbuilt. And, as the effects of ruthless development began to portend the poisoning and plundering of the environment in the name of progress, he began a series of single-subject issues on concerns such as water problems and air pollution in North America. Many more such issues were planned, but the end arrived first. Although the paid circulation of *Arts & Architecture* had risen from just under 8000 in 1962 to 12,500 in 1967, the lack of a parallel increase in advertising support was fatal. After 56 years, first as *Pacific Builder*, then *California Arts & Architecture* and finally *Arts & Architecture*, the magazine ceased publication in September 1967.

Fourteen years later, in September 1981, Barbara Goldstein revived *Arts & Architecture* as a quarterly publication. Changing the logo to *Arts + Architecture* to distinguish it from its predecessor, Goldstein maintained Entenza's commitment to integration in the arts. The new *Arts + Architecture* was notable for its creative graphic design by Joe Molloy and Rip Georges. Georges' style of typography and graphics became widely imitated in other publications.

Rather than being international in focus, the new *Arts + Architecture* featured the work of West Coast architects and artists who had been largely ignored by the East Coast-based art and architectural press. It was Goldstein's belief that much of the innovative cultural thinking was taking place in the West, but that there was little outlet for its publication.

Because of its infrequent publishing schedule, *Arts + Architecture* published themed issues exploring the interrelationship of architecture with the other arts, including issues on utopian thought, the landscape in art and design, artist/designer crossovers and collaborations, housing, and new museums. After fourteen issues, the magazine folded in 1985.

BARBARA GOLDSTEIN

Esther McCoy

Remembering John Entenza

WE MET AT A TIME WHEN LOS ANGELES was the wrong place to be. San Francisco was all right, but in 1932 L.A., even Santa Monica, was déclassé.

John Entenza was in his late twenties, had great dignity and an outrageous sense of humor. He sat in a puce-colored velvet chair left over from his mother's move West. We started quarrelling at once and then howled with laughter at his instructions to an ant pushing a crumb across the table. That was the key to our friendship. That and the fact that we were trying to escape from Los Angeles. But thirty years later we were both still here.

I knew him in at least five houses, only one of which met the specifications for a Case Study House prototype. Although in 1932 the closest he came to architecture was designing a boat that was never built, five years later he was commissioning a house by Harwell Hamilton Harris in Santa Monica Canyon. It was the only Harris house that had any relation to the International Style, an early indication that John's eye was focused toward Europe rather than on the native organic architecture of Frank Lloyd Wright. Then he bought *Arts & Architecture* magazine and in 1944 was writing the program for the Case Study Houses. By then I was winding up two years as an engineering draftsman at Douglas Aircraft and starting to work for R.M. Schindler. I would never have guessed that both our paths would lead to architecture.

The Case Study House program was the answer to the need for well-designed two-bedroom houses that were easy to maintain without servants. But John's own Case Study for himself, designed by Eero Saarinen and Charles Eames, was off the mark for a bachelor who hated big parties—it had a close to fifty-foot-long living room. Nor was he keen on sunlight, yet light flooded into every room except for a windowless library in the center of the house, a place to escape the sunlight and distraction, where he could write.

From 1950 on, when I wrote fairly regularly for the magazine, I would take my story and photographs to John's Case Study House and we would sit at the end of the kitchen. It must have been apparent to him that he was not a Case Study himself, for he sold the house and moved into a Neutra apartment in Westwood.

In 1962, when he finally sold *Arts & Architecture* to David Travers and moved to Chicago to head the Graham Foundation, he moved into a Mies apartment where on my two trips to Chicago we drank coffee close to the kitchen, our backs to the glass wall.

He was a man passionately devoted to the new architecture, yet obviously had sensibilities at odds with what the sun-drenched rooms and flowing plans promised. He sponsored the new furniture, much of it plywood, and yet he called me once from Chicago to ask if I knew of a really modern down-filled chair. I reminded him of his mother's puce-colored velvet chair, traditional and downy. That was the end of his search for comfort. He stuck to plywood—what he called the thirty-minute chair. As always, John's principles took precedence over comfort.

ESTHER MCCOY, 1989

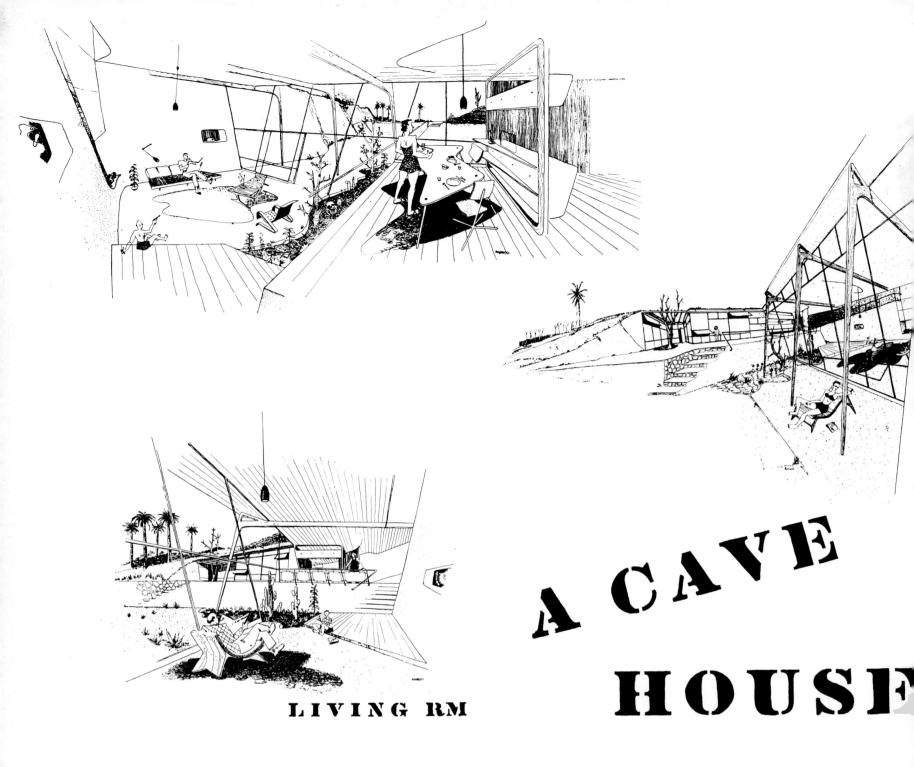

A CAVE HOUSE

LIVING RM

Basically this house is a return to an elementary principle of shelter, one of "digging" into the earth. Psychologically, this return to mother earth would be healthy and vigorous. By hewing out the earth and by covering over the roof with soil and planting, this literally becomes a house moulded around dwellers and site conditions. Although not a complete air raid shelter, this "cave" house does offer much in the way of camouflage and protection. The walls are primarily a chemically treated rammed earth, providing sound-proof, weather-proof, heat insulation and fire, water, and bug-repellent walls. Any variety of dirt can be used, with only the percentage of the bituminous asphalt emulsion varied according to the properties of the earth. The average percentage of the emulsion is 10 to 85 per cent dirt. Since the emulsion

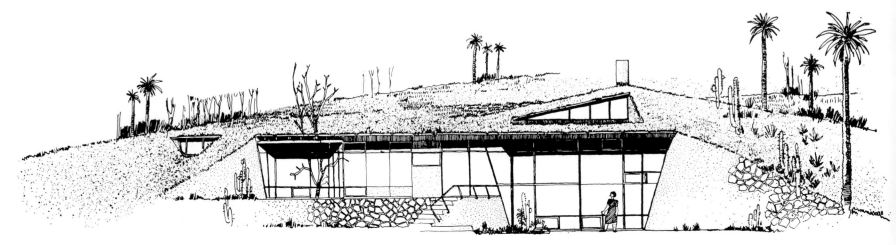

ELEVATION

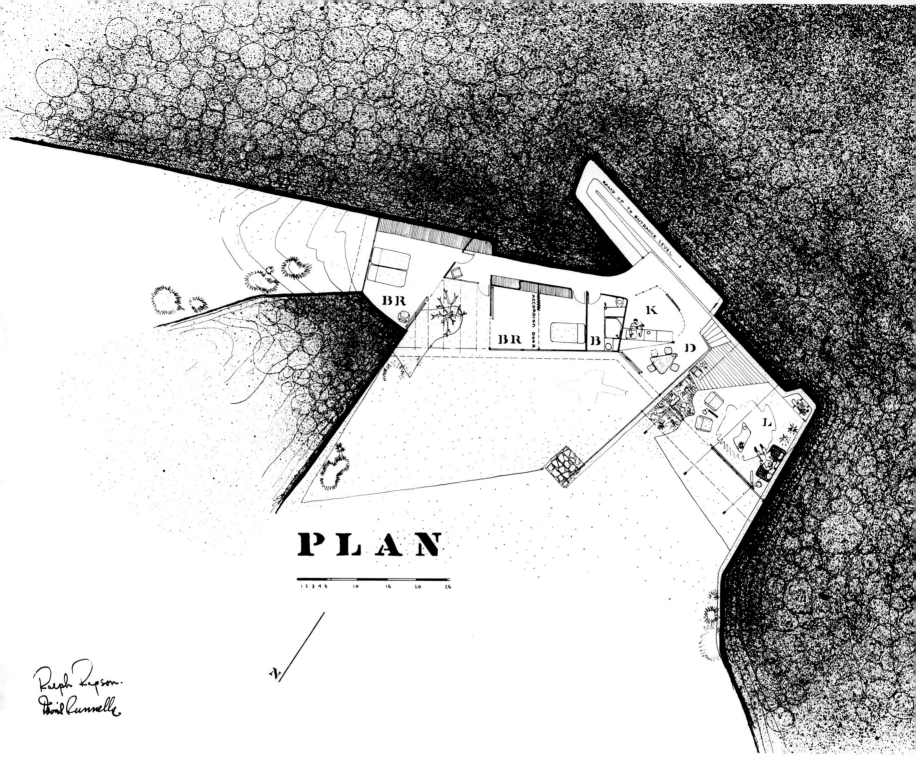

PLAN

(signatures: Ralph Rapson, David Runnells)

costs exceedingly little, 10 to 20 cents per gallon, and since the earth can be dug and rammed by unskilled labor, the resulting structure is economical and durable. In all other respects, the house can employ ordinary construction practice; however, in this case a system of plywood bents are used for the main structural members. For further protection and insulation, earth and planting are laid over the roof. Since earth maintains a constant temperature underground, and since these walls are chiefly the earth itself, very little heat is necessary. Before the walls and floors are rammed in place, pipe panels are laid in for the radiant heating system. Exposed walls can be either the traditional glass or, in this case, transparent and opaque plastics.

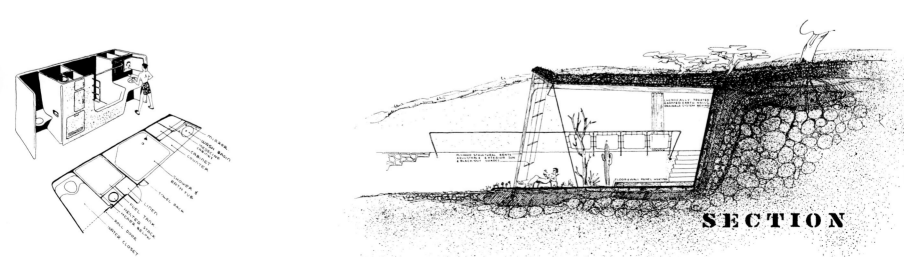

BATH and MECH. UNIT

SECTION

a prefabrication vocabulary
R. M. SCHINDLER, ARCHITECT

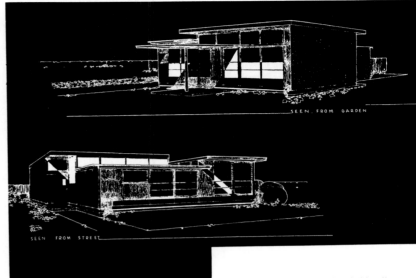

SEEN FROM GARDEN

SEEN FROM STREET

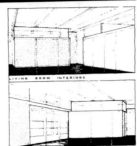

LIVING ROOM INTERIORS

the panel-post construction

1. **BUILDING:** Building is the planning and developing of a shelter problem on the basis of a sensitive response to the conditions of the locale, the time, the occupant, and the available material.

2. **PREFABRICATION:** Any brick is a prefabricated building unit. However, modern technique and transportation helps us to respond to an old tendency in building construction—to use increasingly larger building units. This urge ends in absurdity and completely eliminates "building" if we propose to deliver the whole house ready-made.

3. **PURPOSE:** Intensified prefabrication transmits the bulk of building work into the factory. The consequent increase of efficiency and the use of machinery reduces COSTS and furnishes a better product.

4. **INDIVIDUALIZATION:** The system shall permit individualization of house and garden. Unless a personal relation can be established between house and occupant, both will become meaningless cogs in a social machine without cultural possibilities. Such personal relationship insures maintenance. Prefabricated systems which confine adaptability to wall panels under a standard roof, limit development of the exterior too much to be acceptable. No rabbit hutch housing.

5. **PRODUCTION:** The market does not equal the one of the automobile. Therefore, the system should not require excessive investments in SPECIAL machinery

which would tend to over-concentrate production and increase transportation costs.

6. **STANDARDIZATION:** Machine work requires standardization. However, to safeguard life, only fractional units shall be standardized. The machine is the only tool which may produce units of such precision that they may be assembled freely and assure complete individualization of the end product.

7. **TRANSPORTATION:** Building units shall permit easy packaging and shall be light in weight. Heavy lifting equipment to handle them shall not be necessary. Size of package is limited by loading space of standard truck.

8. **FIELD WORK:** Only excessive standardization will eliminate field work completely. Sensible prefabrication will require that an occasional cut or bore be made on the job. This will be more efficient than to make, list, and ship special units for minor differences.

9. **SIMPLICITY:** It shall not be necessary to provide specially trained erection crews. The assembly shall not require superhuman precision. On the contrary, the units shall compensate slight irregularities in fabrication and erection.

10. **SPEED OF ERECTION:** Important only for emergency housing projects. The individual owner does not require a house overnight. Building his house is one of the great stimulating experiences in man's life.

11. **REGULATIONS:** The system shall be subject to all standard regulations of the various local building ordinances. Stresses shall be below permissible maximums, earthquake resistance possible.

12. **CLIMATIC CONDITIONS:** It shall be possible to adapt the system to various climatic conditions. Uniform weather resistance would be wasteful in milder climates.

13. **SOIL CONDITIONS:** Footings must be free to conform to local conditions and experiences.

14. **BUILDING PLAN:** The Units shall permit the execution of any building plan. The majority of the prefabricated systems used for the recent war housing were restricted to the execution of only one plan. The "knock-down" house is not suitable for peacetime use.

15. **MODULES:** All dimensions horizontal and vertical shall be multiples of a basic module.

16. **FLEXIBILITY:** The system shall permit additions and subtractions of partitions and rooms, and the change of size and location of all openings at any time. This demand will eliminate the "stressed skin" constructions, since alterations of this kind would upset their structural system.

17. **SALVAGE VALUE:** Units shall be demountable and reusable at any time. However, since alteration work will be only a small percentage of the field work, it shall not be necessary to use bolted connections throughout. Some hidden nailing may reduce erection cost sufficiently to compensate for a small increase in alteration costs.

18. **CONSTRUCTION JOINTS:** No attempt shall be made to conceal the joints. They are a natural consequence of a unit construction and as such shall become an architectural feature. All attempts of the "knock-down" systems to simulate monolithic construction will end in failure. Articulated joints will facilitate alterations and repairs.

19. **WEATHER-PROOFING:** All caulking, etc., necessary to tighten joints shall be inconspicuous but permanently accessible and renewable without marring the finish of the building.

20. **VERMIN-PROOF:** All hollow spaces within the construction shall be factory sealed or permanently accessible.

21. **MECHANICAL EQUIPMENT:** Heating, plumbing, and wiring systems shall be installed after building is erected. They shall be permanently accessible for repairs, alterations, and modernization. Their aging is the prime source of building depreciation.

22. **THE UNITS:** No wasteful attempt shall be made to create an artificial similarity between units serving different functions. Wall, floor, and roof panels need to be designed and surfaced differently to satisfy their use.

23. **MATERIALS:** If units are made of standard materials (wood, etc.) they shall utilize commercial sizes without waste.

24. **THE POST:** The contemporary house is not conceived as a box shape with large areas of solid walls. The prominence of its openings is its main architectural character. The only system of construction which will give both openness and flexibility is a skeleton construction. Therefore, all systems using structural wall units are inadequate. All structural loads shall be carried by POSTS separated by no structural interchangeable panels or openings.

25. **THE BASE:** The floor base shall form a dust-proof floor edge in all rooms and shall serve as a spacer for the posts.

26. **THE WALL UNIT:** Not being a structural member, it may be executed of a number of materials such as plywood, boards, plastics, metals, etc. Only a few units in each house may have to be reinforced to withstand lateral forces. (Earthquake resistance.)

27. **THE OPENINGS:** Sash and doors are factory hung and finished in frames which fit between the posts like wall units. Windows may be of any height and may be multiplied to attain any desired width.

28. **TRIM:** No trim, cover strips, or bases shall have to be installed at the time of building.

29. **THE ROOF:** Roof slopes are the necessary consequence of old-fashioned roof coverings applied in small units. Modern technique permits a continuous roof-skin which allows dead-level application. Sloping roofs shall be eliminated to simplify design and erection.

30. **BUILT-INS:** Closets, cupboards, and cabinets shall be prefabricated units.

31. **FINISH:** All units shall be factory finished. Touching up service for minor damages may be necessary after erection. However, it shall not be made impossible to change color and finish after erection if necessary.

32. **SPACE FORMS:** It shall be possible to build rooms of varying heights to permit architectural articulation in the house. Since real contemporary work is "space architecture," this requirement is basic for our architectural development.

33. **CLERESTORY:** It shall be possible to vary roof heights to allow architectural articulation of the exterior. The possibility of clerestory windows is essential for adequate ventilating and sunning of all rooms.

34. **"PANEL-POST CONSTRUCTION":** This construction scheme shall fulfill all specifications outlined above and introduce a new building material for unlimited use - the PREFABRICATED "PANEL-POST" UNIT.

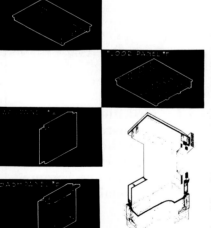

ROOF PANEL *R*

FLOOR PANEL *F*

SASH PANEL *S*

DOOR PANEL *D*

ENDRAFTER *E* PACKAGE

THE POST *C*

ABOVE BASIC UNITS OF PREFABRICATION SYSTEM

CROSS SECTIONS

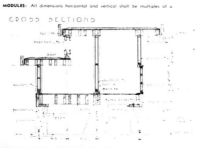

THE BASE *B*   VENTBOARD *V*

PLAN SECTIONS
FLOOR   WALLS   ROOF

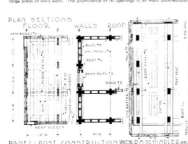

PANEL-POST CONSTRUCTION   R. M. SCHINDLER, ARCH.

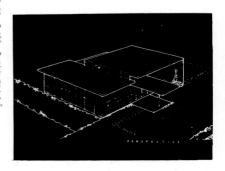

PERSPECTIVE

notes

THE AIR HAS BEEN HEAVY with talk about the world, the house, the life of tomorrow. Everyone and his silly brother has been writing it and singing it and threatening to build it. For months the public has been asked to consider houses that will never fall down and automobiles that will always stand up and ice boxes that will never wear out.

It has been high and heartening talk and the people who have been making it have done a job of tub-thumping. "Just wait, " they say. "Just wait until after the war when we stop making guns we will make the dadgumdest hairpin in the world." "Mr. and Mrs. America," they say, "you just wait and see."

So, all right, we're willing to wait. And up until recently we've been almost ready to believe. Until, on close examination, we found a few small cracks developing in the dream. A truculent gent who makes heaters says that he thinks there's too much talk about the wonderful things that are going to happen, and as far as he's concerned he's going to make the same dammed heater he's always made, and none of this pish-tosh that does nothing but upset his own secure knowledge of the kind of a heater that Americans should have whether they like it or not. Another, who manufactures carloads of ice boxes, is expensively reminding all who will read that "our boys" demand that they return to an America that is *exactly* as they left it.

Obviously, it is no longer considered smart and cagey to be too insistent about this business of merchandising miracles. Of course, miracles don't lend themselves to very precise cost accounting (at least not in the preliminary stages of their manifestation). It is obvious that the boys had to say something about what they intended to do, come the end of the war, but the fact seems to be that they are now overcome by sudden panic at the prospects of a future that might be as bright as the one that they have been predicting. They should know, as any fool does, that miracles are difficult to control and are not in the habit of permitting themselves to be adjusted and confined to neat little grooves with no spilling over allowed. A miracle has a way of spawning all sorts of things that develop from the mere fact of its existence. A miracle is something that you don't fool around with unless you are pretty definitely a part of whatever created it; unless you are a part of the spirit of it; unless you really understand and want it.

The only thing that can possibly delay the future we are fighting for is our own actual fear of it. There's no sense in pretending that it doesn't mean change. In some cases it means very drastic change. Among other things, it makes the maintenance of an economy of scarcity and impossibility in the face of already existing facilities for almost unlimited production. It is going to force upon us considerations and reconsiderations of the complicated systems, *political*, *social*, and *economic*, by which we have lived up to now.

We are at this late date just becoming aware of the nature of the great decisions we will be forced to make. We are only now beginning to realize that when the war ends we will be faced with something that is new, something that is strange, and something that is not going to take "no" for an answer.

There's no point in trying to run away from it, or hide from it, or deny it. It is senseless to look around for a cave, or an acre of land, or a well to jump into. The simple fact is that we are about to face the new world. And the only fear that we need have comes from the weakness of our preparation to become a part of it. The struggle against it will only prolong the agony of our final acceptance.

Frankly, we just don't know what anybody thinks they can do about refusing to allow the future to happen.

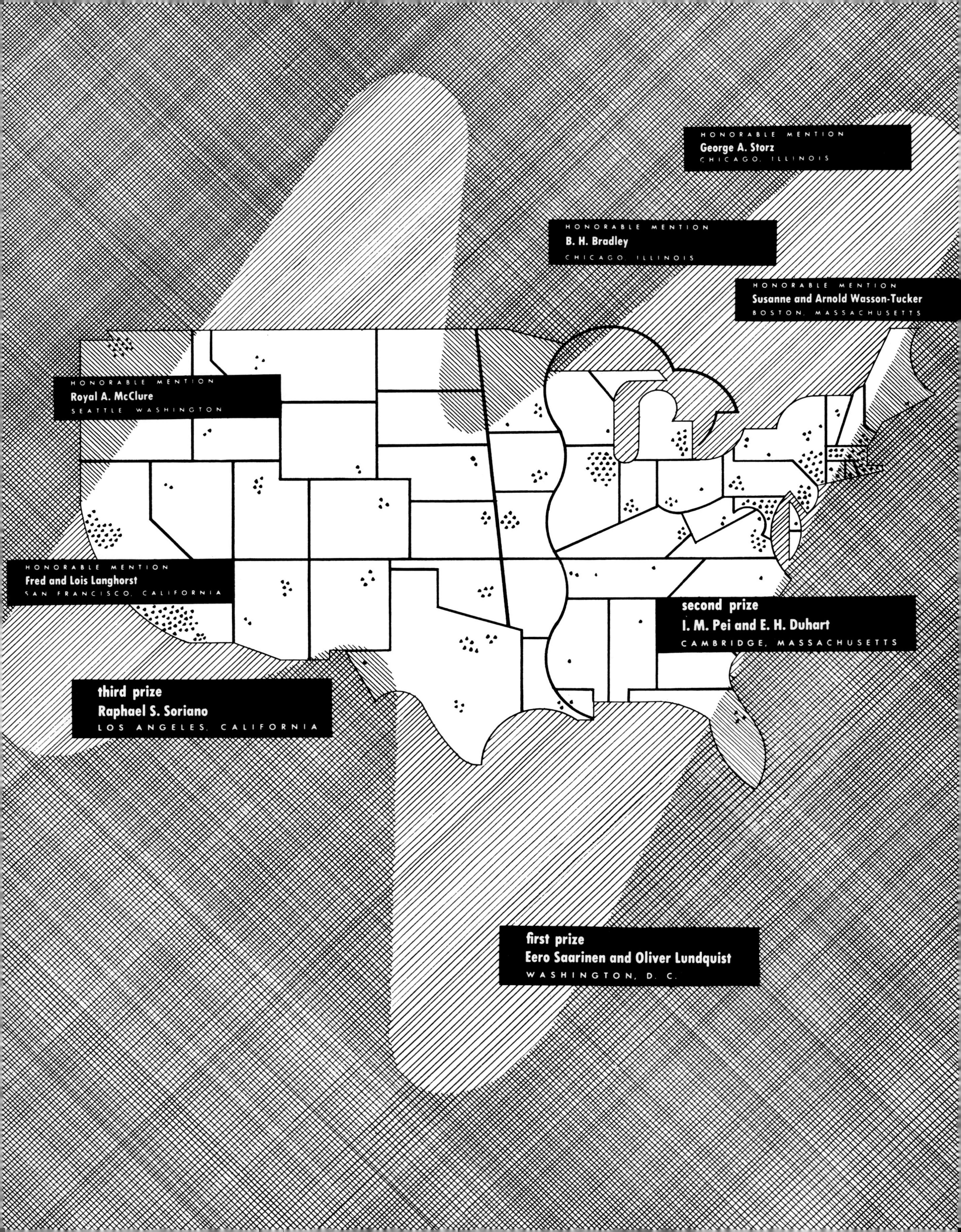

HONORABLE MENTION
George A. Storz
CHICAGO, ILLINOIS

HONORABLE MENTION
B. H. Bradley
CHICAGO, ILLINOIS

HONORABLE MENTION
Susanne and Arnold Wasson-Tucker
BOSTON, MASSACHUSETTS

HONORABLE MENTION
Royal A. McClure
SEATTLE, WASHINGTON

HONORABLE MENTION
Fred and Lois Langhorst
SAN FRANCISCO, CALIFORNIA

second prize
I. M. Pei and E. H. Duhart
CAMBRIDGE, MASSACHUSETTS

third prize
Raphael S. Soriano
LOS ANGELES, CALIFORNIA

first prize
Eero Saarinen and Oliver Lundquist
WASHINGTON, D. C.

■ The final judgment of the many entries has resulted in a good overall selection from the material submitted. While there was considerable disagreement as to the merit of individual contributions, and endless, however enlightening, discussions of what should be where and exactly why, the end of jurying came suddenly with everyone standing his own ground, exausted but firmly convinced. In the light of all the intelligent bickering that went on, it is particularly interesting that the first prize was awarded by unanimous approval.

The winning designs represent a fairly good cross section of the ideas of American designer-architects and what we can expect from them at the moment. What those ideas will be in the next five minutes or the next six months no one can tell, inasmuch as a century of progress and catastrophe and chaos and hope is packed into every moment of these bitter war years.

We are grateful to the contestants for a much better than good try at a difficult problem, and immensely encouraged by the honest thinking that went into most of the work submitted, and wish again to thank the battered jurors for the sincerity of their efforts.
To the co-sponsors, our highest praise for holding onto their hats and letting the competition develop without the slightest interference.

To the magazine this has been a hectic and stimulating experience, and it is our hope that we will soon be able to announce a continuing series of such competitions, believing that American designer-architects will welcome an opportunity to send further trial balloons into the modern air.

We have too many people to thank for the considerable help which has been given in this rather nerve-wracking enterprise. They must take their satisfaction (and justify their nervous breakdowns) with us in the knowledge that they have assisted in a project which has played its small part in giving some hint concerning the shape of the world which might be confronting us some fine morning.

And to everyone, including ourselves, may we wish many happy returns of the day?

co-sponsors of the competition:

The American Rolling Mill Company . . . E. L. Bruce Co. . . . California Panel and Veneer Company . . . Fiat Metal Manufacturing Company . . .Gladding, McBean and Company . . . Harbor Plywood Corporation . . . Klearflax Linen Looms, Inc. . . . Libbey-Owens-Ford Glass Company . . . Marsh Wall Products, Inc. . . . Myers Bros. . . . Pacific Coast Gas Association . . . Pacific Portland Cement Company . . . The Paraffine Companies, Inc. . . . Pioneer Division-Flintkote Company . . . Preskote Paint-Ace Color Company . . . O'Keefe & Merritt . . . Schumacher Wall Board Corporation . . . The Sisalkraft Company . . . The Stanley Works . . . Stewart & Bennett . . . United States Heater Company . . . Washington-Eljer Company . . . West Coast Screen Company.

Honorable mentions and other entries of unusual merit will be shown in subsequent issues.

designs for postwar living

announcing

the winning designs

in the architectural competition

sponsored by

california arts and architecture

jury comments
SUMNER SPAULDING, F. A. I. A.:

Sumner Spaulding, born in Michigan. Graduated from Massachusetts Institute of Technology in Boston. His work includes residential buildings and public works. Chairman of architects committee for the Civic Center of Los Angeles. Architect in collaboration with John Austin on the Municipal Airport, Los Angeles. Chairman of the capital expenditure committee of the Council of Social Agencies. Member of the board of directors of the Los Angeles County Museum Patrons Association.

■ The program for the competition for a postwar house conducted by California Arts and Architecture contained a statement that could only congeal the mind of the competitor: "One thing should be kept in mind: this is to be a house that can really be built when the war is over."

The jurors conceded that baths and kitchens might be prefabricated. However, as long as we must use eclectic forms, deal with long-vested building material interests and established labor customs, we must in no way consider this competition as bringing out a pattern of living which is bound to come.

The evolution of the airplane, resulting in such diversified examples as the helicopter and the flying wing, has produced forms compatible with the actual function of flying with human or freight cargo. Prejudice concerning appearance has never been tolerated in the airplane industry. The automobile, on the other hand, has never completely abandoned the pattern of the horse-drawn vehicle. It has been able to concede to certain prejudices without too much loss of life. Only minor concessions which have been made to safety and speed have helped to dictate the present form. The house, since it is going nowhere, is static both in design and position.

There seems to be little realization that our way of living actually has been changing as much as our methods of transportation. Unfortunately, risk of life and painful death in badly designed houses is so well concealed in secondary causes that the public has never been forced to accept a parallel development in the physical form surrounding our home life.

Most of the designs submitted are rectangular in shape, with the usual room arrangements, and with little consideration of the form that might develop from actual usage, as has been done in the design of the airplane. For example, it is quite conceivable that a kitchen might be circular. Certainly a breakfast table with surrounding seats need not be rectangular. Shower baths, toilets, forms enclosing conversational groups, if built according to modern manufacturing principles, need not stem from the post-and-lintel pattern. The winning designers toyed with these ideas. Two distinct prefabricated units were used. Such units could easily have thrown off the yoke of preconceived forms but failed to do so. The designers might still have eased their consciences in regard to the program as written by making more or less traditional use of the space between the units. They distinctly had their feet well planted in the existing world, but were peering with wistful eyes into the world to come.

Practically all entrants used some form of module system of construction, this being a necessary concession to the existing material manufacturers. Plywood, steel, concrete, and glass can be cut into squares and rectangles for prefabrication. The existing plants and warehouses can still be used. Thus, to a certain degree, the old system of construction can be maintained. Are we to assume that the manufacturer of a new plastic will be forced to copy the old methods of construction to the end that the new shelter will show direct descent from the Cape Cod cottage?

The first two winning designs show a definite consideration of labor custom. Old-time methods are sufficiently used to camouflage, perhaps, the real intent. Certainly in the prize-winning design there is some opportunity for the mason, carpenter, and electrician. The third prize-winning design, however, would certainly be frowned upon by the trades of the building industries. It seemed upon close inspection that should these prefabricated units be made in a factory, they could easily be assembled with practically no use of the old building trades. It is obvious that none of these methods will be fully accepted by labor unions until our social systems can be sufficiently revamped so that the resulting saving in time and energy can be translated into more relaxation, without loss of economic security to the working man. It can be said that the ultimate solution of the house to come is one to be made of flat, easily packed units. However, inasmuch as the house of the future will probably travel but once, isn't it conceivable that in this land of plenty, and with our taste for gadgets, the public might be willing to pay the higher price for transportation of warped surfaces?

Finally, the competitors show only what the ablest designers can do while they still drag the chains of tradition, materials, and system. Let (Continued on page 240)

CHARLES EAMES:

■ The spirit of the program was to a great degree the answer to the problem, but it was very broad and very disciplined, a difficult thing to live up to. When things really got going, one was aware of many preconceived attitudes that stood between us and the program. There seemed to be too much "architecture" in both the solutions and the jury, and values became mixed up with the ego of a specialized profession.

It is fortunate that the first prize is such a clearly stated, well worked out solution, because the other prizes and mentions cannot be taken too seriously as awards. It was an unanimous choice for this place. It is significant that the basic idea was, in a way, similar to that which a number of others strived for and attained in a lesser degree — prefabricated packaging of the more standard units of human activity, combined with complete freedom in those areas serving the special demands of the individual. I believe that the Saarinen-Lundquist solution is one that the contestants as a group will be glad to see.

The mentions are probably representative of a good cross section of the entries, but there were others not included which I feel had more to contribute. The only multi-story solution in the group (Huson Jackson and Henry Shotwell) lost any chance of being viewed objectively by being labeled by the jury "Le Corbusier." The plan of the individual apartments was perhaps weak, but the relation of them to each other and to the out-of-doors space was a real contribution. When unusual thought is presented, most of us seem to have a tendency to spend great energy proving that the thought is not new but has been used by so-and-so. Unfortunately, we can at the same time accept without a mumur the more common, and possibly more dangerous, clichés.

There were solutions that took advantage of the connected row-house scheme to offer the occupant practical privacy in the form of courts and offsets. (Marcel Breuer had a good one.) In general, these seemed to have a more realistic approach than those which placed a house in the middle of a 50-foot lot.

A few structural systems were presented. Ralph Rapson's fabric house was one. However, the merit of his system and his plan was eclipsed by an interpretation put on a part of his statement—"No longer must man be pigeonholed into 'rectangularism,' but can literally clothe himself in his house." This was taken as suggesting the "horrible" thought that the client might be his own architect. He may have overemphasized flexibility, but there was nothing in his statement that would eliminate specialists in planning—in fact, such a system might conceivably grow into a tool which, in the hands of a planner of living space, could prove very useful. One entry, very unarchitectural, came from a housewife whose principal contribution consisted of 15 very significant things she would *not* include in her postwar house. If her list indicates what the attitude of the postwar client will be, and in many ways I believe it does, then the architect had better soon start finding out what *living* could really be like today and tomorrow. It will take more than architectural clichés.

There can be nothing in any sense final about a judgment of this sort. It was a good competition—the majority of the contestants made a sincere effort to design a house in terms of the program with all its intangibles. I, for one, found the business of judging a very stimulating, exhausting, and extremely valuable experience. My present feeling toward the problem differs from my original attitude, and I would like to do it all over again.

RICHARD J. NEUTRA, A. I. A.:

■ Sitting in judgment is no easy sitting. But it is only the deciding and selecting that is really the hard part. The viewing itself was full of appeal and stimulation, and it calls for thanks of the juror to the competitor. It is sad that among so many hopeful workers the greatest number must be disappointed, and that awards are for a minority only. There are part-ideas, fertile fragments and ingredients mixed into many designs which finally may go unpremiated, and the only comfort to me is that such production, once begun, will go on within its producer. His part-ideas one day will become irresistibly integrated.

I doubt that we should underestimate sound and wholesome work because perhaps

Charles Eames, born in St. Louis, Missouri. Studied architecture in St. Louis and Washington Universities. Traveled abroad. Practiced architecture with Robert T. Walsh. Taught design at Cranbrook Academy of Art. Won two first awards in the Museum of Modern Art's Organic Design Competition. Has worked extensively in the field of industrial design. He is identified with the wood industry in the design and manufacture of materials used in the war effort.

it is not of striking novelty. Still among the many entries of a competition, naturally those are automatically more noticed which have arrived at a formulation so rounded out and readable that the whole seems to be permeated by representative newness.

It is a pity that the contestants cannot have the gratification of seeing all the submitted projects, and in argument and counter argument also be heard, besides being seen.

When the problem of this postwar house was posed by the editor of Arts and Architecture, I felt that the design could not well be judged with the same attitude as would be the design of an individual residence on an individual lot. There is implied in this program that at least a large percentage of our American people are meant to inhabit, to occupy, to consume, and to be capable of paying the bill! The solution therefore cannot well be in the singular. A unique panacea won't do. What may look convincing as the home for a long-skilled town worker of an eastern precision tool factory may be quite different from the dwelling of a share cropper, recently promoted to an employee in one of the adolescent industrial districts of the deep South. And the difference between populations of yesterday's dense, tomorrow's somewhat rarefied metropolitan areas, of comfortably reformed small towns and of de-slummed rural districts will make for significant variety.

It was doubly interesting to administer this contest, the first to be juried in the West, and then to note the far geographical spread of its awards. The possibility to multiply them, to distribute attention into still more numerous solutions, would have perhaps been in better keeping with the far-flung areas and varied levels for which postwar homes will actually be designed.

In spite of this evident diversity in purposes, the long rising tide of prefabrication proposals rolled in with might. Still equalitarianism was not championed, standardization was not favored.

Nevertheless, of panel constructions fit to serve in infinite floor plan variations there was, we note, a lesser number proposed than possibly would have been in previous years. Incidentally, these contestants who hinted at the use of such comparatively small unit elements usually did so in a somewhat casual manner, without insisting on this or that material specification, or such and such contraptions of panel joining. Several of the reports voiced clearly the sentiment that details of this kind must necessarily be left to the scope of collaboration with the experts in shop and field work. Shop and field crews and their operations must be systematically observed by the designer; his imagination concerning the processes

(Continued on page 240)

JOHN LEON REX, A. I. A.:

■ Architects and designers from all parts of the country submitted entries to Arts and Architecture's competition, "Designs for Postwar Living." The majority represented a contemporary solution for living, not an antiquated or confused adaptation of architecture of another era.

Most of the contestants considered the fundamentals of a design for living based upon the planned community. The "cell" system was one solution, affording maximum individual convenience, privacy, and larger community play areas. A "row house," or the house as a part of the planned community, was a substantial favorite among the competitive solutions. Many of the designs were doubtless influenced by the large number of public housing projects embodying similar functions. Nevertheless, the large number of contestants applying these principles of housing indicates the widespread acceptance of this plan as a most desirable and permanent solution.

There were very few outstanding designs or original solutions presented. However, a reasonably large group were provocative and deserve recognition for their ingenuity. New materials, building techniques, and war-time laboratory discoveries were specified for construction of the most interesting design solutions. The lasting value of this competition may be to stimulate postwar planning, and extend the horizons of people who live in "hackneyed" houses built by contractors from stock plans on unrelated lot sites.

Richard J. Neutra, born in Vienna, Austria, in 1892. Came to the United States in 1923 after having practiced architecture in Europe. Since he has been in this country, he has practiced in California, Oregon, Texas, and Chicago, Illinois. He was elected as the first American delegate for the C. I. A. M., an international congress of architects. City planner, housing expert, and consultant. He is an active member of a number of committees in the field of architecture, including the Board of Architectural Examiners for the State of California.

John Leon Rex, born in Los Angeles, California, in 1909. Graduated from the University of Southern California, Los Angeles. Member of the American Institute of Architects. Worked with Sumner Spaulding, F. A. I. A., Los Angeles. Is now design engineer at the U. S. Naval Operating Base, San Pedro, California.

GREGORY AIN:

■ The obvious function of an architectural competition is to provide an opportunity and an incentive for the presentation of new ideas. On analysis, the competition will be found to serve another interesting and useful purpose: it offers a clue to the public's needs, desires, and biases in relation to building. And when the jury consists of members of the architectural profession, the final awards may be taken to reveal, in some measure, the objectivity of the planning profession's relation to the public. These incidental derivatives of a competition are as significant as the designs submitted in it, because they suggest the extent to which sound contributions will in reality be accepted and put into practice.

This competition was unusual in that its extremely liberal program avoided specific limiting conditions. Contestants were even encouraged to base their proposals on their hopes and aspirations for the postwar world—that is, they were free to state the problem as well as to offer a solution. The total result was hardly a competitive thing at all, but rather a cooperative symposium. And the "average" of the great mass of entries seems to represent what the average citizen requires to be solved by the architect. It indicates acceptance of a trend toward simplicity and directness. It recognizes the practical advantages of some degree of prefabrication, and the need to consider the relation of one dwelling to another. It affirms the need for "livability" beyond the satisfaction of the purely mechanical functions of a house. Above all, it proves a general willingness to depart from precedent.

Presumably, then, the public is ready to accept a free modern architecture. Is the modern architect equally ready to provide it? From my observation, it is possible that the architect is often behind the public in showing himself unable to distinguish the means from the end. The logic of the newly developing architecture is too evident to require defense, but suddenly it becomes necessary to defend basic principles, not against imaginary detractors but against the misdirected zeal of some of its own sincere proponents.

For instance, instead of acknowledging standardization and prefabrication as the incidental means to economical mass production of good dwellings, we have almost made of prefabrication an ultimate aim in itself. And after having attacked blind subservience to tradition, we finally evolved an almost equally blind tolerance for any suggestion of tradition, regardless of intrinsic merits.

Some examples from the competition will illustrate these tendencies. A few plans, compact and well studied, were eliminated early in the judging, as architectural clichés. They were well organized, had good inter-relation of rooms and gardens, and adaptability to restricted sites, and especially showed intelligent regard for the "amenities of living" (a cliché, incidentally). They were reminiscent of something that has already been done, but something that could well become a respected tradition. But it must not be forgotten that some clichés are so apt and forceful that they eventually become valuable additions to a vocabulary.

The design which was awarded second prize, although not exciting, was nevertheless a workable plan. In what respect was it judged superior to the rejected "cliché"? It was composed of factory-built elements. *But we need no reiteration of the inevitability of prefabrication: we do need plans worth prefabricating.*

Let us examine the third prize design. The construction, at one moment based on the stressed skin principle, at another on the entirely different post-and-lintel, is depicted in large scale details that have little relation to the plan. The utterly arbitrary but dramatic form suggests an origin in a vaulted roof which is non-existent. The major innovation of this fantasy consists in building the roof and two separate walls in one unit. The advantage is unknown, but the disadvantage, in terms of transportation from factory to building site, is enormous. The plan is less amusing, although the inverted relation of service entrance and bedroom to drive is original. This entry was the subject of more discussion than any other. And in that discussion, many more inconsistencies of the plan were brought out than are worth repeating here. The jury evidently thought it good propaganda for prefabrication. There was unanimous agreement on the choice for first prize. This is testimony to the great merit of that design. The PAC system is a logical development of the idea that prefabrication is a tool rather than an ultimate end. This standardized building element need not be used in a standardized way; it allows unlimited flexibility of plan and grouping without sacrifice of simplicity in mass production. And the detail of the unit is beautifully worked out.

Gregory Ain, born in Pennsylvania in 1908. Studied at University of California at Los Angeles and University of Southern California. Private practice in Southern California. Guggenheim Fellowship in 1940 for low cost housing. Five awards in national competitions, one of which was awarded for an entirely standardized structural system that allowed flexibility in individual buildings—that is, the resulting house was not standardized.

1st prize • Eero Saarinen and Oliver Lundquist

PAC

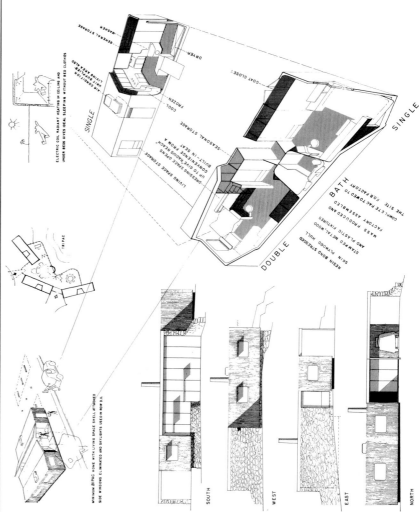

1

Photograph—Betty Cooper

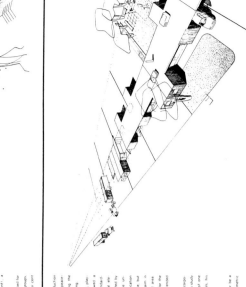

Eero Saarinen was born in Kirkkonummi, Finland, in 1910, and came to the United States in 1923. Attended art school in Paris (sculpture), Yale School of Architecture, 1939. Traveled to Europe. From 1936 to 1939 he did extensive city planning research and other architectural work. From 1939 to 1942 he was associated with Eliel Saarinen and Robert Swanson, building Crow Island School, Winnetka, Illinois. When associated with Perkins, Wheeler and Will; Tabernacle Christian Church, Columbus, Indiana; and Centerline Housing Project, Centerline, Michigan, were built. He has competed in several competitions, including the Smithsonian Gallery of Art Competition, in which the entry was awarded first prize. He is now working for the Office of Strategic Services, Washington, D.C.

Oliver Lundquist, age 26, studied architecture at Columbia and New York University. He worked on world's fair projects and until the fall of 1941 was industrial designer in Raymond Loewy's office. Since that time he has been employed in the Office of Strategic Services in Washington.

- The economic and social demands for postwar housing must be met by extensive utilization of our assembly-line potential.

The PAC (pre-assembled component) method exploits the assembly line by integration of all internal fixtures and conveniences within bulk, size 3x9 meters.

The biological and mechanical functions of the home—sleeping, bathing, cooking, washing, dressing, heating and cooling—are standardized and incorporated into PAC's "A" and "B." "A" contains kitchen utility, bath and single bedroom. "B" double and single bedrooms and bath. PAC's can be used in a variety of combinations—"A", "AB", and "ABB".

By attaching these units to living space which can form a single house or row housing, two-story row housing, motels, or even a tent!, a maximum adaptability is achieved.

Because the PAC's can become standardized for a wide variety of climates and income groups it is estimated that PAC can answer 80 per cent

of postwar housing demands. Mass production of these could so well revitalize our peacetime economy while it distributed among the people a vastly enhanced standard of living.

The social functions of the home—dining, playing, lounging, and studying—are allowed a greater individuality by virtue of the standardization of the biological and mechanical elements. The social functions, vastly affected by climate, income and personal taste are unaffected by this standardization. Prefabrication methods are adaptable to the living space, but local whims may govern. The ultimate aim is to raise the space standard of the social area.

A simple space, 9x9 meters, is desirable for the average worker and possible with our extended economy.

In this B₁-PAC home the living space incorporates a garden, a turnable fireplace, and a study corner, expressing the particular desires of one client, his economic means, local materials, his site, and the climate.

"Incidentally, wouldn't it right after the war be a perfect time for a change over to the metric system?"

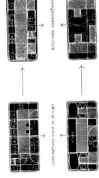

SKETCH OF RADIUS REACH DRESSING SPACE

light — mirror — hats — ties — catch-all — laundry — Comb, brush, gloves, collar, buttons & personal articles — shirts, shorts, socks, etc. — darts, suits, etc. — dressing radius

While the competition drawings showed what we believe should evolve as an ultimate house standard, a period of development starting with a more minimum design is necessary. These later sketches (left) show what we think to be a really good start. Smaller units 8x24 feet would conform to highway regulations and still allow adequate space for the functions within.

We are studying several aspects of this system such as row housing which will be closely dependent on air-conditioning, sky-lighting, etc., the development of the dressing units, and manufacturing potentialities of the PAC's.

We include this brief description of our thought on the development process because we feel that if a definite market materializes, it would be from modest beginnings. Through development and experience the PAC's and the living space could eventually be increased to the size indicated on the competition drawings.

Eero Saarinen and Oliver Lundquist

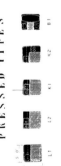

PERSPECTIVE FROM STREET OF MINIMUM HOUSE

SKETCH PLAN OF THE HOUSE COMPOSED OF TWO SEPARATE "PAC" UNITS WITH LIVING SPACE IN ITS ASSEMBLED FORM

street — garden

2

2nd prize • I. M. Pei and E. H. Duhart

parents — study or guest — child — extension

SECOND FL.

dining and sitting — working — playing

FIRST FL.

MODULE 3'-4"

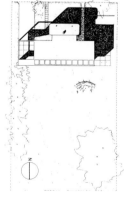

PERSPECTIVE

PLOT PLAN

POST WAR HOUSE

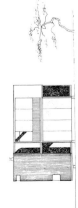

STANDARD SERVICE UNITS

Z strut 8" o. c.
Pressed corrugated thin gauge aluminum sprayed with bituminous mastic on inside to prevent condensation corrosion.
16" o. c.
Horizontal sliding windows.
Aluminum foil with transparent plastic film coatings.
Pressed units.

PRESSED TYPES

VARIATIONS

Alternate combinations

Combinations used in design

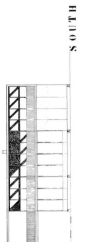
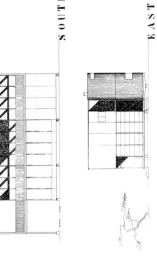
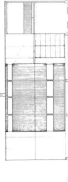

SOUTH

EAST

NORTH

WEST

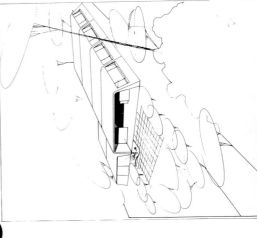

2

3

3 rd prize · Raphael Soriano

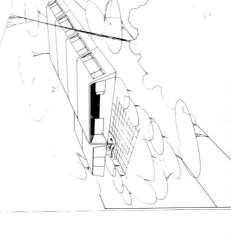

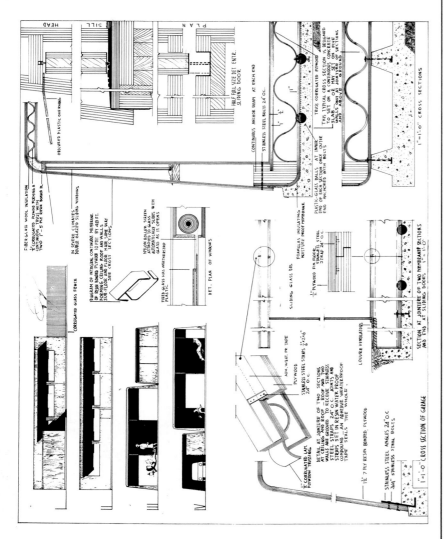

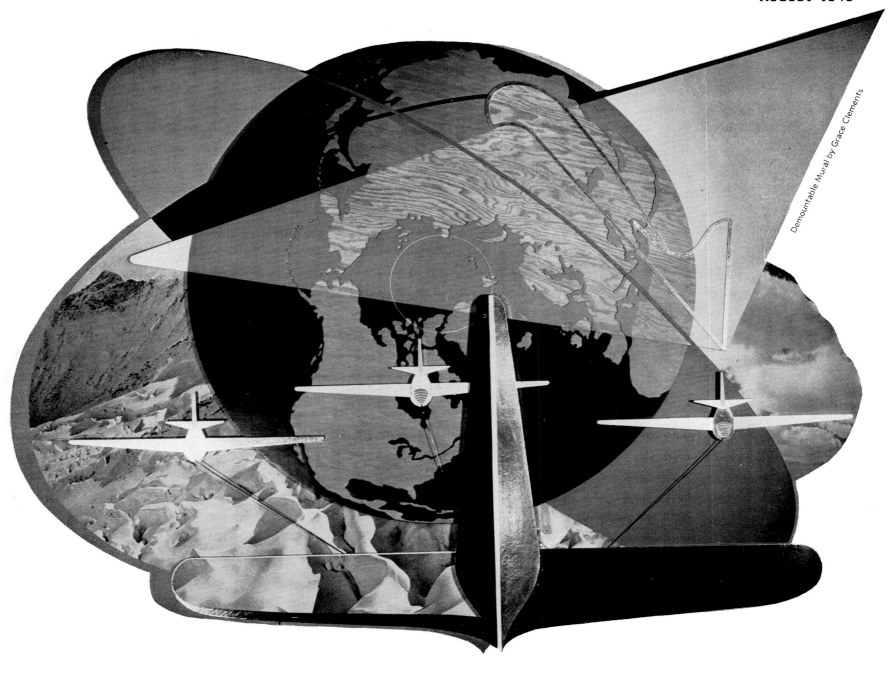

Demountable Mural by Grace Clements

PLYWOOD FOR WAR...LATER FOR PEACE

DESIGNS for post-war living will call for an ever expanding use of plywood, which today we are furnishing in vast quantities for vital military uses . . . when war orders have been filled the George E. Ream Company, having aided step by step in the development of plywood, will continue as the prime source of supply in the Southwest.

26

LINE AND
COLOR DEFINE
VOLUME
THAT VOLUME
CAN BE TANGIBLE
OR NOT BUT THE
SPACE BETWEEN
TWO TANGIBLE
VOLUMES IS
NEVERTHELESS
          A VOLUME

ray eames

it is impossible to talk about painting without bringing up the whole weary subject of aesthetics   philosophy   and metaphysics.

the fact is that without any talk we are influenced by the world in which we live and by the synthesis of the experiences of the world by all creators ● the engineer   mathematician   sculptor   physicist   chemist   architect   doctor   musician   writer   dancer   teacher   baker   actor   editor   the man on the job   the woman in the home   home   and painters

for the past many years the western world has been working back through the maze of surface decoration and meaningless gloss to the fundamentals of form ● sometimes this has been an economic necessity as in the present war years   other times it comes from an aesthetic demand ● where the people through the sensibilities of the creators find it necessary to rediscover values and to cast aside the non-essentials ● hindrances of the past

why is it that today we are more concerned with the materials and design of a chair than with its covering or ornament? why are we more concerned with the quality of the music than with the personal idiosyncrasies of the conductor? why are the uniforms   the word itself becomes strange   so varied and differ so radically from those of former wars? why are our houses being designed from the inside out rather than fitting the living to a predetermined style on the outside? why indeed do we not only accept but also admire and feel intensely proud of the jeep? a superb example of a healthy direction of thinking and feeling

in spite of prejudice and confusion we are becoming aware slowly of true and good and vital and therefore beautiful form.

my interest in painting is the rediscovery of form through movement and balance and depth and light ● using this medium to recreate in a satisfying order my experiences of this world   with a desire to increase our pleasure   expand our perceptions   enrich our lives

space and the relationships of space become
so engulfing ● so important that objects in
themselves lose value ● two left-hand gloves

Jackson Pollack (signature)

The work of Jackson Pollack was shown at the New York Gallery of Art of This Century during November of last year. This, his first one man show, was enthusiastically received and won for him great critical praise.

Where were you born?

Cody, Wyoming, in January, 1912. My ancestors were Scotch and Irish.

Have you traveled any?

I've knocked around some in California, some in Arizona. Never been to Europe.

Would you like to go abroad?

No. I don't see why the problems of modern painting can't be solved as well here as elsewhere.

Where did you study?

At the Art Student's League, here in New York. I began when I was seventeen. Studied with Benton, at the League, for two years.

How did your study with Thomas Benton affect your work, which differs so radically from his?

My work with Benton was important as something against which to react very strongly, later on; in this, it was better to have worked with him than with a less resistent personality who would have provided a much less strong opposition. At the same time, Benton introduced me to Renaissance art.

Why do you prefer living here in New York to your native West?

Living is keener, more demanding, more intense and expansive in New York than in the West; the stimulating influences are more numerous and rewarding. At the same time, I have a definite feeling for the West: the vast horizontality of the land, for instance; here only the Atlantic ocean gives you that.

Has being a Westerner affected your work?

I have always been very impressed with the plastic qualities of American Indian art. The Indians have the true painter's approach in their capacity to get hold of appropriate images, and in their understanding of what constitutes painterly subject-matter. Their color is essentially Western, their vision has the basic universality of all real art. Some people find references to American Indian art and calligraphy in parts of my pictures. That wasn't intentional; probably was the result of early memories and enthusiasms.

Do you consider technique to be important in art?

Yes and no. Craftsmanship is essential to the artist. He needs it just as he needs brushes, pigments, and a surface to paint on.

Do you find it important that many famous modern European artists are living in this country?

Yes. I accept the fact that the important painting of the last hundred years was done in France. American painters have generally missed the point of modern painting from beginning to end. (The only American master who interests me is Ryder.) Thus the fact that good European moderns are now here is very important, for they bring with them an understanding of the problems of modern painting. I am particularly impressed with their concept of the source of art being the unconscious. This idea interests me more than these specific painters do, for the two artists I admire most, Picasso and Miro, are still abroad.

Do you think there can be a purely American art?

The idea of an isolated American painting, so popular in this country during the 'thirties, seems absurd to me, just as the idea of creating a purely American mathematics or physics would seem absurd. . . And in another sense, the problem doesn't exist at all; or, if it did, would solve itself: An American is an American and his painting would naturally be qualified by that fact, whether he wills it or not. But the basic problems of contemporary painting are independent of any one country.

"The Guardian of the Secret," 1943
"The Search for a Symbol," 1943
Courtesy Art of This Century

and the screen

by Dalton Trumbo

● When Ralph Waldo Emerson, one of the most impeccably remote intellectuals of his time, set aside Transcendentalism to defend John Brown and urge arms for the Kansas abolitionists and be shouted from platforms by pro-slavery hoodlums, he summarized his philosophy of writing in a single sentence which, it appears to me, might appropriately become the keynote of our Writers' Congress. "No man," he declared, "can write anything who does not think that what he writes is, for the time, the history of the world."

It is the exciting and occasionally disagreeable privilege of writers today to live and work in a world as full of conflict and great premonitions of freedom to come as the world of Emerson. All writers of integrity during the middle Nineteenth century fought slavery and the racial lies upon which it was founded. Today they fight a much greater extension of slavery called Fascism, with an enormously broadened base of racial lies. Just as Emerson discovered the writer's role in the battle, so we have discovered that we can't write anything—whether we are journalists, novelists, poets, publicists, playwrights or screen writers—without likewise thinking that what we write is, for the time, "the history of the world."

Inasmuch as this is a panel upon minority groups, and since the fate of all minority groups—including writers—is at stake in the present war against Fascism, it might be illuminating to glance backward and discover how we, as American writers, have dealt with our own minorities. For whether it pleases us or not, the fury with which the Fascists attack us constitutes a high, if unpleasant, tribute to our influence. If, therefore, certain Fascist racial falsehoods find serious acceptance in our country, perhaps it is because American writers—all of us—through laziness or ignorance or lack of courage, have nourished them to their present dangerous and explosive state.

It is interesting to note the exact similiarity of character cliches which the American press, theatre, fiction and screen have applied to a wide variety of racial and national minorities. When the great Irish immigration was at its flood tide, and staid New Englanders became alarmed at the possible corruption of their Puritan tradition, the Irishman bloomed as a humorous, drunken, lying, lazy, dirty, unassimilable fellow. But we had also presented the Negro as a humorous, drunken, lying, lazy, dirty, unassimilable fellow. And later, with the flood of Mexican immigration, we turned upon our Southern neighbor and portrayed *him* as a humorous, drunken, lying, lazy, dirty, unassimilable fellow. We did it to the Italians, too, and the Chinese and the Slavs. The similarity of this pattern of ridicule, the complete lack of any sort of discrimination in applying the pattern, strongly suggests that we have fallen victims to the same racial and national myths which so faithfully have served the wretched ends of Fascism.

South Americans, because they did not migrate to our shores in any great number, and Jews, because of their culturally secure position in our society, received different treatment at our hands. We stigmatized all South Americans as panderers, gigolos, thieves and murderers. We dealt with Jews as dialect buffoons, or as sharp business men(or as mysteriously pious folk voluntarily segregated from the community. Almost never have we dealt with them as people. In "Boy's Town" we even subscribed to a particularly obnoxious racial myth by providing a Jewish youngster with one of the largest noses in screen history.

The Irish tackled their problem by political organization. They even established Anti-Stage Irishman societies, which expressed their general discontent by rotten-egging Irish comics. More recently in Buenos Aires a disgruntled audience tore up a movie theatre in protest against our slanderous presentation of their country-men. Such vehemence, in combination with the Good Neighbor policy, has obliged us to modify our lurid concept of South American life. Our desperate need for Mexican labor, aided by quiet work on the part of both governments, has produced a similar revision in attitude toward the country of Juarez. The Chinese are now our Allies, so we have ceased ridiculing them; and the Irish comedian and hockshop owner bring neither the laughs nor the hisses of pre-Hitler days. We have not yet had the courage to treat these minorities in a positive and constructive fashion, but we at least called off our stupid campaign of insult and ridicule. However, we must make certain this is not merely an armistice forced by the exigencies of war, but rather a permanent treaty based upon an enlightened understanding of minority problems.

That there is a certain degree of opportunism, a certain lack of clarity in our sudden tender treatment of the minority groups already mentioned may be demonstrated by the plight of the one group which, unluckily, has not possessed the weapons with which to defend itself. By sheer weight of numbers, by the sheer horror of his condition, the American Negro remains one of the most oppressed and persecuted minorities in the world. Since his status is not that of an ally of America in this war, there is no friendly government whose placation requires an amelioration of his condition. He is, on the contrary, an American citizen, largely deprived of one power which has been conferred upon all other American minorities—the right to vote. While 10 per cent of our general population is born abroad, while less than 70 per cent of our general population can boast two parents of native birth, the 12,865,515 Negroes in the United States are 99.4 per cent native American born. "If nativity were really the measure of citizenship," comments *Fortune* magazine, "the Negroes would excell any other national or racial stock in this country."

In large areas the American Negro is denied the right to vote, although generously accorded the obligation of paying taxes and fighting in the armed forces. He is forced to live apart from the human race in ghettos. In many states he is obliged to travel separately, like an animal. His children receive poorer educations than their white contemporaries. His income is below the national average. But his rent is higher. His infant mortality rate is higher. His maternal death rate is higher. His disease rate is higher. His death rate is higher. Yet as if this were not a cross heavy enough for any race to bear, we as writers in the press and radio, in magazines and the novel, on the stage and screen, have seized upon the Negro as the object of our cruelest slanders.

In Hollywood the most gigantic milestones of our appeal to public patronage have been the anti-Negro pictures, "The Birth of a Nation," and "Gone With the Wind." And between the two, from 1915 to 1940, we have produced turgid floods of sickening and libelous treacle. We have made tarts of the Negro's daughters, crap-shooters of his sons, obsequious Uncle Toms of his fathers, superstitious and grotesque crones of his mothers, strutting peacocks of his successful men, psalm-singing mountebanks of his priests and Barnum and Bailey sideshows of his religion. We have even gone so far in "The Man on America's Conscience" as to traduce and villify the greatest Reconstruction champion of Negro liberties—Thaddeus Stevens.

We have developed a classic caricature of the Negro in relation to the Civil War which brought him freedom. As we present him, he is an ignorant fool, preferring his "franchise in a bucket," rather than the forthright citizen who

accomplished such splendid, progressive work in the so-called Black Legislatures. He loves the conditions of his servitude, and refuses to accept freedom when it comes, despite the fact that hundreds of his fellows participate in scores of slave insurrections, that tens of thousands of them fled north via the Underground Railway before the war, and that almost a quarter million of them actually fought in the northern armies. As for the northern soldier who freed the Negro, he is presented as a looter, a brigand, a barbarian and a rapist, in contrast with the southern soldier, who invariably is generous, courageous and cultured.

Succeeding generations of writers have perverted the whole humane significance of the Civil War to fit the reactionary legend of the old South of crinoline and magnolia blossoms and lovely, gentle ladies, where one could read, in the year 1856, the wail of a Southern gentlewoman in such a newspaper advertisement as: "$300 REWARD—Ran away from the subscriber on Saturday . . . my servant woman named Emeline Chapman, about 25 years of age . . . with two children, one a female about 2½ years old; the other a male 7 or 8 months old, bright color." As writers we can imagine the drama of Emeline Chapman's flight from slavery with her two children; but as practical men and women of letters, we have always chosen to dramatize the travails of her mistress, one Mrs. Emily Thompson, who inserted the ad.

Our current crop of motion pictures, produced in a moment of national crisis when the President has made a direct appeal for racial understanding and cooperation, reveals many of the vicious old lies dressed up and paraded before us as evidence of our stern devotion to winning the war. "Two Tickets to London" presents us with a Negro murderer. "Tales of Manhattan" contains caricatures of the most objectionable sort which were greeted by Negro picket lines. "Holiday Inn" was typically insulting Mammy and Pickaninny bilgewater, while "This Is the Army" Jim Crowed Negro service men into a number with a zoot suit background. "Cabin in the Sky," "Stormy Weather" and "Dixie," despite a few minor concessions to Negro dignity in the first two, contained bad features which far outweighed their virtues.

There are, however, some hopeful signs to report. The Kildare series has been outstandingly progressive in its treatment of Negroes. "Bataan" contained an excellent Negro character, while "In This Our Life" we discover a Negro law student who represented a complete departure from the stereotype. Rex Ingram's role in "Talk of the Town" was sympathetically written and portrayed with dignity. "Stage Door Canteen" delivered a blow for democracy in a sequence showing the decoration for bravery of a Negro soldier. "Mission to Moscow" made splendid and dignified use of Haile Selassie. "Casablanca" provided a strange combination of the stereotype in a position of unusual companionship and trust. "Oxbow Incident" departed widely from the accepted Negro pattern in an excellent photoplay which perhaps placed too much emphasis upon the Negro propensity for prayer in crises. With the exception of "The Little Foxes," there have been no recent good roles for Negro actresses; and even there the screen version seemed much weaker in its delineation of the Negro's character than the legitimate play. (Continued on page 240)

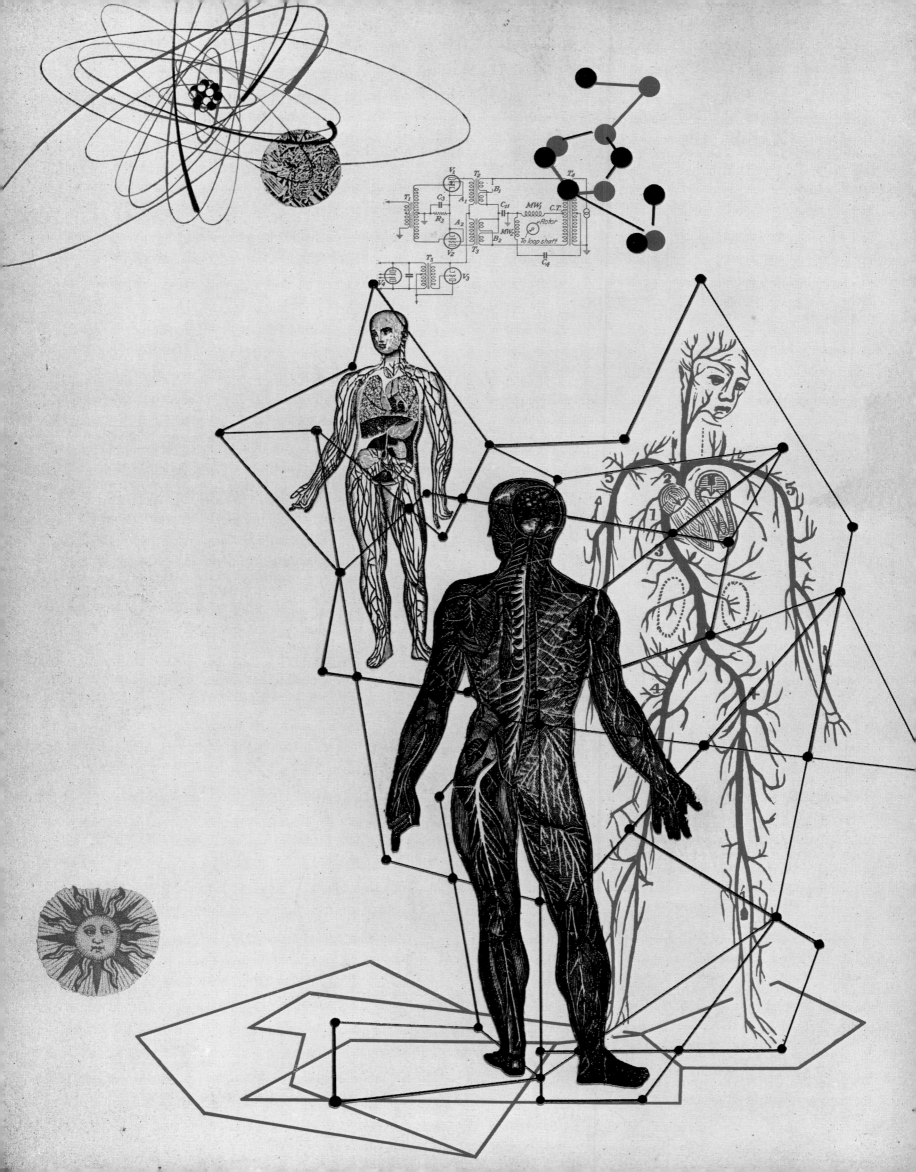

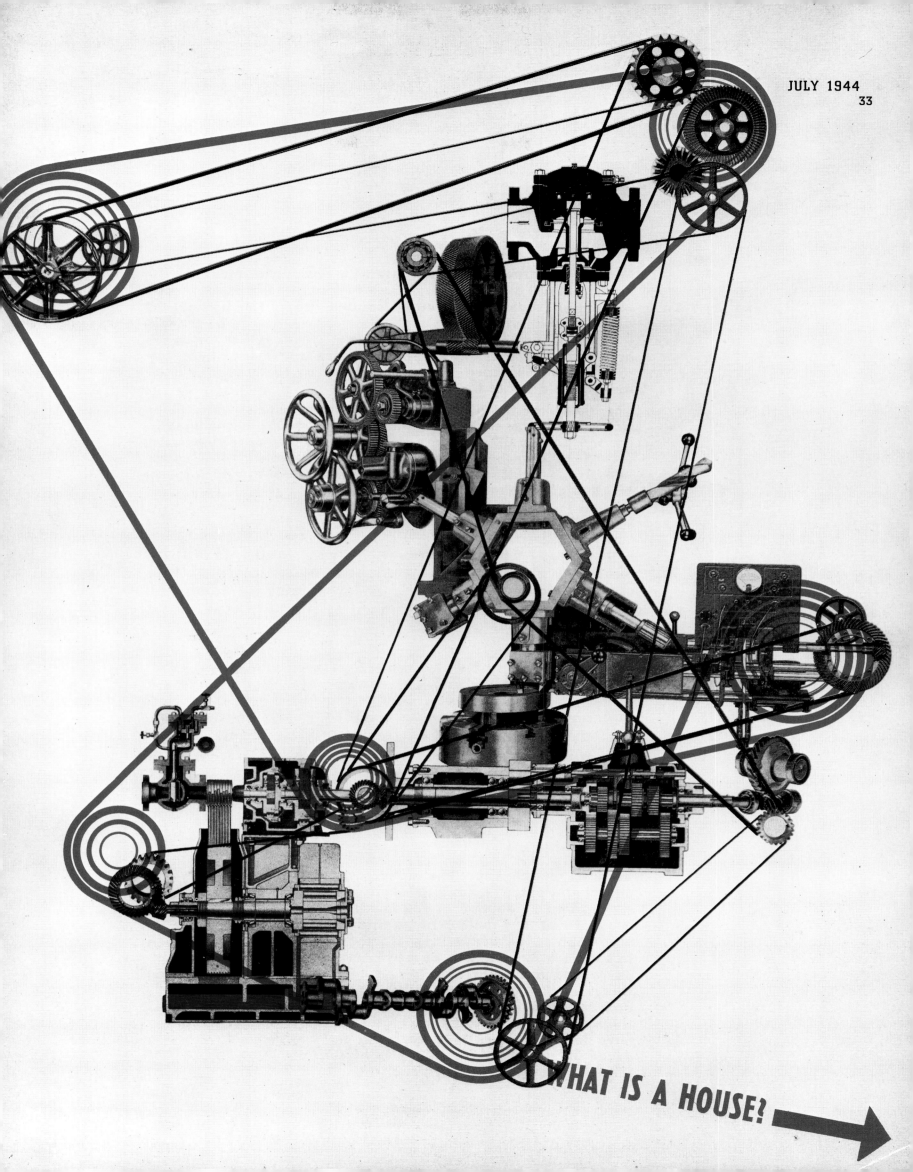

WHAT IS A HOUSE? ➡

HOUSE

(house), *n.*; *pl.* HOUSES (houzes; -iz; 151). [ME. *hous, hus,* AS. *hus;* akin to OS. & OFries. *hus,* D. *huis,* OHG. *hus,* G. *haus,* Icel. *hus,* Sw. *hus,* Dan. *huus,* Goth. *gud-hus,* house of God, temple; and perh. to E. *hide* to conceal. See HIDE; cf. HOARD, HUSBAND, HUSSY, HUSTINGS.] 1. A structure intended or used for human habitation; esp., a human habitation which is fixed in place and is intended for the private occupation of a family or families.— Webster.

We are concerned with the house as a basic instrument for living within our own time; the house as a solution of human need for shelter that is structurally contemporary; the house that above all takes advantage of the best engineering techniques of our highly industrialized civilization. While other attitudes present various possibilities, this approach would seem to be one that can be defended without prejudice as the modern, lucid, realistic solution of living needs.

The history of the house is too obvious to restate. The point we make, at the moment, however, is that NOW is the time in the world when all necessary circumstances and conditions exist in such relationship to one another that we can attack, on an inclusive, over-all scale, the problem of mass housing with a better than good chance for success.

It has been estimated that one million five hundred thousand houses each year for a period of ten years will be needed to relieve the urgent housing problem of this country alone. In the world at large, fifty million families as a minimum will be in need of shelter as the result of war.

The enormity of such a need cannot be even partially satisfied by building techniques as we have known and used them in the past. Large scale industry would seem to be the only logical means by which we can achieve an enterprise of such proportion.

50,000,000

This is a task that will not wait to be done until we decide whether or not we care to do it. It is a job that must be done if we are to achieve order out of the chaos of war; if we are to maintain and expand any of the standards by which we measure our civilization.

Because of the enormous acceleration of world industry for military purposes we now know that insofar as the design, engineering, and production of the house on an industrialized basis is concerned that reality only awaits the desire. That is, desire accompanied by our willingness to restudy, to redefine, and to readjust some of our obsolete attitudes toward living standards and means of distribution. The choice then, between things as they can be and things as they have been, is the only area of controversy. We can only hope that realistic clear-headed thinking will cut sharply through the obstacles that we now know have no reality or validity when the problem of good mass produced industrialized housing is to be considered.

"It has always been obvious that the dynamic life going on within a structure is more important than the static structure, but, like so much else that is apparent, this has been generally disregarded, with the result that shelter has been looked upon as an end in itself, not as a means of life."—BUCKMINSTER FULLER

We have very willingly accepted the products of the machine when those products have added to our ability to get a job done efficiently but we have deliberately avoided the over-all industrial solution when it could be applied to the house itself.

Heretofore we have considered the house a shell into which we have packed selected gadgets—many of them good, too many of them bad. We have yet to find a valid reason for building our houses out of the past and ignoring the techniques of the present or the promise of the future. We have insisted that the house conform to conventional patterns. We have restricted and limited its use as an instrument for living by forcing it into "styles." We have demanded, unreasonably, that it conform to echoes of past elegance which we, as individuals, admire or to which we aspire. We have asked that it be the crutch of our sentimentality, a boon to our vanity, a means by which we prove to our neighbors that we are better or richer or more knowing than they. We have actually submitted the house to the kind of thoughtless faddism with which we accept the season's fashion in hats.

This, the basis for the environment that conditions us; the envelope which encases the most important of our life's functions, we think of in terms of indulgence rather than good sense, and we pay for it by living in the midst of obsolescence, burdened by a lifetime of financing (in money, in time, in health, and environment) what is inevitably a bad bargain.

Perhaps it is because, among other things, we have allowed ourselves to be conditioned to look upon what is known as the machine age with suspicion—the fear of the mechanical—the fear of the logic of precision—the fear of Frankenstein. Man dominated by the machine has for years been a philosophical bogey despite the fact that modern man, if he is great, is great only in relation to what he has accomplished through his creation of the machine. Only now, in this present world, are we forced to realize that the machine, the industrial, the scientific age is the insistent, inevitable manifestation of the physical facts of existence that makes it possible for us to break through into the future.

We now know that we only lose control of what we create if we refuse to take responsibility for the direction and the discipline of the USE of our creations.

We now know that the miracle of industry in war can and must be a part of the peacetime world, a reality no longer possible to deny—an insistent power so much a part of the very existence of modern life that we can no longer have the privilege of choosing whether or not we care to live with it because, by the very nature of progress, it has become a part of ourselves and the MEANS by which we live with one another.

We must, then, accept the machine in the coming age of science as something to be lived by and no longer to be lived for.

"Declarations of rights no longer assure us. We all know that those rights should be,—what we all want to know is just one way by which those rights may be specifically arrived at. And we know that specific way transcends political action. There must be evidenced a formula of advantage gained over environment, comprised of no unknowns but of the leverage principles of universal physical laws. That means a total industry pattern."—B. F.

"That good engineering could be directly causal and IS and ALWAYS HAS BEEN indirectly causal to economics, few have realized. The mechanics of the invention which is all economics is. It is well to remind ourselves from time to time that the word "economics" derives from "ecology," the science out of the house. In such a science, the design and production of the house are causal."—B. F.

Literally mountains of material have been created by

industry under the pressures of war conditions. Not only American industry but also world industry has fully demonstrated its ability to create an abundance of goods for man's needs. But more important than this important fact is man's growing awareness of his real power through the machine. His absolute knowledge of not only an industrial potential but also the accomplished fact of an industrial reality so vast, so overpowering that it becomes the one great common denominator of the life of all mankind.

True mass production has won the respect of all people because it has been able to put into their hands the weapons by which their lives have been saved in war. Man now knows that mass production properly directed and properly disciplined will not only save lives but also set them free. The one outstanding fact of our time is that this c a n be done. We no longer lack the means. It is now only a matter of directing our wills and our intelligence to the proper use of the mountains of materials and technologies at our disposal in order to solve the most pressing problems which concern the material welfare of mankind.

Science in industry cannot be expected to function if it must make compromises in terms of political minorities, committments-to-the-past or prejudices concerning the future.

"Very probably American prefabricators will be called upon to aid in the unprecedented housing emergency which will arise with the liberation of European countries. That emergency relates to 30 million families completely bombed out, who are now doubled up or existing in conditions that will provoke a sanitation crisis. The people themselves will go to work salvaging the rubble and salvaging the industrial materials no longer required for war, improvising many of their own emergency solutions. So enormous is the need, however, that if only one per cent of its requirement were to be referred to the U. S., that would mean more single family houses than the U. S. economy built for itself in its all-time peak year." —BUCKMINSTER FULLER.

Amongst the **heavy industry** categories of the industrial economies, **construction** has always been by far the largest individual consumer of the over-all resources, both volumetrically and tonnage-wise. And within the narrower category of **construction** itself, the **family dwelling** bulks as the largest tonnage consumer throughout the last half-century.—B. F.

This time man is going to convert those intellectual war-instrumented controls to his comprehensive living advantage right down to where the baby comes in. World-wide man is learning about the multitudes of physical advantages inherent in mechanics, technology, cooperative action —of armies that swim and fly and walk through hell. Nothing can divert him from focusing that ability to magnificent realization in his world housing abilities and to the exquisite problem of equilibrium maintained in the living estate.—B. F.

MONTAGE BY HERBERT MATTER

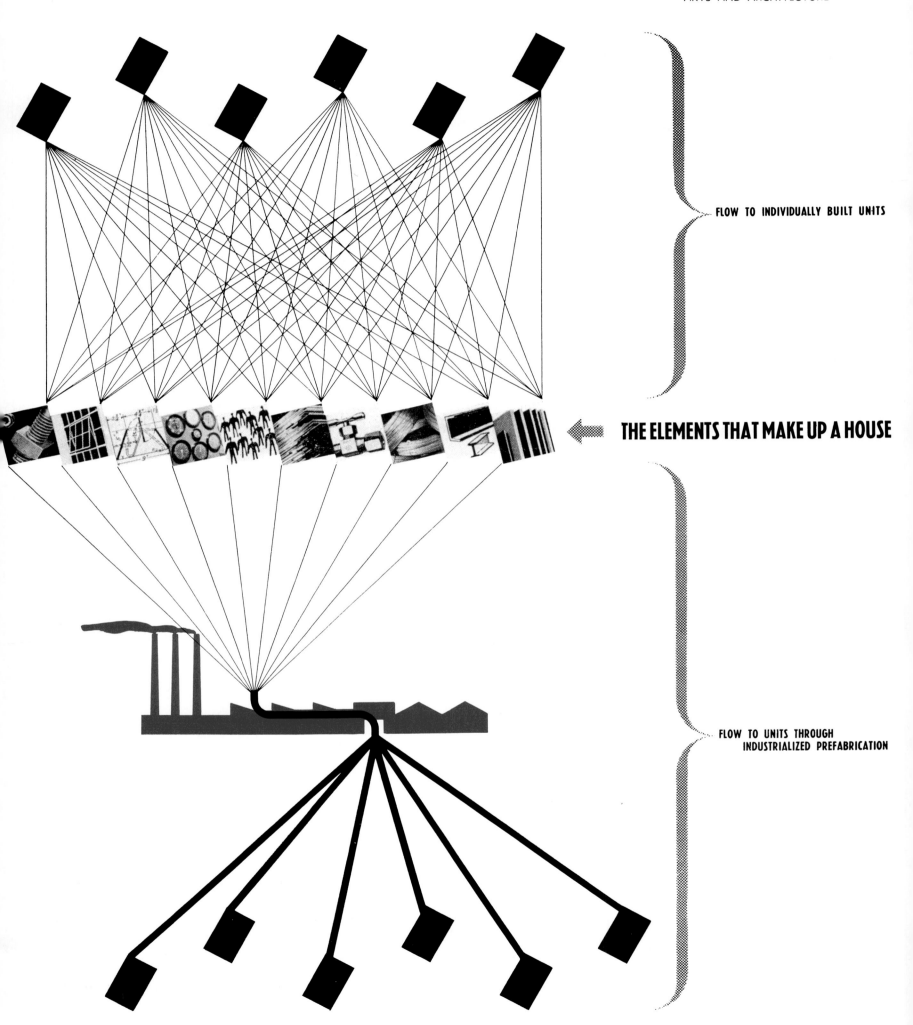

FLOW TO INDIVIDUALLY BUILT UNITS

THE ELEMENTS THAT MAKE UP A HOUSE

FLOW TO UNITS THROUGH
INDUSTRIALIZED PREFABRICATION

Any unit or combination of units manufactured or cut to size before being brought to the building site can, in a literal sense, be called

PREFABRICATION

BUT Prefabrication in the truly industrialized sense is a very special approach to the problem of the "house"—an approach made possible NOW, for the first time, when industry, research and material exist in the right relationship to one another, making possible an intelligent application of these resources to the needs of housing.

PREFABRICATION **IS NOT** Just a trick to save labor in the building of a house

IS NOT a super-industrialized method to be used for the reproduction of the architecture of the past

IS NOT merely an ingenious mechano-set of parts which, when put together, form walls, roofs, shells of buildings

IS NOT the use of the factory as a catch all for obsolete building crafts

IS NOT a new sales promotion package for the purpose of marketing streamlined versions of old products

BUT modern industrialized prefabrication, by its very nature, cannot be disassociated from any of the functions of living related to the house. It is, then, the complete use of all the facilities of mass production aided by the best research, the best techniques and the best materials available, to the end that every living activity will receive the benefits of our enormous industrial energies. It is through the complete integration of all these forces that we will arrive at the form of the product. Form, then, will be the by-product of the end result of our best intellectual and industrial energies rather than a point of departure.

Although the public has knowledge of electronics through the operating principles of the radio tube, it is the war-time expansion of the industry that indicates a vast new application to peacetime uses. House construction of strong light-weight metals or plywoods will be welded by the use of electronics devices. Innumerable low cost additions to home conveniences will change present methods of heating, cooking, and lighting.—Norman E. Bruns, Electronics Engineer.

1

2

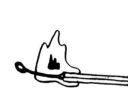

3

4

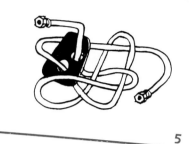

5

6

8

9

10

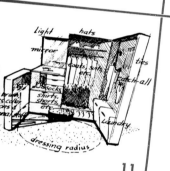

11

12

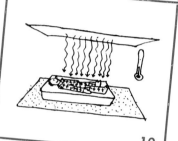

13

1 Under the war pressure of an immediate life and death need for electronic equipment for use in radar communication controls and industrial techniques, an enterprise, rivaling the size of the prewar automobile industry, has been developed. Only on such a scale of production is it now possible to anticipate that things like television will become a reality to the small house, but the development of electronics can and will be expanded far beyond its extensive service in battle and in war industry. It will mean in the immediate future precision control for hot-cold—light-dark—moist-dry—fast-slow—start-stop, plus health and service miracles of which we are just becoming aware.

2 There is in use a chemical when sprayed upon the walls of a room that will keep it totally free of insects for periods as long as six months. It has no effect upon human occupants and there is no unpleasant odor.

3 Acoustical engineers have accomplished wonders in the broadcasting studios, but these wonders have yet to reach the home. The radio, the dish clatter, the telephone, the baby, and the bathroom should not be too difficult for science to treat acoustically.

4 The precipitron is another electronic device first used to clean the air in critical buildings such as those devoted to the polishing of lenses. The air passes through an electronic field where all particles receive a positive charge and are attracted to a negative plate. This device traps particles so small that even some bacteria is included.

5 No longer a novelty, but a very usable material in plumbing, is venylidene chloride which when extruded forms a flexible tubing very superior in combating corrosion and chemical action.

6 A heating unit no larger than a suitcase, and consuming a now secret fuel, can heat a space comparable to the average house. This device is now used for, among other purposes, the heating of interiors of high altitude bombers under conditions much more severe than will ever be encountered in any problem of home heating.

7 We can be sure that no home-owner will be satisfied with a house that is any less fireproof than has been made possible by the development and appliance of wartime science.

8 Such wall-horror need no longer be a household worry if we consider and take advantage of the properties of plastic surfacing and coating materials that now exist in the plastic catalogs of 1944.

9 In the refrigerator, the bacteria destroying lamp will prevent mold and spoilage and thus enable all such units to be operated at ideal moisture conditions, otherwise impossible because high relative humidity encourages bacterial growths.

10 The use of large surface areas (such as floor or ceiling) for heat radiation, produces more uniform and more healthful heat with comparatively low temperature at the source. This principle of heating allows windows to be left open with less consequent loss of heat and reduces the smudging of walls that occurs over most conventional radiators and register grills. An application has been shown that enables one to sleep in cool air in perfect comfort with no bed clothes.

11 Workers in war plants have found that there is a logical approach to the engineering of packaging and filing, and an orderly approach to storage problems. These obviously intelligent solutions can be directed and applied by the same kind of engineering to problems of use and storage of personal possessions, clothing, and accessories. Such convenience has been well thought out in Eero Saarinen's "radius-reach."

12 We know that plywood is now much more than the plywood we have always known. We know now that it can be faced with metal, with plastic, curved, corrugated, formed in strong structural shapes, channels, angles, tubes, cylinders. It can be impregnated and compressed to many times its density and strength. It can have low density cores for light-weight rigid panels.

13 This has become almost a symbol of an approach to prefabrication. It was the first actual evidence of the inferences implied by the application of machine techniques to something directly relating to the scale of human living. It is not this actual prefabrication bathroom but the attitude for which it stands that has had the greatest effect upon modern conception and

Prewar materials and techniques heretofore regarded as hardly out of the laboratory and later restricted to highly specialized purposes have now become commonplace to anyone remotely connected with the industrial machine geared to production for war.

The terrific acceleration in the practical use of science and the almost immediate application of its development to the most urgent military need is no longer regarded as a hit or miss miracle of chance. The laboratory has been put on the production line. The distance between experiment and real use has been compressed into a matter of months. The application of this new and ready vocabulary to a truly industrialized mass production of good family living machines is the logical, practical, and realistic approach to our housing problem.

These things exist no longer in a dream world of gadgets that we will or will not buy depending upon how well they are presented over the air or in the newspapers. They form a part of that mass of material that will inevitably be brought together in order to create the most efficient, economical, and healthful instruments for living.

These things, on the basis of mass production and wide distribution, can no longer be thought of as luxuries when it can be demonstrated that savings in actual time, life, and the conservation of materials and services will vastly outweigh the cost of production. On a very practical economic basis these things are not luxuries because by their functions they save definitely calculable man hours and foot pounds of energy.

acceptance of the engineered house. People will not only expect but demand results from Buckminster Fuller's germinal ideas.

14 Sterilizations lamps, the rays of which destroy bacteria, can arrest the spreading of infectious diseases. They can be used in purifying water supplies and to kill germs in storage units.

15 That wood can be bonded to metal or metal to glass or glass to wood or plastic or any combination of these is now no secret, nor is it a secret that this bonding done by radio frequency can be accomplished in a matter of seconds. With this knowledge the entire field of structural connections in architecture presents unlimited possibilities.

The development of new steel and aluminum alloys has produced much stronger metals than have heretofore been commonly used in building. These more costly alloys can be used economically only by revising the usual conception of structural framing. By resolving a maximum of stress into pure **tension**, which can be resisted by slender rods and cables.

The development and increasing use of metal alloys such as beryllium alloys, which have amazingly high weight strength ratios, will do much to lighten the structure of the house.

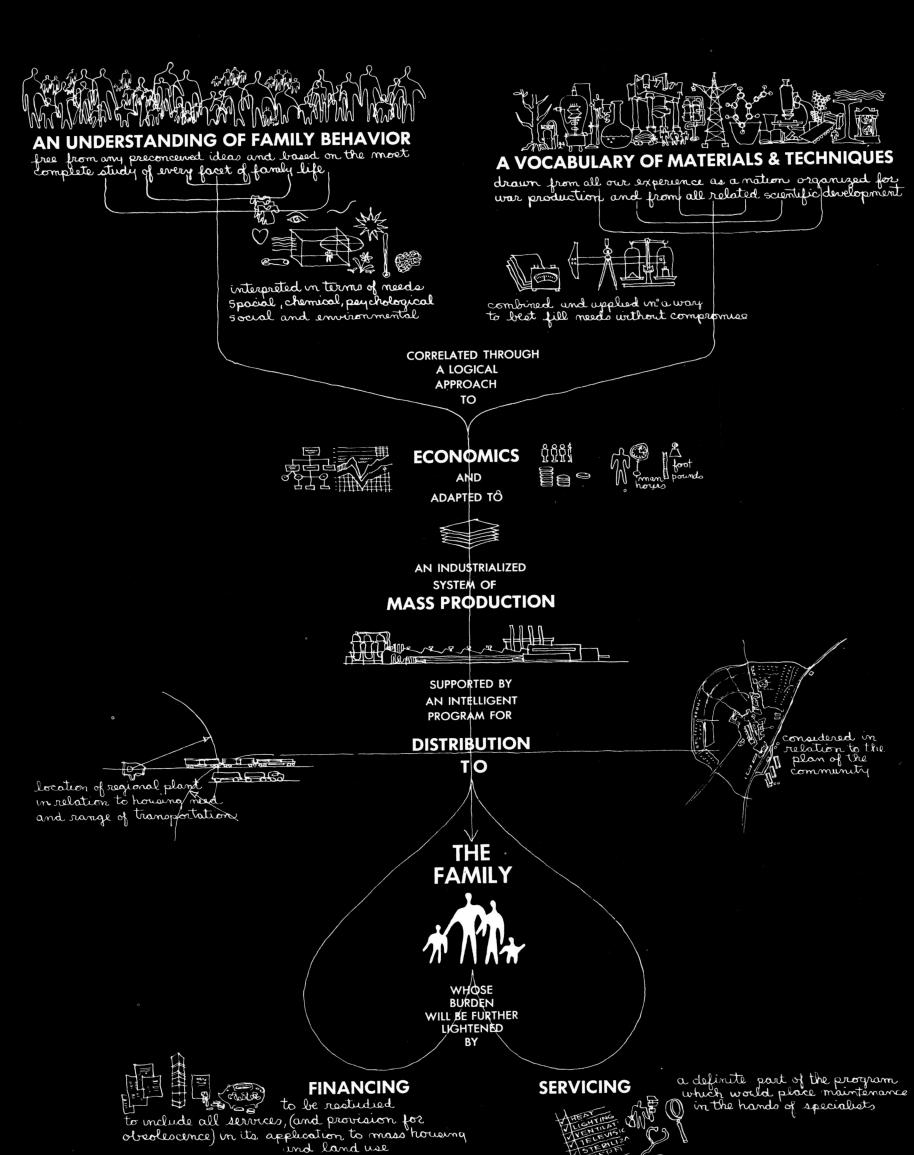

AN UNDERSTANDING OF FAMILY BEHAVIOR

free from any preconceived ideas and based on the most complete study of every facet of family life

A VOCABULARY OF MATERIALS & TECHNIQUES

drawn from all our experience as a nation organized for war production and from all related scientific development

interpreted in terms of needs spatial, chemical, psychological social and environmental

combined and applied in a way to best fill needs without compromise

CORRELATED THROUGH
A LOGICAL
APPROACH
TO

ECONOMICS

AND

ADAPTED TO

man
hours

foot
pounds

AN INDUSTRIALIZED
SYSTEM OF
MASS PRODUCTION

SUPPORTED BY
AN INTELLIGENT
PROGRAM FOR

DISTRIBUTION
TO

location of regional plant
in relation to housing need
and range of transportation

considered in
relation to the
plan of the
community

THE
FAMILY

WHOSE
BURDEN
WILL BE FURTHER
LIGHTENED
BY

FINANCING
to be restudied
to include all services, (and provision for
obsolescence) in its application to mass housing
and land use

SERVICING

a definite part of the program
which would place maintenance
in the hands of specialists

THE ARCHITECTS OF THE PREFABRICATED HOUSE MUST BE

1 THE STUDENT OF HUMAN BEHAVIOR

2 THE SCIENTIST

3 THE ECONOMIST

4 THE INDUSTRIAL ENGINEER

Determining the true need, which is the first step to solving any design problem, becomes many times more complex when the solution is to be arrived at in terms of mass production. Not because the needs of family groups vary in any great degree but because these needs must be basic and cannot legitimately spring from individual fancies. The information to be gathered must be exhaustive. Conclusions must be the result of extensive and complete study of circulation, all phases of space, environment, health, storage problems, and psychological likes and dislikes. All these studies then to be brought down to the most simple common denominator.

With thousands of the final design to be produced, the materials and equipment, designed to meet this common denominator of needs, must be as precisely appropriate as the modern scientist can develop. They must, at the same time, be appropriate to the system of industrialized mass production. There can be no compromise with the demands set up by this basic need. If materials and equipment cannot arrive at the solution of family need with the minimum cost in energy and labor, then the gathering of such data and research will be nothing more than a neat but fruitless trick.

The economist will be called upon to integrate and to redesign the use of capital (either private or government or a combination of both) so that it will function with logic and respond readily to the needs of enterprise without restricting the scientific use of man hours, foot pounds, materials on the one hand and consumer-distribution problems on the other.

The product as it comes together on the assembly line is not just the result of the correlation of all these phases by the industrial engineer inasmuch as the engineering of production itself will contribute to the final form of the conception.

The value of the house that results from such a combination will be measured by the degree to which it serves for the amount of energy it costs. The relation of service to price is so important that nothing can justifiably be added to the house that does not increase its value in service.

The degrees of service are real and can be measured. They are not dependent on taste. If this is true, then this is a house which will not assert itself by its architectural design. In fact the better integrated the services of the house become, the less one is apt to be conscious of the physical way in which it has been done.

Obviously these houses if they are to be industrialized in the sense of the production line cannot be complete within the conception of any one mind but must be the product of specialists in these several fields, each doing his portion of the work without compromise and in direct relation and in coordination with the others.

A house "SERVES" by giving shelter from the elements—assuring privacy and providing for the functions of

eating

sleeping

bathing

dressing

Do I have to live in a box?

Do we all have to live in the same kind of a house?

In our most classic example of mass production, the automobile, no one feels that his car is exactly like everybody else's. Cars parked at the curb all have something of the individuality of their owners, the many models and the wide variety in color gives each a character of its own. In the same way the various "models" in mass produced houses would offer, and to a much greater degree, opportunities for the occupants to individualize their environment.

Suppose there are four major manufacturers

and that each manufacturer produces four makes

$$4 \times 4 = 16$$

and that each make comes in an average of seventeen models

$$16 \times 17 = 272$$

and that each model may be had in six different colors.

$$272 \times 6 = 1632$$

Then in four years there will have been produced and made available

$$1632 \times 4 = 6528$$

cars each different from the other

Is this not conclusive evidence of the ability of industry to offer from the production line a wide choice?

The right to choose when it exceeds the limits of practical good sense can be a prerogative of very dubious value. In fact very often houses are built or bought for everything but the right reasons, sometimes for neighborhood prestige, sometimes for the social consequences of owning something bigger or more expensive or novel or attention-getting. Too many preferences concerning the inside of a house are dictated not by true value, utility, or beauty but by uninformed, high-pressured ambitions to achieve standards that are meaningless in terms of function.

To deliberately insist upon one's personal preferences in, for instance, the kitchen would not make sense if, within the limited budget of the average house owner, a prefabricated kitchen unit, designed and manufactured as the result of the most careful studies in function, space, and motion, resulted in a kitchen more efficient, engineered for every convenience, possessing all good known labor-saving devices, could be made available for a third of the cost of the personal-preference kitchen. It isn't a matter of having a kitchen like everybody else's; it's a matter of being able to have a kitchen that is enormously superior to any that could be conceived by the home-builder within any reasonable budget. So, if one insists upon the right to choose intelligently the only reasonable choice can be a kitchen ten times as good at one-third the price.

It is the kitchen, the bathroom, the bedroom, the utility and storage units that will profit most by the industrialized system of prefabrication. Here the activities of all men are much the same in the use of these basic household utilities, which properly designed and engineered will accommodate the over-all family function, and offer facilities and conveniences impossible to the individual's most ambitious preferences .

It is in the living-recreational areas that variation becomes a matter of valid personal preference where the family desires in terms of differences in activities must be considered. The accommodation of this difference in family activity is perfectly feasible and will be a natural part of the study of the industrialized house.

We choose our automobiles within the limitations of makes and models for the best kind of transportation adapted to our needs but in order to put the stamp of our individuality upon our automobile we do not demand that it have six wheels or two motors.

Unfortunately, personal taste has been considered all out of proportion to personal need and until these war years when more and more people have developed a greater respect for the right machine for the right job the sales promotion techniques which have persuaded a hundred and thirty million people to spend their money has been based upon the slogan, "Let them eat gingerbread."

As the sense of value increases and the demand for better, cheaper, and more efficient instruments for living becomes the criteria of spending, it will be found that the public will be less persuaded by blandishment and appeals to personal vanity than by real value determined by proper use of the machines and labor and materials. When honest use becomes the basis of promotional and sales techniques it will be found that no one really wanted gingerbread anyway, people were lulled into acceptance of the gingerbread diet, aerated whipped cream and all because so little else has been made available.

"Intelligence says, 'conscious inefficiency and non-adaptability to purpose, or change, are SUICIDAL'."—B. F.

"The function of the architect-engineer will be the irrevocable integration into society of an universally accredited into mary survival. This will be done through the adequate disposition of a constantly improving, available 'best' shelter, cloth-ing and sustenance, in a world which can already—through the effort of one man out of every five working but one day a month—produce and distribute the goods and services necessary to all."—B. F.

"The objective of a better, as well as a cheaper, house immediately raises the question: better for what? Obviously the correct answer is: better suited for the activities of family life that will take place in the house. Before the dwelling can be made better for family life, it is necessary to know what family life is—specifically and in detail. It becomes increasingly evident that supplying this need is prerequisite to improving the dwelling. No real progress can be made in housing design until there is in existence a mass of factual data on how families live.

"Before the scientific housing designer can begin his work he must know exactly what families do in their homes, where they do it, and why they do it there. Since families live in time as well as space, he must also know when they do things, in order to have the complete space-time use pattern. The families' possessions must be known, the quantity, type and frequency of use. But it is not sufficient for the designer's purpose to have merely a record of activities and an inventory of possessions; he must also know how much and exactly what shape of space is required to enclose them. He must know the families' habits, customs, and prejudices; what they do and do not like about their present dwellings and why, and what they would like to have instead. Information should be obtained on the families' basic feeling in regard to both space and time in the home; also something should be known of the fundamental dynamics of family life, the chief motivating forces, and the directions in which family life is moving. Finally the designer must know what the house must supply to meet the physiological and psychological needs of the individual members of the family. A handbook for housing designers should present all of the above data in the most usable form that can be devised, with variations for differences in age, family income, family future, ethnic background, occupation, and education, for rural and urban conditions in the different regions of the country.

"Present methods of housing design are a combination of tradition, rule-of-thumb, fashion, personal experience, and the codified experience referred to above. The basic conception is cellular, a cluster of rooms for more or less specialized use. Designing consists simply in establishing the number, size, and arrangement of the rooms. The family moving into the house must adapt itself as best it can to the fixed conditions of the design."

"Time and motion studies, a well known technic used in speeding up factory production, record and measure the motions themselves with the idea of changing them for efficiency in performance. This technic will be useful in studying the work functions, such as housecleaning, food preparation, etc. But here the aim was to measure space needed, as a first step in designing a dwelling that would free the family of all space limitations to healthful and comfortable living. It is recognized that changes in family living itself will inevitably follow design based on family living, and, in fact, that the quality of these changes will be the measure of the success of the design. Our primary purpose, however, is to measure space requirements of family functions in order to redesign the dwelling and not to redesign family living."

In case such minute fact gathering of family behavior seems cold, it must be remembered that any real attempt to make a comprehensive study of the family must include all of those little personal habits that most householders feel apply only to themselves. It is in the full knowledge of all these small and intimate details that the architect-engineer and his associates can design the kind of a prefabricated house that will consider and meet all human needs.

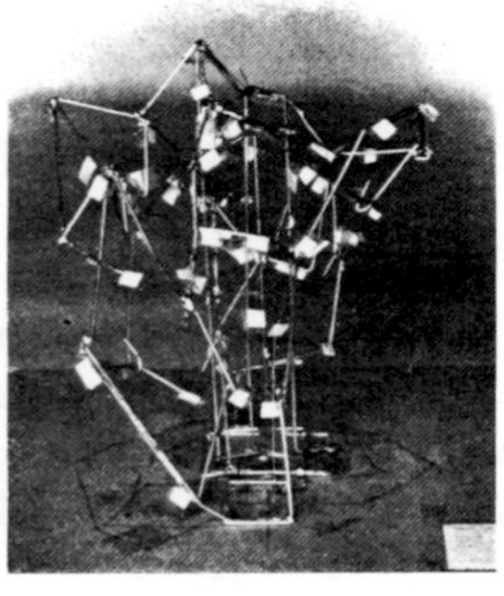

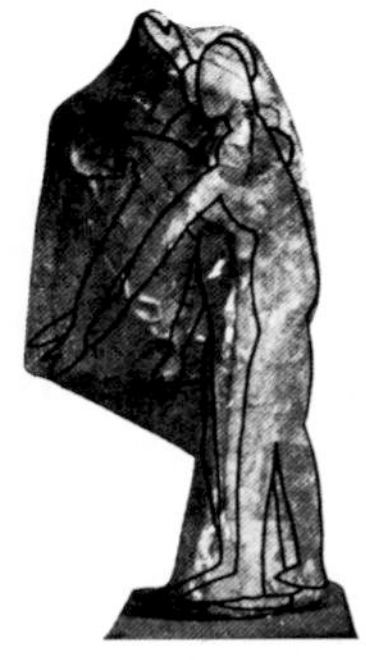

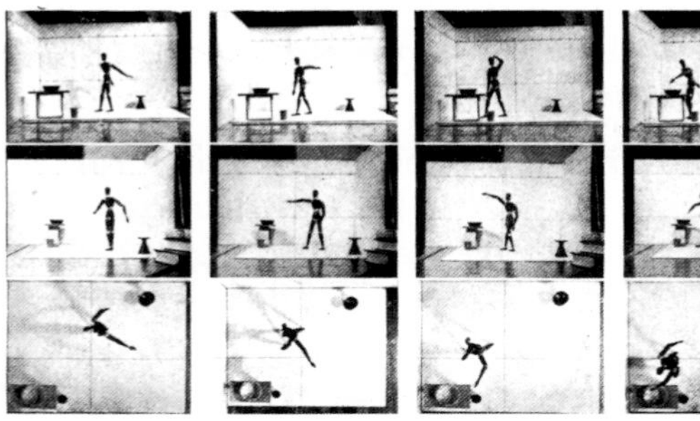

THIS MATERIAL FROM MEASURING SPACE AND MOTION AND FAMILY LIVING AS THE BASIS FOR DWELLING DESIGN, RESEARCH STUDIES 6 AND 4, COURTESY THE JOHN B. PIERCE FOUNDATION.

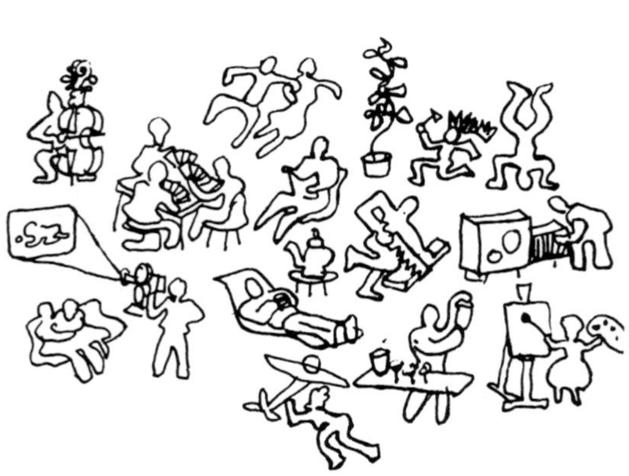

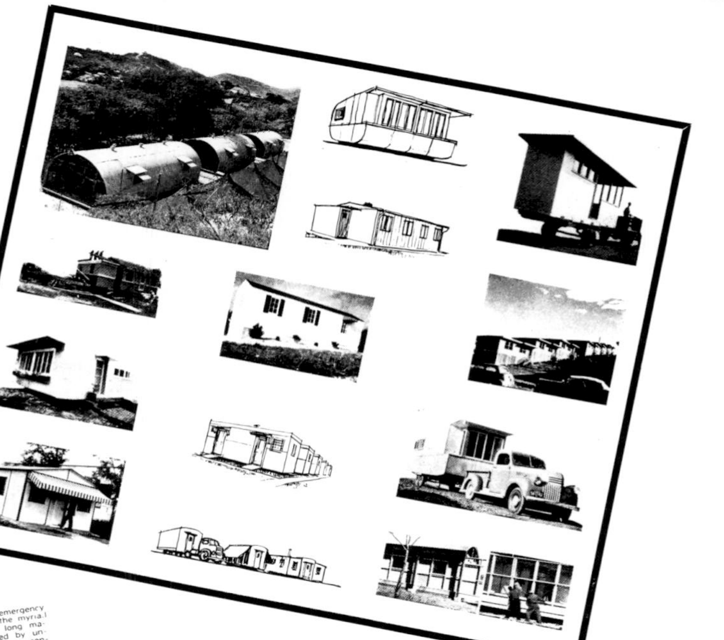

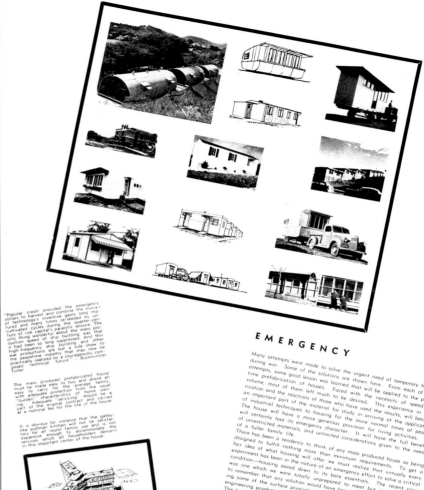

"Popular credit provided the emergency dollars to harvest and combine the myriad of technology's inventive gains long matured and many times re-seeded by uncultivated cycles during the quarter-century of risk capital's paralytic seizure. The only thing wonderful about the mass production speed of ship building was that it had been so long suppressed. And this high-frequency ship building and other war productions are but a side show to the peacetime industry that may now be practically realized by a courageously composed technical future." — Buckminster Fuller.

The mass produced prefabricated house must be made easy to buy and above all easy to carry for the average family, with adequate protection from the usual "burden" characteristics of home owning. Adequate "servicing" should be a part of the original contract and carried at a nominal fee for the life of the house.

It is obvious for instance that the galley-like pullman kitchen will not be satisfactory for all round family use and is not expansive enough to accommodate the services which all householders demand in this important center of the house.

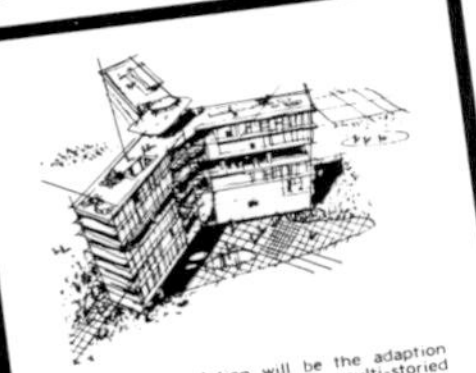

Prehaps one solution will be the adaption of complete perfabrication to multi-storied units with its obvious advantages in terms of land use and the freeing of green areas ... recreational purposes.

EMERGENCY

Many attempts were made to solve the urgent need of temporary housing during war. Some of the solutions are shown here. From each of these attempts, some good lesson was learned that will be applied to the peacetime prefabrication of houses. Faced with the necessity of speed and volume, most of them left much to be desired. This experience in fabrication and the reactions of those who have used the results, will become an important part of the material for study in arriving at the application of industrial techniques to housing for the more normal times of peace. The house will have a more generous provision for living activities. It will certainly lose its emergency character. It will have the full benefit of unrestricted materials, and unlimited considerations given to the needs of a fuller family life.

There has been a tendency to think of any mass produced house as being designed to fulfill nothing more than minimum requirements. To get a fair idea of what housing will offer we must realize that virtually every experiment has been in the nature of an emergency effort to solve a critical condition—housing pared down to its bare essentials. The recent crisis was one which we were totally unprepared to meet but it is important to remember that any solution would have been impossible without applying some of the surface principles of the approach to prefabrication that engineering prophets have been advocating for years.

The big concept of industrialized housing is not to be considered in any way as a stop-gap or tide-over. It is a way of life, a way in which all of the genius and accomplishment of the past can come together for the purpose of expanding and enriching the life of each individual and each family.

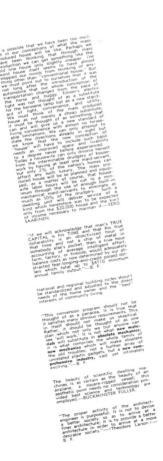

It is possible that we have been too modest in our conceptions of what the mass produced house will be like. Perhaps we have been thinking that through mass production we can get something like the old line house only slightly cheaper. The word house itself seems to have almost stopped our minds from thinking of anything other than "conventional house." But we must point out to ourselves that it was not long after the introduction of the automobile that our whole conception of transportation changed from the pace of the horse and buggy. Edison's electric light was not thought of as a substitute for the kerosene lamp but as a new standard of light, convenience, and utility. We must think of the mass produced house as not merely a cheap substitute; it must be thought of as something that can and will give us a new standard of living convenience with almost no forseeable limitations. We can only attempt to state the directions already in sight but we know that the new conception of "house" will have to include such basic needs as improved space and livability to a degree never before experienced. Today a housewife can only divorce herself from the interminable drudgery of housework by having at least one maid-servant, but only 2% of the nation's homes can afford any such luxury. The mass produced house will be so planned and equipped, as a matter of course, that housewife labor hours will be cut to a minimum through the use of enough built-in mechanical maid-servants to eliminate as much as 50% of the drudgery. Such a dwelling unit will deliver service of a kind which heretofore was to be expected only from the $20,000 house and the kind of income necessary to maintan it.—EERO SAARINEN.

"If we will acknowledge that man's TRUE CAPITAL is his TIME and that his true dollarability is an objectivized hour of that time and not a chip of metal in somebody else's pocket, then a true hour accounting of average intelligent effort, farm, factory, or fireside, would adequately balance costs as now determined by our abstracted fear-longing-and-credit poised dollars which total up to $4710 minimum annual family output."—B. F.

National and regional building codes should be standardized and adjusted to the direct needs of the home owner and the "best" interests of community living.

"This conversion program should not be thought of as a panacea. It is true that it satisfies many obvious requirements. This in itself should not make us skeptical. Rather, it should be thought of as one plan which not only we but anyone can see 'will work.' It is not what **new materials** will substitute in **obsolete mechanics**; it is what comprises the whole family of **new mechanics** which will make obsolete the old troubles; not a further array of unrelated plastic gadgets, but a **new comprehensive industry,** vast yet intimately exciting."—B. F.

The beauty of scientific dwelling machines is as certain as the beauty of an airplane, a square-rigged vessel; this aesthetic point needs no consideration provided best science and technology are employed.—BUCKMINSTER FULLER.

"The proper activity of the architect-engineer is purposeful. It is not to devise a better society so as to arrive at a finer architecture; it is to provide a better architecture in order to arrive at a more desirable society."—(Theodore Larson.)—B. F.

THE ANSWER . . . YES

In a survey conducted for the purpose of finding out just what people are likely to expect of the postwar house, the following figures were so startling and disturbing to the group that got the answers that they immediately embarked upon a campaign to destroy what they considered the **"illusion of the miracle home"** that has **"grown up in the minds of the American public."** If the figures prove anything, they definitely prove what we have thought all along: that the public is not committed to the living standards of the past and they only await the opportunity to accept the benefits of industrial progress when it is expressed in carefully considered use of materials designed to fulfill honest needs.

We quote directly from the survey:

"Prospective home buyers were asked this question about six projected developments in low-cost homes:

"At the price you intend to pay, do you believe that any of the following 'revolutionary' changes will be available?

"Complete air conditioning with cooling in the summer as in the movies	**72%**
"Electronic controls which will make housekeeping far more simple than today	**81%**
"Extensive use of plastics for plumbing, pipes, bathroom fixtures, wall surfaces, etc.	**81%**
"Movable partitions which permit the making of one room out of two or vice versa	**60%**
"Outside walls which can be opened up on a garden or terrace in warm weather	**54%**
"Rooms built as complete units which can be added or removed, depending on family requirements	**56%**

In other words, the overwhelming majority, planning to pay an average of only $52 per month, expect construction features or products which either did not exist in the prewar period, or which were available only to a minority of home buyers in the high income brackets."

In answer to the question **"Would you build or buy a new home if you could not get any or all of the above changes in home construction?"** well over 50% said, **"NO."**

The report continues:

"A further breakdown of the replies disclosed that families willing to pay more than $60 in monthly installments for their home expected the most for their money; those in the $40 to $60 bracket expected only slightly less; but even among families willing to pay less than $40 per month, from one-fifth to two-fifths said they would stay out of the market unless they could get the six typical changes they had been led to believe would be available in the immediate postwar years.

"In other words, the survey clearly indicates that families in the broad, middle income group—the bulk of the postwar market—say they will postpone buying a home until the 'magic house' can be purchased at the price they are willing and able to pay."

The above becomes particularly interesting when the report states its purpose and intention, **"Because of these alarming implications the Association has inaugurated a nation-wide missionary campaign to destroy the illusion of the 'miracle house'."** What do they offer in support of their **"missionary campaign?" Conventional types of homes with reasonable modifications such as wider acceptance of the low sweeping roof-lines of the California and Florida styles."** Concluding with, **"Once the 'magic home' bubble has been pricked, and the public correctly informed on what it can reasonably expect, the industry will be in the happy position of dealing with enlightened customers."**

This, we give to you without further comment.

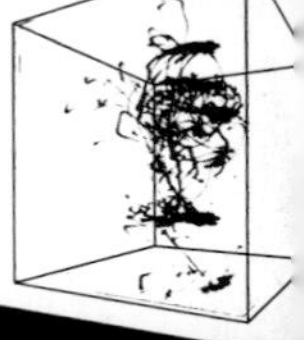

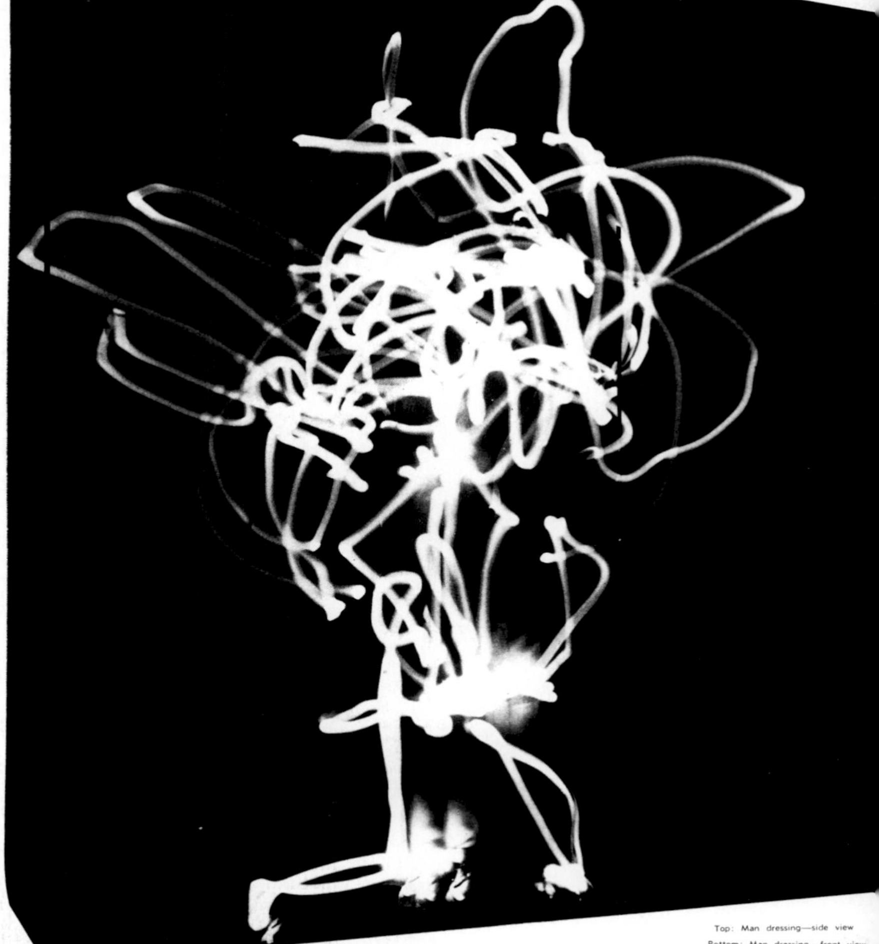

Top: Man dressing—side view
Bottom: Man dressing—front view

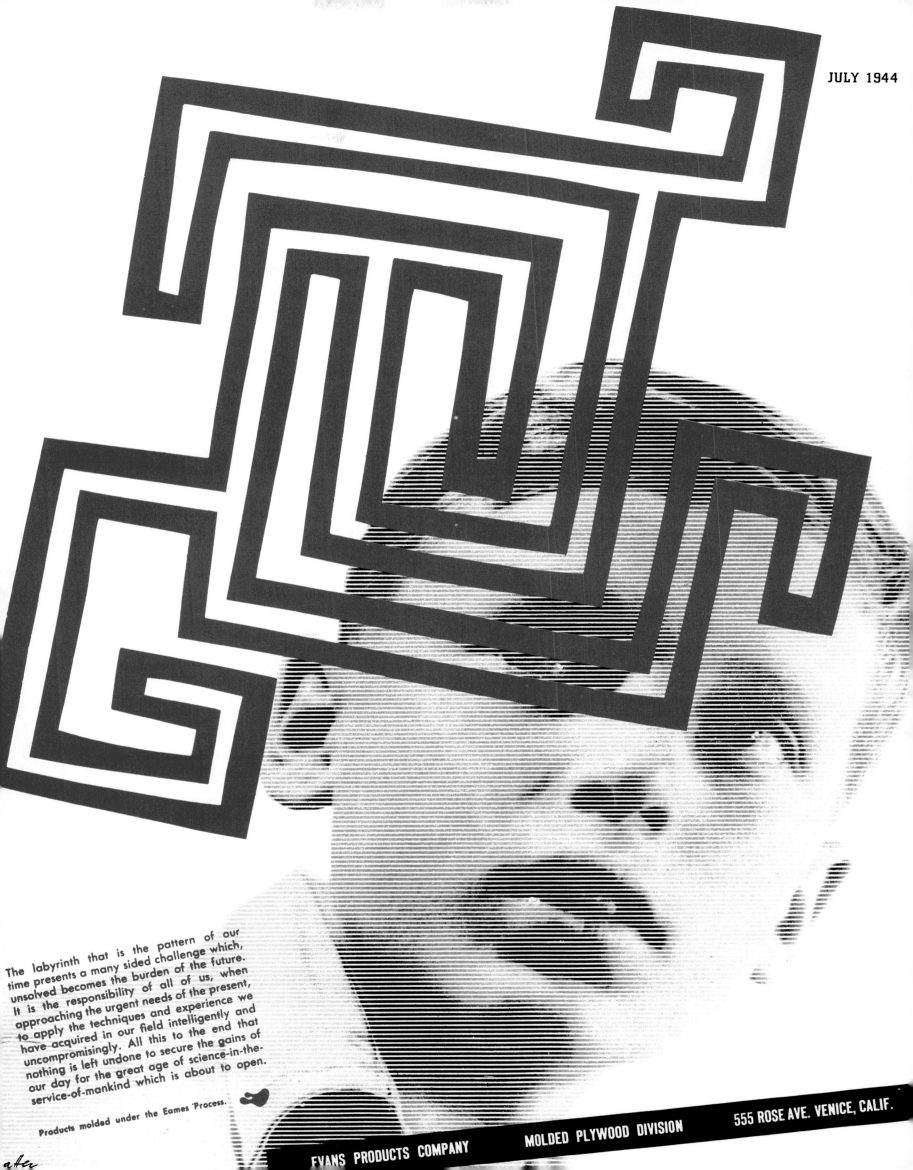

JULY 1944

The labyrinth that is the pattern of our time presents a many sided challenge which, unsolved becomes the burden of the future. It is the responsibility of all of us, when approaching the urgent needs of the present, to apply the techniques and experience we have acquired in our field intelligently and uncompromisingly. All this to the end that nothing is left undone to secure the gains of our day for the great age of science-in-the-service-of-mankind which is about to open.

Products molded under the Eames Process.

EVANS PRODUCTS COMPANY   MOLDED PLYWOOD DIVISION   555 ROSE AVE. VENICE, CALIF.

Abstract and surrealist art in America*

by Sidney Janis

● It is virtually axiomatic that vital thought in any epoch can advance only by means of a cultural spearhead or vanguard. Yesterday's vangaurd art is traditional today. Today's, just entering its second generation, has the drive and spirit of youth, and is still in process of growth and change. In 20th century painting, the virility of its two main trends, abstractionism and surrealism, demonstrates that these have particular meaning for rapidly increasing numbers of our artists and that appreciation on the part of the public goes apace. For, in the thirty years since the famous "Armory show," the handful of vanguard artists in America has multiplied in number, until today there is a nationwide practice of and interest in these dynamic trends.

Science is the open sesame of 20th century art, and artists have entered where angels fear to tread. With the wonder of children and the wisdom of the universe they have investigated, analyzed, dissected, uncovered, painted, pasted and constructed in the process of creating the visual counterpart of the anatomy and structure and inner spirit of the time in which they live—the NEW REALITIES of the 20th century. From the start the whole purpose of painting has been re-examined with scientific precision reaching in several directions and carrying over from one painter to another, from one painting movement to another.

The most important artists of our time are from many countries, and while Paris was the nurturing mother, many painters have developed at home, sometimes in isolation, or moved to foreign lands without a break in the progress of their work. They have appeared everywhere because in this emergence of the innate culture of our era, national borders are of minor moment.

The development of man's visual conception as a basis of artistic activity has gone forward in the 20th century with a tempo true to the pulse of this highly accelarated period. In an epoch throbbing with the vitality and rhythms of a new spirit, a time of courageous exploration and rewarding discovery, perceptive faculties could hardly do otherwise, perhaps than make a proper and consistent response to the force of the age. However that may be, the fact remains that with the opening up of vast new fields in science, the imagination of the artist has responded deeply to the methods and scope involved. That is why, to participate in today's culture, it is only necessary that a country be infused with modernization of its physical equipment. Focusing points both large and small reflect this fact like a kaleidoscope throughout the transpositions found in art.

It may be accepted as a working principle of our time that many artists consider the external resemblance of things only one part of a vast reality, to be utilized or not according to the need, and that they wish to express in a pictorial vocabulary the ramifications of the new forms and rhythms, the mental and emotional images that they experience.

Appreciation—Abstract Art
Effortless training of the eye through everyday experience helped immeasurably to break down those inevitable pre-

---

*From Mr. Janis' book of the same title soon to be published by Reynal & Hitchcock.

STUART DAVIS
Born in Philadelphia, 1894. Lives in New York City.
"Ursine Park," 1942, oil 20x40"
Collection Downtown Gallery

"**Ursine Park** was painted from studies made directly from landscape in Gloucester, Massachusetts. Instead of the usual illusionist method, the emotions and ideas were equated in terms of a quantitative coherent color-space system. Through this method the embodiment of the idea becomes more specific in its terms and more direct in emotional expression."
Stuart Davis, 1944

MARK TOBEY
born Centerville, Wisconsin, 1890. Lives in Seattle. THREADING LIGHT, 1942, egg tempera, 29x19"
Collection Museum of Modern Art

"White lines in movement symbolize light as a unifying idea which flows through the compartmentant units of life, bringing a dynamic to men's minds ever-expanding their energies toward a larger relativity."
Mark Tobey, 1944

judices that come with resistance to change. A vast majority of people not conditioned in advance by personal need or imaginative experience could accept only by degrees a revolution in esthetics unequalled in the history of man.

Influences derived from 20th century art, cubist and geometric abstract art in modern architecture, industrial design, typography, touched the daily lives of the people in innumerable ways. The esthetics of these forms, many of which could be manipulated, and their effectiveness directly demonstrated through use, were for the most part immediately acceptable to a public always quick to respond to the products of scientific research and invention. The original values in the works of art from which these forms derived, though not acceptable to a wide audience at the time they were created, are today more readily understood. Commonplace experience had helped many observers over the difficult hurdle to appreciation and to a more penetrating and conscious understanding of the character of their own time.

Appreciation—Surrealist Art

If America has its organization, its specialization, its worship of mechanics, its devotion to clean, precise, efficient machine appurtenances, it also has their counterpart in the ramifications of life within its machine-age super-structure of fantasy.

Mass producton, the boon and the blight of modern civilization, the hall-

(Continued on page 241)

OPPOSITE PAGE

top left:
RAY EAMES
"For C in Limited Palette"
Collection Mr. and Mrs. Charles Eames

top right:
LOREN MAC IVER
"Moonlight"

lower left:
GYORGY KEPES
Born in Selyp, Hungary, 1906. Lives in Chicago. "Aerial Photography—China," 1942, collage 25x49 collection Mr. Herbert Ziebolz.

"Visual experience is not only the experience of pure sensory qualities. Visual sensations are interwoven with memory overlays. Each visual unit contains a meaningful text; it evokes associations with things, events, and feeling qualities . . . If the plastic organization and dynamic organization of the meaning-signs are synchronized into a common structure, we have a significant weapon of progress. Because these images suggest a new thinking habit, reinforced with the elementary strength of sensory experience, the nervous system can acquire a new discipline . . . "
Gyorgy Kepes, 1944

below right:
FRANCESCO CRISTOFANETTI
Born in Rome, Italy, 1901. Lives in New York City.
"The Comet," 1942, oil 33x45"
Private collection

"This painting with a human figure was made during a period in which for almost two years I devoted my interest to painting moving subjects such as carriages, ships, sails, wings, the importance in the movement itself rather than in the representation. It seems to me that this feeling of movement and flight I tried to express can also be found in this painting of a human figure, as well as in the lighting which is generated by the central subject of the composition."
Francesco Cristofanetti, 1944

A. D. F. REINHARDT
Born in Buffalo, 1913. Lives in New York City.
"Red and Blue," 1941, oil on celotex 24x30"
Collection the artist

"Red and Blue is an abstract or non-objective work neither abstracted from nor representing any other objects. It means what its ordered forms and colors do. And it aims to be a part of the growing body of imaginative plastic learning besides being a personal expression."
A. D. F. Reinhardt

51

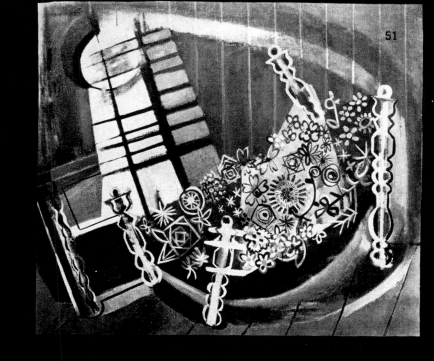

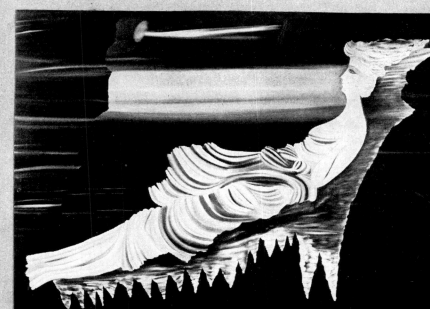

COLOR MUSIC—ABSTRACT FILM—audio—visual music

By James and John Whitney

AS TECHNOLOGICAL CONTROL of new art resources has matured, so has a new generation whose very childhood environment has been a conditioning factor toward acceptance of these resources as material of aesthetic experience. The main outlets of creative and perceptive experience with many individuals of this generation is somehow channeled in the modern technology. When this generation seeks a means of self-expression, they quite naturally take up photography, engage in amateur radio activity, or from old parts build a new automobile of private design. Little can be said here of the exact processes involved, but, in general, it is now clear that this conditioning factor as much as anything else is spreading receptivity to new mediums of creative expression. Contained within the fact is a promise of future arts with a broader base than ever before existed.

Radio, television, and the cinema contain inherent resources of art expression that today have not begun to be realized. This and coming generations will be responsive to the variety and broader scope of these resources. The artist seeking somehow an integration with a new time and society therefore must recognize and determine to employ creatively these resources.

Since the development of techniques of animated moving pictures, an art consisting of movement of visual elements within a temporal pattern has been a possibility. Such an art would possess inherently all the rich potentiality of sensory and structural appeal of music itself. With the development of sound cinematography, audio-visual relationships in complete harmony and unity of feeling became possible, foretelling an art utterly unique in this age. The small but vigorous abstract art movement of today may appear historically as the precursor to its development. That the sound-drama film occupies the entire activity of the present motion picture industry may be only a transient condition. Certainly, there is promise of change here with the development of television. Within the inevitable shuffle incumbent upon the maturation of television, emphasis upon the above currently dominant category of cinematic art may be withdrawn so much as to present in clearer perspective than visible today, the full field of the cinema art. Then, it is probable that the drama film would be seen more exactly as one section on a shaded scale of cinema art. Such a scale would also include in various proportions and interwoven shadings the documentary, the surrealist and the so-called abstract film. The following remarks are based upon experience acquired during the past five years work with animated abstract films. They are intended as an attempt to clarify certain issues centering around a new art medium that derives its existence from the new technological resources that either are in use or are possible today. They are intended least of all as a description of any aspects of that medium which may seem to have become permanently established as formal fundamentals. This is not surprising since here there are no such aspects, just as there are none in any living art.

Perhaps no other art has ever before been so much discussed and experimented with so prematurely. Leonardo Da Vinci speculated on it in *De Sensu*. From the 17th century, the line of experimenters and theoriticians becomes nearly continuous up to the latter part of the 19th century when greatly increased activity followed upon the invention of the incandescent lamp and progress in optics. Today the existence of a variety of means plus the imminent promise of television as agent of communication to dispersed audiences, plus the past thirty years of experiment by two diverse schools—the abstract film group and the experimenters with color-music has brought the medium to the threshhold of actuality. Discussion and definition of its issues and structural problems therefore no longer need be purely speculative in the absence of experience.

It is unfortunate that there exists the term "abstract film." Still more unfortunate that as yet no word has been found to name

descriptively an art having such a variance of unique qualities as to be improperly defined by the catagories of either music or graphic art. "Film" though currently satisfactory in the title, will become more and more misleading as the application of the technology of television modifies techniques by which works are realized. The word, "abstract" has perhaps more misleading connotations today than ever before as it is applied here, because of its present manifold usage in art terminology.

This medium is not more or less abstract than music. It should not therefore be burdened with the issue of abstraction in its very title. That it exists obviously on a level of abstraction should be a natural assumption as it is with music. "Abstract" in the title only serves to differentiate within the cinema medium as a whole that part which is neither dramatic nor documentary. It most certainly does not define or even suggest the range of perceptive experience which therein becomes possible.

The term "Color Music" freed from the history of its experimenters would serve more effectively as a name. But too frequently experiments with color music have been based on unfortunate pseudo-scientific analogies between sound and color. Also, usually, color has been divorced from its essential components: graphic form and movement—a consequence of the shortcomings of the devices invented to produce color-music. Furthermore color-music implies a separate existence from sound-music.

While the separate existence of a visual time art can be assumed, the aesthetic possibilities of the sound film and television dictate greater concern here with the future of a medium uniting sound with image. We will speak of the medium as audio-visual-music. Animation procedures having become the most generally applied means of achieving a moving graphic image, an organic approach to the subject of tempo in audio-visual-music is now possible. The illusion of movement is achieved by a series of static images projected in rapid sequencial order. Television as well as the cinema derives its illusion from this fact known as the Kinematic principle. The audio-visual-music image whether animated frame for frame or however created purposely to be reproduced on the screen or the television receiver only naturally should therefore derive its basic temporal unit from the frequency at which individual frames appear on the screen. With sound film this would be 24 frames per second. As a general principle both sound and image should have as a common time unit, the image frequency of the reproducing device for which they are intended. Music notation where it is used would be converted from metronomic time values to frame unit values.

The fact that movement is not continuous but a series of rapid static images actually limits rhythmic possibilities in the visual element relative to that of sound. For example with the minimum time unit that of one frame or $\frac{1}{24}$th second, the only possible next longer unit is the passage of two frames. Music, notes of shorter duration than $\frac{1}{24}$th second occur infrequently but notes of intermediate duration between this and twice and three times the fraction are very common. The animated image cannot be exactly synchronized to these intermediate durations. Thus it can be seen that the film possesses an inherent rhythm of its own which frequently cannot be tampered with.

(Continued on page 241)

OPPOSITE PAGE: In the film the illusion of movement is achieved by a series of static images. This fact has been employed in non-objective painting which tends to escape the temporal limitations of the frame (Paintings by Rudolf Bauer, courtesy Museum of Non-Objective Painting). A beginning in the search for audio-visual integration in the drama film is shown in the diagram of a sequence from "The Film Sense" by Eisenstein. 1937.

PICTURE FRAMES	SHOT I				SHOT IV		SHOT VI							SHOT VIII	SHOT IX	SHOT X	SHOT XI	SHOT XII
		A		B						A₁					A₁			B₁
MUSIC PHRASES		1	2	3	4	5				10	11			B₁ 13	14	15	16	17
MUSIC																		
LENGTH (in measures)		1	2	1	1	1												
DIAGRAM OF PICTORIAL COMPOSITION																		
DIAGRAM OF MOVEMENT																		

ANNOUNCEMENT

the case study house program

Because most opinion, both profound and light-headed, in terms of post war housing is nothing but speculation in the form of talk and reams of paper, it occurs to us that it might be a good idea to get down to cases and at least make a beginning in the gathering of that mass of material that must eventually result in what we know as "house—post war".

Agreeing that the whole matter is surrounded by conditions over which few of us have any control, certainly we can develop a point of view and do some organized thinking which might come to a practical end. It is with that in mind that we now announce the project we have called THE "CASE STUDY" HOUSE PROGRAM.

The magazine has undertaken to supply an answer insofar as it is possible to correlate the facts and point them in the direction of an end result. We are, within the limits of uncontrollable factors, proposing to begin immediately the study, planning, actual design and construction of eight houses, each to fulfil the specifications of a special living problem in the Southern California area. Eight nationally known architects, chosen not only for their obvious talents, but for their ability to evaluate realistically housing in terms of need, have been commissioned to take a plot of God's green earth and create "good" living conditions for eight American families. They will be free to choose or reject, on a merit basis, the products of national manufacturers offering either old or new materials considered best for the purpose by each architect in his attempt to create contemporary dwelling units. We are quite aware that the meaning of "contemporary" changes by the minute and it is conceivable that each architect might wish to change his idea or a part of his idea when time for actual building arrives. In that case he will, within reason, be permitted to do so. (Incidentally, the eight men have been chosen for, among other things, reasonableness, which they have consistently maintained at a very high level.)

We will try and arrange the over-all plan so that it will make fairly good sense, despite the fact that building even one house has been known to throw a client off balance for years. Briefly, then, we will begin on the problem as posed to the architect, with the analysis of land in relation to work, schools, neighborhood conditions and individual family need. Each house will be designed within a specified budget, subject, of course, to the dictates of price fluctuation. It will be a natural part of the problem however to work as closely as possible within this budget or give very good reasons for not being able to do so.

Beginning with the February issue of the magazine and for eight months or longer thereafter, each house will make its appearance with the comments of the architect—his reasons for his solution and his choice of specific materials to be used. All this predicated on the basis of a house that he knows can be built when restrictions are lifted or as soon as practicable thereafter.

Architects will be responsible to no one but the magazine, which having put on a long white beard, will pose as "client". It is to be clearly understood that every consideration will be given to new materials and new techniques in house construction. And we must repeat again that these materials will be selected on a purely merit basis by the architects themselves. We have been promised fullest cooperation by manufacturers of products and appliances who have agreed to place in the hands of the architects the full results of research on the products they intend to offer the public. No attempt will be made to use a material merely because it is new or tricky. On the other hand, neither will there be any hesitation in discarding old materials and techniques if their only value is that they have been generally regarded as "safe".

Each architect takes upon himself the responsibility of designing a house which would, under all ordinary conditions be subject to the usual (and sometimes regrettable) building restrictions. The house must be capable of duplication and in no sense be an individual "performance".

All eight houses will be opened to the public for a period of from six to eight weeks and thereafter an attempt will be made to secure and report upon tenancy studies to see how successfully the job has been done. Each house will be completely furnished under a working arrangement between the architect, the designer and the furniture manufacturer, either to the architect's specifications or under his supervision.

This, then, is an attempt to find out on the most practical basis known to us, the facts (and we hope the figures) which will be available to the general public when it is once more possible to build houses.

It is important that the best materials available be used in the best possible way in order to arrive at a "good" solution of each problem, which in the over-all program will be general enough to be of practical assistance to the average American in search of a home in which he can afford to live.

We can only promise our best efforts in the midst of the confusions and contradictions that confront every man who is now thinking about his post war home. We expect to report as honestly and directly as we know how the conclusions which must inevitably be drawn from the mass of material that these very words will loose about our heads. Therefore, while the objective is very firm, the means and the methods must of necessity remain fluid in order that the general plan can be accommodated to changing conditions and conceptions.

We hope to be able to resolve some part of that controversy now raging between those who believe in miracles and those who are dead set against them. For average prospective house owners the choice between the hysterics who hope to solve housing problems by magic alone and those who attempt to ride into the future piggy back on the status quo, the situation is confusing and discouraging. Therefore it occurs to us that the only way in which any of us can find out anything will be to pose specific problems in a specific program on a put-up-or-shut-up basis. We hope that a fairly good answer will be the result of our efforts.

For ourselves, we will remain noncommital until all the facts are in. Of course we have opinions but they remain to be proved. That building, whether immediate or far distant, is likely to begin again where it left off, is something we frankly do not believe. Not only in very practical changes of materials and techniques but in the distribution and financing of those materials lie factors that are likely to expand considerably the definition of what we mean when we now say the word "house". How long it will take for the inevitable social and economic changes brought about by the war years to affect our living standards, no one can say. But, that ideas and attitudes will continue to change drastically in terms of man's need and man's ability to satisfy that need, is inevitable.

Perhaps we will cling longest to the symbol of "house" as we have known it, or perhaps we will realize that in accommodating ourselves to a new world the most important step in avoiding retrogression into the old, is a willingness to understand and to accept contemporary ideas in the creation of environment that is responsible for shaping the largest part of our living and thinking.

A good result of all this then, would, among other things, be a practical point of view based on available facts that can lead to a measurement of the average man's living standards in terms of the house he will be able to build when restrictions are lifted.

We of course assume that the shape and form of post war living is of primary importance to a great many Americans, and that is our reason for attempting to find at least enough of an answer to give some direction to current thinking on the matter. Whether that answer is to be the "miracle" house remains to be seen, but it is our guess that after all of the witches have stirred up the broth, the house that will come out of the vapors will be conceived within the spirit of our time, using as far as is practicable, many war-born techniques and materials best suited to the expression of man's life in the modern world.

What man has learned about himself in the last five years will, we are sure, express itself in the way in which he will want to be housed in the future. Only one thing will stop the realization of that wish and that is the tenacity with which man clings to old forms because he does not yet understand the new.

It becomes the obligation of all those who serve and profit through man's wish to live well, to take the mysteries and the black magic out of the hard facts that go into the building of "house".

This can be and, to the best of our ability, will be an attempt to perform some part of that service. But this program is not being undertaken in the spirit of the "neatest trick of the week." We hope it will be understood and accepted as a sincere attempt not merely to preview, but to assist in giving some direction to the creative thinking on housing being done by good architects and good manufacturers whose joint objective is good housing.
—THE EDITOR.

Hella

J. R. DAVIDSON (designer) studied in Germany, England, and France. He came to the United States in 1923 and established private practice in 1925. He is recognized for the first modern designs of stores, restaurants, offices, single and multiple residences and interiors in Los Angeles and Chicago. He has been instructor at the Art Center School in Los Angeles since 1938. In 1937, he received recognition from the Royal Institute of British Architects; first prize winner in the Pittsburgh Glass Competition in 1938. His work has been published in Deutsche Kunst & Decoration, Moderne Bauform, Nuestra Architecture, Architectural Record, The Forum, Arts & Architecture, and House & Garden.

The following architects have accepted commissions in cooperation with the Case Study House Program.

Park

SUMNER SPAULDING, architect and city planner, was born in Ionia, Michigan, June 14, 1892. He attended the University of Michigan from 1911 to 1913, and received his Bachelor of Arts degree from the Massachusetts Institute of Technology in 1916. He has traveled and studied in Europe and in Mexico. He is the designer of many country estates; the Catalina Casino for William Wrigley Jr.; the men's campus at Pomona College, and he is chairman of the American Institute of Architects for the designing of Los Angeles Civic Center. He also worked with John C. Austin in the designing of the Los Angeles Municipal Airport. He has taught architecture both at the University of Southern California and at Scripps College. He is a fellow of the American Institute of Architects.

RICHARD J. NEUTRA was born in Vienna, Austria in 1892 and came to the United States in 1923 after having been in the practice of architecture in Europe. He has been in Los Angeles since 1926. Member of American Institute of Architects. He has practiced in California, Oregon, Texas, and Illinois. He was elected as the first American delegate of Les Congres Internationaux d'Architecture Modern and is now president of this world-wide professional organization. A city planner, housing expert and consultant, he is now architect and consultant to the Planning Board of the Insular Government of Puerto Rico.

EERO SAARINEN of Saarinen and Swanson, was born in Kirkkunummi, Finland, in 1910, and came to the United States in 1923. Attended art school in Paris (sculpture), Yale School of Architecture, Yale Scholarship to Europe.

From 1936 to 1939 he did extensive city planning research and other architectural work. From 1939 to 1942 he was associated with Eliel Saarinen and Robert Swanson, building Crow Island School, Winnetka, Illinois. When associated with Perkins, Weiler and Wile, Tabernacle Christian Church, Columbus, Indiana, and Centerline Housing Project, Centerline, Michigan, were built. He has competed in several competitions, including the Smithsonian Gallery of Art Competition in which his entry was awarded first prize and first prize in Arts & Architecture's First Annual Architectural Competition. Now working for the Office of Strategic Services, Washington, D. C.

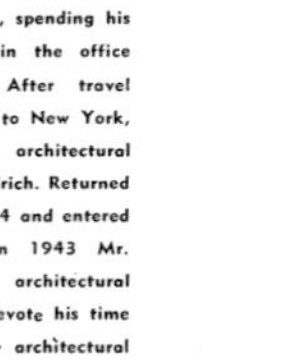

Sturtevant

WILLIAM WILSON WURSTER, of Wurster & Bernardi, born in California. 1895. Educated in the public schools of Stockton, later entered the University of California, spending his vacations working in the office of an architect. After travel abroad he returned to New York, working with the architectural firm of Delano & Aldrich. Returned to California in 1924 and entered private practice. In 1943 Mr. Wurster closed his architectural office in order to devote his time to war and postwar architectural problems, doing special research on Urbanism and Planning. Carried on this research at Harvard as a Fellow in the graduate school of design. Now Dean of the School of Architecture and Planning, Massachusetts Institute of Technology.

CHARLES EAMES, born in St. Louis, Missouri. Studied architecture in St . Louis and Washington Universities. Travelled abroad. Practiced architecture and industrial design in the Middle West. Developed the Experimental Design Department of Cranbrook Academy of Art, working with Eliel Saarinen. Won two first awards in the Museum of Modern Art's Organic Design Competition. He is identified with the war effort through the development of his process for moulding wood and the design of essential items and the techniques for their manufacture.

RALPH RAPSON was born in 1915. He spent two years at Alma College, Alma Michigan, and three years at the College of Architecture, University of Michigan. He received a scholarship at Cranbrook Academy of Art and studied architecture and civic planning under Eliel Saarinen. Co-winner of first prize for Festival Theater and Fine Arts Building for William and Mary College Competition. Prize winner in Ladies Home Journal Small House Competition; Owens-Illinois Small House Competition; Owens-Illinois Dairy Competition; Kawneer Store Front Competition; 1938 Rome Collaborative. He was co-designer of the "Fabric House" and the "Cave House." His work has been chiefly in the residential field and in housing. He is now head of the Architectural Department at the Institute of Design in Chicago. Member of C.I.A.M. In addition to architectural practice he is also designing furniture for several manufacturers.

ABOVE:
Even in Leningrad movie fans queued up to see the latest feature at the October Theater, in this case "Zoya," story of a guerrilla girl who outwitted and outfought Nazis behind German lines. Much of the actual footage was made in German-held territory.

Director Vsevolod Pudovkin in the cutting room.

BELOW:
Director Alexander Dovzhenko, a leading Soviet film maker, and cameraman Roman Carmen, speakers at the Moscow Conference on American and British Cinema, 1942.

Mobile theaters bring the latest films to the front. Though films shown are mainly documentaries and newsreels, features and musicals are rushed to the front as well.

BY ROBERT JOSEPH

• As in no other country in the world the Russians are using motion picture films as a weapon of battle in this war. Films are being used on all fronts, in all theaters of war, at home, in every city and hamlet of every province and Republic of the Soviet Union to keep the Russian people geared to war spiritually and mentally, as well as physically. One of the great stories of this conflict is that one which tells how extensively and effectively pictures have been used to drive the Russian people and the Russian will toward victory.

Although Hollywood and London, entertainment production film centers for the United States and Great Britain, and our own Office of War Information and the British Ministry of Information have made many splendid features, all designed as part of the war effort, respective movie picture-going publics have not seen these non-entertainment films on any wide scale. A few films, like "Fighting Lady" and "With the Marines at Tarawa," were widely shown in American theaters. An announcement by Twentieth Century Fox, the company which distributed "Fighting Lady," a splendid record of the Navy's air fight in the Pacific, that the successful reception of this realistic and dramatic film gave encouragement to try other features in the same vein, suggests that film distributing organizations have been reluctant to give the public anything stronger than the usual motion picture fare, with an occasional strong March of Time or a one or two reel documentary on salvage or saving waste fats.

Long before other nations, the Russians grasped the potentialities of the screen as a medium of information, education, and indoctrination. The Nazis borrowed extensively from the Russians in making their propaganda films, even invented a trick or two; but to the Soviet Union goes undisputed credit for using the screen as a national instrument in the interests of the State. Early Soviet films—Documentaries they were—like "Potemkin" (1926) and "Ten Days That Shook the World" (1928) produced when the Russian Revolution was still fresh in the minds of eyewitnesses and participants, are classics of the screen, and are an indication of how thoroughly Soviet film makers understood what the screen could accomplish.

Nor was the need for a high standard of screen excellence as visual entertainment either ignored or side-stepped by Soviet film makers. The film producers came to the same conclusion as their Hollywood colleagues: to hold the interest and attention of their audiences, producers must use imagination and skill, they must make the kind of pictures people will want to see. Arguments, and they have been vociferous and numerous, that Russian films are pure propaganda, and on that account worthless as entertainment, do not hold true. The film studios before this war—and after, as we shall presently see—were making entertainment films of the highest calibre. Motion pictures like "Peter the Great," "Alexander Nevsky," "We Are From Kronstadt," "Baltic Deputy" are motion pictures of the highest quality, ranking with the best that Hollywood, Paris, or London has produced at any time. These are not personal reactions but the considered opinions of motion picture critics like Frank Nugent formerly of the "New York Times," C. A. Lejeune, England's outstanding motion picture reviewer, Bosley Crowther, film editor of the "New York Times," Pare Lorentz, and reviewers and critics of leading magazines and journals. Soviet film excellence has been well established as a fact by the pictures themselves wherever shown; critics of all shades of political opinion have merely stated the same thing in different terms.

As World War II approached, an interesting change took place in Russian motion picture industry. Paralleling the reliance on heroes of the Revolution and Stakhanovites for picture themes, were the stories out of some of the earlier colorful history of the Imperial era before 1917. Peter the Great, the Imperial General Suvorov, Ivan the Terrible, Prince Alexander Nevsky, Kimelnitzky, a Ukrainian hero, these and other pre-Revolution figures inspired a new era in film making.

Alexander Nevsky, for example, was the Muscovite Prince who met and defeated the marauding Teutonic Knights of East Prussia on Lake Peipus in 1240. Released early in 1939, "Nevsky" could not have failed to impress the Germans who saw the picture in more ways than one.

"Suvorov" was about one of Emperor Alexander I's generals in the Napoleonic war. Suvorov was portrayed as a democrat, the one man who held the Allies together against Napoleon.

Ivan the Terrible, whom history has adjudged a tyrant and despot, a madman and a merciless potentate, is portrayed as the great unifier of Russia. This latest picture by Serge Eisenstein, one of Russia's leading film makers, does not attempt to justify Ivan's barbarism or ruthlessness; but the portrayal of a proud national tradition and of unity is of greater moment to those who guide the destinies of Russia's film industry, than any moral appraisal of a wicked man. Of course, Russian film makers may leave themselves open to charges of historical distortion, or at least historical equivocation. Did anybody in the house see Hollywood's version of Chopin's life and times in "A Song to Remember," or a slice of our own national life in "Tennessee Johnson?"

Speaking of his production of "Ivan the Terrible," Serge Eisenstein said, "We want to show the titonic achievements of this man, who completed the unification of Russia around Moscow. Concealing nothing of his private life, we want to draw the tragic portrait of the man. Today, during the great battle of democracy against this monstrous tyranny of Hitler, it is more than ever obvious that he who proves a traitor to his fatherland deserves terrible punishment; that it is criminal not to be merciless to those who have sold out their native land." Without attempting to get either into interpretations of Russian history or a question of historical morality, the only important point seems to be this: The change in official Soviet policy toward pre-Revolution history is understandable and justified if it has served to unify Russia and sharpen the instruments of public morale which go toward winning the war.

Another and more violent change in the Soviet film industry, and one of the minor epics of this war was the moving of Russia's film industry out of Moscow, Kiev, and Leningrad eastward across the Urals into Central Asia. Judging from the continuing excellence of Soviet films which have come from Russia since June 22, 1941, there was little lost motion and little if any dislocation in this great film exodus. The task was prodigious, for Russia's motion picture industry and its material compared favorably with Hollywood in size. The job of moving cameras, laboratories, building news and sound stages, transporting workers and technicians, literally building cities over night must remain one of the unsung deeds of heroic valor of World War II.

"The Soviet film industry was not caught napping on June 22nd," reports an official publication. Studios evacuated from Kiev, Moscow, and Lenin-

grad were in full blast five months after the day of German invasion, in Kiubyshev, Kharabovsk, Tiflis and Novosibirsk. A new raw film manufacturing plant was operating in Kazan by the same time." Later studios were built in Alma Ata, other Kazakstan and Transcausian centers, and the program of film production continued unabated.

Naturally the World War II offered the industry its chief time. The film was used as a weapon of defense and offense as never before. Cameramen rode into battle alongside riflemen. There was time, too, for lighter moments, and "Leningrad Music Hall," a vaudeville variety show, (of all things,) was literally made in the cellars of that besieged city. However, chief attention was centered on the war documentary, a type of film at which the Russians excel. "Sevastopol," the story of that city's courageous struggle against the invader, has been hailed as an epic of its kind. Cameramen and technicians were dropped into the beleaguered city by parachute to keep the cameras rolling in tune with the incessant fire of mortars and cannons. Days and weeks passed, and the siege of Sevastopol became a national legend, apotheosized by film.

Russia's leading cameraman, Roman Karmen, reports that Sevastopol exploit as follows: "Sevastopol. Years will pass, but Sevastopol's glory will be undimmed. At the Black Sea Naval Base cameramen worked under the bombing of thousands of planes, under the hurricane of shelling. Vladimir Mikosha, Dmitri Rymaryov, and others kept the cameras going without a stop. The months of the war rolled on. There was no sector on the Sevastopol front without the man with a camera. New forces kept coming to this Kinochronika (Soviet newsreel); young students from the State Institute of Cinematography. Assistant operators became fullfledged operators. There were not enough cameras. Sometimes film was lacking. We lost many comrades. Many times in action the cameraman had to put aside his apparatus and take up a rifle or machine gun. But there was never a shortage of men. Hundreds of applications to the Sevastopol front were filled by the Cinematography Committee."

The training of technicians is one of the major features of film production policy. Women and men were given equal opportunity for instruction and advancement. Maria Sukhova, one of Russia's finest documentary film craftsmen, began her work in the Newsreel headquarters as a janitress. She studied at night on her own and was soon promoted to a job as a laboratory technician. From there she was promoted to a post as a cameraman, and later as a producer. Her documentary "Iran," won her the coveted Stalin Prize. At the height of her fame she accepted an assignment to shoot pictures behind the German lines as a guerrilla fighter, and some of the best behind-the-lines films have been her work.

The amazing progress of the Soviet film industry under war conditions, even in the field of experimentation and invention (a Soviet scientist has recently perfected the three dimensional screen to a point where it is now commercially practical) is the result of pre-Nazi invasion planning. On the occasion of his being honored the Order of the Red Banner of Labor, I. V. Pudovkin, a leading director, made this report: "I should like to note this point, that the country has shown its appreciation of the people involved in the cinegraphic profession. It indicates, it seems to me, that the whole organism of the whole Soviet film industry is coming up to wartime requirements. It is working with the efficiency of a wellregulated factory. I think it would be true to say that they have been decorated for coping with wartime difficulties. You will know that for our film industry too these difficulties have been very great. When the war began, Ukrainian and Belo-Russian studios had to stop their work. Several of the studios producing films were in occupied territory. The Moscow and Leningrad studios were evacuated. I dislike that word "evacuated." It would be truer to say that like many other important war industries our industry was moved to new locations. There were difficulties, of course, but they were overcome, just as they were by the rest of the Soviet war economy. The Moscow and Leningrad Studios were moved to Alma Ata, the capital of Kazakhstan. Just like other factories we had to start from scratch on our new site. There was nothing even faintly resembling a studio in Alma Ata. We were given an ordinary theater building and it took much effort and ingenuity to go on. But we had no right to suspend our work for even the shortest time. Millions of people were waiting for new films about the war. We turned into carpenters, bricklayers, electricians and so on. We worked among coils of electric wire. It was in surroundings of this kind that Eisenstein started his monumental 'Ivan the Terrible.'"

Another interesting and in some ways monumental change which has taken place is the closer liason which now exists between Russian studios and distributing organizations and Hollywood companies. Pictures like "Hundred Men and a Girl," the Deanna Durbin film "Modern Times," Disney shorts, "Mr. Deeds," "Mr. Smith goes to Washington," "The Informer" among others have delighted Russian film audiences. It was inevitable that eventually the two film industries would meet, and it was the war which brought them together.

During the past several years there have been a number of notable Russian

(Continued on page 242)

WOMEN WITH CHILDREN I   pastel 21x18½"
Courtesy Bucholz Gallery, New York

GREEK SCULPTURE, GREAT, NECESSARY, LOFTY, has destroyed the mystery of the stone. Twentieth century sculpture: Brancusi, Arp, Henry Moore, have given it back to us. The classical cycle of two thousand five-hundred years has come to an end. But who of the living knows where the end ends, and where the beginning begins. A great destruction has set in in the arts, destruction of perspective, destruction of likeness. And at the same time return, rediscovery, recreation. Not sunshine imitation, yet light glowing from within, not appearance, a defined and definite vision imitated, but form and meaning growing, becoming, in the act of creation *while* created. Transparencies: Cries, silences, allusions, coming, evaporating. Fogs, coalescences. Solutions, enigmas, rhythms, dissonances. And the stone speaks again in Brancusi, in Arp, in Henry Moore. Henry Moore, the son of a coal-miner. Rediscoverer of the life of stones.

What the stone has taught them? That it is hard, impenetrable, granite. Frozen fire—meteor fire locked in stone—spark drawn from the stone. Stone hides—gold in stone. Stone sounds—echoing caves, murmuring shell. Stone reflects—sun and moon over rocks. Stone grows—stalagmites, corals. Stone nourishes—moss, lichen. Stone—form a hundredfold. Crystal—the alchemist's symbol of the universe. Stone a universe. What could the Greek say about it? The stone as such was mute to them, pliable medium of likeness. It was the Greek's great, human contribution to have overcome the magic of matter: As every gain in civilization, it was likewise a loss.

Henry Moore's sculptures are different from Brancusi and Arp's. His is the higher morphology. Early abstract sculpture was enamored with the stone. It remained material. It softened, it balanced, it never added to the stone. It lured it into its own hidden geometry. It aroused it to the feeling of likeness, to flight, to suspense in space. The stone threatened, the stone smiled. The stone became a new bridge between the organic and the inorganic. Incessantly the accent shifted from the one to the other. The stone was alive but it was stone. Henry Moore's concept is wider, more alive, more mysterious. To him stone is not an inanimate matter with the promise of form, to him stone is a mold. And the body is a mold. Both cocoons of the great butterfly—life. This sounds lyrical—no danger, the butterfly never shows its wings. Moore speaks only of the mold of life. This seems the meaning of the magnificent series of (Continued on page 242)

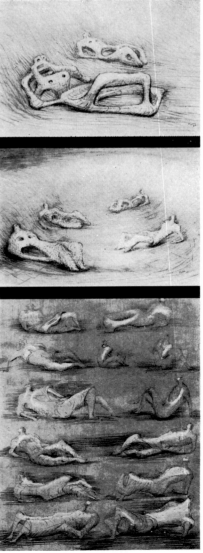

RECLINING FIGURES

what IS landscape architecture?

looks like it might be a chore.....

BY GARRETT ECKBO

Foundation planting?
The garden vista?
Exterior decoration?
Pictures to look at?

So your house is all built and you're about to move in and the grounds around it are a mess—it just looks AWFUL—and the house really cost more than you meant it to and you hadn't really meant to spend anything on landscaping right now. Besides Jane has been reading a lot of garden books, and Aunt Jenny says there are a lot of little shrubs at her place we can have for the digging, and the Windsors gave us those two sweet little holly bushes in tubs. Didn't the architect say something about a landscape architect? We've already spent too much money—but it does look awfully bare, and all the neighbors' places look so nice. Well, let's have that nurseryman who came by the other day plant some grass and bushes in front—that shouldn't cost much. We can fix up the back ourselves later. . . .

So the housing situation is pretty tight, but you've just gotten a swell job here, and you just have to get your family out from Cleveland. So you know the values are inflated 25% by the war, but you finally buy that house the real estate man has been showing you in such a condescending way. And you get your deed and move in to fix it up for the family to move into. It really isn't a bad house—it's on a good-sized lot, the rooms all seem big and pleasant. It looks like a lot of lawn to cut in the front. (I wonder how I manage the mower on that 45 degree bank by the sidewalk?); the front foundation shrubs are so big and overgrown that the living-room doesn't get much light, and that row of shrubs along the porch that's trimmed six feet square looks like it might be a chore. And of course that date palm really is a problem; they tell me it won't even burn; it sure fills up the front yard. It might make a good raft if we could get it to the beach. It's a nice big backyard but it doesn't look as though they ever did much with it. Of course you have to go through the kitchen and the laundry porch to get to it, and the garbage can and the clothes lines are a little messy right by the back steps. I always did wonder why they had to put the garage so far back on the lot: it makes the driveway so long. Of course only one bedroom window looks out back, the others open on the side yard and the neighbor's windows are pretty close. But we can keep the blinds down. . . .

Well, what is landscaping anyway?
First you have the virgin land, the nice flat land and the beautiful rolling hills. And the real estate men and the subdividers come along and lay out streets and cut the blocks up into lots and sell you one and that's going to be HOME.
The piece of land you bought is only the floor or the bottom side of your home-to-be. You live in the block of air immediately above the land, what we fancy designers call SPACE. Space for living, lebensraum, elbow room. If you follow the more or less standard prac-

H just looks AWFUL

tice of planning a house to place ON the lot, you are very likely to lose the use of a lot of this space—the side-yard between houses, the long driveway, most of the back yard because it's hard to get to from the living part of the house. What you have to do in order to get full use and pleasure from your lot—the most for your money—is to plan the development of the whole lot at once, every square foot of it, as a series of rooms, all pleasant, all functional, all the right size and shape, some of them indoors with roofs over, some of them outdoors with no roofs. Planning your home in this way you will realize that home is not just a house; it is at least a house-and-garden, that is, a complete indoor-outdoor unit. You will very likely think in terms of four general divisions of this unit: the public access—front yard and walk, front stoop or porch, entry hall; the general living portion—living, dining and rumpus rooms, terrace, patio, or garden; the private living portion—bedroom and bath, sleeping porch, sun deck or terrace; and the workspace—kitchen, laundry, service yard for clothes-lines, garbage can, garage, wood-chopping, kids' play, vegetable garden, et cetera. You will note that each of these four is an indoor-outdoor unit in itself: it could have a wall around it, a roof over half of it, and just glass between the roofed and unroofed portions. Planning your home in terms of such indoor-outdoor units also makes finally possible the correct proportions among them: general living can have the major part of the lot, public access just big enough to look well from the street (Mexican front lawns are stucco walls), the workspace can have what space it needs, properly screened so it can be as messy as you like, and so on. (Of course the intent here is to suggest that the architect and the landscape architect should get together first thing on the job.)

We mentioned space a few lines back. Just space with a bare lot on the bottom side doesn't mean much to you except room to swing your arms and throw a ball. It's only when we define it with tangible elements—walls or hedges at the sides, roofs or trees overhead—and furnish it with stoves and chairs and kids and dogs, that it really

Doesn't look as tho they even did much with it.......

begins to take shape and mean something to us. The size, shape, and relationship one to another of these defined spaces (rooms) are very important, not only to us sensitive designers, but to you who actually have to live in them. The psychological effect of the size and shape, color and texture, of our physical surroundings upon us is a great field of scientific research in itself.

The qualities of these living spaces are determined by the materials that enclose them. Structural materials and natural materials, wood and glass and brick, earth and rocks and plants. Are plants landscaping? Is home just a house? What is landscaping anyway? It is the organization of outdoor space for people to use and enjoy.

Of course when we think of gardens and landscaping we think of plants. Plants are fascinating. Plants are wonderful. Plants present

designers—professional or amateur—with a vocabulary of form, size, color, and texture that is tremendous in its variety and richness. There is such a variety, at the nursery and in Aunt Jenny's garden, that we scarcely know how to select from it. And we end up with plant frills and plant millinery plastered around our buildings, and with a continuous maintenance problem that makes us cuss the lawn and the perennial border, and really despise that privet hedge.

First the maintenance problem. It is necessary to decide in the beginning how much maintenance you can provide for your home grounds (or any grounds), and then to design those grounds in terms of that amount of maintenance. Plantings which take the most maintenance are lawns, annual and perennial flowers, clipped hedges, trimmed shrubs or trees, and plants which are fussy about soil or water, or have a lot of pests. So to reduce maintenance you plant the front lawn to ivy, honeysuckle, periwinkle, or some other ground cover (there are lots of them), and you plant just as much lawn as you want to walk and sit on, or you put in just a brick terrace, which takes no mowing at all. You make a deal with the corner florist for cut flowers

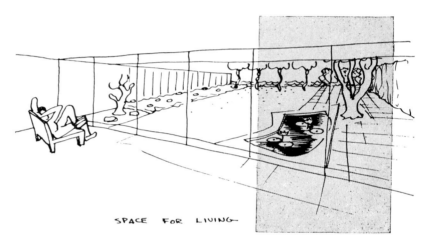

SPACE FOR LIVING

for the house, and you depend upon colorful shrubs and trees, and such old stand-bys as geraniums and day-lilies, for color in the garden. You select shrubs and trees whose natural size and shape, with perhaps an annual pruning or trimming, will stay within the space provided. And you take on only as many rhododendrons and peach trees as you really want to care for.

Now the esthetic problem: that is, how to really bring out and express, with some discipline, harmony, and order, the tremendous richness and variety of plant material. (Sometimes esthetics gets pretty fancy, but really it is just concerned with how we react to the things we see and hear about us. So it is important to everyone.) The principle basic to the solution of this problem is to emphasize the structural, rather than the decorative, role of plants in the formation of the spaces we live in. That is, instead of plastering them in polyglot masses against the foundations of buildings and walls, along streets, at the corners of walks, et cetera, we must establish a simple, clear relationship between the spaces or rooms which are being formed and the plants which are helping to form them. Say, for example, that we are dealing with a rectangular area—one side may be the glass wall of the living portion of the house, another a wood or masonry wall for privacy from the street, another a rough, untrimmed hedge of myrtle or euonymus, and perhaps the fourth, overlooking a valley view, is defined by just a row of small flowering trees. The sides of the rectangle don't have to be all the same or all different, and it may be some other shape, or have less or more enclosure, depending upon the specific conditions of the job. The essential idea is the freely arranged integration of definite structural elements related to the house, and of plants playing a structural role in forming the space, but maintaining their own natural qualities while doing so. **(Continued on page 243)**

Calder doesn't believe in broadcasting theories about his work. It is created in a carefree spirit of playfulness, of feeling his way along as he twists, tears, or bends a piece of wire or metal. Whatever he is creating—paintings, stabiles, mobiles, jewelry, gadgets, or water fountains—grows out of his job of living. His boundless energy and vitality flow through him, into whatever material he touches. Here is no preponderance of European "isms" understandable to a favored few who have travelled and studied abroad, but pleasure for anyone who has eyes to see. Calder has turned to the simple materials we find around us everywhere—bits of iron, wire, wood, and glass—materials which we experience and use in our lives every day—and has combined them with humor and gaiety into plastic forms. To some he has given a freedom of their own—motion—"not a simple translatory or rotary motion, but several motions of different types, speeds, and amplitudes composing to make a resultant whole," to quote his own words.
In using motion along with form and (Continued on page 243)

LEFT AND TOP: GOUACHES—SAMUEL KOOTZ GALLERY, NEW YORK

ON ONE KNEE, MOBILE—BUCHHOLZ GALLERY, NEW YORK

CONSTELLATIONS

notes

WE CONTINUE OUR HEADLONG FLIGHT from reality while frantically screaming over our shoulders that "it can't happen to us." The bitter fact, of course, is that it has happened, and continues to happen, and no amount of running around in circles can accomplish anything but a lot of running around in circles.

The economists and the sociologists talk of trends and cycles and Dow-Jones averages as though possessed of a full knowledge of the alchemy that will allay the spirit of man's world-unrest and exorcise the fevers on the brow of humanity.

Perhaps it is time for sooth-sayer and magic spells. And it might be that the cost-accountants can jiggle and juggle the figures so that they can make sense to the empty bellies of half the world. But also it is just possible that we are in the midst of a social and industrial revolution which we refuse to accept and with which we deliberately ignore our identification. But certainly the troubles of our time begin to take on a pattern which adds up to climactic changes in man's over-all way of life. While we are talking about the shape and size and the climate of the new world, and fighting for the old, reality rushed upon us unawares—and like people caught in a sudden flood, we find ourselves afloat and surrounded in a world in which everything has been torn loose from its moorings. Most of us of course sail sedately on top of the troubled waters, blindly refusing to admit that anything has really happened and stoutly maintaining that nothing can or will happen that won't be adjusted to everyone's comfortable satisfaction.

Somehow we suspect that the cost-accountants and everything they represent will not be the sources of any final answer, or any answer at all upon which we might build a safe security for ourselves or anyone else. First perhaps we had better learn to understand the nature of the revolutionary character of our point in time—and to concede form and substance to the change that is already upon us. We must demand of our leaders that their political horizons be enlarged vastly and extended beyond the parochial interests of their constituents, and for all practical purposes we must resist the currently fashionable retreat into what is called "the revival of spiritual values" as though present standards of morality developed out of mysticism will automatically solve poverty and race-prejudice and disease and the inevitable results of man's ignorance in terms of cruelty and brutality and greediness.

No world worth having is to be constructed out of the thought an action of opportunists and cynics convinced that civilization can have no order other than that which they understand and find profitable.

We speak so piously of progress, but hurriedly deny any allegiance to it whenever it encroaches upon standards which are pleasing to us.

We must, by this time, know that man's life is a changing pattern which will assert itself whether accepted and adjusted with wisdom and reason, or forced to proceed by means of violence. We have just gone through the climactic of a war which was fought not only upon the physical frontiers of the world, but the frontiers of the mind and the spirit. And that war, so violent and so destructive and bloody, was won—though not too many of us are sure of the purpose of winning. "We Won," without any attempt to gain any clearer definition of exactly what was meant by "We."

The enemy that challenged us and is only temporarily destroyed, is now no longer identifiable as a group of recalcitrant power-mad nations, but is actually a disease of society, the seed of which exists in all society. We now turn to the greatest battles of all. To fight within our own bastions and to destroy the most difficult of all things to destroy—that part of ourselves which we selfishly maintain in order to insure the continuance of our own very personal creature-comforts—our own national standards, created out of very special

(Continued on page 244)

Charles Eames

by Eliot Noyes

There is no need to qualify the statement. Charles Eames has designed and produced the most important group of furniture ever developed in this country. His achievement is a compound of aesthetic brilliance and technical inventiveness. He has not only produced the finest chairs of modern design, but through borrowing, improvising, and inventing techniques, he has for the first time exploited the possibilities of mass production methods for the manufacture of furniture. With one stroke he has underlined the design decadence and the technical obsolescence of Grand Rapids.

When you stop and try to analyze how he approached the problem, it sounds very easy and obvious. Whatever good modern furniture we have had in this country has always been expensive. Eames wanted to produce a good set of designs and "take them out of the carriage trade" by designing them so that they could be manufactured economically in quantity and sold cheaply. This meant that he must be able to use the best ways of doing things that the 20th Century could offer. Naturally he wanted his furniture to be as comfortable and useful as possible, because he never forgot that he was making his designs for use. This very direct approach made it comparatively simple. He never worried much (as many designers do) about "what the public wants," or "what the public will accept," because he had a profound belief in the public, and the conviction that if they didn't want or wouldn't accept the furniture which he was designing for their use, the fault lay in his designs, not in the public. He knew very well the absurdity of trying to design to an assumed public taste. It is important to realize that the furniture is an expression of this direct approach; each piece is composed as much of the personal ingredients of Charles Eames as of wood and metal. If you examine this furniture you will find sincerity, honesty, conviction, affection, imagination, and humor. You will not grasp how this furniture came into being or what it really means unless you understand this also about Charles Eames.

The collection includes a wide variety of pieces, using wood and metal as basic materials. There are many types of chairs both for indoors and outdoors, for dining and for conversation, for reading or relaxing. There is also a complete system of unit cases which, with the tables of various heights and sizes, fills out the complete set of furniture needed for living rooms, dining rooms, studies, and so forth. Of the whole group, the chairs are without question the most revolutionary designs.

Two of the most striking features of these

70

chairs in a design sense are their articulation and their sculptural quality. With the exception of the Windsor chair and a few classic pieces of modern furniture, it is hard to think of any pieces in which there is such a clear indication of the nature and function of each part. The success with which lightness and elegance have been combined with strength enhances this articulation. The marvellously clean details of the connections have made it possible for chair frames to be clearly expressed as distinct elements to which seats and backs are neatly and simply attached. To this revealed structure, Eames has added sensitive seat and back forms which give each chair the quality of a brilliant piece of abstract sculpture. On some, the thin metal members are linear elements of a composition in which the seat and back become subtle forms whose shapes and relationship change constantly and delightfully as one walks around the chair. This effect is intensified by the use of a broad range of wood textures, colors, and metal finishes, which also provide a great variation of mood in the pieces. Modern furniture has never before had such a range of woods so well finished. One extremely sculptural piece has seat and back of wood impregnated with a dull jet black, and a thin black metal frame making an elegant line through the composition. The mood ranges from the austere and somber through the broadly comfortable to the gay and even humorous. Some chairs have seats and backs covered in leather or calf hide. Others have bright red, yellow, or blue parts which introduce a new cheery note into modern furniture. There is an unmistakable quality of humor in the tilt-back chair, a completely new type which emerged from Eames' experiments. This design grew out of lunch hour activity in the workshop. During the processes of trying out new leg arrangements, and more as a joke than a serious idea, a chair was assembled with the four legs rearranged so that one leg extended to the rear and another to the front, with only three touching the ground at any time. This made it possible to sit down in a normal upright position, then tilt back and be supported by the rear leg, instead of leaning against the wall or teetering unsteadily in space, or worse. This model sat in the workshop along with other chairs under development and when the lunch hour came around, the carpenters and shop workers all made a dive for this tilt-back chair to sit in. Such spontaneous appreciation was impressive, and the chair was given further study. It has now become one of the most interesting and important features of the group. Great oaks from little acorns. . . .

Since the first showing of this furniture to the public at the Museum of Modern Art in New York last March, there have been many wide-eyed articles written about it. The structural innovations and technical solutions in these designs are so startling that it seemed at times that they were receiving more than their share of attention. It is not possible to overstate their importance, and I shall discuss them all in detail later on.

It will be useful first to review the circumstances which led Eames into making furniture.

Eames is basically an architect. His first excursion into furniture design was with Eero Saarinen when they jointly entered the Organic Design Competition conducted by the Museum of Modern Art in 1940-41, receiving two first prizes. Their designs proposed for the first time the use of molded plywood forms for chairs to fit the human body. The jury, in awarding the prizes, decided that these designs were possible to construct, although nobody, including the technical experts present, had any very exact idea of just how it might be done.

By the terms of the competition, winning designs were to be produced and offered for sale. The next step, therefore, was to search out the means for producing

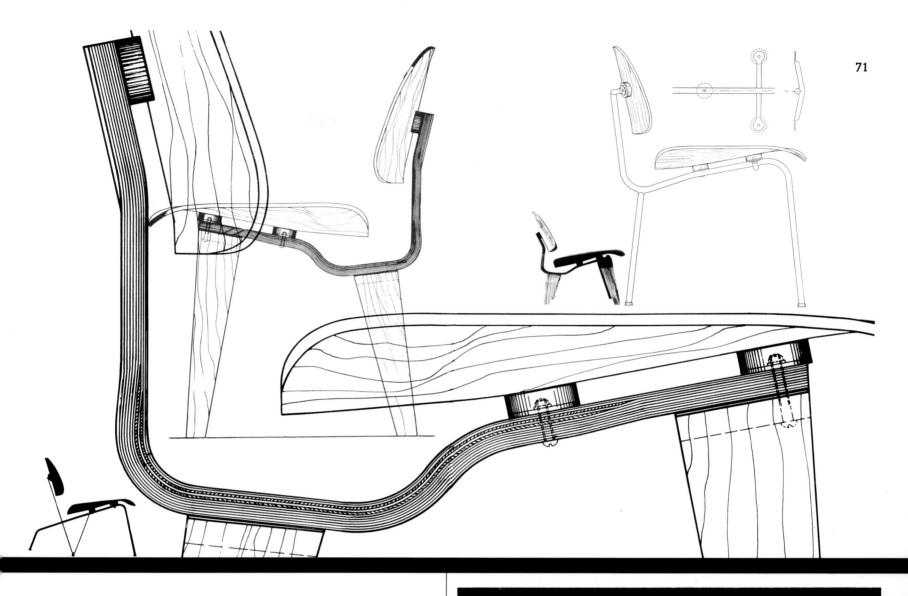

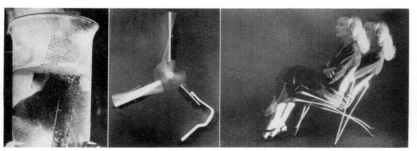

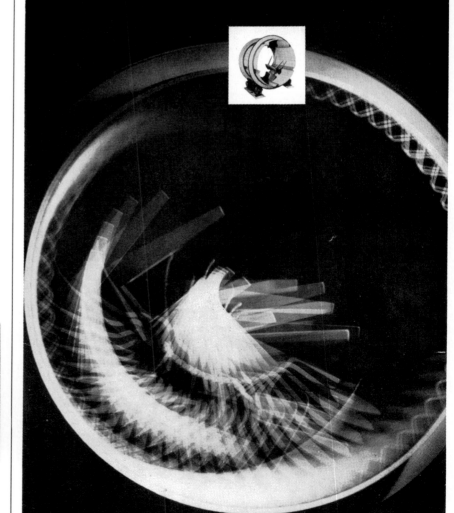

A necessary part of the problem is the consideration of conserving of space or storage and shipping.

and meetings of different materials came up, it became clear how extremely little thought had gone into these important elements of furniture design. Preoccupied with minor adjustments of exterior appearance and "styling," manufacturers were using essentially the same joints and structures that had been standard for centuries. If you doubt this, go to a department store and look at the underside of some of the tables and chairs built in 1946. You will see what clumsy antiquarian techniques are hidden under the slick surfaces. Structural ineptitude has been all too easy to cover up.

The result of the competition effort was that a new conception had been established, a few expensive pieces had been made, and some excellent ideas set in motion. The effort to find a way of producing such furniture cheaply and in quantity had failed for the time being. What had been accomplished was not a hundredth part of what Eames has achieved between that time and the present.

It was at this point that Eames moved to the west coast and started work for a movie company. Convinced that the problems of the furniture program were actually soluble, he decided

to experiment. Furtively and at night, to avoid the landlord's wrath, Charles Eames and his wife, Ray Eames, began smuggling structural lumber into their hillside apartment. From the nocturnal hammering and sawing, and the puffing of the bicycle pump, Eames found that he could make very clean-surfaced three dimensional forms using thin sheets of wood veneer laid up in thicknesses the variation of which he also could control. By this time the United States was at war, and Eames turned his attention to developing traction splints by his new system. This was an interesting problem, and related to the chairs as a problem of making a three dimensional form to fit the human body. The traction splint which he developed was light, strong, easily stacked for shipping, and simple to apply under field conditions. Thousands of them were used by the Navy. As his skill increased, he began making other items for wartime use, including molded leading-edge sections for training planes, and parts for army gliders. In this way, learning as he worked, and inventing as he went along, he developed the tools which made his molds possible, and he evolved his own techniques for doing economically what had been impossible before. In the making of furniture from the competition designs, the factory had used precision tools, but had produced results which were far from precise. Now, as Eames puts it, he had devised a way of doing precision work without precision tools. The difference, he explained, was like this: If you have an ordinary tumbler and wish to close the open top, one way is to take a very accurate measurement of the interior size of the opening, and to machine a part which will exactly fit into it, thus sealing the opening. This would be somewhat expensive, and there still might be leaks. Another way to do the same job is to hold your hand over the tumbler's mouth. Eames' process for making molded plywood has this same basically simple approach.

Toward the end of the war years, while Eames was engaged primarily in making splints and aircraft parts, a connection was made with the Evans Products Company. As the Molded Plywood Division of this organization, Eames was able to carry on, in a well equipped shop, his design and technical experimentation which has led to the creation of the present group of furniture. It is also through the Evans Products Company that the large scale production and distribution of these pieces will be undertaken.

So successful a combining of forces by a large established company and a progressive designer is almost unique in this country. Usually a company's natural

72

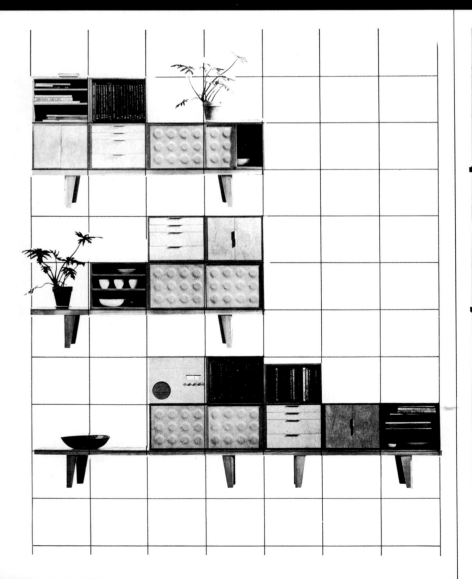

"The unit cases are simply placed on low benches which lift them off the floor. The benches are made in several lengths and there is no limit to the number of different combinations which may be made with the unit."

conservatism has dominated the designer's desire to realize fully his conception, resulting in an unfortunate and unnecessary compromise. It is a tribute to the intelligence, vision, and enthusiasm of Edward Evans, Jr., president of the Evans Products Company, that Eames' designs are to be produced without any loss in quality or character. It is only through such understanding of the fine industrial designer by the modern executive that real progress can be made in producing design for use.

The method which Eames invented is important not only as an economical way of producing molded forms rapidly and in quantity production; it also gave him the means for easily making many design experiments. Without any very great investment in elaborate and expensive tools or jigs, he could try out many different forms, modulating contours, revising thicknesses, and finally arriving at the forms which he wanted.

73

For Eames is first of all a designer, and his technical innovations were tools for design, as well as methods for manufacture. This achievement in molding was only the first of a number of innovations which Eames has introduced to furniture making. Another is shock mounting. All the pioneer designers of modern furniture have been occupied with trying to make chairs which will move or flex as the sitter adjusts his position. Significant progress was made along these lines by such men as Mies van der Rohe, Aalto, and Bruer. Eames has carried this idea farther. His molded plywood chair parts are flexible in themselves to some extent. This flexing is then increased by the use of rubber shock mounts in connecting all the parts to each other. In themselves shock mounts are not new. The mounting of engines on rubber blocks to reduce vibration has long been a standard practice in automobiles and aircraft, but this is the first time that it has been used on chairs. On Eames' pieces, this mount is a thick rubber disc which is used between the various chair parts where they are joined. To make a firm connection between these rubber mounts and the parts of the chair posed still another new problem. Here Eames borrowed a technique which had been highly developed in wartime industries. Instead of attempting to attach the chair back, rubber mount, and wood frame to each other by bolts or by any usual cementing system, a process called Cycleweld was used. In this, a sheet of synthetic resin is placed between parts to be joined. A special electronic instrument then transmits heat by radio wave directly to the resin, which "cures" or bonds the parts to each other without injuriously heating the wood. The process requires only a few seconds, and gives a permanent waterproof joint, which is actually stronger than the wood itself. This welding process is versatile in that it can be used to join almost any two materials, and it offers many important advantages. First, it can be used as the adhesive to bond the various laminations of the plywood itself, giving a finished piece in which the plies will never separate, and which may be subjected to extreme conditions of heat and moisture. Second, the speed and precision of the operation makes it an important technique for mass production. Third, when used as in this furniture to attach chair parts to shock mounts, it distributes stresses over the total area of the mount rather than letting the entire load be concentrated at a single point, which is the case where a bolt is used, for example. Finally, it solves for the first time the difficult problem of making a neat and permanent connection between upholstery material and wood, which becomes another cleanly articulated detail on these chairs. Where, on a chair seat, a foam rubber pad is covered by fabric or leather, this covering material is brought to the edge of the plywood just as if it were another ply, and is bonded there without covering up the expressive plywood edge.

This electronic welding has also been used structurally on Eames' benches and tables. On all these pieces, the legs are detachable. This is not a new idea. Table legs have often been made to bolt to the frame of the table top so that they were removable. There were usually difficulties with this system, since any slight variation in the bolt holes gave slight variations in leg angles, and resulted in wobbly tables where perhaps only three out of four legs touched the ground. This was a shortcoming due to insufficient precision. On the Eames pieces, these joints are handled with the same precision that one finds in the aircraft industry, where there can be no approximations in the way a wing fitting attaches to a fuselage. The joint between leg and table top is made through exactly mated metal fittings. The critical point occurs in the precision of the attachment of these fittings to the table top and to the leg. By means of the Cycleweld process, this can be done quickly and accurately in a jig which allows no deviations.

The fittings on leg and table top are then bolted together with self-locking aircraft bolts.

The precision of this operation is typical of the entire production process; as another aspect of it, standardization of similar parts has been accomplished to the point of complete interchangeability. This has many useful aspects. Similar parts can be stacked or nested for shipping or storage, and when the chairs are assembled by the distributor, any seat and any back will fit any frame. This not only simplifies greatly the problems of handling, shipping, and assembly, but actually helps keep the retail cost of the furniture down, since it becomes more compact for shipment and thus reduces the freight cost per chair.

The group includes pieces for both indoor and outdoor use, though indeed they are interchangeable. This is made possible by the fact that all wood parts have been treated with a resinous impregnation which has two chief effects. First it makes the wood completely weatherproof. Chairs and tables may be left outdoors in the stiffest climate from Labor Day till Easter, and may be washed down with the garden hose nightly if you wish. This impregnation also has the effect of hardening the wood surface so that it becomes much more resistant to scratches and dents. All the metal parts are also weatherproof, having a chrome or cadmium plating which is impervious to weather. These metal parts may eventually be made of stainless steel.

Another type of impregnation has been used most effectively on some pieces. This is the use of brilliant dyes, also weather and alcohol proof, with which the wood has been stained deeply and permanently. These bright reds, yellows, and blues penetrate the wood plies and give a stunning effect but do not cover or blur in any way the natural character or surface markings of the wood.

The case pieces are based on a modular system and advantage has been taken of all the new techniques in their manufacture. A few new tricks have been added here, such as the decorative box-jointed corners, and the molded drawers on metal tracks. This unit design is probably the simplest and most flexible yet devised as well as the best in appearance. The unit cases are simply placed on low benches which lift them off the floor. The benches are made in several lengths and there is no limit to the number of different combinations which may be made with the units. Since the cases may be built up beside or on top of each other without any mechanical connection, the system becomes utterly simple. They provide a perfect complement to the various chairs.

The enthusiasm which Eames' furniture has aroused through its first showings and through publication has been equalled only by the impatience of the public, which is ready to buy as much of it as can be turned out. We are all eagerly awaiting its appearance.

CONSTRUCTION A REVOLUTIONARY STRUCTURAL SYSTEM

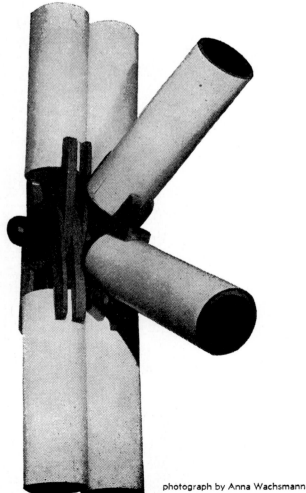

■ The problem of structural fluidity over large areas is approached with a completely fresh conception by Konrad Wachsmann in what he has called Mobilar Structures. What at first appears to be a giant plaything put together from a child's building set, is actually a remarkable half-inch scale model of an airplane hangar of this revolutionary construction. The great truss roof, which would actually measure 140 by 200 feet, is cantilevered boldly out from four supports of incredible lightness. The floor area is almost entirely unobstructed, and the removable external walls permit maximum freedom of circulation.

Mobilar construction was conceived by Konrad Wachsmann, president of the General Panel Corporation, whose architectural inventions had already established him as a leader in developing interchangeable members for building constructon.

Wachsmann worked out details with two partners, Charles and Albert Wohlstetter. Paul Weidlinger calculated the stresses and functions of the construction and the final results were shown recently at The Museum of Modern Art.

Two basic inventions form the root of Mobilar (Continued on page 244)

photograph by Anna Wachsmann

BY KONRAD WACHSMANN

Konrad Wachsmann, architect
Paul Weidlinger, Engineer
material courtesy The Museum of Modern Art

Opposite page:
    airplane hangar—roof structure
    mobilar tube joint—part of a truss

This page:
    main truss and column seen from below
    airplane hangar—general view with doors
    partly removed

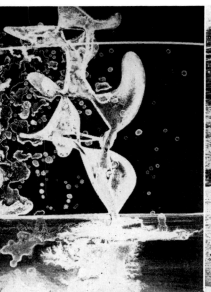 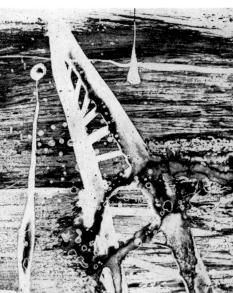  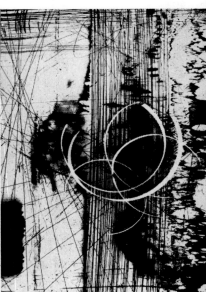

Gyorgy Kepes

Born out of an acquisitive society, photography by nature has tried to appropriate everything in the visible world. It explored and took accelerated possession of newly discovered territories in the visual environment. Things hitherto unseen because they were too fast or too slow, too big or too small, too far or too dense for the unaided eye to encompass, were brought by science within reach of the camera. Optical experiences, which had been confined within the life-span, orbit, and memory of the individual became solid possessions which could be inherited from the past, bequeathed to the future, and circulated in the present.

Photography thus helped to establish a new common world of visual perception.

As a stranger to this new and broader world, unable to comprehend it as an integrated whole, man was afraid. Retreating from the need to grasp this world in human terms, he developed instead a compulsion to possess, collect, and record still further the optical (**Continued on page 244**)

"RED STRUCTURE"   Ink And Gouache, 1945

ABSTRACT PAINTING, 1945   Ink. Crayon And Gouache, 1945

REINHARDT

"The expressive and structural meaning of color space in painting is my main creative interest. The collage with its spontaneous and accidental aspects, along with the completely controlled is an important medium for me. I also believe painting cannot be the only activity of a mature artist."—AD REINHARDT.

COLLAGE. 1946

Ad Reinhardt is a graduate of Columbia University. He has had a series of shows, among them, at the Betty Parsons Gallery, New York; Teachers College, Columbia University; Artists Gallery; and the Brooklyn Museum. He is a member of American Abstract Artists and is represented in the Gallatin Collection, The Museum of Living Art, The Philadelphia Museum, and the Abbot Kimball Collection. Among his many activities there have been Murals for the World's Fair, for the Newspaper Guild Club and the pamphlet done with Ruth Benedict and Gene Weltfish called, "Races of Mankind."

The following pages are from a series by Ad Reinhardt which is in the nature of a preview of a book soon to be published. The material is a part of his creative work as an activity in the field of an educational campaign undertaken for the Daily Press.

HOW---TO---LOOK

by Ad Reinhardt.

A sixth and a summation of a series on modern art   (more to come)

We saw that pictures these days are only imitations and substitutes of real things and therefore not "high" art. If you think that a "picture" of a sunset or a nude is real, then you don't have much fun, do you?

We saw that "pictures" belonged to another age, when human beings (after years of concern with religious salvation and the supernatural) discovered the natural world and what it looked like (the Renaissance).

We saw that perspective, shading, anatomy, naturalistic drawing are simply a bag of illustrative tricks and that anyone can do it better with a camera, huh?

We saw that an artist who makes "pictures" and purveys subject-matter is a peddler of phoney spaces (buckeye) and optical illusions. We saw that "pictures" are a kind of opium of the people and not good.

We saw that surrealists spend their space-time satirizing the tricks, tools and techniques of the "picture-making trade." Not only one picture or story, but numberless pictures, endless stories, infinite subject-matter.

Because surrealist painters ran the "picture-art" tradition into the ground, and out-illustrated the illustrators, we called it "low" art, see....

We saw that both light and time is space, that you yourself are a space, that a painting is a flat space. We saw that an abstract painting is not a window-frame - peep - show - hole - in - the - wall but a new object or image hung on the wall and an organization of real space relations, line structures, color activity.

Because it paralleled the condition of "pure" music, we called it "high" art and no "picture.".....

Now we can go on to really look.

(Five minute break, boys, to refresh your memory.)

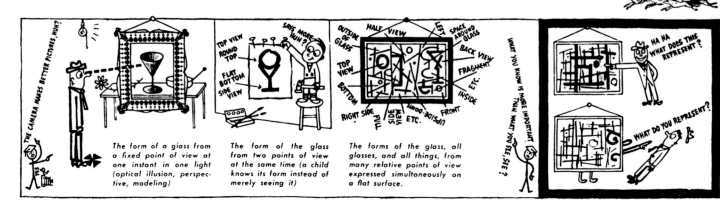

The form of a glass from a fixed point of view at one instant in one light (optical illusion, perspective, modeling)

The form of the glass from two points of view at the same time (a child knows its form instead of merely seeing it)

The forms of the glass, all glasses, and all things, from many relative points of view expressed simultaneously on a flat surface.

HOW to LOOK at SPACE

All through history a man's idea of what was "real" depended mainly on how he felt and what he thought about "space." Each age developed its own ways of describing its space (and time). The history of modern art is a history of modern space (time) too.

During this period people thought that what they "saw" was "real." Things were "seen" in space and a "painting" was thought to be a "picture" of this space.

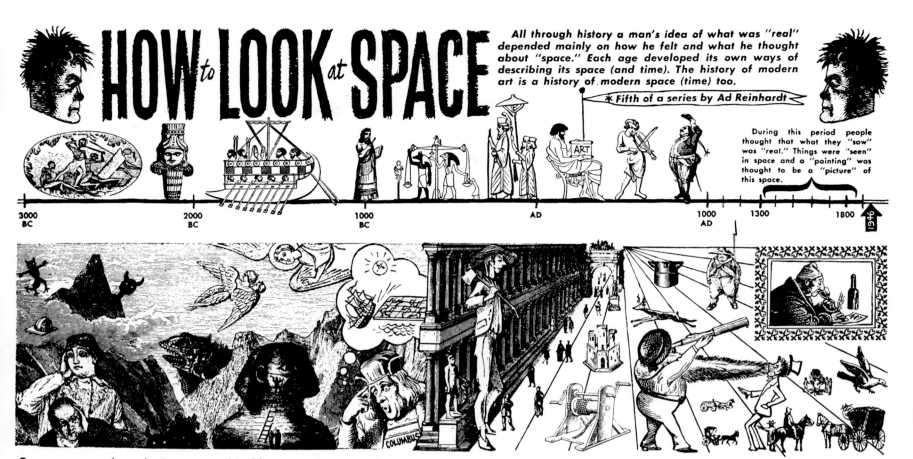

3000 BC   2000 BC   1000 BC   AD   1000 AD   1300   1800   1946

Once space scared people. Space was a big, blooming, buzzing confusion. Even now, what space (or people) represent is still a big mystery but we know more about what they "do," today.

Somewhat later, space was thought to be a quiet and immovable something into which things and people fitted. And an empty space was a thing, too, an ether—or something.

A "picture" was a one-sided representation of this space and after the horse-and-buggy (and Hoover) era, a machine began to make pictures that moved (movies, you know).

Space was a three-dimensional thing until Einstein showed that it had a "warp in a fourth dimension." (A ray of light traveling for 500 billion years would come back to where it started.) Space is a relationship between things and time (space-time).

A drawing is a division of space, a line is an edge of a space, shapes and colors are spaces, and a painting is a flat space. (Architecture is the Art of spaces, movies is the Art of pictures.) ("Art is science in the flesh.")

Spaces in surrealist art are lost, buildings empty, objects, usually bones, are dead — a shocking picture of the low spiritual state of a world which endures greed, race-hate and human exploitation. Spaces today have neither natural nor human dignity.

Abstract paint areas are real spaces—lofty, alive, emotionally ordered and intellectually controlled. A Mondrian painting represents "the maximum in the elimination of the irrelevant." If you like a "picture" of trees, cows, and nudes you like trees, cows, and nudes, which, as you well know, are not the flat spaces of a "painting."

Maybe you think things are o.k. and that you're "doing all right." But someday the monotonous and ugly spaces you live and work in will be organized (by your children) as intelligently and as beautifully as the spaces have been in some paintings. A painting of quality is a challenge to disorder and insensitivity everywhere. . . .

An abstract painting will react to you if you react to it. You get from it what you bring to it. It will meet you half way but no further. It is alive if you are. It represents something and so do you. YOU, SIR, ARE A SPACE, TOO.

HEY, LOOK AT THE FACTS

a page on modern art by Ad Reinhardt

"In scorn of nature, art gave lifeless life"—Shakespeare ✦ "Forms, colors, densities, odors—what is it in me that corresponds with them"—Walt Whitman

ARCH., SCULP., PIC., & REV. DEPT.'S

PAUL CEZANNE TO EMILE ZOLA

"The answer to the question 'What does it mean' will come from much looking at good pictures rather than answers received to the questions."—Stuart Davis

---

HOW TO LOOK AT THINGS

THROUGH A WINE·GLASS

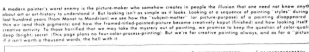

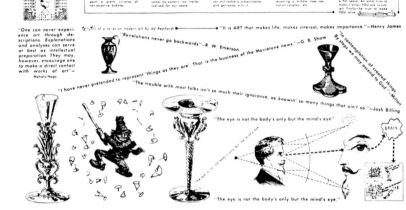

"One can never experience art through descriptions. Explanations and analyses can serve at best as intellectual preparation. They may, however, encourage one to make a direct contact with works of art"—Moholy-Nagy

"Revolutions never go backwards"—R. W. Emerson

"It is ART that makes life, makes interest, makes importance."—Henry James

"It is in contemplation of created things that by steps we may ascend to God."—Milton

"I have never pretended to represent 'things as they are.' That is the business of the Movietone news."—G. B. Shaw

"The trouble with most folks isn't so much their ignorance, as knowin' so many things that ain't so."—Josh Billing

"The eye is not the body's only but the mind's eye."

HOW TO LOOK

AT MORE THAN MEETS THE EYE

The Artist as Reporter—a page of news-flash-reports from the Art-World by Ad Reinhardt

REPORT FROM THE PAST ▪ *REPORT FROM THE MICROCOSMOS*

HEY, LOOK, COMICS

SPORTS REPORT

NAKED-MIND'S-EYE-TO-EYE-WITNESS-REPORT

HOW to LOOK at an → ARTIST

fourth of a series by AD REINHARDT

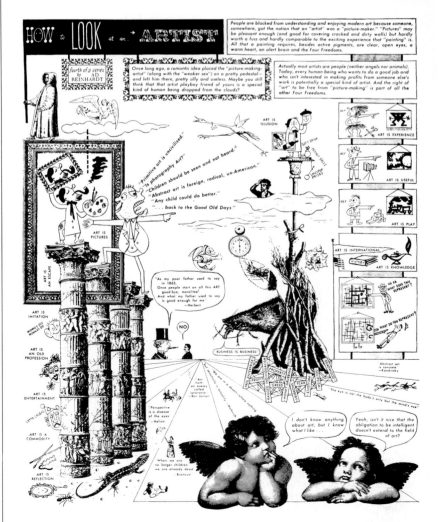

TWO GARDENS

ECKBO, ROYSTON & WILLIAMS
LANDSCAPE ARCHITECTS

The primary function of the landscape architect is to work as closely as possible with the architect and whatever other designers and/or technicians may be on the job in order to provide for the clients a maximum of use, pleasure, and experience from the site space within property lines. This means the development of a concept of the integrity of the site, and the development in landscape design of a concept of space-form comparable to that developed in modern painting, modern sculpture, and modern architecture. It means further the development of an approach to the use of plants which gives them a structural rather than a decorative role in the garden and which gives them an opportunity to develop a maximum of their native qualities, rather than having preconceived qualities forced on them. It means finally a conviction that people are important, and that the artist works for them rather than for himself.

photographs by Halberstadt

DE PATTA

What happens to an artist when the demand for his work exceeds his ability to supply it? If he is realistic, he reaps the benefit of raising the price to the point where a temporary equilibrium is established between supply and demand. What then happens to this artist's work? It necessarily becomes the possession of the very few who are in a position to pay these luxury prices. This is the situation I found myself in—a multitude of friends of my work who were unable to own and enjoy it.

For quite some time I had become aware of contradictions between my social viewpoints and my method of work. Contact with the Bauhaus in Chicago clarified and strengthened the tendencies toward social integration. However, I was justifiably apprehensive of the time demands of business that would interfere with my working and designing time—also the cost factors of even simple production plans appeared appalling. Believing firmly in the modern production potentialities to produce better articles in greater volume, I attempted to become an artist craftsman accepting the challenge of bridging the gap between the craftsman and production. Here then was the aim—to produce more than one piece of each design and to sell these pieces at a lower cost. It would have been possible to proceed upon another path—to produce more pieces and by increasing the number of retail outlets to place these at the same figure as formerly.

I wanted to place my designs upon the market at a figure to compete with the comparable material quality costume jewelry. The problems entailed in this production venture can be best understood only by other designers also engaged in however small industrial production.

In the entire field of jewelry production I found a perpetuation of traditional technics and in spite of the innovation of a few modern processes the designs were still of past eras. A good design reflects the technics and the view points of its age, therefore no matter how beautiful an old design may be it is still a sad mistaken thing when copied or imitated in our own day. That vital element necessary to good design—the interaction of the tool and material upon the designer, and of the designer upon tools and material had been completely lost. Here we are living in an age of high precision machine production and the effect of this upon jewelry design, production, and stone cutting has been less than nothing. What are the factors that perpetuate this lack of contemporary expression in a field apparently so unlimited?

Goods are purchased on the basis of previous sales—automatically continuing the life of the old and excluding the presentation of the new. The purchaser taste is thus conditioned by the choice between one conventional design and another just as bad.

I am proud of the fact that the popularly priced piece is indistinguishable from the "one of a kind" piece. It delights me to display a group of these things and see the baffled frustration on the faces of the "handcraft for handcraft's sakers" as they realize their inability to distinguish one group from the other. The design and the model are produced by me. The materials used are the same sterling silver and semi-precious stones. The workmanship and finish are of exact same quality. The remaining difference being in the number of pieces produced of a given design. This might be a legitimate objection if a tremendous number of pieces flooded a small area, (Continued on page 244)

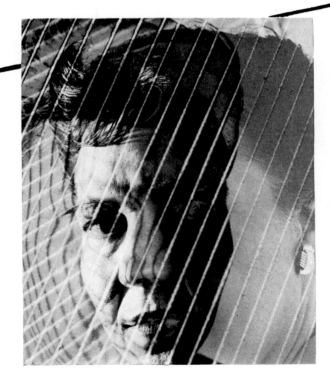

Photographs by Halberstadt.

styling
organization
▶design

by george nelson

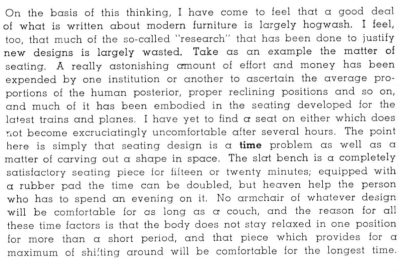

On the basis of this thinking, I have come to feel that a good deal of what is written about modern furniture is largely hogwash. I feel, too, that much of the so-called "research" that has been done to justify new designs is largely wasted. Take as an example the matter of seating. A really astonishing amount of effort and money has been expended by one institution or another to ascertain the average proportions of the human posterior, proper reclining positions and so on, and much of it has been embodied in the seating developed for the latest trains and planes. I have yet to find a seat on either which does not become excruciatingly uncomfortable after several hours. The point here is simply that seating design is a **time** problem as well as a matter of carving out a shape in space. The slat bench is a completely satisfactory seating piece for fifteen or twenty minutes; equipped with a rubber pad the time can be doubled, but heaven help the person who has to spend an evening on it. No armchair of whatever design will be comfortable for as long as a couch, and the reason for all these time factors is that the body does not stay relaxed in one position for more than a short period, and that piece which provides for a maximum of shifting around will be comfortable for the longest time.

At the present stage of furniture design that piece is an upholstered slab to sit on, an upholstered slab to lean against, and at least one padded arm. Visually, this is not a very exciting piece of furniture.

One can buy fairly acceptable versions of it anywhere.

Since it is in the nature of the designer to want to feel that he is making some kind of contribution through is efforts, he is likely to be somewhat frustrated by the very real technical limitations which turn him into a stylist. One possibility that exists lies in a different organization of a piece of furniture which produces shapes that may be new, and at least have validity based on a different appraisal of the functions involved. In our desk, for example, the design arrived at stemmed from a dislike for drawer storage, a preference for visible storage above the desk top, the need for a built-in portable typewriter, and the use of a Pendaflex file—a unit so constructed that no drawer is required.

The result is a piece of furniture which turned out to be somewhat unusual in appearance as a natural result of an organizing process.

Even here, however, nothing terrific happened, for the desk fundamentally is not very different from many English writing tables developed in the middle of the 18th century. Similarly unspectacular examples will be found in the illustrations.

Many of the weaknesses of modern furniture are the same as those of modern houses, stemming from an attempt to make one material look as if it were another. The International Style house, while a valuable negation of what preceded it, was fundamentally dishonest in that it used the oldest of materials and techniques while attempting to create the impression of a product turned out by a sheet-rolling and stamping mill. A good deal of solid wood furniture is being turned out today in forms that could properly be achieved only through the use of metal, or wood laminates. To some extent this misuse of materials is inevitable, for the new forms which have evolved through industrial production have an almost irresistible attraction. The Eames chairs are immensely satisfying for this reason: they have the shapes we have come to like, and these shapes were naturally arrived at through materials and processes.

Another weakness of modern furniture is the result of a craving for "originality" (perhaps novelty is a more accurate word) which in turn comes from the continuous pressure for something "different" to satisfy department store buyers and consumer magazine editors. Perhaps the hardest obstacle for the designer to overcome is this idea, that originality has any validity whatever as an an objective. In reality the original contribution is always a by-product; the designer tries to see and feel the problem as completely as possible and to work out the most natural solution; should there be any new elements injected into this process, the result is something "original." Which is fine if things work out that way. On the other hand, the forms developed in the course of a search for something new and different are rarely good for more than a season. One of the most offensive offshoots of the obsession with "originality" that has appeared within the last couple of years has been the emphasis given by several of the home magazines to the

"American" quality of such and such a piece of furniture. The idea put forth is that a piece with no dubious foreign ancestry is to be greatly admired. As a matter of fact, any piece designed and produced in America is bound to show its origin, although it is hard to see why this should be a matter for self-congratulation, and it is equally inevitable that it will show influences from other countries. To take the most "American" of our best modern furniture, the Eames chairs, these simply could not have come out the way they did without the earlier work by Aalto and Matthson in Finland and Sweden, which is the way design has always developed. Possibly the excitement being generated about the "Americanism" of modern furniture is somehow related to our current hysterical behavior on the international level. But whatever the cause, it is doing no good to either designers or consumers, and a logical extension of this approach would be to advertise a bedroom suite as "100 per cent Aryan." Which, as demonstrated in the past few years, would do even less good.

Another matter that comes to mind in connection with modern furniture design is the matter of distrbution. It is fairly characteristic of the younger architects and designers that they want to relate their activities to as large a group of people as possble. In furniture manufacture this has led to a rather exasperating contradiction. There is mass production of furniture, but to date the mass product has been conceived on a completely false period basis, or it falls into the indescribable category known as "borax." Mass production of furniture—even without radical technological upheavals—is a fact. But what is also a fact is that virtually every one of the manufacturers producing furniture acceptable to the modern architect is a small manufacturer. The furniture of Aalto, Eero Saarinen, Edward Wormley, Paul Laszlo, Ralph Rapson, Robsjohn-Gibbings, Charles Eames and others is all in the hands of relatively small producers. Thus, while the idea of modern furniture includes mass production, the present state of affairs is quite the contrary. It is true that the Mengel Company gave a competent modern designer freedom to work out a problem in his own way in conjunction with its "Module" line, and possibly the meaning of the success of this furniture will not be lost on the rest of the industry. Nevertheless, at the moment, most modern furniture is almost custom made by comparison with the rest of the output of the industry.

Another fact to toss into the general picture is this: virtually every technical development of importance that has been made in furniture has come from outside the industry. The reason is not far to seek, of course. The large manufacturers tend to resist change, and the smaller ones (assuming they are in favor of design progress) lack the needed facilities for experimental work. The result has been stagnation for the larger part of the industry and high-priced modern furniture coming out of those few factories which have been willing to gamble. In this situation there is nothing particularly remarkable—the first modern

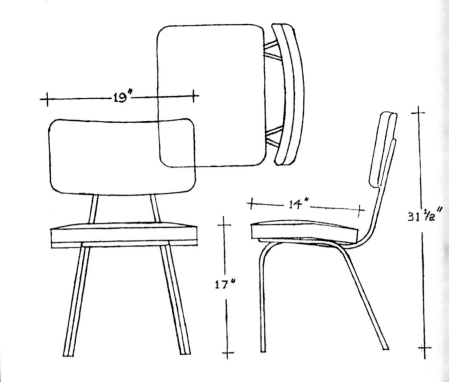

houses were done for individuals, not operative builders, and the first cars were developed for a small group intrigued by a new sport, not by the possibility of faster transportation. There is ample indication that more and more manufacturers will bring out contemporary furniture, and that the price level will gradually spread out. This will happen even if all the postwar dreams of furniture stamped out like doughnuts come to nothing; anyway, technical changes will merely speed up the process. The job for the designers is not to lament over a situation that is admittedly short of ideal, but to solve their design problems as honestly as they can within the existing production framework, and at the same time, to make obsolete that framework as rapidly as they are able.

The pieces shown on these pages are part of a collection designed, over a period of about two years, for the Herman Miller Furniture Company. As few of them represent anything radical in the way of concept or fabrication, there is relatively little to say about them which the photographs do not make perfectly clear. They do represent an experience, however, which has some bearing on the whole problem of furniture design and which may have interest for those who have considered working in this field.

For some reason or other, architects are always intrigued by the idea of designing furniture, and I was certainly no exception. Accustomed to the complexities of even small buildings, one imagines furniture design to be child's play—as a kind of creative relaxation. I also suspect that one has the feeling that no one else's furniture is quite appropriate for one's own buildings. Then too, there is the quite legitimate attraction of the idea of designing for production, an experience denied the average architect in the present state of building technology Which of these reasons intrigued me most strongly, I do not know, but in any event I signed a rather casually worded contract in the summer of 1945, with high hopes, a light heart and not the faintest idea of what I was getting in for.

The first major discovery came with my first visit to the factory, when it became apparent that however complete the mechanization of the plant, the designer is not much better off than Duncan Phyfe. He has at his disposal machines which differ from primitive woodworking equipment only in speed, accuracy and power, and he is still limited to sticks, boards and sheets of plywood His "designing" therefore is actually more accurately defined as "styling" since he is merely reshaping certain objects without necessarily improving them. This point

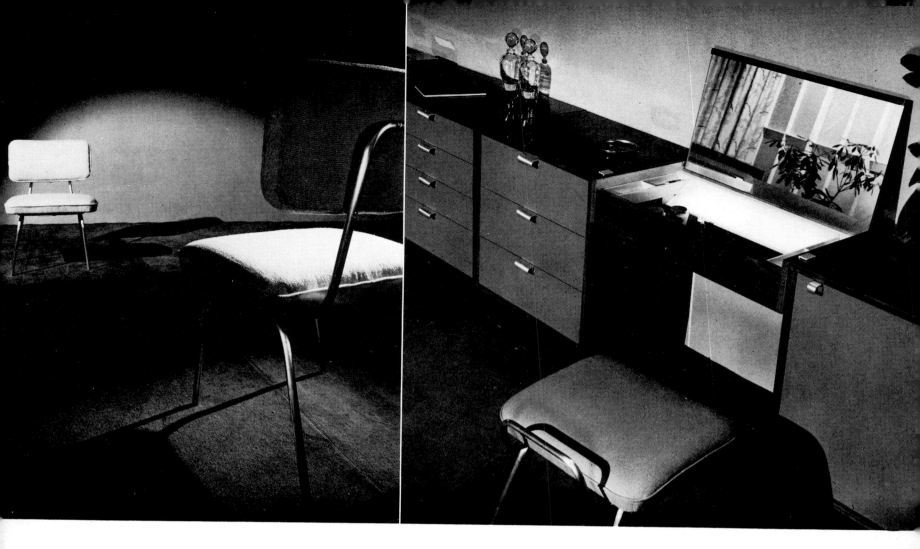

is important, and there has been so much irresponsible talk around it that clarification is in order.

The design process is one in wich materials, functions and production methods are so closely welded that ultimately an object is produced which has an inevitable quality similar to things in nature. Once this state of relative perfection is reached there is no further design development—any changes then made are superfical and merely represent a kind of styling, or variation on a basic theme. Styling is not "bad" necessarily. It merely represents an activity which is not as fundamental as design. There are many objects which reached a completely designed stage quite early: the wheelbarrow represents a fundamental design concept unaltered for centuries, and so does the scissors. The only way in which the latter has been improved was by a fundamental change in the process of cutting, which involved the introduction of motors and a whole series of new movements. This change produced new designs for cutting, but the man does not exist who is capable of redesigning the scissors. The umbrella is another interesting example of an object which reached its final design stage a long time ago. Now to return to furniture.

The designer who works in furniture faces roughly the same functional

requirements designers have always had to meet: a chair has to support someone's bottom, a chest of draws has to store objects of small size, and so on. Unless there is a basic technological change involved, the furniture designer will necessarily function as a stylist, modifying standard models only superficially. When the younger Thonet arrived at his bentwood chair he met an old function wit a new technique; so did Aalto, Breuer and Eames. In each instance we find these designs exciting because they open new vistas and make possible the creation of chairs which are more satisfying esthetically because the process of manufacture leads to shapes which are felt to be more in keeping with the feeling of the period. Attached to a traditional furniture plant, however, the designer can only attempt to capture this feeling by re-shaping the old materials using old techniques. The results may be pleasing, but the basic patterns will not be greatly different from those of the cabinet makers of the 17th and 18th centuries.

All illustrations from furniture designed for and manufactured by Herman Miller Furniture Company by George Nelson, a practicing Architect, co-author of Tomorrow's Home, and editor of Fortune Magazine, and crusader against the useless.

Photographs by Ezra Stoller

house in "industry"

A system for the manufacture of industrialized building elements by Konrad Wachsmann and Walter Gropius

The General Panel system of construction is based on the manufacture of industrialized building elements. These elements consist of load-bearing, standardized panels and such additional parts as fillerstrips, columns and joists. They constitute the supporting, as well as the enclosing members of the structure. Not only exterior and interior walls, but also floors, ceilings, roofs, and even trusses, are composed of these elements.

The panels are completely finished in the shop with all windows, doors, glazing, hardware, insulation and wiring installed. In fact, any detail which may occur in a building is incorporated. The old distinction between "rough" and "finished" construction is eliminated.

The building elements are joined together by a unique method of connection. Every part, of whatever nature, is put together with the same device called the "wedge connector." This method of connection, shown on page thirty, is, furthermore, three dimensional because it is exactly the same, whether horizontal or vertical members are joined together. With the General Panel joint it is not necessary to know beforehand which panel goes into which part of a building. That the uniformity of the edge and the connection have great usefulness for the manufacturer need not be emphasized.

The General Panel industrialized housing plant does not produce finished houses and, therefore, differs from a factory producing trucks or airplanes; which, in the last analysis, is an assembly job. The sacrifice of leaving the assembly to the field is, however, compensated by important advantages.

The standard size, shape and construction of the panels lends itself easily to an assembly-line, mass-production technique. From lumber pile to shipping platform, parts move through the machines in a straight flow. Because the panels are flush, and because of their uniform thickness and light weight, they are easily handled, stored and shipped. For instance, a 35-foot long trailer with a hoist-equipped tractor will ship and deposit at the site a complete three-bedroom house with all appliances, closets, cabinets, fixtures and plumbing materials. Of the scale of this material one may say: What formerly the hod carrier was to the brick, the lift truck is to the panel.

Any house can be constructed merely by joining these elements together like an Erector set. The architect, designer or builder can play with the material without being specialized. This applies not only to houses, but also to schools, hospitals, garages and similar structures of one-story, and later of two-story, height.

Theoretically the design variation is unlimited. Without change of tooling, but merely by operating the indexing machines, types can be varied according to the customer's wishes or local conditions. No insipid uniformity of a "model" will be forced upon the public, superficially disguised by meaningless variations of attributes or decorations. Individual needs can express themselves in the plan, while the uniformity of the detail will create a restful unity and discipline.

Another advantage of versatility is the possibility of production for a mass market. The need for housing will not always be as pressing as it is today, and other outlets must be found. Industrialization, with its high-powered and expensive machinery of great capacity, depends on a fast turnover and the subsequent reduction in product price. In the General Panel plant a house can be produced every thirty minutes. It is clear that this will also revolutionize present methods of home distribution and selling.

The panels which are being built in the factory at Burbank consist of plywood glued to wood frames with which it forms a structural unit. However, the system is adaptable to any other material or finish. The product as it is today has been approved by local and federal agencies and, therefore, is ready to be used. For further development it is important that as much of the field work be transferred to the shop as is feasible with existing technological processes, and every new material be investigated. Doors, windows, roofing and many other accessories are still following the traditional pattern. As mass production of the building elements grows, they, too, will change gradually, and entirely new types will evolve which are typical for industrialized housing.

Today, houses are still built essentially as they were 150 years ago. In transferring construction to the plant, the workman is not simply given a roof, but the whole process is changed by the scientific use of modern tools. This requires new principles of design and will finally create a new form. The house of the General Panel Corporation, as shown on the following pages, is only a beginning of such a process. To express it in the words of Mr. Konrad Wachsmann:

"If we want to analyze a contemporary house for its modern design, we may do the following. We may take a section, say 2 feet by 2 feet, out of this house and compare it with a similar section taken out of a house of conventional construction. Not knowing anything about the design of the two houses, we would very quickly see which of the two is modern. The modern house is one which, through its materials, its precision and workmanship, shows that in its construction the tools and methods of our time have been used. If it is constructed in a conventional method, it is not a modern house, regardless of what it looks like. It has changed the surface, but the body is still the same."

Panel system invented and developed by Konrad Wachsmann and Walter Gropius.

System, process of production, design, quality control and plant layout developed by General Panel Corporation of New York under technical direction of Konrad Wachsmann.

Assistant technical director Curtis Fremond.

Licensee for present production shown: General Panel Corporation of California.

General Panel Corp. of California

Executive Personnel:

President: Carl B. Dahlberg

Vice Presidents:

Albert Wohlstetter, Production
S. Southwell, Technical Director
N. H. Wendell, Jr., Treasurer

Production and Technical Personnel:

Quality Control: Thomas Budne
Production Control: Paul Fisher
Mfg. Superintendent: Larry Green
Field Operations: John J. O'Sullivan
Consulting Engineer: Colin Skinner
Methods Engineer: Louis Jennings
Electronic Engineer: Norman Bruns

FOUR-WAY

THREE-WAY

TWO-WAY

ONE-WAY

POST

CORNER

Wedge connectors, spaced 3' 4" apart through all vertical and horizontal joints consist of four stamped steel parts and four die cast wedges which are shop inserted into the framing.

In the assembly, three parts are first nested together, the fourth is then driven home with a hammer. The diagrams above show how, by means of an unsymmetrical edge, it is possible to effect any desired combination, whereby all elements are interchangeable and surfaces are flush after assembly.

1 MILL

2 MOLDING

3 SLOTTING

4 CONNECTOR INSERTION

5 ASSEMBLY

6 ELECTRONIC PRESS

7 CONVEYING

8 SPRAYING

9 DISCHARGING

10 STACKING

11 SHIPPING

12 ERECTION

photographs by Anna Wachsmann and Dick Whittington

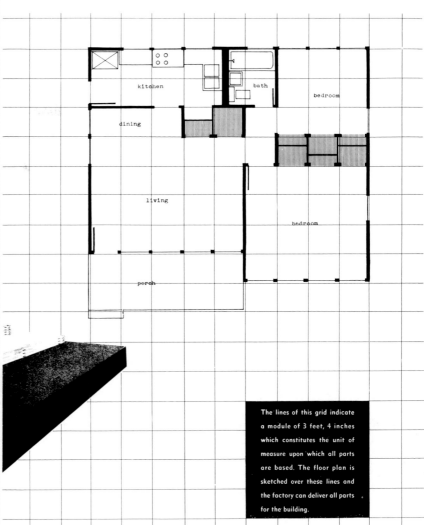

Details of the house by Konrad Wachsmann using standard elements of the panel system

The illustrations on these pages show parts of the small two-bedroom house of preceding page, de-designed by Konrad Wachsmann. In principle they could belong to any kind of building. All detail is integral with the product. A designer confronted with a building project is relieved of the task of having to start all details from scratch, then see them cut to pieces on the site. He can now devote hmiself entirely to the best possible layout. On the other hand great care and thoroughness can be applied to even the smallest detail which, when developed in the shop, will give it an aspect of finality and perfection.

THE MODERN MOVEMENT in architecture and industrial design began, as all rebel movements in art begin, as a protest. It was directed at the decadence, the over-elaboration, the essential ugliness of so many of the existing styles. Its exact roots are nebulous but they are generally traced to William Morris, or, if you will, to the Crystal Palace in the London show of 1851.

The founders of the modern movement were crusaders in behalf of a new esthetic that was a wedding of current technologies and current social needs. They fought for a design idiom that inevitably emerged from the simplicity and efficiency which they favored. On their drafting boards designs took shape possessing a stark new beauty of their own. The most characteristic expressions came from the Bauhaus school which did more than any other single force to give three-dimensional form to the image that impelled the founding fathers of the modern movement.

But even at that early date there were designers who adhered to other concepts and who were indifferent to Bauhaus principles. In France, for example, Ruhlmann worked in the French Empire manner and designed cabinets of rare woods with fine ivory inlays, a sort of contemporized late 18th Century furniture. The rebels never carried the field entirely.

what is modern
by alfred auerbach

Regardless of the divergences that may have marked the early exponents of European modern, there was a certain genuine rationale underlying the better work. If Ruhlmann expressed himself as he did, it was essentially because machinery and mass production did not interest him. So that one of the basic tenets of the Bauhaus school . . . simple machine-made products for the masses . . . was a matter of no concern to him. His work was executed on a custom cabinet-shop basis for a few discriminating clients. In northern Italy, too, a sort of modern provincial furniture came along, but this also had a certain integrity for it sprang from the tools at hand and from the people's needs. In short, though the European expressions varied, there was justification for these variations, at least among the better work.

In America, however, there is a jungle of confusion about modern. Everything goes. Things are called modern that have no relation whatsoever to any of the basic urges that prompted the modern movement. We have jumped on the bandwagon with characteristic American enthusiasm, but we have allowed the horses to run off in different directions. Surveys are made showing that modern accounts for 25% or 35% or 45% of current sales . . . but what is it that they term modern? A furniture dealer in Grand Island, Nebraska visualizes one thing when you say modern to him; a department store buyer visualizes an entirely different thing, and even among department store buyers there is by no means unanimity.

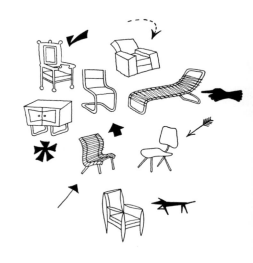

It seems to me that in the interest of order and sanity we ought to have a trade vocabulary that is more precise and definitive than our present one is when it comes to talking about modern design. I have tried to develop for you here a suggestion for such a nomenclature by itemizing ten different types of modern furniture now on the market. You may reject my terminology and devise your own, if you wish, but of the need for a set of identifying labels there can be no doubt.

The ten types I now find on the market speak for themselves in demonstrating how far some of them have drifted, and how confused, how varied, how contradictory, how groundless is the thinking of most of us about this thing called modern designing. And now for the ten types themselves:

unrelenting modern

This is intolerant and uncompromising. I call it unrelenting because it won't yield as a result of pressure to water its principles. It may sound like a harsh definition but I don't mean it to be. It is the standard bearer for the slogan "Form follows function." Its kinship with the Bauhaus principles is clear and direct. It is honest, straightforward and logical. It happens to be the type I personally like most. Perhaps that explains why I feel there is too little of it on the market.

nostalgic modern

This has a yearning for another day. It is wistful about 18th Century designs. It streamlines the old and in doing so renders a real service. Much of it has an elegance and suavity that is often missing in the school that I have termed Unrelenting Modern. As a species it lacks the rebellious courage of the Unrelenting Modern but it is essentially a very popular type and it is not difficult to understand why.

floradora modern

This is a lush and full-blown species. Sometimes you hear it called baroque modern. It uses Venetian sconces, distressed mirrors, and elegant Louis XV color schemes. It is luxurious and elaborate, indifferent to cost, and addressed in the main to cafe society. It has little to do with mass production or the general stream of humanity. It is the darling of some of our best known decorators. It essentially is a type that developed in the hands of decorators rather than in the hands of industrial designers.

smorgasbord modern

This aspires to take its cue from Sweden. I have often felt that a good deal of the American furniture sold as Swedish Modern offered the Swedish government a fine justification for a libel suit. It appeals to those who love anything that smacks of an import tag. Some of it, however, has real merit. It has influenced U. S. designers to some extent, particularly towards lighter scaling and the use of blond woods.

lane bryant modern

This is best known by its huge, overblown chairs which look as though they are going to have little ottomans any moment. It is a type especially popular in Hollywood. It recalls klieg lights, private swimming pools and huge derricks, the latter needed mainly to move the furniture around.

chinese modern

Because Chinese art and Chinese room decoration have for centuries represented the height of simplicity, it was inevitable that a kinship be established between Chinese design and American modern. Some of this is good, much of it is clumsy and awkward. Don't blame the Chinese. I should add that Chinese Modern seems to be a style that appeals particularly to those who have said goodbye to Mr. Chippendale.

kodak modern

Kodak Modern is the special pet of those designers who are more concerned with the reactions of editors and with the reactions of other designing colleagues than they are with the needs of the market. Everything that they design is undertaken with an eye for the camera. Is it photogenic? Will it look well in House Beautiful or House & Garden? Will it make me seem smarter, more gifted than this designer or that designer? If the chair designed by one of these designers is not comfortable he won't concede the design is bad but will contend instead that the human anatomy is at fault.

hothouse modern

This is a limited, rather exclusive species which blooms in the form of curved lucite leaves supporting crystal table tops and many similar convolutions of material that have nothing to do with serviceability, nothing to do with the natural properties of the materials that are employed, nothing to do with current trends in general. Despite the fact that this species has never had real sales acceptance, it seems to be a rather hardy lot, as it has been on the scene a long time and shows every intention of remaining on it.

monotonous modern

This is a type that has extensive acceptance in bedroom and dining room furniture. It is boxy, uninspired and unobjectionable. It isn't as refined or as polished as a type I referred to earlier, namely, Nostalgic Modern, which is a streamlining of 18th Century furniture. It's cruder but essentially uses the same kind of carcass. It would be quite an acceptable type if it had just a bit more eye appeal and were not so obviously self-conscious about its determination to be inexpensive, resonably efficient, of questionable quality and unquestionable dullness.

juke box modern

This is the contemporary version of so-called borax furniture. It needs very little description, for I am sure you get the picture quickly enough. It uses sunburst veneers, long plastic handles placed against plastic escutcheons. It is busy, noisy and, like a juke box, never stops talking to the people in the room. It is a more important species from a sales point of view than most of us like to admit. We generally don't visit the showrooms that specialize in this kind of torture of perfectly innocent lumber and so we don't know that it remains a fundamentally important selling type in many stores. But no inventory of the modern school is complete without including it.

And so there you have the ten. What a kettle of fish! It's true we've left the early chromium-and-ebony days, and the days when galvanized iron was glorified as a neglected Tiffany material and when cork walls were an applauded innovation. But have we made progress or merely changed? I hold no brief for a modern school that has only one insulated expression. I welcome an alive, mobile, many-faceted modern movement. But there must be some standards of taste, some fixed basic principles, some ideology, to guide the hands of our designers and the understanding of our manufacturers and retailers. Without these the present tangled, blurred mass of chaotic outpourings will continue.

At the outset I indicated there was order and sanity in Europe's modern. This is not true except for the work of the better designers; there is plenty of humdrum and questionable work done there, too. But I am not content that we do no better than Europe. The setting is ripe for us to take the leadership role.

The moment is at hand for a reiteration of basic principles. Let us hope that the competition sponsored by the Museum of Modern Art will do much to clear the air and establish once and for all a set of basic criteria by means of which we can better understand modern and more intelligently differentiate between the good and the bad, and move on to that foremost position that is properly ours.

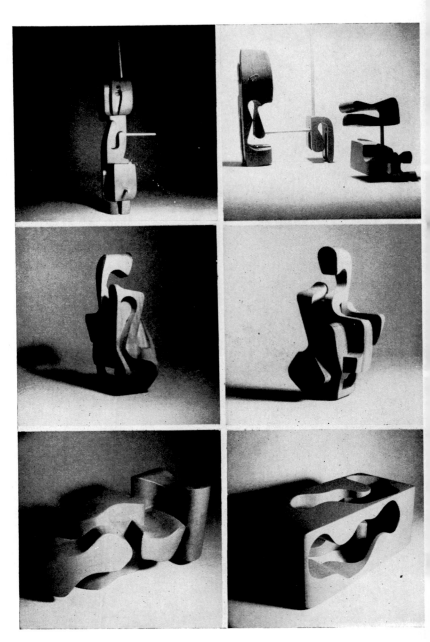

design and the machine

by jan de swart

A most rewarding project, both from a practical and an inspirational viewpoint, is an intensive, explorative study of the machines involved in the making of objects. The more familiar the machine, the more likely we are to find that it has been invested with a very limited repertoire. An experimental approach alone can yield insight into its manifold potentialities and clarify its limitations and compulsions. A study of the bandsaw is one example that illustrates this point.

Characteristically, the bandsaw cuts a straight or curved line, leaving an unfinished saw-marked surface. The process of setting the saw-teeth, even when done mechanically, leaves some teeth protruding farther than others, so that the wood is torn rather than cut apart. By experiment it was found that by using two carborundum stones and pressing one gently against each side of the blade so that it does not vibrate, the protrusions can be eliminated. At the same time the saw is sharpened to such a point that it polishes as it cuts. Since the hand-finishing of a saw-cut surface, particularly an intricate one, is by far the most tedious and time-consuming step in making a study, it is a decided advantage to let the machine, with its speed and precision, do this work.

A second experiment concerns the tilting table. This is ordinarily used to cut a piece of wood on a certain angle, an operation bearing no relationship to the reassembly of the segments. By tilting the table at various degrees the taper of the cylinder cut out of a block, and its protrusion from that block, can be controlled. When

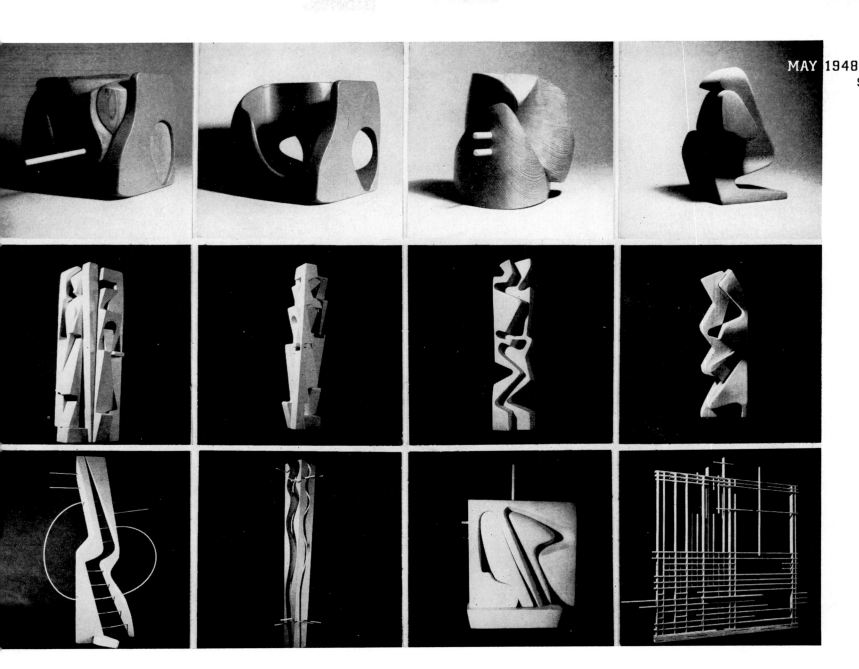

the table is level the cut-out cylinder is separated from the original block. When the table is tilted the cylinder becomes a cone. This is only partly released from the original block because its taper limits the movement outward. The greater the degree of tilt, the less is the protrusion of the cut-out part. With this technique one can "explode" a block into any number of related segments. Their fit is so perfect and their seams are so invisible that the effect of a solid mass can be retained.

As many as twelve compositions can be made from the fragments of a single block. The various segments may be assembled unglued so that they can be interchanged to invite the creation of new designs. Care should be taken in the original cutting that each piece is a beautiful form separately, as well as a beautiful part of a balanced composition. A simple way of accomplishing this is to repeat the design in different sizes. Harmony, results, no matter how intricate and small the segments. An astonishing phenomenon is created by gluing the various fragments into an interesting composition, then taking this to the bandsaw and again cutting it into segments.

The complexity of such studies is overwhelming. And yet the method is so simple that a boy of fourteen with clear instructions can succeed in a project like the following: On the top and one side of a block of wood, mark two circles, one larger than the other. Set the tilt of the table so that you create a cone instead of a cylinder. Enter the blade with the grain of the wood so than an invisible glue-joint can later be made. Now follow the marked circle with the blade. Remove the blade through the same cut you used to enter. Before cutting the next circle, decide whether to remove the cone just cut or to wedge it into the block, eliminating the slight space the saw-cut has made. Two completely different effects are possible. If the wedge is left in, and the second circle is cut in the same manner, the two cones, when removed from the block will pierce each other and leave an intricate inversion of their forms in the hollowed block. The results of this simple cutting along two lines is a group of three interrelated separate pieces which seem to be carved out of one block. The whole project does not take more than ten minutes. Its variations are unlimited. Its effect on the boy is astonishing: his interest captured instantly, his ingenuity challenged. The perfection and professional appearance of the result give him a feeling of mastery that could be acquired from handicraft only after long and laborious apprenticeship. Any teacher who has despaired of finding a program that can compete with the diversions which threaten a creative impulse today will realize the value of this stimulus.

To me, as a designer, such studies are more than a persuasion . . . they are are a revelation. Thus, when I cut into a block, lineal continuity becomes an adventure in the third dimension. I am catapulted into a realm of space and volume, line and shadow, where I am released completely from all that is limiting and binding. The harmony that emanates **(Continued on page 244)**

(Continued on page 244)

The Jan deSwart "Exploring Plastics" exhibition will be held at the Modern Institute of Art in Beverly Hills, California from June 1 to July 4.

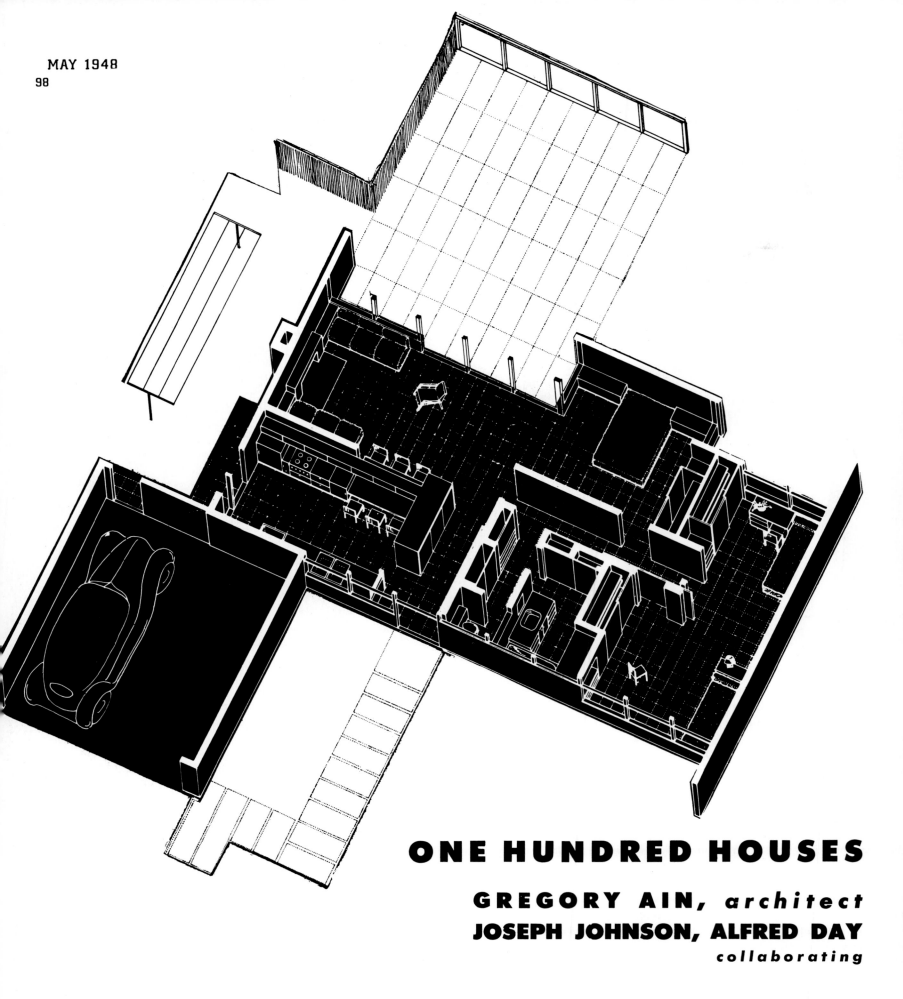

ONE HUNDRED HOUSES

GREGORY AIN, *architect*
JOSEPH JOHNSON, ALFRED DAY
collaborating

FOR THE ADVANCE DEVELOPMENT COMPANY

Individually designed and individually constructed houses are almost negligible, numerically, in relation to the total of all houses built. The great majority of houses being erected today are the product of operative builders, who provide the lot as well as the finished house to purchasers who have little or no active part in expressing their preferences, or in determining the character of the structure.

Most operative builders, like most radio writers and most movie producers, assume that they know "what the public wants;" and their assumption is usually insulting to the public's intelligence. This is not surprising, since the object of most construction is a quick and profitable sale, rather than the genuine satisfaction of a common general need. To the typical operative builder, a house is a **commodity**,

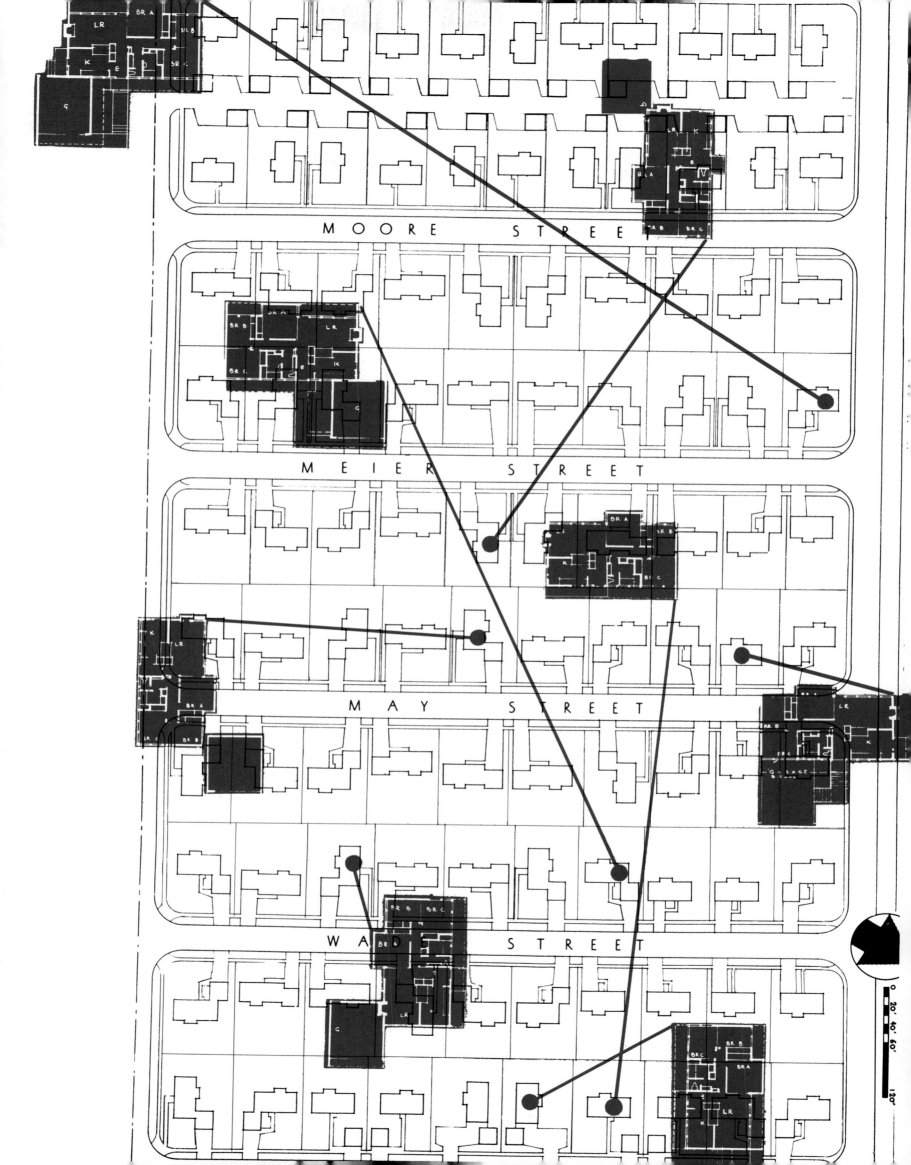

MOORE STREET

MEIER STREET

MAY STREET

WARD STREET

an object to be bought and sold. But the word **commodity** has another and equally correct definition: "the quality or state of being commodious; convenience; accommodation; benefit; advantage" (Webster).

The architects chosen to design the subdivision illustrated on these pages were at first incredulous, then delighted and stimulated to find that their client thought of his contemplated tract in terms of the broader and more human definition of the word **commodity**. This subdivider proposed to build a hundred houses for a hundred average veterans' families. These houses, with a floor area of approximately 1050 square feet on more or less average lots, were intended to bring to the typical home buyer the advantages of modern planning: full use of necessarily limited area; removal of living room from the main line of traffic through the house; direct connection of the living room with garden area away from the street; ease of maintenance, etc. It was required, moreover, that the plan satisfy the practical and realistic requirements of the Federal Housing Administration, and of the Veterans' Housing Administration.

To achieve maximum economy, through the efficiencies of standardization and repetition, it was decided to employ a single basic house type, allowing for considerable variety in exterior appearance by recourse to different relationships of garage to house. Further variety was produced (at the request of the lending institution), by turning some of the houses at right angles to the street.

Since the street pattern was largely predetermined by existing adjacent streets, the major problem resolved itself into establishing a floor plan. No one of the hundred hypothetical average families could be presumed to be really "average;" the house plan must be flexible, and adaptable to varied family compositions. Hence the liberal use of sliding partitions.

The two smaller rooms (most probably children's bedrooms) can be readily converted into a single larger room by rolling the intermediate partition alongside a blank wall in the hallway. Similarly, the room adjacent to the living room (normally the parents' bedroom, study or den) can be opened to and made a part of the living room. And one half of the width of the wall between living room and kitchen can be opened or closed at will. When opened (the normal position), the family eating space is accessible from both sides, and the housewife in the kitchen can participate in social activities in the living room. The plan finally developed is normally a five-room house, which can be advantageously converted, for different uses, into a four room, three room, or two room house.

The project (now under construction in the Mar Vista district in Los Angeles) employs the post and lintel system of construction, allowing generous window areas with no interruption of structural framing. Exterior and interior wall surfaces will be cement plaster. Asphalt tile on a cement slab provides a dry, resilient and easily washable floor only one step above the garden level.

JAMES PRESTINI

James Prestini is a craftsman of exceptional sensitivity. In the few years he has worked on a wood lathe, he has attained a unique place among contemporary craftsmen. Many exhibits of his work have been held, and his pieces are represented in the museums as well as private collections.

The forms he creates are born directly out of the process of wood-turning to which he has devoted himself. But the common denominator which distinguishes his plates, trays or bowls from all others is the exquisite refinement of these simple forms. Again and again one is astonished by the beauty achieved in a medium rarely treated with artistry.

Moreover, Prestini reveals to us the special characteristics of various woods by his penetrating exploitation of their properties. We discover

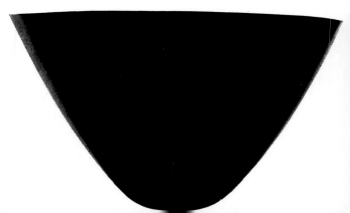

photographs: Barbara Morgan

the amazing delicacy of pattern in curly maple, the vigorous organic substance apparent in the fibrous greens and yellows of Zelany Topal, the hardness of mahogany's closely grained surface, the elegance of polished blond birch, the deep richness of color and the extraordinary sensuous texture of ebony brought to its fullest bloom.

All of these qualities are reinforced by the shapes in which they are cut. Like a sculptor striving for absolute perfection of abstract form, Prestini turns wood, often cutting it within a hair's breadth of its tensile strength. His own pleasure in creating shapes which excite and satisfy the eye of the beholder leads him to guide the curve of bowl in its most expressive form. No craftsman approaches his work with any greater enthusiasm or sincerity of purpose.

There are in Prestini's background three major factors which seem to have contributed to the growth of his particular creative ability. His

natural skill in working with his hands may have been acquired to some degree from his father, an Italian stonecutter. The study of engineering at Yale undoubtedly laid the foundations for his honest approach to design, for the engineer does not tolerate superfluity in dealing with problems which require facts and exact judgment in determining what forms a material is capable of assuming. Finally, his mature development as a craftsman came from actual experience gained in a workshop where tools and materials are an organic part of creating. Consequently, unlike many American Craftsmen who suffer from the unassimilated knowledge acquired from textbooks and teachers, Prestini has developed a thoroughly personal insight and conviction rare among our designers.

Since his real sense of design has grown out of his own experience, involving an intense application of himself toward solving practical and aesthetic problems, his book, DESIGN SENSE, will prove a valid thesis for manufacturers, educators and designers alike—ELODIE COURTER.

This remodeled Drive-in Restaurant, inside and out, is distinguished by the mark of the confident planning of the designer. Facilities included are: a lunch counter, fountain, dining room, and bar. Visible to automotive traffic as a Drive-in Restaurant, the building requires but a minimum of signs and neon lighting.

The dining room and bar are open to a garden for outdoor dining and waiting. An incombustible metal trellis forms a patterned acoustic ceiling in the dining room and extends into the garden, providing diffused light inside and out.

Natural textures and a warm color scheme, together with the planting, contribute to an inviting atmosphere day and night. The large concrete planting boxes, integral with the building, were formed with rough lumber and stained.

photographs: Garber-Sturges

drive-in restaurant
john lautner

designer

Office building
Raphael S. Soriano
architect

photographs: Albert L. Bresnik

This building, which occupies a lot with 45' street frontage and 123' depth adjoining a 20' alley on one side, consists of two floors, the first to be used as a sales and display room, the second as offices.

For maximum flexibility of room arrangement a light steel construction was devised which permits clear spans across the entire 44' width of the building on both floors. Expanded 24" steel joists set 4'-0" on center were used with 2" x 6" tongue and groove diagonal sheathing for both the second floor and the roof. All interior partitions are non-bearing and may be rearranged easily and inexpensively to satisfy various occupancy requirements. Utilities have been so located that they do not interfere.

The front facade consists of a glass partition covering the two-story surface and set at an angle to provide shade from the afternoon sun without the use of awnings. All of the outside walls where glass is not used are made of expanded steel studs, wire mesh, and 1½" of cement plaster. A 4" concrete slab was laid for the lower floor.

The recent project for a California beach house by the young Brazilian architect, Oscar Niemeyer, is the culmination of thirty years of development in architectural design.

This house represents today's final synthesis of two important Twentieth Century stylistic trends: the strict mechanical formalism of Le Corbusier and the Cubist-Constructivist movement, and the organic shapes and free form fantasy of the tradition of Miro and Arp.

The rectangular prism of the main section of the Niemeyer house, raised above the ground on stilts, derives directly from the purism of Le Corbusier. The tightly geometric curves that were part of Le Corbusier's precise architectural idiom in the twenties, and which were expressed both in his buildings and paintings, have been replaced, a generation later, by the less restricted, free shapes of Miro and Arp.

These irregular, free-flowing shapes came into architecture in the thirties in the work of such men as the Brazilian landscape architect, Roberto Burle-Marx. The Niemeyer house demonstrates the successful architectural integration of these complex and varied influences from the related arts.

The process of cross-fertilization by which creative influences are transmitted in the arts remains a mystery despite all that is written about them. Yet the study of the models and drawings may help to suggest how contemporary architecture has arrived at its characteristic visual forms.

The new Brazilian gardens designed by, the painter, Roberto Burle-Marx carry the free-form, fantastic tradition of Arp and Miro into direct contact with architecture. They are less "psychological" than the painting and sculpture in this style, since they must approach the utilitarian. They seem to be as direct a translation of non-mechanical abstract painting into gardening terms as the English parks of the Eighteenth Century were of the classical landscape paintings of Poussin and Claude.

OSCAR NIEMEYER, architect
detailing and execution
LUTAH MARIA RIGGS, A.I.A. AND ARVIN SHAW, III

PROJECT FOR A

LANDSCAPE DESIGN: ROBERTO BURLE-MARX

Material courtesy of The Museum of Modern Art and the office of Lutah Maria Riggs and Arvin Shaw, III.

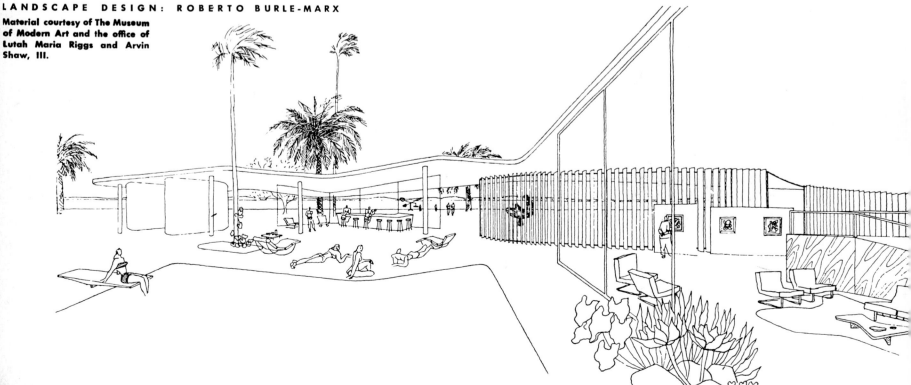

the plan

the solution adopted, in accordance with the living requirements as especified and the local conditions, is very well suited to terrain and further, which is important, takes maximum advantage of the marvelous view offered by the Pacific Ocean. With this in mind we tried to avoid, initially, any plan dividing the property into two parts, thus shutting the view from the entrance (fig 1) Hence the adoption of "pilotis" and the disposition of grand floor construction contrary to that of the second floor block (fig 2) the solution allowed the living to face the east, protected when necessary by varandas and "brise soleils". the bedrooms, which we thought should look toward the sea, were facing to the south, where provided with w to the north, thus permitting good ventilation and light (fig 3) From this standpoint we tried to provide every pa of the building with pleasant atmosfere. the living and dining room in the grand floor were connected with the garden and swiming pool by a large "marquise" under which were located resting places such bars, etc., protected against the wind fixed glass panes. A music room 3 ft above the floor in the living room has also been planned which will perm dancing around the bar and the swiming pool during parties. the service reasonably distributed meets the requirements of program; the laundry was provided with a dumb-writer and tube connecting it directly with the clothing-store located on th top floor. On this floor the rooms as well as the main apartment are connection to the swiming pool by means of external s A wooden trellis serves as a sunshade to the rooms forming at the same time private and pleasants varandas. "Brise soleils" h been foreseen to protect externally. Easy to handle they will enable to control the rays of the sun and excessive light w shutting out visibility. In the bedrooms they will work as courtains giving light protection and privacy.

Architecturally, the solution is simple and pure — composed by two definite forms; one formed by a rectangular block corresponds to the second floor and the other contrasting with the first one constitutes the grand floor construction (fig 4) Sculptu paintings have been planned not as independent elements but as integrating part of the whole — enriching and completing

Oscar Niemeyer, Soares Filz
Rio. 1948.

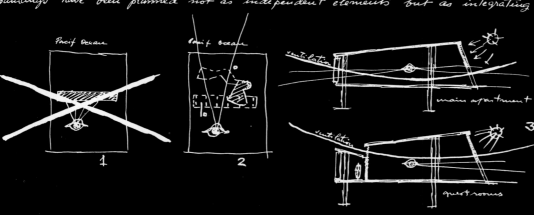

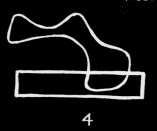

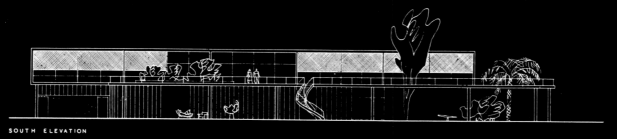

SECTION A

HOUSE IN SANTA BARBARA

SOUTH ELEVATION

NORTH ELEVATION

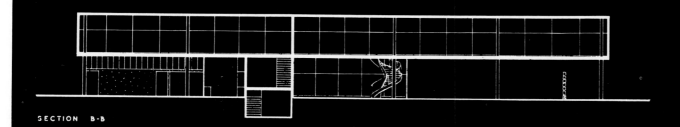

SECTION B-B

1 LOBBY
2 TERRACE
3 LINEN
4 MASTER DRESSING R.
5 MASTER SLEEPING R.
6 BALCONY
7 GALLERY
8 GUEST BED ROOM
9 GUEST BATH ROOM
10 BALCONY
11 MASTER BATH ROOM

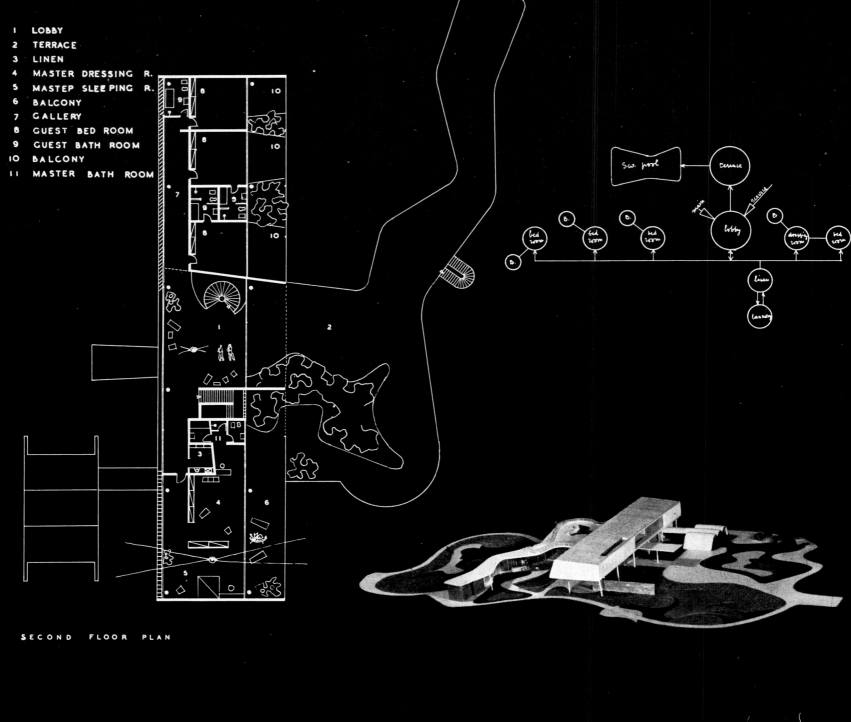

SECOND FLOOR PLAN

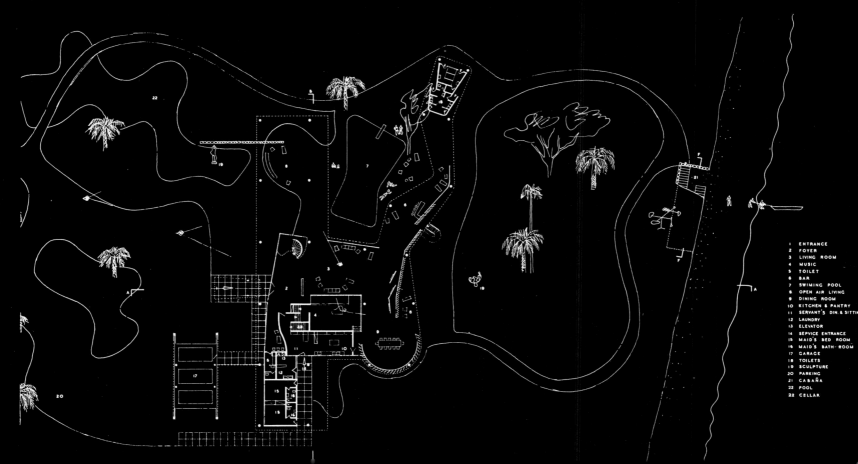

1 ENTRANCE
2 FOYER
3 LIVING ROOM
4 MUSIC
5 TOILET
6 BAR
7 SWIMING POOL
8 OPEN AIR LIVING
9 DINING ROOM
10 KITCHEN & PANTRY
11 SERVANT'S DIN. & SITTING
12 LAUNDRY
13 ELEVATOR
14 SERVICE ENTRANCE
15 MAID'S BED ROOM
16 MAID'S BATH-ROOM
17 GARAGE
18 TOILETS
19 SCULPTURE
20 PARKING
21 CABAÑA
22 POOL
22 CELLAR

OSCAR NIEMEYER, architect
detailing and execution,
LUTAH MARIA RIGGS, A. I. A. AND ARVIN SHAW, III

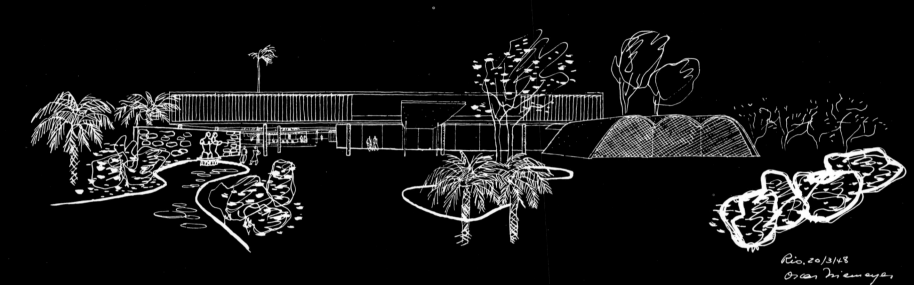

Rio. 20/3/48
Oscar Niemeyer

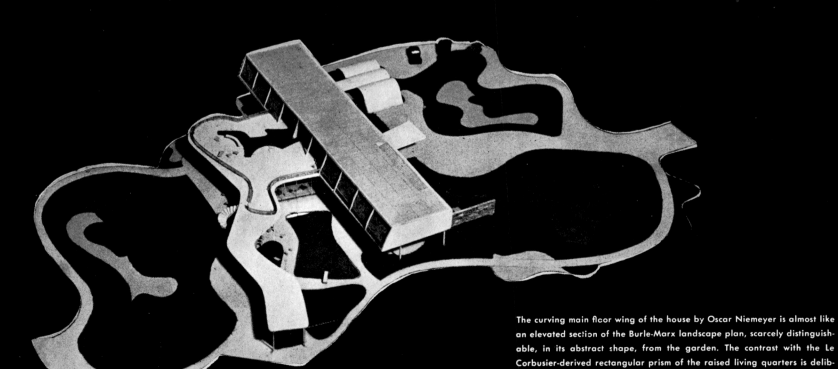

The curving main floor wing of the house by Oscar Niemeyer is almost like an elevated section of the Burle-Marx landscape plan, scarcely distinguishable, in its abstract shape, from the garden. The contrast with the Le Corbusier-derived rectangular prism of the raised living quarters is deliberate and dramatic. The biomorphic shapes of Arp and Miro have come the full way from three-dimensional experimentation to large-scale architectural expression, incorporated finally in the structural shape of the building itself.

project:

This exhibition is a part of a client presentation prepared by design students of California School of Art in a design-for-use project. The problem as it was originally specified required that the ten advance students design and execute, for actual sale, a collection of large scale garden pottery. The pots were to be formed and fired on the premises of a local pottery factory. Arrangements had been made in advance for the work to be shown and sold at Evans and Reeves Nursery.

Soon after the first field trip to the pottery factory the problem was restated and required that the students strive for a design commission to establish a commercial line of garden pottery for national distribution. This design emphasis was shifted from one individual pot per student to a group effort in coordination.

The pottery firm expressed enthusiasm for the problem as originally outlined but was unable to commit itself to a design service. On the other hand, the nursery saw distribution possibilities in the pottery and was willing to be shown its potentiality. At this point the present exhibition was conceived.

Several existing molds with which the factory produces its present line of garden pottery were selected for experiments. Each student was asked to prepare sketches of contemporary pots based upon the selected molds. One of the students was made responsible for layout of the exhibit. The sketches and exhibition plan were presented and upon the merits of their design and graphic quality funds were made available by the nursery for the purchase of the experimental pottery and necessary exhibition expenses.

All schedules for the project were prepared and supervised by individual members of the class. Contacts, whenever possible, were made by delegated members, and all work including pottery design and execution, exhibit design and construction, promotional design and production, and research was handled by student members of the class. Critiques were held to a minimum. Credit for outstanding work was given to Jack Morris for research; to Steve Pefley, a photographic student assigned to the class for the duration of the project for all photographs; to John Follis for the exhibit designed within a budget of $40. The exhibition was completed one day before the announced opening.

As a result of enthusiastic public acceptance of the pottery in its present experimental stage, the group has been commissioned by Evans and Reeves to design the line and plan its merchandising. A design fee and royalties have been established, and the complete line will be ready for national distribution in about three months.

LIGHTING COURTESY OF GENERAL LIGHTING OF LOS ANGELES
FURNITURE COURTESY OF VAN KEPPEL-GREEN

photographs: Steve Pefley

GARDEN POTTERY

LAGARDO TACKETT, *instructor*

MARK BRUNNER	BOB MARVIN
AL EGGLESTON	JACK MORRIS
JOHN FOLLIS	PAUL SODERBURG
REX GOODE	MEL WEITSMAN
FRANK KRUEGER	JOHN WELLS

STUDENTS AT THE CALIFORNIA SCHOOL OF ART

photographs: Gardner-Rand

ONE OF A HUNDRED

DESIGN PROBLEM:

To design a small house to be built in a tract of 100 houses of the same plan for selling to the average family.

To comply with the requirements of all the various institutions involved in financing the project, including the owners, the insurance companies, and the Federal Housing Authority.

To provide maximum flexibility in the use of space to meet different requirements of family life and retain the minimum amount of actual floor space.

To incorporate the simplest division of space possible in order to achieve economy in construction.

DESIGN SOLUTION:

Basically a three bedroom house was determined as the best house to meet the requirements. Flexibility of use was then achieved by use of sliding walls to actually permit use of the house as a one, two, or three bedroom house, or any combination of them. This also permits expansion of the living room from a length of 20 feet to 32 feet. In a similar manner the two end bedrooms can be converted to a single room for use as a nursery or playroom.

The conventional dining space connected with the living room and the dining alcove in the kitchen were combined by placing the dining table between the two. This allows feeding of the young children in the kitchen where they can be closely supervised with the remainder of the family on the other side of the table. It also allows the woman of the house while in the kitchen to participate in the conversation in the living room. Visual connection between the two areas may be cut off by dropping the venetian blind over the dining table and the hinged panel under.

Special conveniences incorporated in the house include built-in drawer sets in each bedroom with mirrors over, separate toilet compartment, thermostatic heating control, special lighting for the dining table, sliding glass doors at the tub, and built-in storage facilities.

Blank walls at the ends of the houses assure privacy while using the maximum width of the lot.

Centralized circulation permits direct access to all rooms without passage through any other room.

GREGORY AIN, *architect,* **JOSEPH JOHNSON** · **ALFRED DAY,** *collaborating*

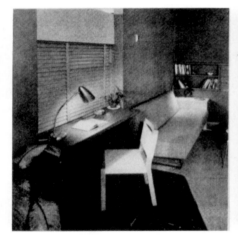

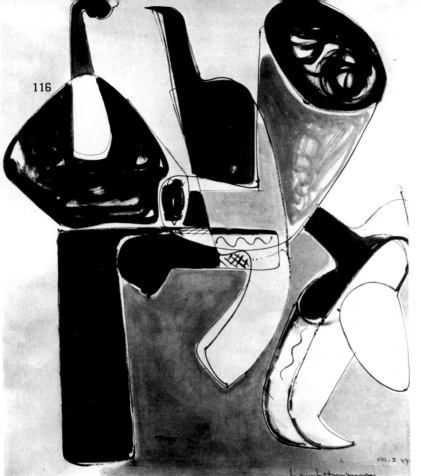

LIBERATION—Oil painting, photograph courtesy Kootz Gallery, New York

Hfofmann

**reply to questionnaire
and comments on a
recent exhibition**

Following two pages:
Statement THE PERFECT ARCHITECTURE—Ink and wash drawing

INTERIOR—Oil painting, photograph courtesy Kootz Gallery

article and material
assembled by
PAUL ELLSWORTH

SEATED WOMAN—Oil painting, photograph courtesy Kootz Gallery

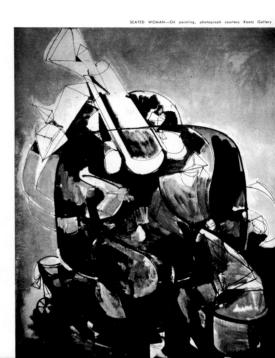

Hans Hofmann is a modern artist who has dared
to be logically progressive for nearly a half century developing a procedure system of physical
laws that are propelled by spiritual intuition.
While many a modern artist dwelt in lulling confines of cultivated visual happenstance, he demanded bold expansion of conceptual vision as
a basis, technique its consequences. Hans Hofmann's philosophy emerged with measurable distance from his contemporarys.
Perhaps no other man to the same extent has
clarified the myriad aesthetic principles of new
directions in the plastic arts. Here is valid proof
of recognizing the limits of any given medium.
The flat surface of the picture plane and restric-
tion of color pigments allow refreshed selection
of elements from nature which are then transfer-
able in the idea of the medium; the idea being
realized in the intrinsic life and the inherent
qualities of the medium. Such rejuvenated pictorial reality is conceived when the artist is un-
remittingly intuitive and possesses the desire to
derive imagination from his inner creative life.
Hans Hofman's philosophy is one of constant sur-
veillance of what physical laws allow greatest
possible independence in the pursuit of building
plastic expression. Line and plane concepts can
be utilized in construction, however the real aim
of art is to overcome all construction.
Too often a basic approach to composition is
neglected allowing platitudes of individualism to
overcome the first four lines of the picture plane.
Hofmann insists these lines are the first lines of
the composition and at any given point when
the artist draws on this plane, that point must be
in relation to those primary lines of the composition. The first lines are the spacial limitations
for imagination and without this limitation no
spacial fixation would be possible.
His protean spirit has exerted a great influence
in the visual arts with the axiom of 'push and
pull' forces in the depth of a picture plane. Hans
Hofmann claims this is the basis for all art approaches producing enormous pulsating volume
and is not a mere device.
His synthesis is that inside every great work of

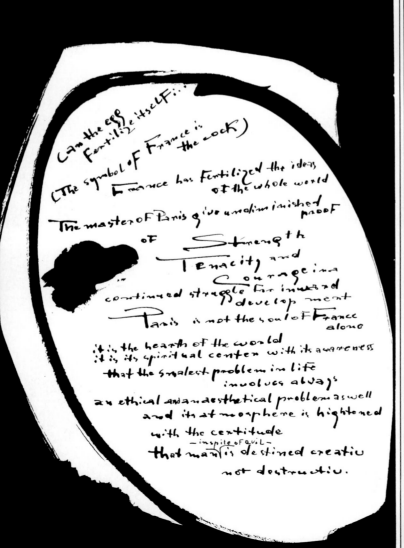

(Am the egg
Fertilize itself...
(The symbol of France is
the cock)
France has fertilized the ideas
of the whole world
The master of Paris give undiminished proof
of Strength
Tenacity and
Courage in a
continued struggle for inward
development
Paris is not the soul of France
alone
it is the hearth of the world
it is its spiritual center with its awareness
that the smalest problem in life
involues always
an ethical and an aesthetical problem as well
and its atmosphere is hightened
with the certitude
—inspite of evil—
that man is destined creativ
not destructiv.

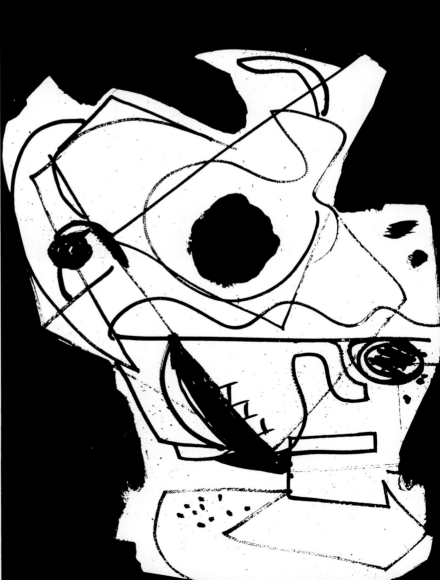

RED TRANSITION—Oil painting (most recent completed work of Hans Hofmann)

Pablo Picasso and Hans Hofmann at the Galerie Maeght, February 1949, Paris France. Photograph: Paul Ellsworth and Edward White

NOVEMBER 1949

COIFFURE—Oil painting, photograph courtesy Kootz Gallery

art a great architectural wall rests majestically in space created with resounding planes.

"The plane is a fragment in the architecture of space. When a number of planes are opposed one to another a spacial effect results. A plane functions in the same manner as the walls of a building. A number of such walls in a given relation creates architectural space in accordance with the idea of the architect who is the creator of this space. Planes organized within a picture create the pictorial space of its composition."

Hans Hofmann's complex definition of how planes are carriers of movements within the idea of 'push and pull' is similar to a physicist's resultant conclusion. The forces of 'push and pull' function three dimensionally without destroying other forces functioning two dimensionally. The movement of carriers on a flat surface is possible only through an act of shifting left and right or up and down. To create the phenomenon of 'push and pull' on a flat surface one has to understand that by nature the picture plane reacts automatically in the opposite direction to the stimulus received; this action continues as long as it receives stimulus in the creative process.

It is impossible to give the reader a complete appraisal of the varied directions of this versatile artist. The most thorough history of Hans Hofmann is found in the book "Search for the Real" published last year by the Addison Gallery of American Art, Phillips Academy, Andover, Massachusetts.

The following is Hans Hofmann's reply to a questionaire, August 20, 1949, concerning his views of American art today.

"Weldon Kees, the painter and poet, and Fritz Bultman, a very promising young American artist, conceived the idea of establishing a weekly for-

um during the summer of 1949 at Provincetown, Mass., for the purpose of discussing the position of all the arts today. The forum was titled 'Forum 49,' and an exhibition of abstract art was held at Gallery 200 where works of most of the leading younger American painters were shown. I was asked to be one of the sponsors, and was one of the speakers at the opening forum which presented the question: 'What is an artist?' I admitted frankly: I don't know what an artist is, but I do know what makes an artist. I said that I do know that only the man equipped with creative instincts and a searching mind is destined to become an artist. And as an artist I do further know that only the highest exaltation of the soul empowers the artist to transform the deepest and the weightiest experiences into the new dimension of the spirit that is art. Creation is a mystery and so is the artist in the act of creation. Every great work of art is a (continued on page 45)

Student working—Hofmann School, New York. Photograph: Paul Ellsworth and Edward White

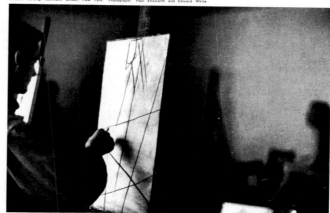

the house of GEORGE NAKASHIMA, *woodworker*

Photographs by Ezra Stoller

The rough outline of the specificatians are: framing—mostly oak, milled by owner; roof—corrugated transite and 1 inch thick concrete tiles, cast by owner; walls—stone, ⅜ inch pressured pure asbestos (war surplus), and walnut, cherry, and cedar paneling; ceilings—20" wide solid poplar, ⅜" pressed asbestos with insulation batts; floors—wide planks of walnut, oak, ash, birch, and beech for various rooms; sash—sliding of cypress with double strength glass and inner sash of paper shoji; heating—a combination system of a circulating fireplace, oil, and United States Rubber radiant heating panels.

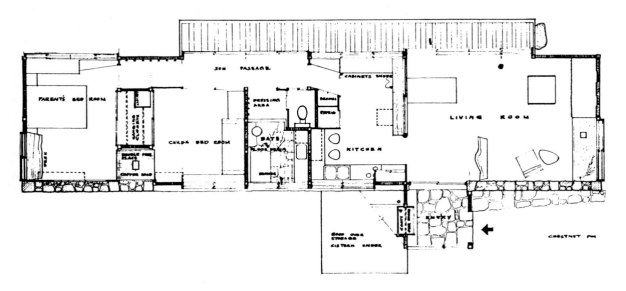

This house does not pretend anything from the point of view of design. The approach is more an expression of expediency in the need of housing within limited available funds and the techniques of building tempered by the background of the owner. Whatever design there is evolved from these requirements.

The house was built without plans and the detailing was developed from the material on hand or that which was available. The existing plan was drawn after the building was more or less finished.

Perhaps the greatest drawback in domestic architecture is that only the forms change, but the methods are the same, whereas the greatest need today is a creative study of "method"—not merely the mulling of forms on paper or the building of models, but a synthesis of the techniques of building within our present requirements.

Too many of our fresh forms have bones of 2 x 4's held by nails. The bones are forgotten. But our study should start at the bones. With our wonderful machinery we should come to better conclusions.

The esoteric we can do without. The fuzzy third-rate mysticism, we can do without. Building is essentially a practical problem, and we must face the hard fact that the fundamentals are tools and not paper. The greater needs today are not always being answered honestly, and probably cannot be answered without a new mentality.

The fundamental factor in this house is that it was about 90% owner-built, including millwork, cabinet work, masonry, carpentry, roofing, ditch digging, wiring, plumbing, etc. Also it included a large part of the manufacturing of framework, flooring, cabinets, and many odd items from rough material. Material was purchased when funds were available. Time used was what is generally allotted to entertainment or leisure—George Nakashima.

Grass seated chair, walnut or cherry

Furniture cannot fundamentally be disassociated from building—the problems and precepts overlap. There again it should be the expression of "method" and less of "style" or "design." There is essentially nothing "modern," nothing traditional," but preferably honest and dishonest results. "Modern" can be just as dishonest as even our worst periods. Here we must examine the bones. There is also personal preference, such as one's reactions to plywood. It has definite utilitarian uses, but it is often esthetically and economically doubtful. In a personal sense what we do in furniture is mostly the outcome of a way of life which to us is important—George Nakashima.

Low table of walnut, custom made →

NAKASHIMA, woodworker

Arm chair, walnut

Cushioned chair, cherry wood, rubber foam, denim cover

Straight backed chair, walnut with poplar seat

SANTA BARBARA HOUSE

by Richard Neutra, architect

Siegfried Giedion: Only one case may imply how far the development within a quarter of a century has led Neutra. Not without hesitation we single out one: Many of his houses are situated in far more spectacular landscapes than the Tremaine house, which is hard to find, as it is almost hidden in the wooded gentle slopes above Santa Barbara. But nowhere so much as here does the house seem to merge into the landscape more naturally and easily, yet differentiating themselves from it at the same time. Between the naturally growing and the artifically created by human hand, between nature and artefact, a living dialectic relation develops, which only a masterhand could have contrived.

The house is completely open, and yet, where the demand arises it maintains a certain reserve. Its core are the social quarters, flowing into one another without distinct separations. Typically, the social quarters and their elongation over the western terrace form a bridge into the landscape. (Even in his student projects Neutra had developed similar relations between inner and outer space.) The only rooms that hold themselves apart are bedroom, kitchen, servants-quarters and the guest-room.

The social quarters with their glass walls are broadly opened into the landscape, but the entrance drive is stopped by massive walls. But just here the interpene-

tration of the structural framework with architectural expression has caused something wonderful to happen. The heavy walls of the guest wing forbid admittance, but at the same time, the structural skeleton protruding from the interior of the house and forming a canti-levered roof, protects the porch and invites entrance. The porch has become no longer an annex, but inseparable from the main body of the building.

What has happened?

On pillars of reinforced concrete, which are regularly spaced throughout the house a network of superposed beams and crossbeams rests. Through the slender slab-like beams and the thin slabs of the roof, an unaccustomed structural lightness is produced. For the Health Center in Puerto Rico, in 1944, Neutra had already proposed the same shading and rainprotecting overhangs for continuous subsoffit airchange over lowered spandrels. Cross ventilation and diffusion of light right under the ceiling is also the reason for this airy construction. The slim beams set on edge, together with their thin roof-slabs give the Tremaine house a hovering quality, and yet, by their anchorage in the depths of the structure, an air of tranquility is achieved. Neutra states (page 120) how early (1923) the differentiation of structural elements emerges in his work. Only in the Tremaine residence the transcendence of mere function into psychic expression is accomplished.

A Close-up into Landscape: F. L. Wright grew out of prairie earth. He can almost transform himself into a piece of material; a stone, wood, or a plant.

R. J. Neutra is a city-dweller. He approaches nature, man and materials with the analytical eye of an explorer. Through his love for these and a sensitivity which is ever alive to them, he is near them in a particular way. This is not so much a reference to the use of dramatic contrasts that can be seen in some of Neutra's houses: Panoramic view of the ocean on the one side, view of a swimming pool, garden enclosed, on the other.

Here too, we think of a single case; the contact between the master-bedroom and nature, in the Tremaine residence. The waking man is not interested in wide panoramas and dazzling light. He prefers to see things close at hand and only gently illuminated. The master-bedroom faces the mountains, and the eye wanders along gentle slopes, losing itself in the intimate nearness of green plants and rough stones, and the structure of furrowed, evergreen oak-trunks.

What has been done by the architect? Almost nothing. He simply left the site undisturbed, so that the ground nearly reaches the window sill. And yet, a view into a microcosm of nature has been created—unknown to me anywhere else. This power to leave nature undisturbed and simultaneously to draw her into a specific emotional situation, reveals the artist, no less than the power to transfuse a ferro-concrete skeleton with psychic value.

Introduction by Siegfried Giedion to Architect Boesiger's Book "RICHARD NEUTRA." Publisher Girsberger, Zurich, Switzerland

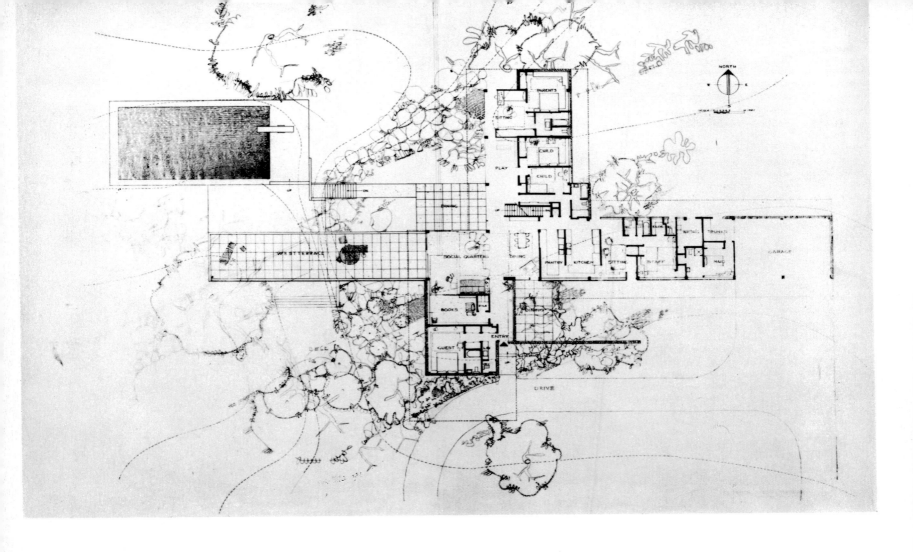

SANTA BARBARA HOUSE BY RICHARD NEUTRA

Opposite page, below: Living room furniture was designed by the architect—couch formed of sectional ottomans can be taken apart to seat informally a number of guests. This page, left from top to bottom: The dining table may be lowered to coffee table height—partitions disappear, portholes to pantry close, and the dining area becomes a part of the living quarters. These quarters open to a radiantly heated dining terrace with a mountain vista in the background. The elastic changeability of interiors increases the usefulness of the floor area. Looking from outdoor dining terrace to the mountain vista. Right, above: Detail view over living room couch in front of walnut paneling with dining space to left. View from staff dining room into kitchen and pantry bays.

Figure 1. The Petition of the Chippewa Indians to the President of the United States, 1849

In 1849 the Chippewa Indians sent a petition to the President of the United States, asking for the return of a piece of land with fishing privileges on Lake Ontario. (Fig. 1) A wampum belt indicated the money involved, the totem animals identified the chieftans, and the heart-strings of men and beast led to the bosom of a tail-coated, boot-wearing president. But the petition failed. The Erie Railroad was built where the Indians once speared the fish, and in 1850 the Bible Society of America distributed two thousand Bibles among the aboriginals of the North-west. In addition to all the other horrors of civilization the Indian was suddenly confronted with a method of communication he could not understand. For him idea and form had always been one. The archaic Greek identification between "idein-to see" and "Idea-semblance, or nature" had never been broken. What he thought took on form, and what he had to express became image. His identity with the surrounding world rested on the IDEOGRAM. He could not comprehend why the white man had replaced ideas as formed, sensuous images with typographical abstractions. Plato's theorem, removing the idea from the visible world into an esoteric realm of universal essence, had been lost on him.

A juxtaposition of the Chippewa petition and a page from the Bible furnishes proof of one of the deepest schisms in human development. During the course of three thousand years, the slow emergence of philosophical ideology extricated the archaic root of "idein-to see" from the consciousness of Western civilization. The identity of idea and form was broken. Even the artists, whose concern should have been the affirmation of the harmonious accord between concept and image, fell under the spell of the abstracted verbal symbol. With the victory of Humanism over medieval Mysticism, art succumbed to the dull pomp of the allegory.. One thing was described under the guise of another, a visual charade which the spectator could only solve with the aid of a literary scaffolding. In order to explain to himself the story contents of the allegoric presentation, he had to rely on the heard and read word. The champions of this art were numerous, from Poussin to Ingres, to Bouguereau, to Watts, to Klinger. While art historians recorded their tableaux faithfully, and the new ruling class, emerging after the French Revolution, invested millions in these literary transcripts, the intense images of the inner vision went unrecognized because the visual essence of the idea no longer knew its form.

And then came Gauguin. With the fury of the savage and the cynicism of the intellectual he smashed the allegory and in its place he put the symbol. In his wood-cuts he started to heal the millenial breach between the ideogramatic unity of non-hellenic cultures, and the muted soul of modern man. No one had taught him. His technique was crude, and his range of form limited. (Fig. 2) But he stripped his vision of all Renaissance trappings. Naked he embedded himself in the cyclic rhythm of a primitive society. Slowly and not without horror he established contact with the vast realm of ideological meaning that was too tremendous in its impact to bear allegoric disguise. The light he held up to the archaic symbol was "kindled by a weak and trembling hand but destined to become"—says Gauguin's testament—"a big thing in the hands of others."

For almost forty years this symbolic image of the inner reality grew in meaning and visual depth, "bodying forth," in the words of Odilon Redon, "imaginary beings, built in terms of material logic." It was an "uprush of the unconscious" that multiplied in form and meaning with the growing multiplicity of modern man. Imagination and image fused, creating the fabulous flower world of Redon, the gentle insanity of Marc's colored animal souls, Maurer's desperate Twin Heads (Fig. 3) and Klee's frightened faith in the unassailable purity of this inner world. The naturalistic image was not abandoned, it was transfigured by meaning. Finally with DADAISM this identity of form and message tried for an all-embracing universality and collapsed. Shocked into action by the insanity of the first World War, the young artists rallied for a total protest that would denounce **all** manifestations of a refuted social order. But bound to the model as they were, they found no longer any images that did not carry the identification marks of this refuted social order. The railway tickets and string ends of Kurt Schwitter's MERZ Collages, the newsprint of Raoul Hausmann's portraits, and the screws and bolts of Picabia's compositions, were meant to demask the false esthetic values of academic art, but they also symbolized a hopeless involvement with the manifestations of the society that supported this academic art. The search for new visual means to protest the materialistic triviality of nature imitation and of literary allegory, had to reach back farther than aboriginal primitivism or archaic simplification. It became evident that Gauguin's return to pre-historic imagery had been a necessary purification process but that it could not annul the complexity of contemporary existence. This existence could only be perceived through a synoptic vision—through a creative process that focussed complicated life patterns in a vis-

Figure 2. Paul Gauguin, Woodcut from "Noa Noa," 1892

Figure 3. Alfred Henry Maurer, Twin Heads, Circa 1930

Figure 4. Yves Tanguy, La dame l'absence

ual unity, based on fundamentals. The remaining traces of verbal identification had to be wiped off the canvas. The traditional limits of pictorial comprehension, based on the recognition of the model, as they had been maintained by the Cubists, had to be surpassed. The physical logic of an object and the common sense of its existence in three dimensions was challenged by a new knowledge of relativity. It was a gradual transition. The best among the creators of this syn-optic world withdrew cautiously from verbal identification. For a while—roughly between 1930 and 1936—the isolated plastic form remained as subject matter. This form was seemingly part of the surface world, yet it was without physiological attributes. These were "as if" forms, attracting the imagination through familiar proportions and poses, but remaining aloof of man's

penumbra between reality and dream, had become conscious of the disembodied character of inner vision. Psychological succession rather than psychological perspective was charted like the fluctuations of a graph. Color became self-purpose, often resembling a frantic scream like the outcry of an inarticulate being. Lines balled, looped, stretched, like cross currents on an electric tension field. Automatic reactions to subconscious stimuli guided the hand that created fumages, or arranged patterns according to the law of chance. The abandoned background-foreground relationship of forms emphasized the astral plane. There was no time to anchor the instantaneous experience in defined space. Infinity was like a screen on which to project the unconscious self; and the only possible approach of the spectator was self-surrender, a shedding of the skin to

Figure 5. Gordon Onslow-Ford, The Luminous Land, 1942-43

IDEA AND PURE FORM by Sibyl Moholy-Nagy

interpretation by lacking human characteristics. The picture plane retained the aspect of the naturalistic landscape. (Fig. 4) Depth perspective and horizontal-vertical articulation were maintained. But it was a landscape without spatial limitations, a surface unrelated to topographical characteristics. The "geological substructure" of which Cezanne had spoken, had finally risen to the surface.

But even the unfamiliar form of the familiar object retained a traditional identity that obscured the relationship of idea and pure form through the ever-intruding verbal explanation. The three-dimensional shape, related to an imaginary horizon, was replaced by configurations, surpassing all that could be perceived in the sun-lit world of material reality. The macrocosm of the inner self was revealed as the new subject matter, a panorama of emotional responses. The significance of each inner experience was expressed in fantastic forms and hues, in concentric or eccentric rhythms, pulling the ego either toward a position of central importance or dissolving it in a universal space that seemed to extend beyond the limits of the picture plane. (Fig. 5) Besides the panoramas there were close-ups. One form, one facet, one spot of color, mirrored the complexity of the whole creative being, as one carefully forged link stands for the quality of the whole chain. (Fig. 6) It was a revolution that dislodged the spectator from a position he had held for some three thousand years. Traditionally, he had been addressed by the artist, spoken to from the picture frame. The museum relationship between painter and layman rested firmly on their common understanding of vanishing point, foreshortening, and conical perspective. But these new images invalidated the museum approach. They could not be grasped under the aspect of the "visual axis" or identified with the thematic word. The fellow being had to be absorbed by the image. His own ego had to center in the center of the fabulous dream. Aerial and linear perspective had been replaced by PHYCHOLOGICAL perspective.

But the forms of this new art were still biogenetic. They had developed from the transfigured models of symbolic expressionism. Like all genetic forms, they had outline, structure and tactile surface. They congealed the vision that created them in their rational frame work. The flight through inner spaces came to a halt when it met its image. And in about ten years of development the new expressionists verified what Cezanne said had taken him forty years to discover, namely, that painting is not sculpture. The problem of form plasticity changed into the problem of form dynamics. The inner eye, now accustomed to the

feed the impact on the exposed nerves. (Fig.7)

In the forty years since Paul Gauguin had died in 1903 the search for the identity of idea and pure form had gone through three decisive stages. There had been an illustrative symbolism (see Fig. 3) transforming the traditional model through the idea. Configurative symbolism (see Fig. 4) as the next step had derived from the memory of biological shapes a new form morphology that surpassed the model but petrified the idea through a coagulation of the emotional intensity. And finally there had emerged dynamic symbolism (see Fig. 7) shedding all formal connotations and all structural organization to record nothing but inner force. With this development the search for a new vision had reached anarchy, meaning the undefined state of primordial matter. At no point in the development of western art had the rift between creator and public been so deep. Art was indicted of being mere chaos. But it was in the nature of this chaos to hold forth the promise of a new vision. Its antithetical contrast to the harmonious order of classical art gave a reciprocal function to this anarchic conclusion of the long retreat from the allegory. No creative chaos could be envisioned without the protest against petrified harmonies, and no future universe could emerge without a deep experience of the power inherent in chaos. Experiencing both, order and chaos, the new expressionists could start building a lasting entity between spirit and image. The painted surface took on a new meaning based on the premise that painterly form is substance and consequently endowed with the basic properties of all substance. These properties were not those of biological substance, but those of physical fundamentals: Warmth and cold, polarity or identity, spatial tension or equilibrium, mobility or rest. Pigment became a visual clay, shaped in the image of inner necessity. (Fig. 8) The egocentric obsession of the creator was sublimated. It fused with the essential reality of the idea. Each color element contributed to the perception of all painterly factors—radiance, gradation, line rhythm, weight and mass. Combined on the picture plane these fundamental elements formed a dramatic subject matter that surpassed in intensity all possible illustrative meaning. A new contents emerged that was no longer superimposed upon the abstracted form element like a stencil labeled hope, fear, love, desolation. Contents was shaped by the innate energy of substance, a substantiation of emotional experiences, not a transcription. As color, light, line and space fell into their place on the picture plane there occurred as, one might (Continued on page 245)

Figure 6. Robert Jay Wolff, Impression, 1938

Figure 7. Fritz Winter, Black Painting, 1936

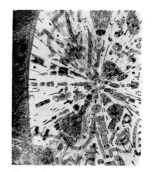

Figure 8. Lee Mullican, Agawam, Fourth Quarter, 1950

Figure 9. Wolfgang Paalen, Face Planetaire, 1947

(Continued on page 245)

SAM OF WATTS   "I had in my mind to do something big and I did."

Watts is a small industrial community on the outskirts of Los Angeles, and on a triangular backyard plot heavily fenced one finds Sam (or Simon). His project was begun in 1921. He drew up a set of plans, presented them to the local building code office where they were promptly turned down as being unsafe. He immediately entrained for the State capital, at Sacramento, and after presenting his project to the authorities there he was granted the right to go ahead with it.

There are three tall towers, one of 104 feet, at the center of the pie-shaped lot. Beginning with a modest 25 feet, his plan of procedure was simple and direct. He started at the bottom again and carried the outside structural members up to another fifteen or twenty feet. By this means, and working alternately on all three towers, he brought them to their astonishing height. The project half completed, he found it necessary to stop in order to build a fence around his yard so that neighborhood children would not endanger their lives.

Sam (or Simon) wires the steel reinforcing rod in place, wires mesh around it and then applies by hand a special mixture of waterproof cement which he carries up in a small bucket. Not wishing to go beyond the 104 feet of the highest tower now completed, it is his

intention to bring the other two, at present 100 and 80 feet high respectively, up to what he has set as his limit.

The impressive quantity of material used amounts approximately to 7,000 sacks of cement, 75,000 seashells, hundreds of broken dishes, thousands of pieces of broken tile, and several truck-loads of broken bottles. Sam (Simon lives alone; he was born in 1879 in Rome; he is a tile setter by trade and came to the United States when he was nine years of age.

These strange, steel and concrete, spider-webbed, Cambodian-like structures, encrusted with sea shells, broken bottles, incised lines, multi-colored and fragmented dishes, and the imprints of tools, hands, and corn cobs, are the bid for immortality of Simon Rodilla, tile setter and cracker barrel philosopher. Since 1921, without benefit of preconceived design, the three towers and many small walls, loggia, fountains and pathways, have taken shape as a series of meandering impulses. As a result, one enters a bizarre yet pleasant world, one enters a naive, and disturbing, for the ill-assorted quilt work of the textural designs lacks the discipline of a genuine folk art.

Simon Rodilla reads the Encyclopedia Britanica devotedly and for him Alexander the Great, Julius Caesar, Joan of Arc, Amerigo Vespucci and Buffalo Bill are presences more vital and alive than the people in the streets of Watts. "A man has to be good good or bad bad to be remembered," said Mr. Rodilla, glancing up at what he calls his Tower of Babel. It becomes apparent in talking to him that this project expresses the longing of a dignified, lonely, indomitable mite of a man who seeks the immortality of the historic figures he admires.—JULES LANGSNER.

PHOTOGRAPHS BY JAMES REED

THE LADERA PROJECT

A. QUINCY JONES

FREDERICK E. EMMONS

ARCHITECTS

DEVELOPER: EICHLER HOMES, INC.
SITE ENGINEERING: GEORGE NOLTE

In presenting this, the latest of the Eichler Homes projects, which is now in process of construction, it is well to remember the success with which these community developers have demonstrated in the past that a progressive attitude and a willingness to work with contemporary architects is productive of not only a series of good living solutions but also demonstrates rather conclusively that there is a large and eager public for good modern design in housing. As in their other very successful community projects Eichler, Inc., has worked in close cooperation with first rate architectural talent and with a sincere interest in providing the best all around results at a reasonable price for the ultimate owner.

In this case, the problem was to design three or four-bedroom houses at the medium cost level on rolling terrain. The street layout and lot sizes were previously established by earlier developers. The site is located near Palo Alto, California, on rolling hills with view throughout 360 degrees. The lots were previously laid out with 80-foot frontage and 180-foot depth with the exception of shaped or cornered lots. The lot types vary from level through medium sloping to steep. Rather arbitrary setbacks were already established by the County Planning Commission and were not susceptible to any substantial change.

It was the developer's desire, as well as the architects' to use dry construction throughout. The houses, therefore, are wood frame with wood and masonry exposed surfaces. The system of construction is based upon two types of laminated roofs with spans from 12 to 16 feet with no intermediate beam or wall support required. All houses are on concrete slabs with wood interior, and exterior wall surfaces either redwood siding or plywood.

In approaching the project, the architects divided the lots into types: level, medium, sloping, and steep, and houses were designed to fit them. For the level lots, as illustrated, houses 304, 403, and 404 were designed; for the medium sloping lots, houses 302, and 303D; for the steep lots, houses 302, 304U. Careful consideration was given to view, orientation, privacy between outdoor living areas on adjacent property.

The architects considered that a successful solution would have to include a consideration of full land usage and the kind of living permitted by the climatic conditions of the area.

The houses will be sold equipped with dishwashers, disposal units, built-in electric oven and range, Formica counter tops, and radiant heat. In all houses there will be much more than normal cabinet and closet storage space, as well as much more than normal built-in items—bookcases in each living room, raised hearth fireplaces with cantilever hearth slabs providing additional sitting space and built-in brazier type barbecues on each terrace. Each house will have a fencing scheme to provide for screened service yards in order to provide privacy.

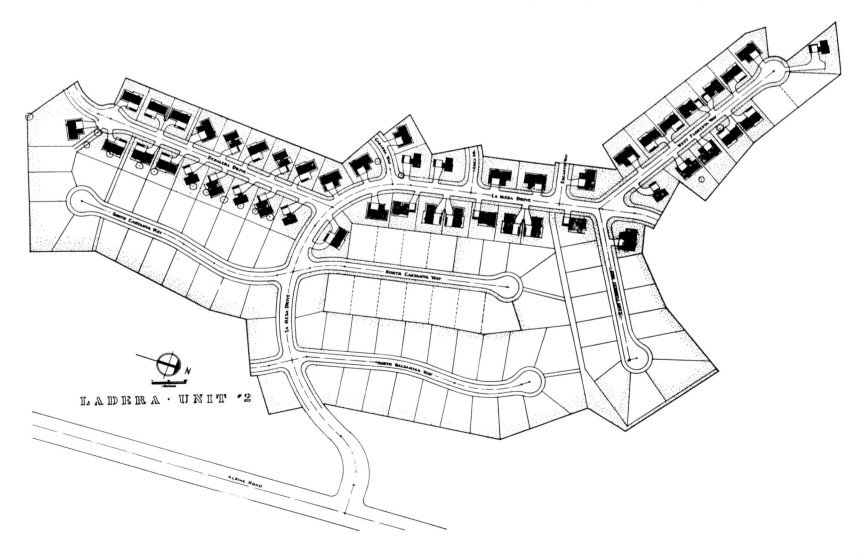

LADERA · UNIT #2

3()2

A. QUINCY JONES

FREDERICK E. EMMONS

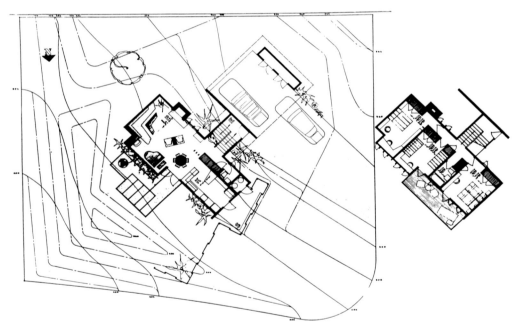

House 302 was designed for medium to steep slopes. The entrance and garage is at an intermediate level half way between the first and second floor. From the entrance, the drop to the living-dining-kitchen area is 4½ feet; the sleeping area is above. All rooms are oriented for views in one direction. Privacy is insured for the side walls of the house have no openings. The living areas open to a sun terrace as well as a shade terrace, the latter made possible by a second floor balcony. The stair well in the house makes it possible to bring planting through a glass wall into the living area.

3()4u

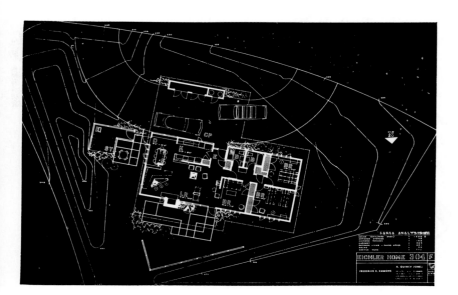

House 304 is a three-bedroom house with two baths designed to fit level building sites. The living and dining area is laid out in a manner to permit views in two directions. On one side of the living area there is a 8 x 24 porch, which gives shade and protection for the garden furniture. One of the three bedrooms is adjacent to the living area and the method of closing off this room is optional with the buyer. He may select a solid wall separation or a sliding partition. Or, the buyer may choose the simplest of all—a complete opening to the living area. In this house, as in all of the houses, the quiet or sleeping area is zoned completely from the living or more noisy areas.

House 304U is a three-bedroom house designed for steep lots and the plan is similar to 304. It was designed for a lot either steep up or down from the road. In the cases where the lot is steep and rises up from the road, half of the house cantilevers away from the terrain on steel beams and forms the car shelter. In the reverse case (when the lot is steep and down from the road), the car shelter is handled in a similar manner to house 304 and the part cantilevered from the terrain then forms a shade garden for outdoor living. In all cases this house is intended to be adapted to the building site so that the living, dining and kitchen areas open at floor level to the terrain and the bedrooms are over the cantilevered porch.

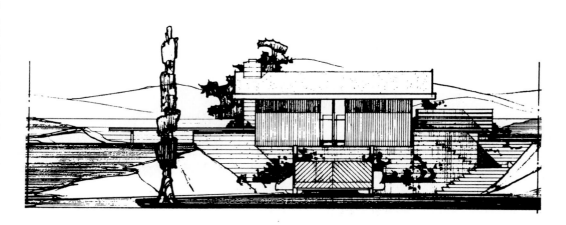

303D

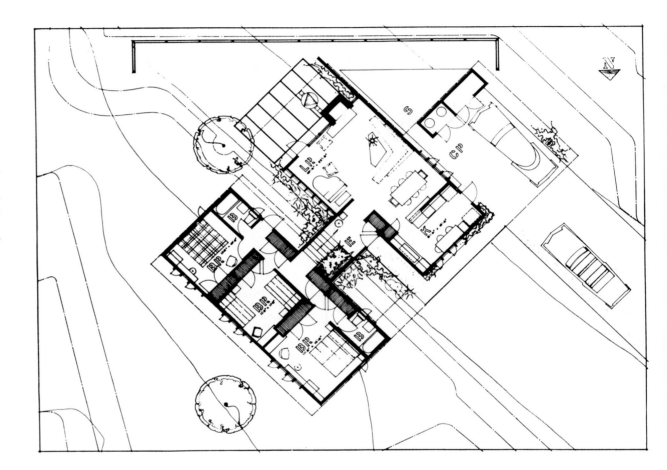

Houses of the 303 type are all three-bedroom and two-bath houses designed to fit medium slope lots. Basically, the plan is two simple rectangles, one housing the living-dining-kitchen area, and the other housing the bedrooms and baths. The link connecting these rectangles houses the entry and stair that makes the two levels possible. In all cases, the bedrooms are either 3½ feet above or below the living area. The open glass connecting allows planting to be carried through the house. A roofed porch 8 x 14 provides a shade terrace and protection for garden furniture. The brazier type barbecue is within this porch.

A. QUINCY JONES

FREDERICK E. EMMONS

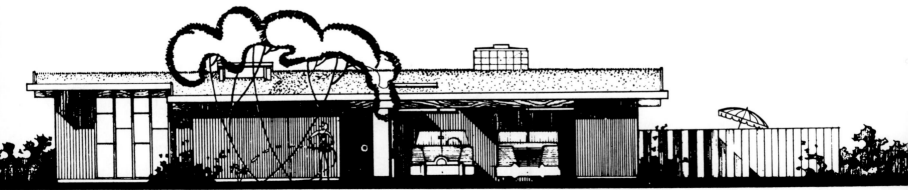

404

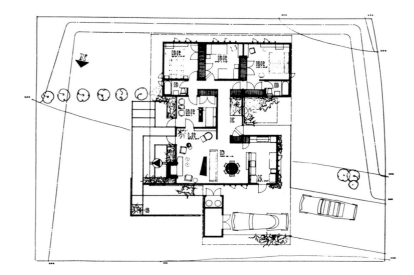

House 403 is a four-bedroom level lot house. It was developed after house 303 was designed and provides an extra bedroom. This house is one that has the view provided for in one direction only, giving privacy from adjacent property.

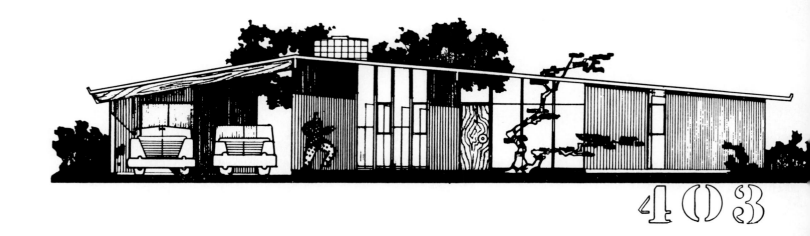

403

House 404 is a four-bedroom, two-bath house designed for level lots. From a square footage point of view, this is the largest of all the houses, and if the owner chooses to leave the fourth bedroom open to the living area, it provides a living space 40 feet in length along the fireplace wall. The living area has views in two directions.

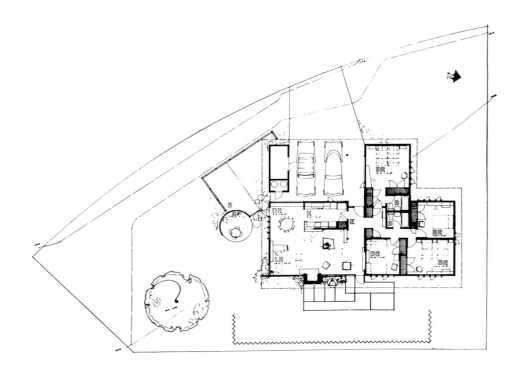

JARDINES DEL PEDREGAL DE SAN ANGEL

"After thousands of years there has been discovered one of the most beautiful spots in the Valley of Mexico, El Pedregal. It can be described only as a sea of great waves of lava, suddenly solidified, and which as it cooled off formed numerous crevices.

"This fifteen square mile lava bed, formed some five thousand years ago by the eruption of Xitle, is now the site of Mexico City's unique and beautiful housing development, Jardines del Pedregal de San Angel.

"The discoverer of El Pedregal and of its potential value as a residential zone is due primarily to Architect Luis Barragan. He has created out of his talent and his toil a marvelous garden in an arid land covered by volcanic lava, and has indeed brought water to the rocks.

"There exists a special interesting type of vegetation in El Pedregal, the palo bobo tree, rock flowers, cacti and succulents, all nourished in the soil deposited during thousands of years.

"The development of Jardines del Pedregal in this unique and exotic atmosphere is a special type for residences or villas placed on the site in such a manner as to preserve the natural contours of the terrain and its plastic beauty.

"A few years ago some architects proposed the construction of the University of Mexico City in El Pedregal, using zones not covered by lava, and this idea has culminated in the great work of the university project now under way.

"The directors of the project are architects Enrique del Moral and Mario Pani, the executive director Architect Carlos Lazo. The University of Mexico City in El Pedregal will be officially opened November, 1952, and architects from many countries will be invited."—CARLOS CONTRERAS

To obtain an harmonious relationship between volcanic rock formations and architectural design in El Pedregal, certain restrictions have been placed upon construction and landscaping.

All houses are required to be of contemporary design. (The style known as "California Colonial" is expressly forbidden.)

The minimum lot is to be approximately one acre, and the area of the house not exceed ten per cent of the total area of the lot, the rest to remain in gardens and free spaces.

The lava rock is to be protected, the amount to be removed to facilitate building or for use in roads and walls being limited to the immediate and minimum need. Only a part of one of the three lava caps which constitute the one hundred foot thick basaltic blanket may be removed.

Native vegetation is to be preserved, and other planting is required to follow the natural lines of the terrain.

The first house in El Pedregal was constructed in 1945. At present 42 houses have been completed or are under construction. Thirty two more houses are in the design stage. Seven hundred lots have been divided.

Two thirds of El Pedregal will always remain in gardens.

Opposite page, left: Looking from El Pedregal across its choppy black sea of basaltic rock to Mexico's great landmarks, the peaks of Ixtaccihuatl (The White Woman) and Popocatepetl.

Right: The lava formations are protected by tract restrictions.

Below: Concrete sculpture by Mathias Goeritz in the entrance court of El Pedregal.

EL PEDREGAL

PORTRAITS BY ELIZABETH TIMBERMAN

Above: Luis Barragan
Opposite page: Fountain in forecourt of El Pedregal.
Above, right: Walk into El Pedregal gardens.
Right: Entrance gates to El Pedregal are steel painted with luminous red paint. The entire development, including roads, houses and gardens, adjusts itself to the volcanic rock.

Comments by Luis Barragan on his approach to Architecture in Mexico:

"It is fitting that the first residential development in Mexico City which requires all houses to be of contemporary design should be situated on lava beds formed approximately five thousand years ago by a volcanic eruption."

"I first became captivated with El Pedregal when I introduced some fragments of the lava rocks into my garden. Rock formations are as satisfying an element in a garden as grass or flowers."

"In the design of my houses I have attempted to state new relationships between modern materials and the popular house of the villages and farms of my country, while in my gardens I have suggested new relationships between rocks and vegetation."

"It is meaningless to set design restrictions for a residential development without also restricting landscaping. An excellent house can be degraded by a garden—or a neighbor's garden."

LUIS BARRAGAN

"I constructed my house to satisfy my personal taste, which is the solution of two problems: first, to create a modern **ambiente**, one that is placed in and is a part of Mexico, and is basically influenced by the architecture of the ranches, villages and convents of my country; and, second, to utilize primary and rustic materials required for modern comfort. "I have used a reinforced concrete frame and concrete block, and in the living room-library I have used 8x10 commercial pine beams.

"I have left large plain walls without window openings, both for plastic beauty and because they are required for book shelves, pictures and furniture. By the use of large wall surfaces one can also obtain spaces with varying luminosity, which creates an **ambiente** more comfortable and intimate."

RESIDENCIA DEL ARQ. LUIS BARRAGAN EN LA CALLE DEL GENERAL FRANCISCO RAMIREZ NUM.14, TACUBAYA, D.F.

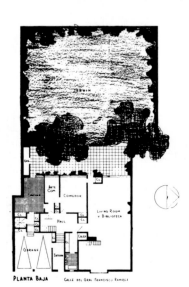

PLANTA BAJA   CALLE DEL GRAL FRANCISCO RAMIREZ

FACHADA

PLANTA ALTA   AZOTEA

Upper left: Studio terrace; lower right: Living room facing garden.

Opposite page, upper left: Deck on top of house; right: Stairway from library to mezzanine-study. Risers and treads of unrailed stairs are anchored into the masonry wall. Below, left: Garden elevation showing living room with 16-foot ceiling. Outdoor canvas curtains shield glass. Right, Studio with aerial map of El Pedregal. Leather chairs are butaques.

The site for the house is a 100-foot front lot on a narrow street in Tacubaya, an outlying section of Mexico City. The house has been placed flush with the street and stretches the full length of the frontage. Following the lot line on both sides, it forms a rectangle 50 feet wide. The flat lot is 140 feet deep and all important rooms face the garden which extends back 90 feet. The garden is walled on three sides with a convent-type buttressed wall of plastered adobe.

PHOTOGRAPHS BELOW AND RIGHT BY ELIZABETH TIMBERMAN

142

"It has become necessary again to introduce doubt and discomfort into academic smugness..."

JUAN O'GORMAN

PHOTOGRAPHS BY ELIZABETH TIMBERMAN

"It is necessary for architects to remember that the time in history in which developments occur is of importance. The functional or once-called International type of architecture in Mexico, which started around 1928 with European influences (Le Corbusier, Mies van der Rohe, Gropius, etc.) and with cries of horror from everyone (including the architects who today are its advocates) and which became the movement of the avant garde up to about 1935, had at that time a social importance. Its main asset was the abolition of the old molds, of two or three academic mannerisms and the liquidation of a certain amount of stupidity in planning according to sets of rules which had no human meaning.

"The principal function of functional architecture in Mexico during that time was to destroy. Its positive and human side was the idea that a poor country cannot waste in esthetics what it should gain in efficiency. Unfortunately this formula was applied with very little efficiency and for an esthetic reason.

"Today architecture in Mexico has taken from functionalism its forms. It has great pride in its up-to-date modernism, and has become thoroughly academic.

"Everyone does today the 'right' thing, which was the 'wrong' thing in 1930, and as a result we have all the boring stuffiness of correctness.

"Just a few years ago the disguise for bad architectural planning was the symmetrical layout of Greek columns; today this disguise is the simplicity of bare walls, large areas of long windows (whether you need them or not) and the puritanism that is the style of abstract beauty.

"It has become necessary again to introduce doubt and discomfort into this academic smugness for the sake of vitalizing and rescuing our architecture, now sick with functionalitis.

"So today the task is to try to produce an architecture which, irrespective of all functional rules, will be more functional, that is to say,

(Continued on page 245)

Juan O'Gorman established a precedent in 1928 when he built his first concrete frame house stripped of all ornament. Today he returns to Mayan culture for the inspiration for his new house in El Pedregal.

The spiral of an open stairway from living room to roof continues in the exterior wall, terminating in a Mayan head. The cross was placed on the head by workmen to honor Santa Cruz, patron saint of the masons. All buildings under construction on May 3, the Day of the Masons, are guarded against the evil eye by garlanded crosses.

ARCHITECTURE

IN

MEXICO

BY

ESTHER McCOY

"A recent tendency in architecture is to express through the material of a house the Mexican tradition, whose essential characteristic is concern with the life within the house, which makes the exterior secondary," Architect Enrique Yanez of the School of Architecture of the National University said, in speaking of the first exhibit of contemporary Mexican architecture held this spring at the National Institute of Fine Arts in Mexico City.

In the foreword to "18 Residencias de Arquitectos Mexicanos," he says, "A new decorative sense is being applied to the use of our native materials, volcanic rock, wood and brick, all rich in architectural qualities, texture and color.

"It is perhaps a sign of dissatisfaction with the degree to which we have achieved national expression that we use in our interiors archeological artifacts, clay figures and statues, in an attempt to recapture the Mexican spirit.

"In the same way folk art, such as masks, textiles and toys are combined with modern furnishings in a logical and happy desire to unite tradition with the dictates of the new architecture. We have fused with our present day environment these manifestations of nostalgia to form an artistic unity."

Among the architects interested in the exploitation of the Mexican tradition is Luis Barragan, whose work shows the influence of indigenous building, especially convent architecture and the popular house of the village.

The popular house of Mexico is the only truly native style. The popular house has always been restrained, in contrast to the embellished house of Mexico City. The further away from the city, it has been remarked, the more sparing the ornament.

The exuberantly ornamented church to be found in every Indian village is often considered the only expression of the Mexican architectural temperament, while the straightforward instinctive house is overlooked.

In the popular house the art of building was reduced to its simplest and plainest forms. Indeed the International Style (that description persists in Mexico) that gripped Mexican architecture after the fall of Diaz was in its clean surfaces closer to the Mexican spirit, as revealed in the popular house, than the eclecticism of the Diaz regime. Although both the modern house of the thirties and the popular house were simple declarative statements, one was a literal translation and the other idiomatic.

Other architects are digging deeper into Mexico's architectural past. Juan O'Gorman, one of the leaders of the modern school of the thirties, whose lean, well-organized buildings were "stripped for action," as the expression went, has returned to Mayan culture for the forms of his new house in El Pedregal. The house may perhaps be more sculpture than architecture, but there is evident the growing respect among Mexican architects for native traditions.

The skeletal style of concrete construction which one sees everywhere in Mexico City was certainly launched in the early thirties by Tolteca Cement Company's smart propaganda campaign and design competitions, but it was the acute shortage of schools, hospitals and other public buildings that prolonged it. The shortage could be remedied faster and more economically by employing the more direct forms than by clinging to the time and material-consuming Spanish colonial and eclectic forms.

Tolteca's reign has also been extended by the scarcity of wood in most parts of Mexico. Today practically all residences in Mexico City have a reinforced concrete frame, and wood is confined usually to structural beams. Instead of wood sash, steel casements are used almost entirely in residences, and light steel doors—selling at 150 pesos—similar to ones used industrially in the United States are widely used in residences.

The instability of the soil in Mexico City, where the water content is three times the solid, requires a special type of foundation which consumes enough concrete to keep Tolteca Cement Company in business for some years to come. For the National Lottery Building a system of mechanical jacks was used between a flexible T-beam grille and concrete trusses. Because of the compressible nature of the soil, long horizontal buildings have a tendency to sink, and in the last twenty-five years the new designers, working without precedent, have produced buildings that have been adjusted to the special soil conditions.

When Architect Enrique Yanez was asked what he thought of the embarrassingly ornate Palace of Fine Arts, designed by an Italian imported for the job, he replied, "It is sinking, thank God!"

The returning interest in native materials is noted in new commercial buildings, which are less rigid in form and more textured and colorful. Jose Villagran Garcia has used glazed brick in colors as a facing for his new buildings on Cinco de Mayo and the auto parking building on Gante. The lower half of the Hydraulic Resources Building was faced with this decorative material, and one facade of the building housing the United States Embassy.

In the new university buildings, Architect Mario Pani has used a native glazed brick as an exterior and interior finish.

Fortunately for Mexico, the architect enjoys a place of honor that is reserved for the engineer in the United States. Architects under thirty are given important commissions. This is not new. Villagran was twenty-four years old when in 1925 he designed the Institute of Hygiene. He was then architect for the Department of Public Health.

On the other hand there is a tradition of responsibility on the part of the architect to the community. At twenty-seven Juan O'Gorman founded the School of Construction under the Secretary of Public Education. This was a time when design far outstripped construction methods, and the school was something of a laboratory where there was developed means of getting buildings off the board. The building trades, receptive to the new design, were consulted, and cooperated with the architects.

Young architects joined together during that period to study the problem of low-cost housing. Juan Legarreta built a minimal house as his thesis for his degree in architecture, which was the prototype of many units constructed later.

Today there exists the same responsible attitude on the part of the young architects, and they continue to receive important commissions. Half of the architects whose work is represented in this issue are under thirty-five; three of them are in their twenties. Ramon Torres Martinez, who designed the adobe-wall-house also designed the National School of Medicine in University City, Mexico, and planned the Islas Marias Prison. Luis Rivadeneyra, as Zone Chief for the Federal Committee for the Construction of Schools in the State of Veracruz, has designed numerous schools.

Mexico has its full share of ill-considered residential work. In the thirties, many of the older residential sections did not permit modern design. In Polanco, however, there flourished a modern concrete house that is often referred to as "Hollywood Modern." It is pompously scaled and the orientation is irrational. It has the same picture window looking out to the street as the marble mansion next door—although that the glass is usually larger and without protection from glare. Except for the absence of applied ornament, there is little to distinguish the Polanco modern from the Polanco colonial. But Polanco is changing. The current interest in the rich native materials has started a rash of over-textured houses.

El Pedregal is not without its imperative houses, despite careful design restrictions. One of the newer and more costly houses, designed entirely for show, has a nine-car garage. "Not all Cadillacs," the owner said. (Mexicans are fond of Cadillacs, preferring cream-color or black.)

Stories about poor construction in Mexico are abundant and often well-founded. North Americans find the hardware on the doors awkward, ceilings unnecessarily high, and acoustics in the concrete frame structures abominable. One serious defect to a North American used to a servantless house is the cramped and characterless Mexican kitchen. It was not, however, until the United States ran through its servant class that our kitchen became a pleasant room. In Mexico today the entry hall, boasting a rubber plant, is often larger than the kitchen. The criado, or servant house, may one day, let us hope, borrow a little space from the master's large house.

The cost of construction at present for luxury builidng in Pedregal averages 350 pesos per square meter, which is about $4 per square foot. Labor cost is approximately one-fifth of the total cost of construction in El Pedregal. Carpenters, paid by the job per square meter, average 13 pesos a day. Masons customarily receive 9 pesos for an eight-hour day.

One of the impressive things about Mexican residential architecture today is the imaginative use of water as decoration. Max Cetto uses a declivity in a volcanic rock formation for a natural pool. Luis Barragan has borrowed the village watering trough, placed it at an intersection of two walls in a garden or on a roof terrace, and down one wall is a slow almost imperceptible movement of water. The texture of the wet wall is of a richness that apparently only a century could have produced—yet it is but a few years old. The acid colors used on the wall to help produce this magic were developed by the muralist, Xavier Guerrero.

Interior pools are used everywhere, in residences, hotels, public buildings, supper clubs. No two are alike. In a dining room of a hotel is a free form pool whose edge is marked by a

143

(Continued on page 245)

144

LUIS RIVADENEYRA

Mexico's most typical and least noted structure is the one-room house, a modest rectangle constructed of the available materials of the region. Now two young designers—both are under thirty—bring a new and modern interpretation to this national institution.

The house by Jaime Lopez Bermudez was consructed at a total cost of 11,700 pesos (below $1500) and utilizes no imported materials. The **tepatate** excavated for garage is mixed with cement for the masonry blocks that form three walls of the house.

The framing is a shop-fabricated steel

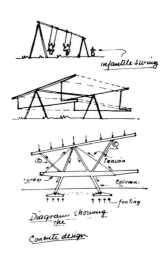

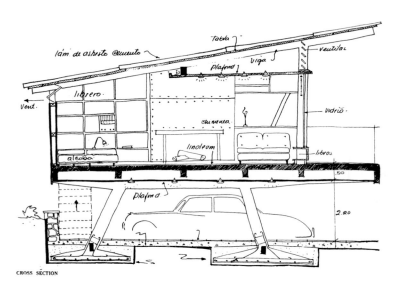

CROSS SECTION

PHOTOGRAPHS BY CHANO ROJANO

JAIME LOPEZ BERMUDEZ

structure composed of ½″ and ¾″ angle irons, welded together by ¼″ steel rods.

The slab floor has circles of colored cement set in. The roof is corrugated asbestos. Insulation is cocoanut fiber, one of several industrial materials used for the first time in residences. The fiber, light and porous, is commonly used as a padding for burros; its name **sudaderm de burro** deriving from its use.

There are no interior bearing walls. "The tendency to do away with unnecessary interior walls is growing in Mexico," says the architect. "The one-room is a natural way of living."

Jaime Lopez Bermudez is a painter as well as architect, this dual role being a commonplace among young and old of his profession in Mexico. The mural on the front of the house is his.

The house is in the Santa Fe district, 13 kilometers from Mexico City, and is placed on the site and glass areas planned to take advantage of the entire Valley of Mexico.

The one-room house by Luis Rivadeneyra in Jalapa, Veracruz, is also raised to take advantage of a view, and at the same time to form a car shelter. The structural principle employed is that of the children's swing found in public playgrounds. The light-weight concrete house is hung from steel columns, which have been set in concrete.

The architect in Mexico has always been fortunate in being commissioned to do important work before he reaches middle age. Rivadeneyra is Zone Chief of the Federal Committee for the Construction of Schools in the State of Veracruz, and his work includes the design of many schools in the State of Veracruz, the Jalapa railway station, cemetery chapel, a large cements work and many residences.

MAX CETTO

"The difference in construction in Mexico from what I had been used to in Germany, and during the year of work with Richard Neutra in California, is due to one basic fact: the lack of skilled workmen in Mexico.

"There are explanations of this lack to be found in history, the sociological structure and the human qualities of this people. The regular workman in the whole booming building trade of Mexico has no chance to acquire sufficient technical knowledge either by tradition or by education. His tools are poor, and house construction is accomplished without mechanical equipment. Considering these, and other odds, including the fact that only a small number of foremen are able to read working drawings correctly, the actual completion of so many thousands of houses in Mexico obliges us to give the highest credit to the extraordinary

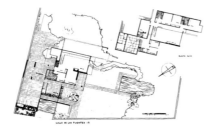

natural resourcefulness, the imagination and the passionate addiction of everybody involved in the activities of building.

"In Mexico houses cannot be built by a complete set of drawings and specifications, as in most European cities and in the United States. If the architect cares to see the building finished according to his concepts, he has to supervise the work every day, playing the part of a general contractor himself. Knowing that even the most careful preparation on the drawing board would not free him from spending at least half his time to put them through on the job, he very often prefers to rely on sketches and oral directions.

"This method is not as bad as one would imagine. What is lost in efficient preparation is gained in directness of approach, new suggestions coming out of the work in progress, and a flexibility which allows one to make improvements on a moment's notice.

"Under such circumstances it seems considerably wiser to renounce certain ideals of mechanical perfection which we adored in the first years of functional architecture, and accept the blessings of a rather rustic, handmade and more human touch, which is probably the most adequate expression of the natural and spiritual resources of this country."

The first two houses constructed in El Pedregal were designed by Max Cetto, former head of the Industrial Construction Department in Frankfurt, Germany and Professor of Planning at the Offenbach School of Applied Art. He has practiced architecture in Mexico for the last ten years.

Opposite page, center: When constructed, the lava rock formed a portion of the living room wall leading the garden into the house. Later, the owner had it chipped out. Center, right: Carport with service patio beyond; gate at right to living room garden. Below: Paved walk leads from motor entrance by pool to living room garden.

This page, left: Pool is cut out of lava rock. Soil for entire garden is river silt and coral trees were planted in crevices of the rock. Below, center: Steps to bedroom wing from service patio. Steps at right to portero's quarters. Below, right: Service patio.

This house was the second one to be built in the Pedregal and was designed to be sold. To build for an unknown client introduces an unreality into the work similar to carrying out the whole *faena* of a bullfight without ever facing the bull. One must accept the prejudices of an imaginary client as a fact, without being able to modify or dispel them. If the dimensions of the house are slightly exaggerated, and the ground plan formal, it is for this reason. His own house in the Pedregal is more reticent and is closer to his thinking.

To refer to a specific problem: the servant's rooms. The relationship of that quite extensive group of rooms to the rest of the Mexican house of higher standards is complicated in that it has to be separated and independent, but on the other hand, if possible, have direct access to entrance, kitchen, laundry and bedrooms. The plan shows the solution to that cross puzzle.

As to orientation, all bedrooms face east, living rooms south, according to the best sun exposure and view.

The master key to the house has unfortunately been lost. When the house was constructed a rock was used as a wall in the living room, penetrating the total length of the ground floor and leading the garden into the interior. When this was removed by the owner, because it was hard to clean, the room no longer accommodated itself to the topography of the rocks.

ENRIQUE DEL MORAL

In the middle 20s a group of architectural students that included Enrique del Moral and Juan O'Gorman formed itself around Jose Villagran Garcia, founder of the modern movement in Mexico, and at that time architect for the Department of Public Health. The students left their drafting boards to work with Villagran on such projects as the Granaja Sanataria and other hospitals.

Out of this association, in which theories of modern design were put into practice, there emerged a standard of construction for the new skeletal-type structure. Also there was developed a group of excellent constructionists educated not only in the rigid economy of the new architecture but in a civic responsibility.

Much of the planning for the new University of Mexico City, to be opened in November, 1952, is Enrique del Moral's. In collaboration with Mario Pani he has coordinated the extensive project. Architects throughout the world are to be invited to Mexico City on the occasion of the opening of the first buildings.

Enrique del Moral's house is on the same short narrow street in Tacubaya as Luis Barragan's. It is placed close to the street to allow for generous garden spaces, and all important rooms face the gardens.

The key to the house and to Mexican living is the covered terrace, used for outdoor living and dining as in the humblest Mexican house. The terrace extends out from the living room, to form an L, with one end unwalled and the other with sliding glass. A tile floor continues beyond the covered terrace as a garden paving.

Servants' wing and service patio have been placed to form a buffer between garden and street.

PLANTA BAJA

PLANTA ALTA

Opposite page, above: House forms an "L" around the garden. Concrete block wall encloses the bedroom garden. Below, left: Corner of the living room. Batague chairs and polychrome figure give a Mexican emphasis to the room.

This page, above: Corner of the patio.

Below: Terrace room is open at one end to the garden. Right, from top to bottom: Covered terrace extending from the living room; two views of the living room; bath room with specially designed tile tub and glass wall on closed garden; bedrooms are separated by storage wall, both sharing the garden view.

PLANTA BAJA   PLANTA ALTA

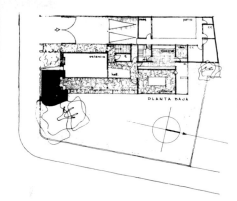

Left: Front elevation. Below: Pool at end of southwest wall of living room. Opposite page, center: Living room looking toward pool and toward dining room. Below: From the garden looking through glass wall to living room.

PHOTOGRAPHS BY GUILLERMO ZAMORA

"Modern materials combine well with ancient materials, such as tile and **piedra braza**, a stone used in the foundations of colonial and pre-hispanic buildings. I like especially to combine glass and tile because of the contrasting texture. The tile used in my house as an exterior facing is 15 x 30 centimeters and is one inch thick. It is made of clay and is manufactured in Mexico. Colors are yellow and beige.

"The construction is concrete frame, with a concrete slab floor and roof. Floors are carpeted except for the bathrooms, which are tiled, and the breakfast room and office are paved with **piedra braza**. Volcanic ash acts as insulation for the roof. Steel casements are used throughout.

"I have combined motor entrance with door grille in order to avoid the hole-in-the-wall front door and to produce a continuous flow of line and material. Also, I hesitated to introduce a new element at this point in a house where variety of material has been kept at a minimum. The motor entrance and door grille are of steel bars backed with a stainless steel mesh. I have related the rectangle of the bars to the upper mass of the house in scale, contrasting the openness of the modern mesh with the solidity of the masonry."

VICTOR DE LA LAMA

This house in Las Lomas de Chapultepec designed by a 31-year old architect treats the high garden wall as a boundary of the house itself, the unbroken wall of glass of the living room setting no limit for the house. The wall, planned as part of the house, closes off the garden from the street and makes plausible the handsome glass areas. The upper story, supported by steel columns, forms an overhang for the glass, the glass hanging as a curtain.

The use of the pool at the end of the living room gives richness to what might otherwise have been a monotonous wall, an excellent example of the felicitous landscaping to be found everywhere in Mexican houses.

RAMON TORRES MARTINEZ

PHOTOGRAPHS BY GUILLERMO ZAMORA

The adobe wall and the enclosed garden are characteristically Mexican, and here they are combined with glass and modern planning by the 27-year old architect, Ramon Torres Martinez, designer of the National School of Medicine building in University City.

The absence of setback requirements makes it possible for the adobe wall, which follows the property line, to serve as three masonry walls for the house. The fourth wall is glass, and faces the garden.

Entrance is through the carport, which has been placed away from the garden, thus insuring privacy for the important rooms of the house.

The house recalls another typical residence in Mexico City, which makes use of the same structural principle, fitting itself between existing walls. It is to be found in the affluent districts near large apartment houses and is occupied by the families of street merchants, or others of that low economic level. The house borrows two walls from an existing structure, and they serve as supports for roof of cardboard or corrugated tin. The only other structural member required of the homemaker is a post. Two sides are left open, or one may be surfaced with palm fronds. The floor is dirt.

From humble beginnings, where necessity determined form, is evolved the developed thinking of the Torres house.

The basic points followed in the construction of the house are these:

1. A plan which allows one to look continually between garden and interior, treating the whole as one indivisible element.

2. The use of materials of purely Mexican character, such as adobe, which is employed for the walls; and tile paving for the floors.

3. In coloring, basically the natural colors of materials are used: brown of adobe, red of tiles, green of grass and foliage, combined with black walls.

4. Seeking the greatest flexibility of plan, and placing bath and kitchen with future extension of the house in mind.

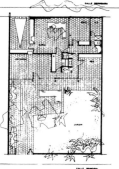

ROBERT MOTHERWELL

ROBERT MOTHERWELL: THE RISE AND CONTINUITY OF ABSTRACT ART—From a lecture given at the Fogg Museum, Harvard University.

I have placed emphasis on the modern artist's existence as a solitary individual. I would be misleading however if I left the impression that this solitariness is caused solely by his desire, whether conscious or unconscious, to remain aloof from the world surrounding him, as when the Chinese artist argued that the best place for a studio is on a mountain top, that is, that withdrawal from the world is a necessary condition of contemplation. Only psychological analysis of each modern artist as an individual could adequately demonstrate how far his solitude is brought about by his own character in the sense that, whenever we encounter an aloof individual, artist or not, we suspect that his isolation derives in part, from his own secret desires.

Still, if we assume the hypothesis—a false one, I am sure, whose fruitfulness is not affected by its falseness—that every modern artist wants to come into intimate contact with the world—that is, with other human beings—as an artist, then it is immediately apparent that the general ignorance of plastic culture as a whole among other human beings—laymen of course, but most intellectuals too, often even critics and museum directors—is such that a modern artist often has difficulty in being granted some of the simplest things that he is, intelligent, accomplished, cultivated—since hardly anyone but his confreres can "read" his work and consequently his basic characteristics. Perhaps it is for this reason that in modern times artists have written and spoken in public so much, and issued manifestoes by the dozens.

It is true that modern art has a unique amount of experimentation in it, and that perhaps only people very close to these experiments can at once "read" them. But it is true too that much of the so-called "unintelligibility" of modern art is a result of the enormous extension in modern times of the background of art, a background which was for everyone until a century or so ago, and still is for most people the realism of Greece and Rome and the Renaissance, and modern modes of illustration. If I may give an example from my own experience, which I am certain is that of every advanced artist who

Adolph Gottlieb

*Photographs Courtesy of
Kootz Gallery, New York*

Adolph Gottlieb

I have always worked on the assumption that if something is valid or meaningful to me, it will also be valid and meaningful to many others. Not to everyone, of course. On the basis of this assumption I do not think of an audience when I work, but only of my own reactions. By the same token I do not worry whether what I am doing is art or not. If what I paint is expressive, if it seems to communicate the feeling that is important to me, then I am not concerned if my work does not have known earmarks of art.

My work has been called abstract, surrealist, totemistic and primitive. To me these labels are not very accurate. Therefore, I chose my own label and called my paintings pictographs. However, I do not think labels are important.

After spending a year in Arizona around 1938, I came back to New York with a series of still lifes. Everyone said my paintings had become very abstract. The thought had never occurred to me whether they were abstract or not abstract. I simply felt that the themes I found in the Southwest required a different approach from that I had used before. I think the same is true of my pictographs. The material I use requires the style I have built around it. If I should find other subjects and forms that interest me more, I shall no doubt find it necessary to use a different method of expression.

People frequently ask why my canvases are compartmentalized. No one ever asks this about a house. A man with a large family would not choose to live in a one room house. It is ununderstood that for convenience and privacy it

ADOLPH GOTTLIEB

earns his living by teaching, my students come to me—all themselves teachers of art, by the way—with their chief experience in painting from the model as it has been taught in academic institutions from the time of Delacroix and Ingres down to our own day in, say, the Art Students League of New York or the Chicago Art Institute. This narrow background—self-evidently narrow, when one compares it with the totality of world art, which is now available to everyone, less, as Andre Malraux points out, because of the ease and speed of modern travel than because of the enormous diffusion of reproductions—leads the students to believe at first sight that I propose to teach them radically experimental techniques (even the idea of experiment seems radical to them), "wild" and irrational beyond belief (one sees very well even now how inevitable it was that such terms as "fauve" and "dada" should come to be accepted, with malice by the public and humor by the artists), tolerated at first only by the authority of my position as the teacher of the class. One of my pleasures, and one of the students', is when the day comes, more rapidly that one expects in a studio class, less rapidly in a lecture course, that students can "read" a Mondrian or a Miro or a cubist collage as feelingly as they already could a Vermeer or a Chardin or a Goya; an equally great pleasure on my part, and one unexpected on the students' part, is that they can also "read" with equal ease an Italian primitive, a Cretan clay figure, a Byzantine mosaic, a New Hebrides mask. It is interesting that once this range of perception is added to (Continued on page 245)

is desirable to divide a house into compartments and it can at the same time be beautiful.

I am like a man with a large family and must have many rooms. The children of my imagination occupy the various compartments of my painting, each independent and occupying its own space. At the same time they have the proper atmosphere in which to function together, in harmony and as a unified group. One can say that my paintings are like a house, in which each occupant has a room of his own. —ADOLPH GOTTLIEB.

Robert Motherwell

ART SUMMONED BEFORE THE INQUISITION

1573 - 1951

In the year of Our Lord 1573 Paolo Caliari, called Veronese, was hailed before the Tribunal of The Holy Office and there accused of sacrilegion in his painting of The Last Supper, now called **Supper in the House of Levi**, one of the great masterpieces of Western art.

The following excerpts, taken from the archives at Venice, possess an unexpected relevance 378 years later.

Saturday, the 18th of July, 1573

Mr. Paolo Caliari Veronese, living in the parish of San Samuel, was summoned to the Holy Office, before the Sacred Tribunal, and was asked his name and surname.

He answered as above.

He was asked his profession.

A. I paint and make pictures.

Q. Do you know the reason why you have been summoned?

A. No, my lords.

Q. Can you imagine it?

A. I surely can.

Q. Tell us what you imagine.

A. For the reason told me by the Reverend Father, that is, by the Prior of SS. Giovanni e Paolo, whose name I do not know, who told me that he had been here, and that your most illustrious lordships had directed him to make me substitute a figure of the Magdalen in the place of a dog. And I replied that I would willingly do this or anything else for my own credit and the advantage of the picture, but that I did not feel that a figure of the Magdalen would look good there, for many reasons which I am ready to state whenever I have an opportunity.

Q. In this supper that you painted in SS. Giovanni e Paolo, what is the meaning of the figure of the man with the bleeding nose?

A. I did him for a servant, whose nose, owing to some accident, may have been bleeding.

Q. What is the meaning of those armed men, dressed in the German fashion, each with a halberd in his hand?

A. Here I need to say a few words.

Q. Say them.

A. We painters take the same liberties as poets and madmen take. And I painted those two halberdiers, the one drinking and the other eating near the staircase, who are placed there that they might perform some duty, because it seemed fitting to me that the master of the house, who was great and rich, according to what I have been told, should have such servants.

Q. Are you not aware that in Germany and other places infected with heresy there is the custom of using strange and scurrilous pictures and similar inventions for mocking, abusing, and ridiculing the things of the Holy Catholic Church, in order to teach the false doctrine to the illiterate and ignorant?

A. Yes, my lords. That is wicked. But I shall repeat what I said before, that I am obliged to follow what my predecessors did.

Q. What did your predecessors do? Did they ever do anything like that?

A. Michelangelo, at Rome, in the Pontifical Chapel. He painted our Lord Jesus Christ, His Most Holy Mother, St. John, St. Peter, and the Court of Heaven, all of them naked, from the Virgin Mary down, with little reverence.

In the year of our lord 1951 the Los Angeles City Council, convened as a tribunal, summoned the modern artists of the city, and without due process of law brought certain artworks into the chamber of the Council on suspicion of heresy.

November 6th of this year 1951

The City Council (Edward Roybal dissenting) adopted a resolution, after hearing testimony from" both sides," which states, in effect, that any kind of painting or sculpture other than illustrative realism is suspect of subversion and sacrilegion. For the first time in the history of the United States an elective body has gone beyond the bounds of constitutional propriety to infringe upon the right of artists, freely and without fear of doctrinal conformity, to express themselves in the idiom of their own time.

Shades of Paolo Caliari, called Veronese.

Jules Langsner

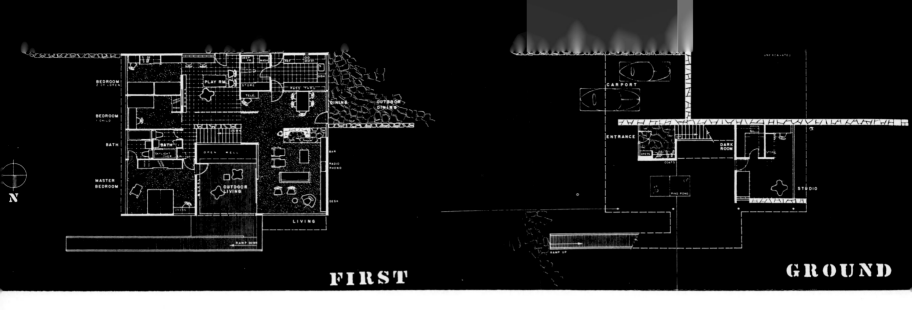

HOUSE NEAR SYDNEY AUSTRALIA   HARRY SEIDLER, ARCHITECT

The expansive property, which extends into the surrounding typical Australian bush land, made possible a building that is freely exposed on all sides. The sloping ground resulted in a main living floor which is accessible from the ground on one side and elevated on the other.

A flexible open plan provides for all members of the family. The central play room, which forms a link between the living and sleeping portions of the house, can be used in conjunction with the two alcove-type children's bedrooms, by closing a free hanging heavy sound curtain—or it can be incorporated with the adults' living space for entertaining by closing the full-height sliding doors to the children's bedrooms.

Separation of the outdoor areas on various sides of the house provides for children's play space next to the service yard for easy supervision from the kitchen. The adult outdoor living terrace is formed by a wind-sheltered open-air "room" which is spacially part of the general living area with its decorative mural (illuminated by continuous overhead lighting at night). Access to the garden is provided by a fully suspended plywood-core ramp.

The rectangular mass of the building which is hollowed by this open center is further lightened by a two-story open well, piercing the center of the building vertically and admitting sunlight to the play space below. From the rigid rectangle of the building "tentacles" reach out into the surrounding land in the form of retaining walls, the ramp and the louvre fence.

HOUSE NEAR SYDNEY, AUSTRALIA

Construction: Local sandstone, steel columns, concrete floor, timber walls and roof. Exterior: Painted vertical tongue and groove boarding. The mural was designed and executed by the architect.

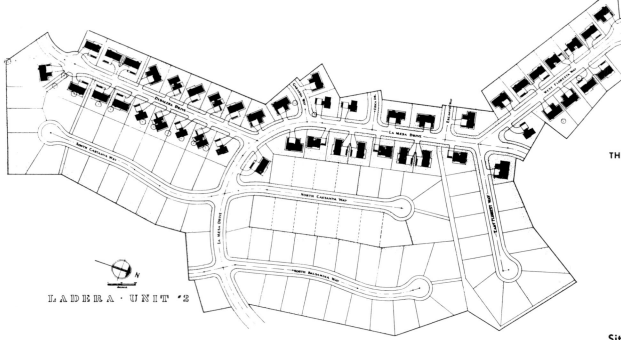

L A D E R A · U N I T · '2

THE LADERA PROJECT BY A. QUINCY JONES, JR. AND

FREDERICK E. EMMONS, ARCHITECTS

DEVELOPED BY EICHLER HOMES, INC.
SITE ENGINEER: GEORGE NOLTE

ARCHITECT·BUILDER·SITE·HOME AND COMMUNITY

Site

The Ladera project is located in an area of rolling hills just outside the city limits of Palo Alto with views throughout 360°. The architects have given careful consideration to the nature of the terrain and adapted the houses so as to insure absolute privacy as living units. The climate through a great portion of the year permits a great deal of outdoor living, and in general plan all of the houses consider the ease of circulation to the garden and terrace areas as well as easy food service for outdoor dining. The lots had been laid out when the architects began, and were of an average size of 80' x 110'. They varied from level to slopes up to 20 per cent.

Construction: Dry construction with concrete floors covered with cork. Stud walls with redwood exteriors and mahogany plywood interior walls. Laminated wood ceilings with spans of 12'-0" between supports. The roof is laminated, using 2" x 2" and 2" x 3" Douglas Fir in alternating boards, giving a corrugated interior finish. The ceilings and beams were stained. All houses are radiant heated with automatic control. Roofs are all built up with gravel surfacing.

Equipment: All kitchens are equipped with dishwasher, garbage disposal unit, refrigerator, built-in electric range and oven, and provisions for automatic washer and dryer, and are planned to be as nearly "servantless" as possible.

General: In all of the houses the plans have been devised to give privacy of circulation from outdoors to the bedroom and bath facilities, a particularly desirable feature when it is realized that too many group projects use the living area as "entry" and circulation "hall." More than normal storage of all types has been provided, with large bedroom wardrobes, general interior storage, and, in all cases, large exterior storage closets. In each house the kitchen is open to the living area though arranged to screen preparation and clean-up activities.

Through this system of group planning Eichler Homes, Inc. has been able to provide facilities usually not found in houses of this price range. Wall and ceiling finishes are stained woods—redwood and mahogany, masonry—brick or concrete block, and glass. The floors are cork with the exception of the baths which are asphalt tile. All houses are two-full-bathroom houses with either three or four bedrooms. Each bedroom is provided with a built-in drawer unit as well as a dressing table.

This project, one of several recently undertaken proves the enormous value of real cooperation between the architect and the builder with the result that the buyer is invariably assured of a better way of living at a much more reasonable cost.

Through skillful handling of the problem of "house to site" adaptation, as well as variations in material and the thoughtful use of fence location, the project is entirely without the usual monotony of the average residential street and the feeling of a "house tract" is eliminated.

FLOOR PLANS AND ELEVATIONS ON THIS PROJECT WERE PUBLISHED IN THE JULY, 1951, ISSUE OF ARTS & ARCHITECTURE.

PHOTOGRAPHS BY RONDAL PARTRIDGE

Actually this is more than the cooperative planning of a group of houses; it is an intelligent approach to the development of the community in terms of people. The Southwest Research Institute in evaluating this particular project has said: "The general development has been thoroughly reviewed by the Foundation and found to be of exceptionally high quality. The project is commended on many counts, but particularly for the general excellence of the architectural design and the attractive appearance of the houses, inside and out."

THE BREAD OF ARCHITECTURE

BY BERNARD RUDOFSKY

Gardens, as we have known them through the centuries, were valued mostly for their intimacy and order—that is, order of a geometric kind. Both qualities are conspicuously absent in most contemporary gardens. Intimacy, so little prized today, was the key note of ancient gardens, skeletons of which have been preserved, for instance, in Herculaneum, Pompei and Ostia. Some of these gardens were even replanted quite accurately with the help of archaeological information and furnish us today perfect and good examples of how a diminutive and apparently negligible quantity of land can, with some ingenuity, be transformed into an oasis of delight. Though they were miniature gardens, they had all the ingredients of a happy environment.

These ancient gardens were an integral part of the house; they were contained **within** the house. All were true "Wohngarten," outdoor living rooms, rooms without roof, and they were invariably regarded as **rooms.**

The wall and floor materials of Roman outdoor rooms were no less lavish than those used in the interior parts of the house. Stone mosaic, marble slabs, stucco reliefs, mural decorations from the simplest geometric ornamentation to elaborate paintings, were employed to establish a mood particularly conducive to spiritual composure.

The vegetable element was by no means of the first importance; paradoxically, it was least in evidence. But then, some of the celebrated gardens of medieval Japan do not contain **any** living plants at all. One may argue that a grapevine pergola—Pompei abounded in arbors—is esthetically more gratifying than the stoutest tree. Or, that, in the absence of a pergola, there always remains in the inventory of nature that component which never fails to enrapture the more sensitive souls: the sky. The spectacle of the ever-changing sky can be truly enjoyed only out of doors; viewing the sky through even the most generous expanse of plate-glass,

PHOTOGRAPHS BERNARD RUDOFSKY

is a poor substitute for the genuine article. It almost seems that the use of glass walls in recent years has alienated the garden. In some instances, the arrangement recalls a show-window; the garden has become—to borrow a word—a **spectator garden.**

Contemplating nature from a sort of sentry box has its advantages in a harsh climate. But even outdoors, to fully appreciate the changing patterns of light, the configurations of clouds, one ought to watch the sky not in a shapeless garden but rather within four, possibly white, walls—an enclosure as definite as a frame.

A wall is the bread of architecture. Yet it has never occurred to anybody to celebrate the wall as one of the great inventions of man. No doubt, man was well along his path when he knew how to make tools and weapons, but even when he painted his first decorations, he was still living in natural caves. By erecting the first free-standing wall he arrived at a point in his evolution that was as sharply defined as when he got up from all fours and stood on his legs. Building his first wall, he became, **mentally,** a biped. With the wall, man created space on a human scale, and in the many thousand years that followed, he came sometimes quite close to the mastery of space, architecture.

The prehistoric event of building the first wall was not immortalized by any cornerstone or memorial tablet. (It is this downright lack of evidence which often makes the business of the historian and archaeologist such a source of pure conjecture.) Perhaps, the first stone-layer, in his playful mood, was intent on building nothing but a wall—tall, square, and free. The idea of using it to support a roof may have come to him much later. But even a naked, free-standing wall—for all its abstract beauty—serves a purpose. It unfailingly provides shadow, being more dependable than a tree which sheds its leaves periodically. It braves the wind, defies the beast; it is a symbol of the upright man.

With time, the business of erecting a wall became an art, sometimes a secret art. We can not duplicate some cyclopic walls built thousands of years ago. We don't even know how they were built.

But then, we are quite ignorant of the beginnings of architecture. The Bible tells us about the beginnings of Man. But, for the truly inquisitive mind, it is so full of pitfalls that after centuries of readers' response, it still has to be explained from the (Continued on page 245)

BERNARD RUDOFSKY, ARCHITECT

MURALS BY COSTANTINO NIVOLA

WATER PLAY

A FOUNTAIN BY WAYNE THIEBAUD AND JERRY McLAUGHLIN

This fountain which was done as a part of the Art Exhibit at the California State Fair is an amusing and often rather wild composition in moving water. While its several parts are in motion there is a constantly maintained interest, and within the interplay dazzling confusion becomes part of a very engaging pattern and texture. The devices which are ingenious in material and form take on a lively life and vitality under the compelling movement of the water. The variety and the unexpectedness of the activity, the sometimes frantic, sometimes serene water in motion is fresh and cool and stimulating.

Thiebaud and McLaughlin have freely and playfully used the propelling power of the water itself to move the objects, and in turn this movement within the water creates a beautiful and sometimes hilarious experience.

HARRY BERTOIA

Painter, printmaker, sculptor, designer, Harry Bertoia enjoys the rare good fortune (in these days of the corporate Table of Organization) of being able to bring to bear a common body of skills and insights to each of several kinds of creative activity. Both "abstract" metal sculpture and new wire cage chairs (illustrated here) emerged and took shape as facets of the same impulse. The problems (and the solutions Bertoia has found to the problems) while given different stress in the chairs than in the sculpture, are so closely bound together as to be, in a sense, one and the same.

It would be rash to assert categorically that sculpture or chair (or for that matter earlier paintings or monoprints) best express the Bertoia charm and inventiveness.

Result: integrity of conception in both chair and sculpture. At once elegant and sturdy, esthetically satisfying and humanly habitable the Bertoia chair takes metal furniture completely out of the category of the fashionable new look that has a period date stamped upon it two years later. Though the use of the metal rod in furniture too quickly degenerated into the novelty and the oddity, the production rationale for such an approach made sense. Unfortunately the esthetic adaptation of the material too often reveals an incredible poverty of resources in the handling of formal values. Without felicity of form, coherence of shape and color to space, a piece of furniture suffers every bit as much as a painting or sculpture.

There is an absolute clarity of design and uncompromising validity in the use of material in the Bertoia version of wire and metal rod furniture that is a hopeful signal of the end of the elephant-on-stilts school of design.

PHOTOGRAPHS | LAYOUT | HERBERT MATTE

Here Bertoia's background as artist enabled him to proceed with assurance. His feel for aerated, rectilinear forms suspended in an atmosphere peculiarly their own dates back to student experiments at Cranbrook. Crystalline transparency, subtly adjusted, shifting movement of squares and rectangles, open space as a buoyant medium, all entered into the making of the Bertoia chair, and are traceable to the earlier paintings and monoprints.

The diamonded, wire cage of the chair, padded in

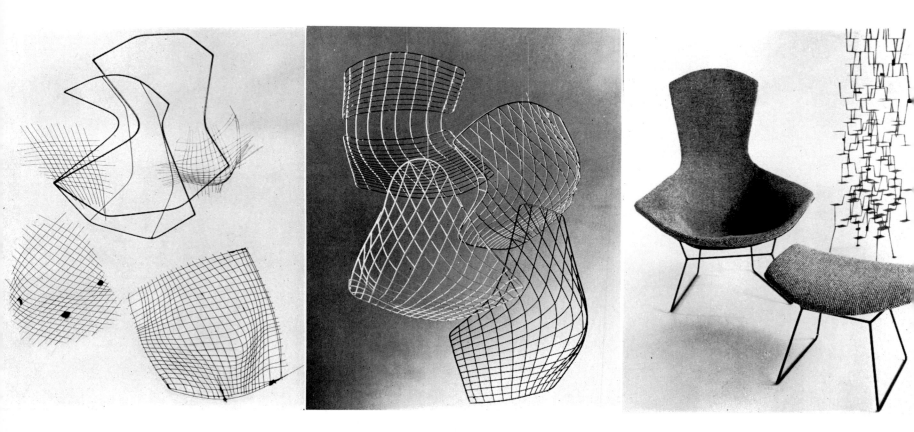

colorful, receptive material, provides "allowance" for the changing stresses of the human figure. Your engagement with a Bertoia chair is not an athletic contest. You are not snatched, imprisoned, immobilized, gripped within an implacable wrestler's hold. To enlarge the user's freedom of movement, the chair seat is pivoted with a rubber "brake" permitting just enough leniency backwards and forwards to allow shifts of posture; a sheer physiological necessity fatally overlooked in so much of the string, wire, plastic and plywood furniture of the last decade.

Result: a fusion of form and function in the chair that enhances its position in the room as an object pleasurable to look at.

The sculpture was conceived by Bertoia as a construction for the purpose of contemplation of geometric forms in space. Yet so interrelated are the parts of the Bertoia creative program that the sculpture possesses the properties of an architectural screen, providing the kind of semi-privacy often desirable in a contemporary building.

Whether useful baffle or contemplative geometry, the sculpture presents to us the Bertoia cellular construction in its purest state. In the sculpture the eye benefits from the observer's mobility, flowing in and around the units, catching reflections of braised metallic surfaces, giving life to hollows as well as solids. The identical principle can be seen in the pictorial space of a Bertoia painting and in the engineering of the Bertoia chair accommodated to the oddities of the human frame.

It is difficult to understand why the metamorphosis of art into useful objects raises a tumult among certain designers and architects. No amount of backing and filling can obscure the deep, rich influence upon contemporary designs of painters like Klee or Mondrian, sculptors like Brancusi or Arp. The Bertoia achievement erases, once and for all, any lingering doubts about the complementarity of art and design.

—**Jules Langsner.**

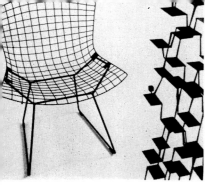

Harry Bertoia was born thirty-seven years ago in Italy.
He calls himself an "amateur in the field of art." He might well
call himself a professional in certain fields of science.
He found that the fundamental principles that unite the fine arts
applied equally to the useful arts of architecture and furniture
design: For buildings he has produced glittering metallic wall
elements; for interiors, he has produced elegantly formed wire
chairs. Through combination of pure art and pure science he
produces objects that are both useful and beautiful. His works
in sculpture, painting, and furniture were on exhibition at Knoll
Associates, Inc., New York City, through December.

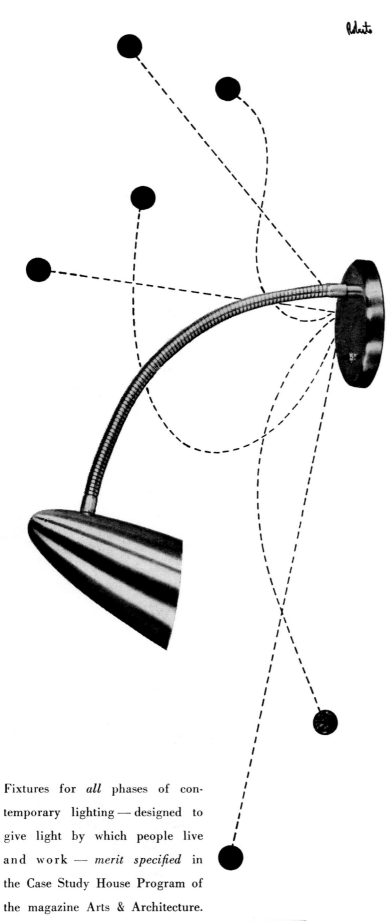

Fixtures for *all* phases of contemporary lighting — designed to give light by which people live and work — *merit specified* in the Case Study House Program of the magazine Arts & Architecture.

8336 West Third St., L.A. 36
32 Union Square, N.Y. C. 3

designed by Finn Juhl

BAKER FURNITURE, INC.
Holland, Michigan

CHICAGO
6TH FLOOR MERCHANDISE MART

NEW YORK
THE MANOR HOUSE
305 EAST 63RD STREET

LOS ANGELES
8778 BEVERLY BOULEVARD

EXECUTIVE OFFICES; EXHIBITORS BUILDING. GRAND RAPIDS 2, MICHIGAN

arts and crafts

dubois
8030 west third
los angeles 48

courtyard apartment

By Craig Ellwood, Designer

Mackintosh and Mackintosh, Consulting Engineers
Jocelyn Domela, Landscape Design
Henry Salzman, General Contractor

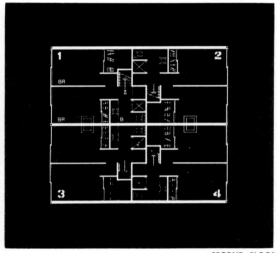

SECOND FLOOR

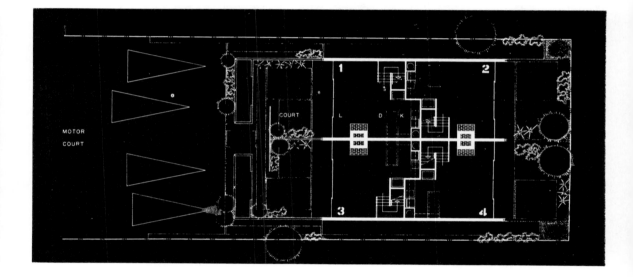

PROJECT: To design a four-unit apartment building; each unit to have two bedrooms; each unit to be approximately 800 square feet; basic materials to be masonry, wood siding, and glass; structural system steel frame; budget $10 a square foot.

SITE: A typical city lot, 50' x 110'; level.

SOLUTION: The conditions of the client's program—the relation of the budget to the requested materials and structural system—required that the plan and details be developed with numerous economical considerations. These, though economical in concept, did not limit the quality of materials and workmanship. A partial list of cost saving factors:

—each unit is alike in size and detail.
—North and South elevations are duplicates.
—East and West elevations are duplicates (except for courtyard walls).
—mechanical equipment—plumbing, venting and ductwork—is centralized.
—the masonry is Davidson hollow clay block; this unit "lays up" for the same cost as concrete block and is more economical than brick.
—the fireplaces are "hung" back-to-back on the central masonry wall.
—the three walls of solid masonry allowed a minimum of structural steel; a steel frame at each open end of the structure was designed to withstand all lateral seismic forces; the 6-H-20 columns of the frame

CRAIG ELLWOOD

are fixed at the base with a continuous 12" x 24" reinforced concrete beam, and the truss of 4-I-7.7 fixes the columns at midspan to place inflection points so that structural analysis was simplified and column size reduced to a minimum.

Living rooms were placed on ground level to give each unit a private, individual courtyard. Open planning and glass walls visually extend the rooms beyond their real limits. The compact kitchens are open to the living rooms, and Miller steel-framed sliding glass door units open the living rooms to the courtyards. The gardens thus become roofless extensions of the living areas.

An open feeling has been achieved in the apartment furnishings. The scale has been kept light, with particular attention given to maintaining a low height in all pieces. Fabric and texture have been used to bring a garden feeling into the living area. Soft earth tones of green and brown are relieved by vivid color in a scattering of pillows. There is a notable absence of clutter which creates an illusion of spaciousness.

The steel-framed bar tables of the kitchens are unattached, and may be moved into the courtyards for outdoor dining. The sliding panels of the kitchen cabinets are Masonite, painted black, white, and primary blue. The use of electric hot water heaters conserved considerable space and eliminated the two-story venting problem; the water heaters are concealed in the cabinet adjacent to the range. Kitchens also include garbage disposers, stainless steel sinks, Pryne vent fans, Globe recessed tube lighting.

To aid in counteracting the compactness of plan, and to supplement the general openness of space, the treads and landing of the lower stairs are open cantilevers. Fireplace hoods are 1/8" sheet steel, painted black.

Bedrooms and baths are upstairs. The sliding wardrobe panels of steel-framed Masonite are

(Continued on page 246)

steel frame house

by Pierre Koenig, Designer

This small steel and glass house takes full advantage of a heavily wooded site by opening to the front and rear with large expanses of glass and sliding doors. Except for the covered passage leading from the carport to the front door, there are no overhangs in order to admit the maximum of light and sun. With the exception of the bath, the house is one large room with sliding doors closing off the bedroom when desired. A storage cabinet serves as the dividing wall between kitchen and bedroom. There are no bearing walls as the cantilevered columns support the roof and take up seismic forces.

Columns, beams, roof deck, sliding doors and window frames are all arcwelded. The result is a simple, light and spacious structure. One side wall is a concrete block retaining wall, the other side wall is corrugated steel "hung" on three horizontal channels and insulated with cork. The interior living area wall and entry closet is of birch plywood. The bedroom wall is finished with natural colored insulation cork.

In keeping with the general character of the house, the kitchen cabinets as well as the storage units are of welded angle frames and brightly colored masonite doors and panels. The underside of the exposed roof deck is painted a soft gray. The draperies are bright yellow and the mastic floor tile is light tan. Heat is provided through a forced air system that serves as an air circulator in the summer.

PHOTOGRAPHS BY JULIUS SHULMAN
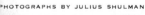

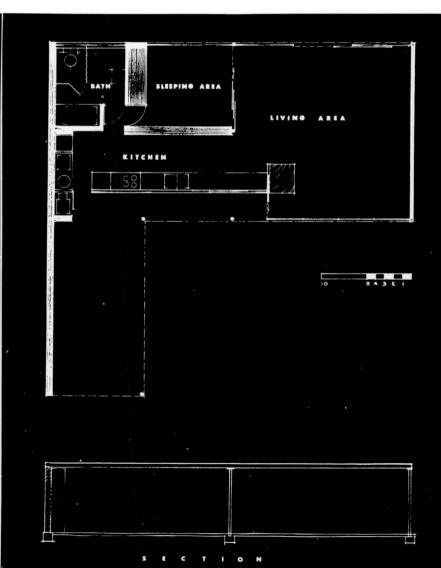

BATH   SLEEPING AREA

LIVING AREA

KITCHEN

SECTION

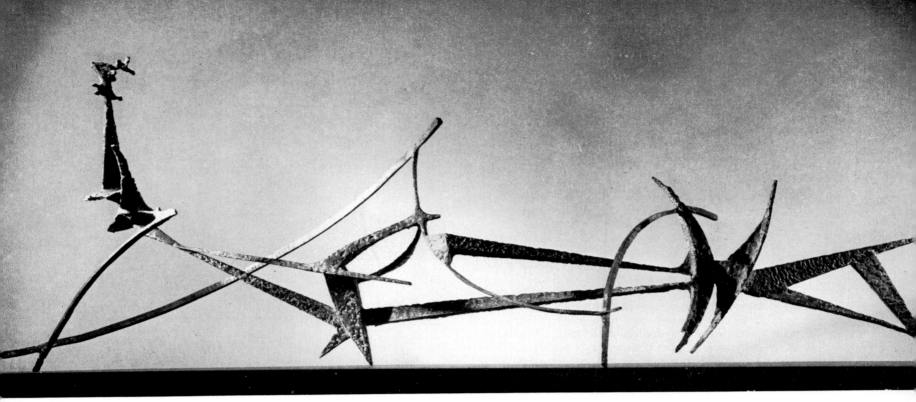

Reclining Woman

ROSENTHAL

The most recent group of bronzes by Bernard Rosenthal represents an important moment of achievement for him. His busy career during the past few years is both rewarding and illuminating. Surprisingly, he is perhaps better known for his uncanny ability to bring new life to contemporary architecture with his numerous fountains and commissions related to the art of building than he is for his independent works; however, unlike so much of the ponderous monumentality of the not too remote past, he has been able to provide a new definition of the "architectural sculptor." He is one of the rare few of the younger or second generation of creative workers of our century who has assimilated the significance of those intensely experimental developments which took place in the twenties and early thirties. He clearly perceived the import-

Odalisque

ance of the creative tradition of our time which is by now importantly historical and may be understood with the surety provided by the passage of almost a quarter of a century.

Realization and creative accomplishment at a high level in the modern world is characterized by many layers of discovery. The artist—whether he is called architect, sculptor, painter or designer—must find himself, pick his way through a complex maze of many pasts impinging upon the immediacy of the present moment. Rosenthal has helped clarify and define the vitality of those basic patterns of creativity for today. Moreover, he has expanded the range of the sculptors' place in society and once again proves that sculpture is a necessary part of any important architectural environment. He discovered, too, in his own terms the universal fact that all significant sculpture conveys meanings which are architectonic by the nature of its three-dimensional life. Spatial relationships are central to both architecture and sculpture, and however loosely we use the overworked word "space," we do know the dynamic revolution in our aesthetic perceptions has produced the need to accentuate qualities of lightness, transparency, openness with which the daring architects and engineers ushered in the twentieth century.

The validity of the experimental paths of our time in sculpture and building are further reinforced by the work of Rosenthal. He uses traditional materials, bronze and brass, for all the sound virtues each has had through the centuries, but he has the capacity for freeing himself of academic processes of working. Techniques and materials are merely the means for finding fresh, vivid solutions to a widely differentiated group of problems.

Although autonomous and independent creations, these new works imply an architectural setting. They envelop and electrify the expansive dimension of their ordered world. The vibrant tracery of patinaed rods and richly textured planes establish complex patterns of movement. These crisp, linear statements evoke overtones of myth, legend and religion. Symbolic content is contrapuntally imbedded in the wholeness of conception. Each piece develops and grows out of the basic theme. Content and form are more than hyphenated; these inseparable and constituent ingredients of any meaningful expression are literally welded into another level of reality.

Whether the work grows playfully out of the idea for an *Odalisque,* or seriously from a stirring symbolization of *Moses* and *The Three Kings,* each is an adventure in space. The range of varied thematic compositions are generally developed into either an emphatically vertical or horizontal scheme. Whatever the formal disposition, the works are pleasant to be with. They are lyric with the gaiety and gravity of a superbly wrought ballet. Not tense, nor desicated, they convey a sense of ease, a grace, an elegance of which our world has all too small a portion. They are richly dry without being astringently ascetic.

It is reassuring to find an authoritative, venturesome craftsman who speaks quietly, with restraint and sophistication. His works do not shout or rant with terror or pity. Without being clamorous, they are alive, resilient, energetic and often moving. Rosenthal clearly points a way for adding another felicitous dimension to the house, garden, or square. Sculptors, architects, and the citizenry may well profit by the pioneering sensibility of a major American artist.

Gibson Danes, Chairman
Department of Art, UCLA

These works are being currently shown at the
Catherine Viviano Gallery—New York

NOVEMBER 1953

Moses

174

Eurydice

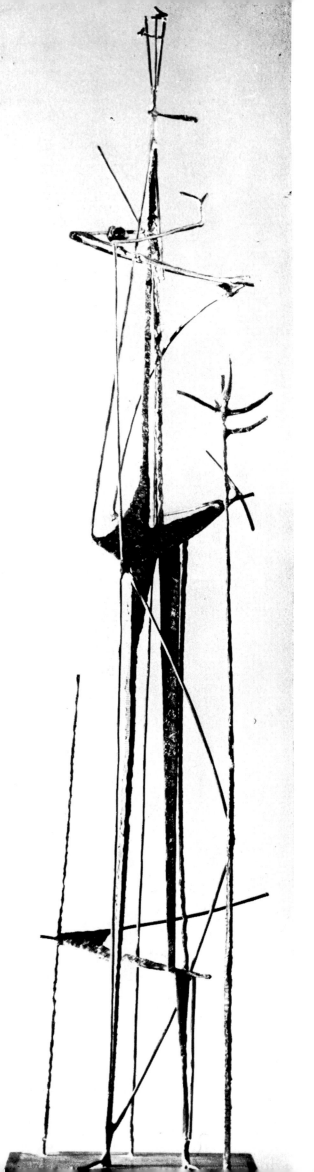

The Three Kings

Japanese Packaging

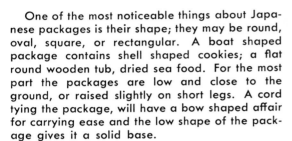

One of the most noticeable things about Japanese packages is their shape; they may be round, oval, square, or rectangular. A boat shaped package contains shell shaped cookies; a flat round wooden tub, dried sea food. For the most part the packages are low and close to the ground, or raised slightly on short legs. A cord tying the package, will have a bow shaped affair for carrying ease and the low shape of the package gives it a solid base.

There is a subtle use of natural materials. Wood, bamboo, rattan, jute, or banana leaves are often used. It is interesting that paper is usually a secondary material, and is seldom used as primary wrapping.

Since much of the packaging is done by hand, close attention is given to details. For the most part, wooden bamboo pegs are used. Many of the products are contained in baskets, the tops laced on. A copper band secures the sides of a wooden box.

The textures are interesting in these materials. Silk threads appear in conjunction with hemp and heavier rope used for binding or tying the package together. A wooden box may be left in its natural finish, or a box may have a lacquered or painted finish. Here again, there is a careful consistency maintained, and a unity in finishing. Seldom are two different finishes used on the same package.

The rice paper labels are almost an art in themselves, and yet, an integral part of the package. The labels accentuate the shape of the container, rather than the conventional square or rectangular fold. Some are folded in kite shapes, or pointed like arrows. The label may be designed with great care, and its position on the package may show evidence of modern design, it might be tucked under the cord wrapping the package, with several other labels and a traditional symbol for "a pleasant gift" tucked in beside it.

With the use of native materials, texture and color become part of the final packaging art. In many cases where the container is left in its natural finish, a surprise element of color seems to complete the over-all design. Purples, cocoa, bright reds and blacks are subtle and carefully placed highlights.

The calligraphy on the label is designed to augment the over-all design. Japanese design depends heavily on detail, by using it in scale with the product of package, it seldom supersedes or outweighs the initial shape.

The placing of labels is important and often the finishing touch, usually there is a progression of labels of varying shapes and colors, inside as well as outside.

The modern Japanese package is functional. Some of the labels are so designed and placed to serve as napkins and the package may be contained in an ingenious use of mats wrapped around the package or they may serve as the bottom of a box. In either case the mat is something which may be removed and used later.

Just as a liquor or wine is often purchased for the bottle, so a package in Japan might be bought for the package.—*Theodore Little*.

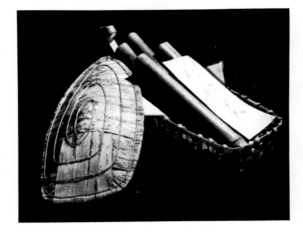

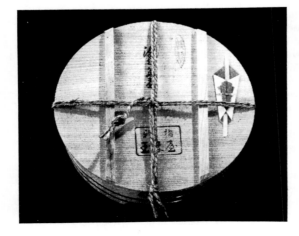

R. M. SCHINDLER

1890   1953

Gregory Ain:

I first met Schindler when I was a college sophomore, majoring in physics. He was the first architect I had ever known, and his house was the first stimulus toward my interest in architecture. That house revisited recently arouses the same wonder and delight that it did almost thirty years ago. Powerful, yet delicate, vibrant yet serene, it is distinguished in detail by innumerable innovations which have since become the common language of modern domestic architecture, but which have rarely since, I believe, been used with such sensitive meaning or to so rich a cumulative effect. The house and the garden are literally one, and the garden is as private as the house. How different from the current cliché of "indoor-outdoor integration" in which the house is as public as the garden! Schindler's garden was planted with near weeds—castor bean, tobacco plant, and bamboo; but it had the rare charm and depth and excitement that marked all of his work, and which revealed a genius of composition which is still too little recognized because the artist was so unconcerned with publicity.

Schindler was an architect who had not merely mastered engineering. He felt and thought in terms of structure, which was an inherent element in his design. He invented, successfully employed, and then discarded dozens of structural systems and mechanical devices which, if patented and commercially exploited, could have earned him a fortune. Three decades ago he poured concrete wall slabs on the ground and tilted them up vertically; he developed an inexpensive vertically sliding form for high concrete walls poured in place; he shot pneumatic concrete against one-sided forms to obtain thin ribbed bearing shells; he employed stucco not merely as a skin but as a load bearing structure by plastering it over light cages of metal lath; he made flush ceiling lights, pin-point spotlights and concealed garden lights long before these appeared on the market; he built flush front cabinets, remote window operators, pullman type lavatories (out of kitchen sinks), sliding sheet metal framed doors and windows, and a multitude of gadgets for two-way fireplaces, folding chairs, and drainboard stoves. And these ingenious inventions were regarded by him merely as incidental elements in the execution of small and inexpensive buildings. Many of these ideas developed on the building site, where much of his actual designing took place. He rarely built from finished working drawings. His plans were usually the roughest sketches of a building, just as his buildings were sometimes just rough sketches of a subtle and wonderful idea.

(Continued on page 246)

1916: *Buena Shore Club, Chicago, work of Schindler in his middle twenties, designed two years after his arrival in the United States. Building pays tribute to his beloved teacher Otto Wagner as well as Louis Sullivan. In 1918 Schindler was invited to Taliesin, where the Imperial Hotel was on the board. He spent four years in Wright's drafting room.*

1922: *Kings Road house, Hollywood. After supervising construction on Wright's Barnsdall house, Schindler remained in Los Angeles to open his own office. The S-shaped house is built on concrete slab with walls of tapered concrete panels cast on ground and tilted into place, panels joined by ribbons of glass through which light and space filter. Sliding canvas doors open rooms to gardens.*

1926: *Design for one of the group of League of Nations buildings is work of Schindler and Richard J. Neutra, who shared an office for two years in the Kings Road house. League of Nations design was one of the award winners. (Buildings never executed.)*

1927: *Sachs Apartments, Silverlake district, Los Angeles, was first of a number of apartment houses in which Schindler eliminated the long central hall, using instead covered outdoor passages, and opened all apartments to private garden spaces or terraces. This plan did much to overcome bad lot subdivision.*

1928: *Entrance detail of Wolfe house, Catalina Island, shows the strongly articulated forms which were becoming characteristic of Schindler's work. Three-story house appears to hover over steep slope of its sea-edge setting, rather than adding to the hill mass.*

1937: *House for Henwar Rodakiewicz, Beverly Hills, set in a citrus grove, follows the slope. Outdoor living area extends out from main or second floor level. By 1937 Schindler had abandoned the balloon frame and was developing his own system, which allowed for a free use of clerestories and varying ceiling heights. By placing his plate line at door height the horizontal continuity of the design became a structural reality.*

1944: *Bethlehem Baptist Church, Los Angeles, breaks with cliches to utilize a limited area sensibly. Street side where traffic is heavy presents solid wall. Church has two wings to seat worshippers, these resulting in an interior patio which, together with roof terraces, affords space for outdoor gatherings.*

R. M. Schindler brought to the small house a personal kind of urbanity. He has taken the cottage out of the small house and given it a private, self-sufficient character, his plan equalling in its wisdom the indigenous adobe of California, whose chief virtue was that it allowed for access of all rooms to outdoors, as well as providing privacy.

His small houses were in many respects substitutes for the city apartment, with the advantage of having one's own garden.

In keeping the floor area small, Schindler has by use of high glass achieved a continuous flow of space through the rooms. Early in his career he arrived at a separation of floor plan from ceiling plan, each having its own integrity in his building. His use of large glass areas in partitions delivers the small house from the tyranny of walls.

Schindler's plans must always be read on two, sometimes three levels, because of his frequent change of ceiling height and wide use of clerestory windows. —Esther McCoy

House for Mr. and Mrs. Robert Erlik, Los Angeles, 1952. Street elevation: House is raised above slope to provide for carport below deep balcony. Entrance on level ground at right.

Breakfast table and living room have access to deck. Built-in buffet at dining end of living room backs up against bedroom storage wall, with 4x12 glass area above eye level opening one room into another.

House for Mr. and Mrs. Maurice Ries, 1950, is in Hollywood hills above the county strip. Four rooms of house all face view of city. With only minimum level land on street front, main body of house is lifted above 45° slope and rests on wooden posts.

Extended beam develops into lighting fixture to illuminate entry.

Memorial exhibit of photographs, plans and models of the work of R. M. Schindler will be shown at Landau Gallery, 702 North La Cienega Boulevard, Los Angeles, through June 5.

Material correlated by Esther McCoy

PHOTOGRAPHS BY SHIRLEY C. BURDEN
                ROBERT C. CLEVELAND
                LOTTE NOSSAMAN
                PETER JAMES SAMERJAN
                JULIUS SHULMAN
                W. P. WOODCOCK

Stone and glass desert house for Maryon Toole, Palm Village, 1946. Walls are reddish granite bolders set in cement mortar in such a way as to suggest, the architect said, "the somewhat savage character of the desert." Glass is used above the stone, "the whole shaded by an ample but lightly poised roof reminiscent of a giant oak leaf."

The mountain cabin for Gisela Bennati, on a wooded slope above Lake Arrowhead, was built in 1934. "Local restrictions stipulated 'Normandy Style,'" said Schindler, "so I carried the roof down to the ground and filled both gables with glass. All rooms are composed within the resulting triangular cross section formed by the rafters and the lowest floor joists. The stone is from the site."

Falk Apartments, 1943, Silverlake district, Los Angeles. "The lot does not face the lake squarely, but the living room of all apartments was turned toward it, and the resulting angular relation between the two wings became the basis for the development of the building. The first and second floors were interlocked to comply with minimum ceiling heights without producing long flights of steps. The units arranged in tiers one above the other were related in height in order to screen the large roof areas of the lower apartments from view."

Patio of Bethlehem Baptist Church, Los Angeles 1944. Garden space for social functions, with steps to open-air theatre on roof terrace. Covered passages for off-the-street, after-service chats among members. Church has wood frame with stucco exterior. Base of cross is surrounded by skylight so worshipper can see cross from their pews. "Instead of retaining the traditional two-dimensional symbol of agony, the cross is here four dimensional and with outstretched arms invites the congregation to gather under its shadow."

Waiting room of Medical Arts Building, Ventura Boulevard, Studio City, 1945. The architect designed furniture for most of his houses. All interiors for this building were executed from his design.

In 1934 Schindler wrote in the magazine *ARCHITECT AND ENGINEER*, that an architect's "power will be complete when the present primitive glass wall develops into the translucent light screen. The character and light issuing from it will permeate space, give it body and make it as palpably plastic as is the clay of the sculptor. Only after the space architect has mastered the translucent house will his work achieve its ripe form."

Witty low-cost house for Ellen Janson was designed "to explore the possibilities of translucent material for walls." Plastic sheets are used on north and east walls in continuous areas without division bars.

Laurelwood Apartments, Studio City, 1948. The design uses the knoll and the view toward the valley to give each apartment an unobstructed outlook. A two-story unit containing an apartment on both floors was repeated ten times and grouped in a fashion so that principal rooms face the view. Each ground floor apartment has a private garden, and second floor apartments have a private roof terrace with view.

Metal sandwich course between ceiling and upper floor is used as sound insulation.

Kallis house, North Hollywood, 1947. House for an artist and his family is divided into two units connected by an artificial terrace which cuts across the branches of the oaks. Studio and living room open out onto the terrace. Living room is composed around a valley view and a stone fireplace "laid in a pattern suggesting the oak leaf." Insloping walls trap the north light for the artist's studio.

In the house for Adolph Tischler in West Los Angeles Schindler uses corrugated plastic as a roofing material, with temporary floating saucers to produce shade areas until trees and vines are established. He uses blue Alsynite in order, as he said, "to introduce color into the atmosphere rather than on the wall surfaces." Fireplace has stack and hood of aluminum.

House for Richard Lechner, Studio City, 1946. Schindler wrote in the ARCHITECTURAL RECORD of May 1947 that his struggle with the tradition-bound carpenter had finally caused him to develop his own system of framing.

"The standard system of wood frame construction is not suitable for the execution of the contemporary dwelling. The balloon frame presupposes a box-shaped building and cubicle rooms, with large wall areas and small openings, solid partitions, a superimposed sloping roof with small projection of decorative character only."

Schindler thought of houses in terms of "large openings which reduced walls to a minimum, ceiling heights that varied without disturbing the rambling, low-to-the-ground and open-to-the sky character of the building. Careful orientation of rooms makes clerestory windows and large shady overhangs mandatory.

"The traditional stud is cut to wall height and provides for a double plate at ceiling. Varying ceiling heights make it difficult for the carpenter to ascertain and locate the various stud lengths required. It also interrupts the top plates wherever ceiling heights change, thereby weakening the important horizontal tie these plates should provide for the building."

Schindler's framing eliminated all these difficulties by cutting all studs at door height and thus providing a continuous belt of plates at that level. Doors and window frames were set in above and below these wall plates.

1. *Stepping stones crossing the lake at the heart of a garden; these stones continue in the grass, bringing about a foreshortening of the landscape.*

2. *Garden planted years ago by Roberto Burle Marx; two different colored grasses are used in the lawn, in free flowing design; semi circular bench covered with colonial traditional blue glaze tiles, a link between two groups of aloes; trees and shrubs link the garden with the forest on lower slopes of a sheer rock mountain.*

3. *Free standing wall with glass mosaic design completed by scultural plants, color plants, trees; stonepaved pattern.*

4. *Pool created in a depression of terrain; waterplants all planted by Roberto Burle Marx; different colors and textures in ground cover; conifers already on the terrain were left in the site.*

ROBERTO BURLE MARX

1

A garden is a complex of esthetic and plastic intentions, and the plant is to a landscape artist, not only a plant, rare, unusual, ordinary, or doomed to disappear; it is also a color, a shape, a volume, or an arabesque in itself. It is the paint for the two-dimensional picture I make of a garden on my drawing board.

A garden, in its broader sense, I think is a careful selection of certain aspects of nature, water, rocks, flowers, foliage ordered and arranged by man, in which man may have a direct contact with plants; an area in space, however small, in which he may find rest, relaxation, recreation, and above all the feeling that he is living in and integrated into this space. It is also a complex of plastic intention with a utilitarian purpose, and it should, whenever possible, fuse with the surrounding landscape while seeming an extension of the architecture for which it is designed. For it is not only as a botanist and as a working gardener that I think of gardens. I was trained as a painter; I worked under Portinerie on the "Products of Brazil" Panel for the Minister of Education's private office in Rio. The problems of color contrast in harmony of structure and form are as important to a two-dimensional painter as they are to me in a three-dimensional or four-dimensional garden. My two professions complement each other.

It seems to me, in fact, that the principles on which I base the structure and the arrangement of my gardens are in many points identical with those which are at the root of any other means of artistic expression, whether the idiom used be music, painting, sculpture, or the written or spoken word. In each case the creative impulse comes first and is essential, but the expression of this impulse is consciously controlled and measured, eliminating any chance solution. A work of art cannot, I think, be the result of a haphazard solution. The development of the creative impulse is carried out by means of rhythms which will produce what the artist knows to be the considered results. In any art the artist learns how to stress a sound, a word, a color, a line, a shape, a volume by means of contrast, comparison, repetition, tension, and relaxation, slowing down speed for suspense, racing speed for climax. And this, whether he is dealing with Marc Anthony's funeral oration, with the construction of Dostoevski's "Idiot", with the counterpoint in a Bach fugue, with a Debussy sound picture, a Picasso, or Braque cubist canvas, a Matisse color juxtaposition, a Mondrian, or a Moore sculpture. In a Beethoven symphony, for instance, the parts are linked from the statement of the theme to the conclusion.

In the garden the theme stated may be the predominant place given to a certain plant, or it may be the use of cylindrical flower boxes repeated at various time intervals. If I wish to stress the vertical of a colonnade in a garden, it must be contrasted with the horizontal of the mosaic stone path, in which I may at intervals plant low-growing volumes such as a series of philodendron, all different, but all closely linked with the familiar family characteristics.

The great difference, of course, between the two-dimensional painter and the three-dimensional landscape architect is that the plant, the raw material is not static, it has its own cycle of bud, flower, seed, and withering, and then again a gust of wind, a cloud, a shower, a storm will alter its color and its very structure. In the creation of these effects, the artist must use every means at his command. The painting on the drawing board is not the garden itself, any more than a photograph of a Calder mobile can give you any real idea of the emotion aroused by a mobile in the open air. It is this esthetic quality, which, if the garden is properly planned, will produce in the spectator a constant state of exaltation and surprise.

2

3

4

U P A

These are scenes from UPA's unusual presentation of the Edgar Allen Poe story, "The Tell Tale Heart."

This is a scene from "Magoo Goes Skiing,"
Pete Burness directed.

This is a scene from "When Magoo Flew."
UPA's latest Magoo adventure.

This is a background scene from "Destination Magoo,"
a story of Near-sighted Mister Magoo at Coney
Island. Myopic Magoo believes he is on the moon.

These are scenes from the third Gerald McBoing-Boing cartoon, "How Now Boing Boing." Gerald, the little noise-making boy, succeeds in saying a few words
over the telephone company's unscrambling device. Robert Cannon directed.

Anyone who has been to the movies in a G.I. theater will have no difficulty in recalling the stomps, whistles and whoops of the audience when the cartoon came on the screen. This noisy demonstration of affection, by no means confined to military audiences, must be attributed in large measure to the magical power of the cartoon film to whisk the spectator into a captivating flight of fantasy. In the cartoon film the viewer is transported instantly to an imaginative realm he knows quite well violates outrageously the logic of everyday life.

Cartoon characters blithely disregard "'insurmountable" obstacles. They may suffer momentary set-backs, be flattened into cookie shapes by crashing head-on into immovable objects, but quickly bounce back, their physical identity unimpaired, their taunts to fate more impudent than ever. The inhabitants of the cartoon world call upon reserves of magic excluded from mundane life. They thumb their noses at "'laws" of time, space, energy imprisoning their viewers. Natural and man-made objects surrounding the cartoon character are endowed with similar powers, and can shift from being objects to acting as protagonists

with insouciant disrespect for the "facts" of the situation.

So it is not surprising that in the surrender of individuality, of personal identity implicit in the military life, down to the presence of identical clothing—everyone in uniform, the G. I. (and for that matter most of the rest of the population) delights in the improbable world of the cartoon film.

Recognizing the "hold" the cartoon film has on servicemen, the U. S. Navy astutely decided during World War II to make animated training films for pilots. Putting young men at the controls of "hot" flying machines created behavioral problems that were not being coped with adequately by ordinary methods of indoctrination. A pilot might be a model of conformity on the ground, in the air, with hundreds of horsepower at his fingertips, he might regress to an infantile state, flying recklessly and as a result all too often fatally. The Navy commissioned a fledgling cartoon organization, Industrial Films and Poster Service, to dramatize the infantile feelings of omnipotence that may overcome a pilot alone in the air and released from military regulations. The success of the

notably effective Flat Hatting assured subsequent calls upon the company from the Army, the Office of War Information, the State Department and private business for cartoons featuring human subjects that were fresh and imaginative.

The young animators who had formed the nucleus of United Productions of America, as the company became known in 1945, were dissatisfied with the rigid conventions of storyline and visualization that dominated the film industry. Working for well-entrenched organizations they had had no chance to deviate from the animal fable in a naturalistic setting that the cartoon industry was content to exploit endlessly. These young animators, many serious, knowledgeable, and established painters, believed that the cartoon, as it then existed, failed to do justice to its visual and narrative possibilities. They were convinced that the creative innovations of twentieth century painting, not only could be adapted to animation, but more importantly would enhance immeasureably both visual and narrative quality. They felt that the creative potential of the cartoon film had scarcely been tapped.

The U.P.A. staff, once the opportunity pre-

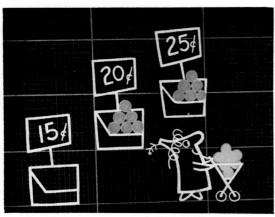  

These are scenes from "Fudget's Budget," a story of the family Fudget who try to live within their budget. Robert Cannon directed.

These are scenes from UPA's animated interscenes from the feature film, "The Fourposter."

sented itself, quickly extended these generalized ideas on the possibilities of animation to the thesis that the cartoon medium would gain impact as fantasy by stressing human foibles in human (rather than animal) characters existing in an invented (rather than naturalistic) setting that utilized the pictorial devices of twentieth century painting. Drawing upon the rich diversity of directions developed in modern art enabled U.P.A. to vary the styles with which different kinds of characters in different kinds of stories are presented. *Gerald McBoing Boing,* the ingratiating tyke with built-in sound effects in lieu of speech, exists in a different visual milieu than the aggressively myopic *Mr. Magoo,* while the *Madeline* series is Bemelmans in every accent and *The Unicorn in the Garden* treats the Thurber fable Thurberesquely.

No matter what the story, however, a common visual denominator runs through all U.P.A. productions. That is to say the screen is seen as a flat surface whether kept to the single surface plane as in *Fudget's Budget,* the action of which takes place on graphed paper, or in *Tell Tale Heart* (of Edgar Allan Poe), which slopes, leans, and tilts objects instead of anchoring space firmly in conventional perspective.

This flattening takes full advantage of the fact that a cartoon is a fantasy and that the audience delights in the transmutation of appearances. Whole episodes occur in which action transpires on little more than a platform, the characters simplified to linear essentials. The audience is responding to visual cues which are in themselves visual puns that heighten the sense of fantasy. This freedom of invention extends to the use of color, which in U.P.A. films is boldly "unreal," applied in flat, even, frequently brilliant tones with no attempt at modelling to suggest the rounded dimensions of the every-day world.

Certainly one of the keys to the imaginative zest of U.P.A. films is the studio's emphasis on creative invention. Once a story idea is approved it is turned over to a group of artists under the leadership of a director. Everyone working on the project contributes ideas to the story-line and to details of execution. Rather than a job, each project is a challenge "to come up with something"; consequently the atmosphere at U.P.A. is closer to that of a studio in the artist's sense than that of a place of employment.

Yet despite the acclaim of audiences all over the world, the success of U.P.A. has not been achieved without a running battle to maintain the integrity of their films. To continue to be creative, there must be growth, changes, departures from accepted innovations. The distributing end of the motion picture industry has not always known what to make of productions that, being different, are "off-beat" and therefore present the element of commercial risk. Many distributors are fearful that the appeal of U.P.A. is too sophisticated for the "corn-ball" audiences constituting the financial backbone of the industry. Nevertheless, though the most vociferous admirers of U.P.A. pictures are to be found in the more articulate segments of the community, films like Mr. Magoo, Gerald McBoing Boing, and the Hans Christian Andersen fable of *The Emperor's New Clothes* are entertainments designed to captivate audiences of all kinds. True, there is fey wit, and a fresh way of presenting animated images, but U.P.A. films are above all fantasies, carrying on the cartoon tradition of providing moments of improbable hilarity—collective waking dreams, if you will, to compensate for the dull, predictable, and oppressive realities we must all contend with in everyday life.—**Jules Langsner**

These are scenes from "Flat Hatting," a UPA training film produced for the United States Navy.

A scene from "Unicorn in the Garden," James Thurber's sardonic fable about a henpecked husband.

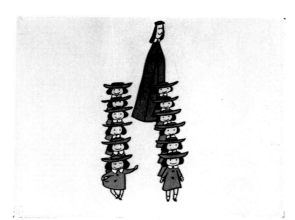

These are scenes from UPA's "Madeline," the delightful children's story by Ludwig Bemelmans. Robert Cannon directed.

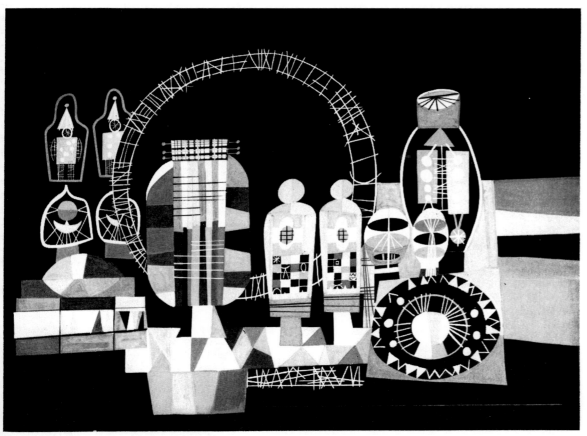

An opening scene from "Tune in Tomorrow," UPA's third film for CBS.

RICO LEBRUN

By Jules Langsner

The spectator viewing Rico Lebrun's huge collages and paintings at his studio in West Los Angeles is unprepared for the driving energy of these monumental pictures, for the violence of imagery wrenched, fractured, ripped from specific local context, for passages dramatically contrasting intensely-hued with fuliginous color. The one-time ballroom that is Lebrun's studio appears, at first glance, to be the site for the activity of a cadre of artists: mural-length collages are tacked to the walls, enormous canvases concurrently in process of development stand on easels, cut-out swatches of ducoed paper representing stages in the growth of ideas are spread across vast expanses of floor. These works possess at once elemental vigor and sophisticated concepts, are charged with emotional impact, and beg to be incorporated in an architectural site bold and secure enough to measure up to the challenge of an empowering pictorial vision.

A Neapolitan transplanted to the West Coast, Lebrun seeks to infuse his native Baroque sensibility into contemporary painting. For this artist, steeped in the pulsating grandeur of architects like Guarini and Borromini, and the dramatic rhetoric of painters like Tintoretto and Tiepolo, the idea of a picture or work of sculpture serving at best as a minor accent to an architectural conception needs to be re-examined. Now it is true that so far no architect has beaten a path to Lebrun's studio. Nevertheless, the validity of the Lebrun enterprise—making pictures powerful enough to push beyond the scope of the architectural site—is in no way lessened by the absence of architectural commissions. What Lebrun is doing pictorially is premised on the possibility of once again rejoining architecture and painting, creating a new, fructifying synthesis appropriate to the second half of the twentieth century.

This effort to invest architecture with the vitality of pictorial forms runs counter to the prevailing notions of regularity, pure, clean, unobstructed space, to the judicious restraint, some would say "decorum," of many present day buildings, with their insistence on austere structural efficiency. The battle against 19th century eclecticism in architecture is over. The danger now is in the solidifying of style and concepts

(Continued on page 247)

PHOTOGRAPH BY JERRY CHESEBROUGH

CLAIRE FALKENSTEIN

by

MICHEL TAPIE

The recent work of Claire Falkenstein lies at the very heart of the adventure which is today's art, that *art autre* which, after the structural terminus of the classic spirit that Cubism was, and after the cognizance of its total liquidation by Dada, came to life about fifteen years ago with, at the start, Mark Tobey in the United States and Fautrier in Europe. In a movement begun in an atmosphere of total anarchy — and it could not have been otherwise — among several isolated (and alas quickly imitated) individuals, the very slight distance we have come still puts at our disposal several hundred, soon perhaps several thousand *autre* works of indisputable value. Any confusion now can lead only to an academism of anarchy; we are almost there already. But this sterile trap, the greatest danger that attends the art of our time, can be avoided by throwing up as soon as possible— *a posteriori* in regard to existing works — the bases of an esthetic itself *autre,* without any retrospective tie to classic esthetics (and hence without systematic opposition), an esthetic at once on the scale of the authentic new works and on that of the new philosophico-scientific necessities which obtrude unavoidably upon our psycho-sensory reflexes.

At this historic point, we can see to what extent Claire Falkenstein's recent work is situated in the new zones of efficacity. I wish to cite her sheared and vigorously fired surfaces, and especially the series of "Suns" which, as an outgrowth of her techniques, suggests a possible future synthesis.

Claire Falkenstein joins to a vivid and rich intuition a sort of pantheistic governing wisdom which springs no less from a deep intellectual apprehension of the structural problems essential to our time. Departing from long research on forms structured not only from the pythagorean geometries and rhythms, but even more clearly from the organic, and the most freely dynamic rhythms, she has made the crucial element of her forms *continuity,* that concept which is one of the bases of present topology, by which our whole perception of formal and spatial relations has been challenged. But this is only of the so pertinent aspects of her work.

Her extraordinary "Sun" series deeply interests estheticians, philosophers, architects, at the same time that it attracts the subtle antennae of true collectors and art lovers, because these works, bearers of a mysterious magic issuing from forms and spaces conceived on the plane of our needs, reveal to us the current problems of tensorial calculus, of the dynamic logistics of contradition, problems of abstract space of complex relations decipherable only by the most contemporary notions of what 'number' can be (infinitesimal, real transfinite, hypercomplex . . . .). All these things concur to endow the new forms with sensory efficacies so rich that with them and by their means, it will one day be necessary to reconsider the Human Adventure, Eroticism, Drama, Love, and Life which, if these forms be not vitiated by useless academisms, must be the foundation of their *content.*

Claire Falkenstein is probably the artist who has led sculpture closest to the heart of that which must be the artistic epos of Now.

Translated from the French by Julia Randall

PHOTOGRAPH BY PAUL FACCHETTI

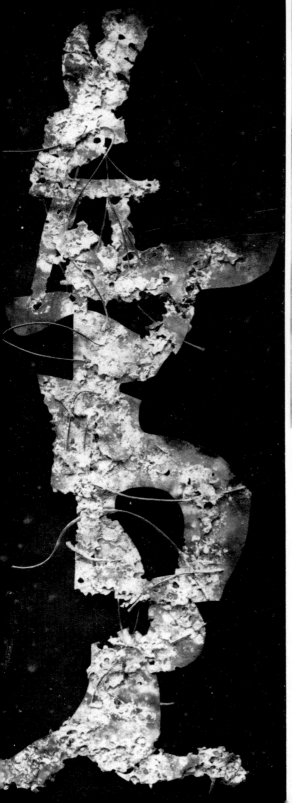

PHOTOGRAPH BY NIGEL HENDERSON

PINWHEEL HOUSE   Designed by Peter Blake

Paul Weidlinger, Structural Engineer

PHOTOGRAPHS BY HANS NAMUTH / PAINTING BY ALFONSO OSSORIO

Idea: Most vacation houses are designed to work, roughly, like a camera: a box, glazed on one side, with the glass wall pointed at the view. The designer felt that he could make the project more interesting if he could find a way to open the house to a variety of views with a possibility of shutting out a view occasionally. It also seems that summer living poses certain distinct problems, i.e.: how to keep cool, how to keep away from bugs, how to cut out the sun if and when it becomes too insistent. Finally, the concept of summer-living as different from all-year-around living suggests that in a summer house the sleeping quarters and utilities be reduced to a minimum, and the living quarters made as spacious as possible, all to be designed for a minimum of upkeep.

Solution: The pinwheel house seemed both an obvious and a disarmingly simple solution to these problems. It consists of two elements: a 24′ by 24′ living area upstairs, and a 19′ by 19′ sleeping-bathing-utility-storage area below. The upstairs area has four identical exterior walls. Looking at each wall from the inside, and reading from left to right, these walls consist (1) of a 6′ wide fixed glass panel; (2) of a 12′ wide opening that can be screened; and (3) of a 6′ wide wall panel faced with plywood.

The key to the pinwheel plan is a very large —18′ long and 8′ high—sliding wall hung from an overhead track. This wall can be moved along the outside face of the house, to cover up or open up the 12′ wide opening at the center. There are four such sliding walls—one for

(Continued on page 247)

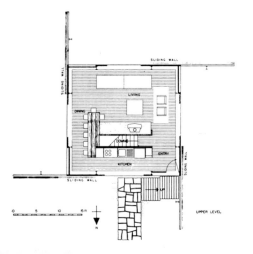

UPPER LEVEL

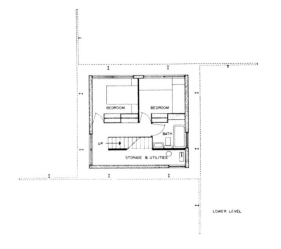

LOWER LEVEL

TWO INCOME-UNIT STRUCTURES

By Raymond Kappe, architect

Problem: To design a 4-unit (2 one bedroom and 2 single) apartment on a portion of a lot which the owners had felt was unbuildable. Set-back and yard requirements limited the building site to a 25' x 70' rectangle; another 4-unit already exists on front portion lot. An alley which provides access to the lot near the rear portion makes it possible to unload materials . . . however concrete has to be craned in and it is not possible to get any excavating equipment to this portion of lot. The budget was set at $20,000.

Solution: The initial aim was to solve the excavating problem. This, coupled with the restricted site, established a split-level one bed-room apartment which would most closely follow the natural contours and require at most a small amount of hand digging. The split-level plan for two of the apartments also had the advantage of requiring a minimum ground area, at the same time affording maximum visual spaciousness due to increased volumes and general openness. By setting the floor level of the two single apartments at the same elevation as the bedroom in apartment 2, the excavating problem was again solved and the massing was kept more pleasing. Wood decks were employed in order to avoid retaining walls and again keep the natural grade as close as possible . . . private outdoor areas for each tenant were taken for granted in the program. Each has such an area facing existing trees which were saved on this piece of property as well as those on the adjoining property.

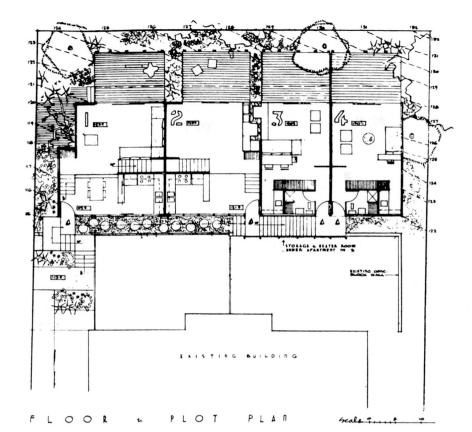

BEDROOM LEVEL · APTS. 1&2

EXISTING BUILDING

F L O O R & P L O T P L A N   scale

ECKBO, ROYSTON and WILLIAMS, Landscape architects

The photographs relate to an already completed structure; the drawings, to a working project.

HOTOGRAPHS BY RENE SHERET

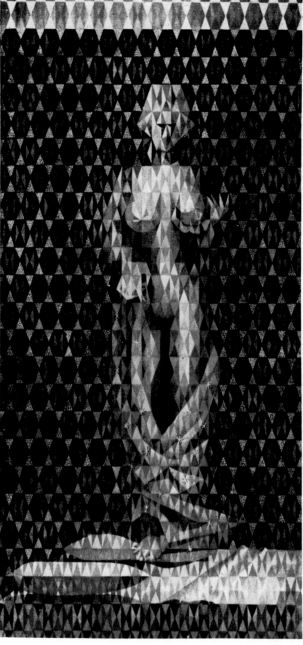

THE BRIDE—OIL

THE ADVOCATE—OI'

JUNE WAYNE
imagist

Art experience, it is held, somehow must remain mysteriously pure and undefiled. I do not accept the premise that contemplation of a visual object is an autonomous experience. The psyche, as I understand its nature, consists of overlapping rings of experience and is not compartmented into sealed-off chambers. An immaculate art experience is psychologically untenable.

Now to get on with considering the art of June Wayne. This painter and printmaker is that rarity among contemporary artists—an authentic imagist. The word "authentic" is of essential importance here. It stands for that unique capacity to create an order of imagery at once personal to the artist and compelling for the spectator.

The imagist in the visual arts, to define the term as it pertains to Wayne, is a *pictorial poet*. That is to say, like the poet of words she presents metaphors and similes, but visually rather than verbally. Her images cluster constellations of feelings, ideas and sensations into unique and meaningful relations, coalesce kinds of experience otherwise isolated from each other.

Now you may ask, and rightly, exactly what visual images in a poetic sense may be. For one thing, the poetic visual image draws suggestions from the familiar world but eschews reproducing everyday surroundings accurately. Resemblance to familiar objects sometimes is tenuous, often

barely perceptible. Indeed, in the poetic image the familiar world is transposed by an act of imagination. The connection to the visible world is psychological, never descriptive.

These imaginative traces of the visible world are endowed with the kinetic power to stir our inner selves. For example, in Wayne pictures you are likely, at one time or another to encounter figures she calls "the mushroom people." You can recognize these creatures by their mushroom-like heads. The mushroom, to this artist, is freighted with associations: it is a delicacy and a poison, a sensuous shape and the form of the atomic explosion. The mushroom people are recurrent images, transformed by the situation in which they find themselves, appearing now in one context, now in another. They are, in effect, the raw material for poetic metaphors. Thus in *Final Jury*, the mushroom people are positioned in isolated chambers, just as each juror is impelled to come to terms with himself. Or again, in *The Messenger*, one of the mushroom jurors catapults out of the jury box, metamorphosizing as he travels into a light that reveals a pair of defendants.

The modern imagist is deprived of an established system of potent and meaningful symbols. Consequently he invents images he hopes possess the magical power to touch the inner recesses of the spirit. It is hardly sur-

THE TRAVELERS—LITHOGRAPH

THE MESSENGER—OIL

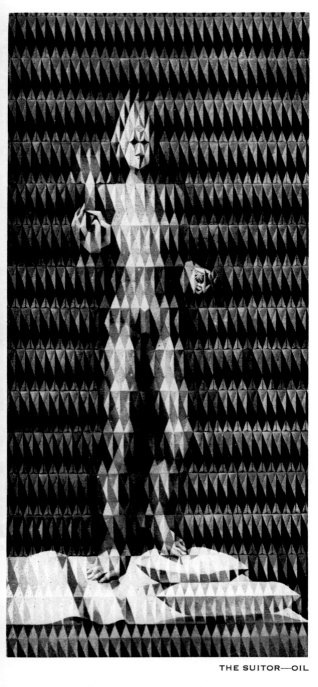

THE SUITOR—OIL

prising then, that June Wayne's images initially are private rather than public. The test of the modern imagist resides in the force of the invented image to strike a responsive chord in spectators who are not privy to the personality of their maker. Fortunately we respond to private imagery in the same way we respond to the images of cultures not our own. The successful image transcends local restrictions, reaches beyond its maker by somehow giving shape to common experience. In this sense, it seems to me, June Wayne is a successor to artists like Blake, Redon, Ensor, pictorial poets whose private imagery we incorporate in our personal imaginative life. Like the art of these predecessors, her invented images overlap our experience, touch something vital in ourselves, are incorporated within our imaginative life.

This incorporation of her images occurs because they are visually conceived. No amount of verbal elaboration can substitute for a direct confrontation of the images themselves. By visually conceived I mean that the images are experienced optically, and could not exist except in a visible dimension. The pictures by June Wayne are not only visible manifestations of ideas, but are emotionally weighted and always sensuous. Sensuous especially in the satisfying language of sight. In pictures like *The Advocate, The Suitor* and *The Bride,* though figures are immersed within a precisely diamonded atmosphere, the idea is poetically right and

the emerging forms are visually sensuous. The figures are images inseparable from their environment. The result is an exhilarating tension between the precision of the diamond shapes and the way in which the figures quiver and tremble into life. In short, these are images whose being is pictorial.

The imagery of these prints and painting is poetically persuasive, persuasive because it results from the most intense and passionate concentration. It is not so much a matter that the images bespeak passion, and intensity, but that they arise from an initiating emotion that is intense and passionate. That initiating emotion is transmuted into images that may be lyrical, tragic, comic . . . but always involving. The artist possesses this gift for transforming initiating emotion into poetic image. Consequently we do not duplicate the emotion presented, but experience it poetically. This is an important distinction, for that transportation of emotion into imaged form is the difference between art and non-esthetic experience.

Sir Thomas Browne had the last word to say on this matter, and what he said applies to the art of June Wayne. "There are many things delivered Rhetorically, many expressions merely Tropical, and as they best illustrate my intention; and therefore also there are many things to be taken in a soft and flexible sense, and not to be called into the rigid test of "Reason."—JULES LANGSNER.

the language of the wall

This unique subject, the scrawls and pictures carved and drawn on building walls in Paris during the past twenty years is the theme of an exhibition of photographs by the French artist, Brassai, shown at the Museum of Modern Art.

Graffiti, an Italian word meaning scribblings or scratchings, are rudely scratched inscriptions and figure drawings found on rocks, walls, vases and other objects. Brassai feels that graffiti give a spontaneous testimony as to the character and life of an epoch and for two decades has been collecting "these ephemeral and savage flowers of art, blooming everywhere on the walls of Paris' boroughs." He has divided his photographs into five categories, according to the subjects he found: faces, magic, death, love, animals. Most of the faces are dominated by two deep holes used as eyes with other features scratched in varying ways into the wall. The diversity of drawing is illustrated by the different kinds of expressions these faces appear to have: sad, fierce, comic. Drawings characterized as "magic" include variations on devils, faces that resemble our Halloween pumpkins and witches. Death is represented by a series of drawings of a skull and cross-bones, ranging from extremest detailed pictures to an abstraction consisting simply of two crossed lines, each ending in a knob. Love is a pierced heart, and birds, beasts and fish are both imaginary and real, or sometimes a fantastic combination of people and animals, or of animals alone.

"This exhibition stands as a postscript to the memorable group of 64 Brassai photographs exhibited here at the Museum in 1951, wherein his robust curiosity about the every-dayness of life produced a vivid portrayal of Paris and Parisians. Here he takes us with him prowling around Paris where for over a period of 20 years he has looked at the images scratched on the walls of Paris by many anonymous youngsters. Brassai the photographer sees these graffiti just as he has seen people and places. Like his other photographs, these images come to life with an existence of their own. Here is evidence that youngsters have had their imaginations stimulated by the weathered aspect of a wall's surface or by accidental or deliberate mutilation. I believe the visual image, as children and young people see it in films, in the magazines, in newspapers—the comic strips, on Paris kiosks, has had an influence on young minds, interesting them not only in the shapes and patterns but also in the emotional expression these images may have. Brassai has obviously been impressed with how many of these graffiti begin with two holes in the wall, and he has found and photographed many faces so that the eyes create an extraordinarily dramatic impact."
—Edward Steichen.

CONCRETE SHELL FORMS — FELIX CANDELA

A MAJOR EXHIBITION OF THE WORK OF FELIX CANDELA IS BEING SHOWN
AT HARRIS HALL, UNIVERSITY OF SOUTHERN CALIFORNIA,
FROM MAY 7 THROUGH JUNE 12; SPONSORED BY
THE UNIVERSITY OF SOUTHERN CALIFORNIA'S FINE ARTS DEPARTMENT
AND SCHOOL OF ARCHITECTURE
THE ARCHITECTURAL PANEL, AND
THE AMERICAN
INSTITUTE OF ARCHITECTS, SOUTHERN CALIFORNIA CHAPTER;
ARRANGED BY DON GOODALL, CHAIRMAN OF THE FINE ARTS DEPARTMENT
OF THE UNIVERSITY OF SOUTHERN CALIFORNIA, AND ESTHER McCOY

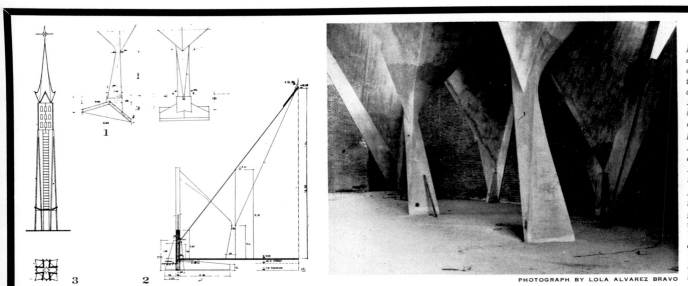

PHOTOGRAPH BY LOLA ALVAREZ BRAVO

IGLESIA DE LA VIRGEN MILAGROSA.

Drawing No. 1: Structural section and elevation of one of the interior columns of the nave. The surface of the column is formed by three warped surfaces arising from a triangular base. The shape of the column was not dictated by, but actually does coincide with the diagram of downward thrusts at this point.

Drawing No. 2: Structural sections taken at two points of the roof of La Milagrosa showing the relationship of the edges of each paraboloid.

Drawing No. 3: Plan and Elevation of the Bell-Tower. In keeping with the general design of the church, this tower is also composed of warped surfaces. The intermediary campaniles, considered by Candela an unsatisfactory feature, were introduced during the course of construction to increase the height of the tower.

PROJECT FOR A MARKET

Drawing No. 7: Cross section and elevation of scheme a. This project, if built, will surely be one of the most beautiful and awe-inspiring structures of all time. Not merely because of its gigantic size, but because of the delicacy of the forms, and the fact that there will be no visible beams throughout. The design is entirely formed of repetitive units, but they are so merged together as to give a completely uninterrupted flow, and it would be hard to imagine anything less monotonous. Around the perimeter of the great vaults is a continuous rippling band of doubly-curved shells, whose forms are also derived directly from the groined vaults. To see how this is so, we must imagine two groined vaults placed along side each other: a common parabolic arch is thus formed by the juncture of two of their perimetral arches. Now taking this arch as the diagonal of a square, the contingent paraboloid on each of its sides is removed. The new structure which results is square in plan and supported at its two lower corners which are joined by the diagonal cross arch. Each elevation of this structure is seen to be a half-arch, and when several of these forms are placed together, the apparently continuous effect in drawing No. 7 is obtained.

Drawing No. 8: Aerial perspective of scheme b. This scheme uses the same solution for the perimeter area. In the great hall, however, the larger vaults are replaced by those of 26x26 mts., except for one at the intersection of the cross, and these smaller vaults are staggered in height to get extra lighting.

Drawing No. 9: Elevation of scheme b.

Drawing No. 10: Elevation of scheme c. This scheme entails covering the entire plan with the half-vaults described in scheme a. At points of juncture, the roofs are again opened. These apertures are covered by small elongated paraboloids in the form of arches, to enable the windows to be vertical and the lighting indirect.

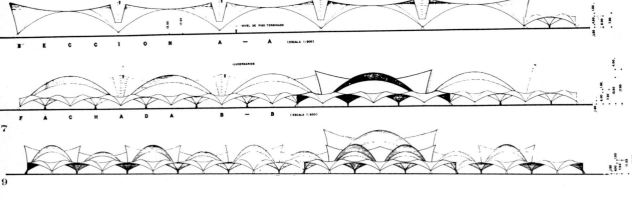

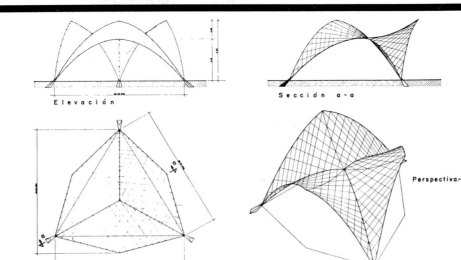

Elevación

Sección a-a

Planta.

Perspectiva.

11

PROJECT FOR THE CASINO OF THE SAN JOSE HOTEL IN PUERTO RICO.

Drawing No. 11: Plan, elevation, section and perspective of shell. This drawing shows one of the solutions studied for the new casino now under construction in Puerto Rico. It provides for a structure of almost hexagonal plan, supported at three points. The shell is formed by three similar hyperbolic paraboloid sections. Max Borges, Jr., is the architect.

Shells are as old as nature, and it was from nature that Felix Candela learned his first lesson: all shells have compound curves, and their strength is derived from their shape rather than their thickness. The stresses in the surfaces of a shell are so evenly distributed that no one point is more vulnerable than another.

To apply this principle to architecture required more than an understanding of how nature works, for she does not pour her shells, and she needs no supporting framework to build them. Her creations are free in space, while a work of architecture is fixed.

To the architect and engineer a shell means a continuous curved surface whose supports are integral with the structure. There are numerous kinds in architecture, the simplest of which is the cylindrical shell. This was the first type to be built, the Zeiss factory in Jena, Germany, in 1924. A culmination of a century of investigation, which started in 1828 when Lamé and Clapeyron, French engineers, presented the first analytical approach to shells, the direct application of theory to structure became possible only after the development of a monolithic material, reinforced concrete, in the last quarter of the 19th Century.

Man is a close observer of nature and has enjoyed amassing knowledge of the way she builds, but the shapes he is accustomed to using—cubes, flat surfaces—are unknown in nature. She is not a classicist; she has no post and beam construction. Her products, including man, all have compound curvatures, and are held together by tension.

The shell roof of Candela's El Atillo Chapel reminds one of no shells in nature, rather of a single leaf gently twisted in the wind. The membrane drape of the roof surfaces of Iglesia de la Virgen Milagrosa is like the webbing of a bat's wing. But the roofing systems for both are hyperbolic paraboloidical shells, which are generated by stretching an elastic web of concrete over four points. The surfaces, as noted, do not depend upon their thickness for their strength, but rather upon the membrane action.

It is in the design of hyperbolic paraboloidical shells that Felix Candela has committed his genius.

Between 1924 when Carl Zeiss designed his factory in Germany, and 1950 when Candela executed his first hyperbolic paraboloid, an understanding of the theory of shells had spread rapidly. This

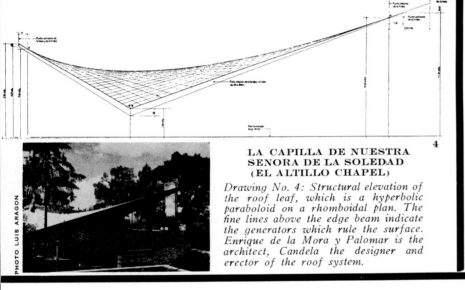

4

LA CAPILLA DE NUESTRA SEÑORA DE LA SOLEDAD (EL ALTILLO CHAPEL)

Drawing No. 4: Structural elevation of the roof leaf, which is a hyperbolic paraboloid on a rhomboidal plan. The fine lines above the edge beam indicate the generators which rule the surface. Enrique de la Mora y Palomar is the architect, Candela the designer and erector of the roof system.

PHOTO LUIS ARAGON

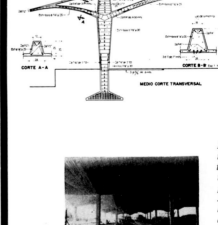

CORTE A-A   CORTE B-B

MEDIO CORTE TRANSVERSAL

5

ADUANAS DE MEXICO (MEXICO CITY CUSTOMS WAREHOUSE)

Drawing No. 5: A half-section taken through one of the columns showing the steel reinforcing in the column and the stiffening rib. The structure is composed of short cylindrical shells with a span of 20 mts., with a six mt. cantilever wing on each side. The tie-rods are over the roof.
Carlos Recamier is the collaborating architect.

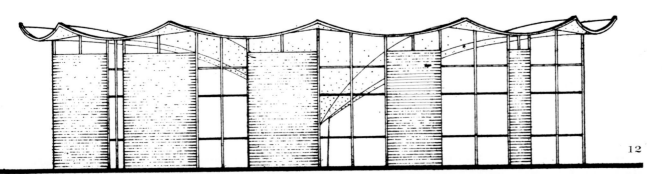

12

OFFICES FOR THE PENNSALT CO. IN MEXICO.

Drawing No. 12: Elevation of building showing the staggered system of walls and windows, and the enormous (20x20 mt.) dodecagonal umbrella which is the roof. The almost circular shell is divided equally into twelve equal hyperbolic paraboloids which spring out radially 10 mts. from the one supporting column at the center. The curved borders and groins give an almost liquid and enate appearance to the structure.

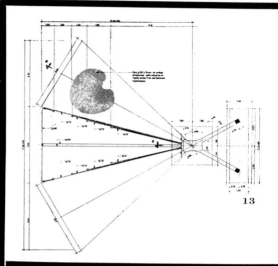

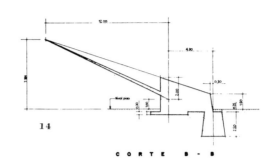

13

14

CORTE B - B

BANDSHELL IN SANTA FE HOUSING PROJECT, MEXICO CITY.

Drawing No. 13: This bandshell is built in the new housing development of the Instituto Mexicano del Seguro Social, under the direction of architect Mario Pani. The structure, although seemingly complicated, is simply a triple-cantilever formed by six hyperbolic paraboloids. Each paraboloid commences at the base as a vertical and ends at the edge a horizontal. The structure was designed and calculated in a single day. The solid bastion below ground to the rear (see drawing No. 14) is a weight to compensate the cantilever. Drawing No. 13 shows the plan with the placing of the reinforcing rods. Drawing No. 14: Schematic section showing arrangements of masses.

new and imaginative approach to the roofing of large areas gave latitude to structural layout, and it made the most economical use of materials of any other system of construction.

In the intervening years came some significant examples, among them Freyssinet's hangar at Orly, France, the first application of shell design in this field, a primitive shell, the simplest kind of doubly curved paraboloid, Torroja's cylindrical shell for a fronton court in Madrid in 1947; and Maillart's temporary shell for the Zurich Exposition of 1939, his only essay in shell design.

Nervi has contributed some superb designs for the roofing of large areas, particularly his Exhibition Hall in Turin, Italy, but his structures are articulated and joined, and he makes use of pre-fabricated concrete roof elements, of great beauty in themselves, which excludes his work from pure shell construction except in a few isolated cases.

An architect who was intrigued with the shell was Antonio Gaudi, who used hyperbolic paraboloidical surfaces for roofing parts of his Casa Milá, a chapel in Güell Park, and for certain portions of his church, La Sagrada Familia, in Barcelona early

in the century. Unlike Candela's work in this type of shell, they do not act alone in a structurally logical way. The function of the structure and its economy are Candela's first preoccupations.

There existed an even more important difference between Candela's shells and others. His are thin, and the essence of the shell is its thinness. If upon the appearance of the new plastic material —reinforced concrete—the shell form was proved, there awaited its development as a thin roofing surface before it could emerge from the experimental stage to take its place in architecture.

It came in 1950, when Candela designed the roof for the Cosmic Ray Pavilion for Mexico's University City. This shell was not experiment for experiment's sake: a roof thin enough to admit cosmic rays was required.

Reinforced concrete is the standard building material in Mexico, because of its economy, the scarcity of steel, and also because concrete responds to handcraft methods. It happens that little steel is necessary for shells, for the stresses are so evenly distributed that almost no bending moments exist. And shells are easy to build with unskilled labor; they are no more difficult that the

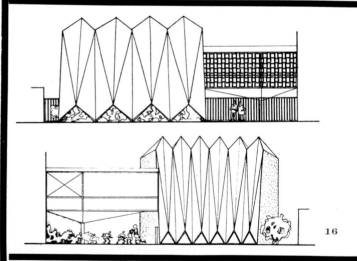

16

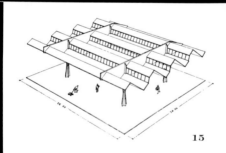

15

PROJECT FOR THE THEATRE OF THE ANGLO-MEXICAN CULTURAL INSTITUTE IN MEXICO.

Drawing No. 16: Street and back elevations of this small theatre, showing the folded shells covering the auditorium, and the elevated lobby which connects the theatre with the existing Institute building. Another example of the great structural and aesthetic possibilities of prismatic shells. It is interesting to note that similar structures to these might be executed using the hyperbolic paraboloid.

PRISMATIC SHELLS FOR INDUSTRIAL BUILDINGS.

Drawing No. 15: Perspective of Folded Plate Slab structure with suggested dimensions. This drawing is part of a series which Candela devoted to the study and mathematical analysis of prismatic shells some years ago.

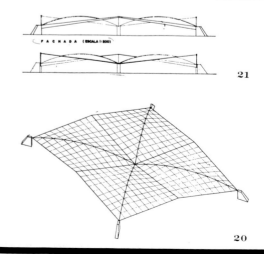

21

20

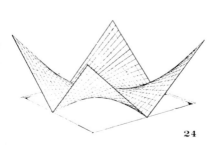

24

PROJECT FOR SYDNEY ROSS LABORATORIES, MEXICO CITY.

Drawing No. 20: Aerial perspective showing the generators of the surface. This huge shell for an American chemical company will serve as a warehouse. The structure is square in plan, with one column in each corner and another in the center. The roof consists basically of four hyperbolic paraboloids, each with a support at its lower corners. However each paraboloid is divided again into two sections by a diagonal arch springing from each support: this is to keep the rise relatively low. Drawing No. 21: Elevation and section through the shell. Alejandro Prieto is the architect who is in charge of the design of the whole complex.

SHELL STRUCTURE FOR ARCHITECT JOSE LUIS SERT.

Drawing No. 24: Perspective of shell. This structure consists of four hyperbolic paraboloids on a square base, with supports at the center of each side.

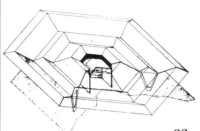

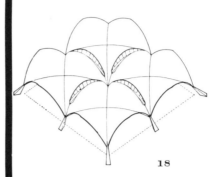

TWO DESIGNS ON A HEXAGON BASE.

Drawing No. 22: This solution is an another prismatic or folded plate shell. Drawing No. 23: Elevation of a second solution, also hexagonal in plan. The structure is composed of six hyperbolic paraboloids of rhomboidal plan; each edge in each paraboloid is half a parabolic arch. The structure is supported at six points.

Both these designs are solutions proposed for a storehouse by Architect Luis Rivadeneyra.

GROINED VAULTS FOR ECONOMICAL SPANS OF 100 FEET IN INDUSTRIAL BUILDINGS.

This drawing No. 18 is an aerial perspective of a project for a factory in Mexico City demanding the most economical possible method for spans of 100 feet in each direction. The vaults are opened at points of juncture to permit a hanging catwalk and natural lighting.

Enrique de la Mora y Palomar is the architect of this church. Candela was contracted for the execution and structural design of the shells only.

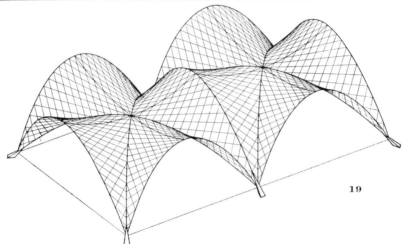

PROJECT FOR CHILDREN'S TRAIN STATION IN CHAPULTEPEC PARK, MEXICO CITY.

Drawing No. 19: Perspective of groined vaults, showing system of generators. This is another example of the use of the groined vault formed by doubly curved surfaces. In this case it is play architecture, and the lightness and small scale (12x12 mts.) of the vaults seem especially adapted to the program.

traditional vaulting work done in Spain with hollow bricks, which Candela had watched masons build from memory.

How the Cosmic Ray Pavilion was to be constructed by handcraft labor was a factor as important as the extraordinary thinness required. The solution was two hyperbolic paraboloidical vaults coupled along a principal parabola, and stiffened by three concrete arches to avoid buckling.

"The two director planes form an angle of 60°. Each generatrix of a system intersects all the generating lines of the other one, but does not touch those of its own system, being in parallel planes with them. The formwork was made of ½″ tongue and groove flooring laid, in an approximate form, according to a generating system, on 2x4″ wooden joists disposed exactly along the other system of straight generatrix. The reinforcement, disposed along the principal parabolas, was a mesh of ¼″ mild steel wire placed 4″ on centers." Thus Candela describes the method of construction.

After the forms were in place the concrete was troweled on by hand, and was then vibrated. The roof was the thinnest ever to be constructed: ⅝″ thick, increasing to 2″ at the springings.

Up until the construction of the Cosmic Ray Pavilion, shell forms were an architectural indulgence. Now they became economically feasible. They were ready to take their place on our landscape.

Felix Candela was born in Madrid in 1910. He became interested in shells in his student days at Escuela Superior de Arquitectura, from which he was graduated in 1935. But, he said, "The mathematical barrier so cunningly laid by the German scientists who developed the method restrained me for some years from seriously considering the possibility of building shells myself."

The fact was that during the years of experimentation the natural evolution of the shell was being obstructed by the mathematician. The solution of the shell was wrapped in a tight cocoon, woven of such heavy cables of statistics that the butterfly was caught inside.

There were more equations than shells. By a miracle some were built. But a few butterflies do not declare a summer. The shell

(Continued on page 247)

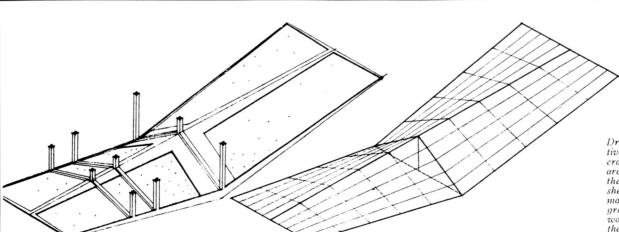

PROJECTED ENTRANCE CANOPY FOR RICHARD NEUTRA, ARCHITECT.

Drawing No. 17: Axonometric perspective and perspective showing the generators of the shell projected for Richard Neutra as an entrance canopy to the new U.S. Embassy in Karachi. The shell was to hang from beneath the main building, which is mostly open at ground level. One side of the shell would thus cantilever about 50 feet over the entrance walk and drive, while the other would extend beneath the building.

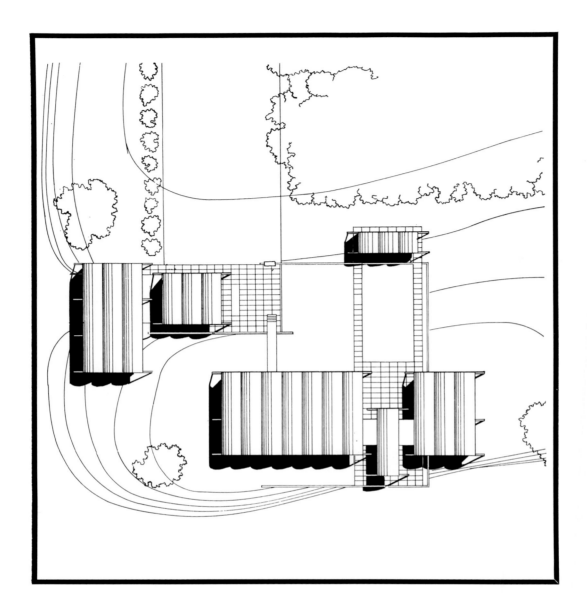

HOUSE IN FLORIDA, BY PAUL RUDOLPH, ARCHITECT

This house is an attempt to expand space by bending plywood and supporting it on a steel primary structure. A kind of open shelter, it is well isolated from its neighbors on the bend of a beautiful river on the west coast of Florida.

The project includes a boat house, shop and swimming pool to augment the usual facilities provided. Glass areas with rolling windows sections expose most of the general living area of the house. Those portions where privacy is necessary are enclosed in concrete brick walls. Entrance is through a glassed-in area way which divides the living and dining section from the sleeping quarters, and leads through to a semi-enclosure which becomes a part of the terrace, swimming pool, recreation center. The open living area occupying the center of the structure has the quality of a glassed-in pavilion. Enclosure again occurs beyond the living, dining areas and kitchen unit for a small study. Separate structures house the car port and boat house which is immediately adjacent to docking facilities.

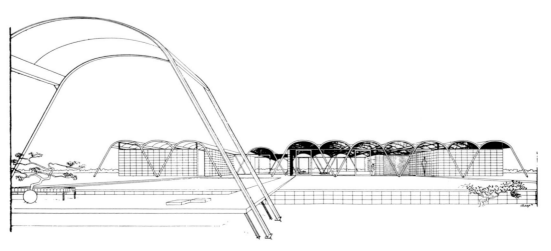

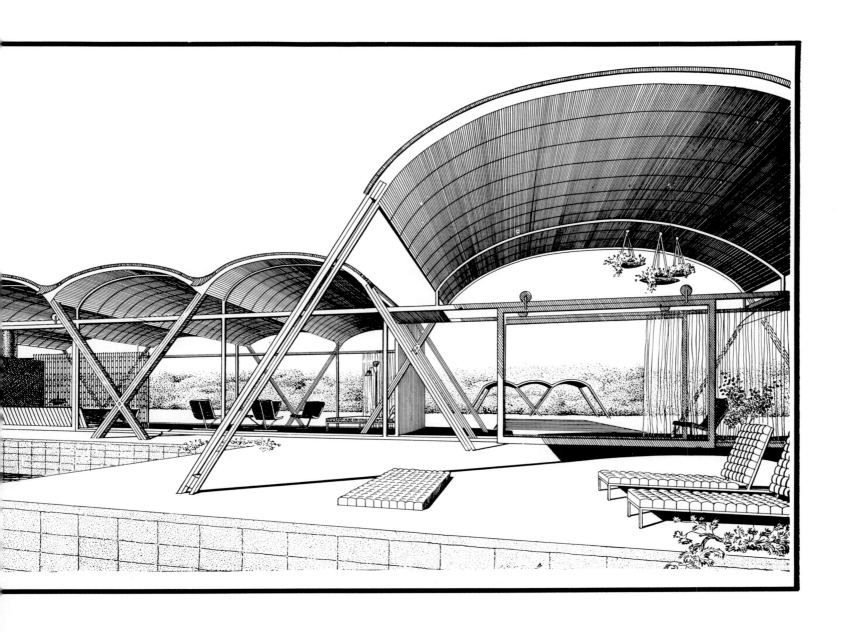

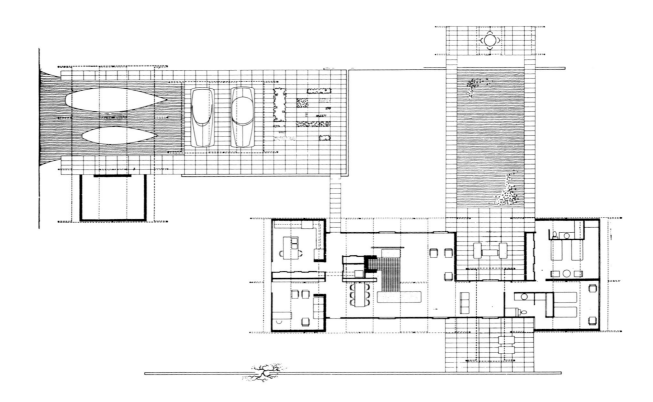

House
Thornton M. Abell, Architect

The site is in a quiet suburban neighborhood near the ocean and slopes slightly to a group of large trees at the edge of a wide canyon. There is a fine northwest view across the canyon toward the mountains. One of the most important requirements of this house was that there be extensive storage facilities located in proper places for specific needs. The house has been planned for the accommodation of considerable art work with many walls for paintings. The living and dining area is informal and spacious and arranged to open on to the garden and the view. The kitchen is very complete, with seated-height work cabinet in the center containing mixing equipment and basic supplies. Dish storage and sinks are toward the dining area, the work pantry and utensils, near the range. The refrigerator is centrally located. There is a large skylight that floods the work center with light. Breakfast space, laundry and storage pantry complete the kitchen area, with general storage outside.

From the living room a wide gallery leads to the guest room. In the gallery there is storage for linen and cleaning equipment. The guest bath also serves as a powder room. The owners' suite was planned to be a room of many uses; one part, a study, another for writing and sewing. The problem in designing this house was a matter of developing an orderly background for a very complex but pleasant pattern of living.

The construction is wood frame, with T & G cedar exterior and drywall interior finish. The insulated roof plane is flat, with drywall ceilings and gray slag surfaced composition roof. Floor finish is carpet except for vinyl tile in baths and kitchen areas over plywood floor construction. The studio has a mastic floor over a concrete slab. Precast pebble surface masonry units are used on the exterior at the car shelter. Glass areas are fixed, with sliding steel doors, and white opal glass for all louvered ventilating units. Wall coverings have been used on all walls: grass cloth, burlap and vinyl. The color is generally neutral; the cedar is stained oyster; concrete units are slate color with natural pebbles; the exterior fascia and trim is green slate; all ceilings and overhangs, light gray.

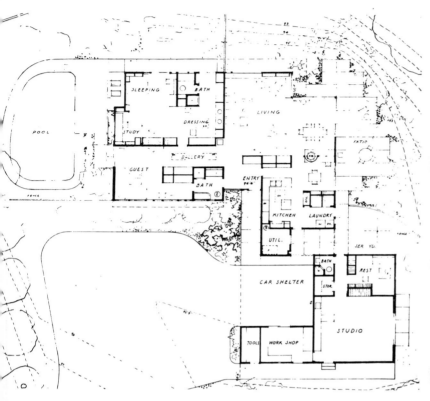

PHOTOGRAPHS BY JULIUS SHULMAN

POCKET GUIDE TO ARCHITECTURAL CRITICISM   Jules Langsner

The purpose of this guide is to alert the intelligent layman to the euphemisms, arcane jargon, incantations, fustian and obfuscations commonly found in architectural criticism. It may help the unwary to avoid some of the baited traps of this occult corner of criticism.

By and large, criticism of architecture (or what passes for it) falls into readily identifiable species. Let us isolate those specimens likely to be encountered.

ACCOLADES-TO-GENIUS-CRITICISM

Critics in this category must have a genius to salaam. Paeans of praise to a dazzling innovator characterize the Accolade-To-Genius-Critic, "His daring, profound intellectual grasp, unmatched intuitive powers, and complete independence of conventional solutions, assure our time the designation—Epoch of the Master."

Accolades-To-Genius tend to be uncritical, are weighted with superlatives and quotations from the discourses of the Master. His buildings are always without flaw—total statements, self-sufficient works of art.

Geniuses are either Venerable Giants surrounded by devout disciples or crew-cut, bow-tied Boy Wonders of forty. Both types are very helpful to critics. Both types make good copy. It might be noted in passing that writers of "genius copy" are 1) ecstatic acolytes, or 2) cynical publicists.

CRITICISM-BY-ROUND-TABLE-PROPHETS

Polar opposite to the Accolade-To-Genius Critic is the We-Must-Have-An-Anonymous-Architecture spokesman whose natural habitat is the Round Table discussion platform. Exuberant and eloquent by nature, advocates of Anonymity are apt to call for COLLECTIVE TEAMS OF ARCHITECTS, DESIGNERS, and ARTISTS to SINK THEIR ROOTS AMONG THE PEOPLE.

We-Must-Have-An-Anonymous-Architecture prophets can be detected by such sounds as, "We must bring industrial anonymity to the esthetic level of medieval anonymity. Architecture becomes great when the individual designer and craftsman loses his identity in the common effort. The best products of the Machine Age bear no single imprint, and neither must the Machine Age house. Besides, what about African art?".

We-Must-Have-An-Anonymous-Architecture critics prefer to have their names placed prominently on the program.

ARCHITECTURAL-SCIENCE-FICTION-CRITICISM

This school can be identified by the heady concoction of evangelical fervor, nineteenth century Utopianism, and twenty-second century technology. It is Utopian in the assumption that inner man can be changed for the better by placing outer man in a plastic ellipsoid. It is nineteenth century in the belief that technology moves us ever onwards and upwards.

The science fiction aspect is clearly seen in visions of glistening spheroids and ovoids spread before the homeward-bound, helicopter-borne electronic computer operator. Once inside his all-in-one-piece ejection-molded retreat he can, if he likes, hose down his cornerless, washable plastic interior. An additional side benefit is that the house weighs only 13 pounds.

OUR-WAY-OF-LIFE-CRITICISM

Our-Way-of-Life-Criticism revolves around the idea that NATIVE ARCHITECTURE must spring from NATIVE SOIL. It speaks in behalf of NATIVE MODERN—human, true, honest, valid because it is indigenous. The *bête noire* of Our-Way-of-Life-Criticism is FOREIGN MODERN — skimpy, deprived, impoverished, stemming, as it does, from enervated cultures alien to our virile, fecund society.

Our-Way-of-Life-Criticism has a recognizable patter, "This warm, gracious, friendly house, serene, poised, dignified under its canopy of native pitched roof fearless in its adherence to Native Traditions, harmoniously furnished in rare Sung ebony and modern old New England birch, previsions the NEW LOOK that is the NEXT US."

Native Modernists transgress on the domain of the Science Fiction Space Cadets by assertions that the GOLDEN AGE IS HERE. All we have to do to enter this millenium is make sure Modern is Native. The reader is buoyed by allusions to the Frontier coupled with eulogies to the Golden Age of the Deep Freeze. There are goggle-eyed references to the NEW ELEGANCE OF OUR TABLE SETTINGS, NEW CREATIVITY OF OUR COOKING, all under the aegis of Native Modern Architecture.

Our-Way-of-Life-Criticism suffer from the nervous habit of glancing nervously around the room to see if their hosts have been corrupted by FOREIGN DESIGN.

BUILD-FOR-THE-WHOLE-MAN-CRITICISM

This group closely resembles, and may easily be confused with, Our-Way-of-Life-Criticism. Both claim squatter's rights to such architectural verities as PROVISION FOR THE FULL HUMAN PERSONALITY and INTERIORS FOR THE INTERIOR LIFE. Consequently, a certain amount of encroachment can be expected.

However, Build-For-the-Whole-Man critics eschew the regional idosyncrasies of Native Modern. They prefer the grand abstractions: "A Humanist Architecture to shelter the spirit of Man from the onslaughts of the Machine Age. We must provide Modern Man with the spiritual grace, harmony, security, integrity provided Medieval Man in the walled town. We must bend technics to human purposes, or be automated."

Once readers grasp the nub of Build-for-the-Whole-Man Criticism, they agree. So does everyone else. If the drafting room could be floated on Cloud 9, our problems would disappear.

Build-for-the-Whole-Man criticism can be spotted by references to architecture or earlier, less-complicated, "organically-integrated" times. WE NEED TO RETURN TO HUMAN VALUES is the recurrent motif. LET US GO BACK TO is the thematic counterpoint. The reader is warned to see if ways of effectutating the grand abstractions are indicated. If not, beware of the narcotizing power of Build-for-the-Whole-Man rhetoric.

HOSANNAS-TO-PURITY-CRITICISM

Here rhetoric flourishes under hothouse conditions of self-bemusement. The idea of this school is to surround us with virginally-pure, esthetically-uncontaminated, complete-unto-themselves modern buildings. This Elysium of Architecture is within our grasp.

Hosanna-to-Purity critics extol the virtues of FUNCTIONAL ESTHETICS, CLEAN LINES, INTERPENETRATION OF OUTER SPACE. There is a great to-do about DESIGN INTEGRITY down to the last piece of flatware in the kitchen cabinets.

The arch rivals of Hosanna-to-Purity critics are painters and sculptors eager to paint ceilings and place sculpture on walls, thereby smirching the immaculate purity of the building. Part and parcel of the credo is the slogan ARCHITECTURE IS THE ONLY COMPLETE ART FORM. For Hosanna-to-Purity critics, architecture is not only the most significant of the arts, it now effaces painting and sculpture. More sophisticated Hosanna-to-Purity critics acknowledge (reluctantly) the contributions of Cubism, Mondrian, de Stijl, Kandinsky, Brancusi, Calder etc. But in their creed architecture has sifted out the best of these artists, who properly belong in museums as curiosities. Research indicates this patter rarely succumbed to outside the clan, and there most avidly by starry-eyed students.

Hosanna-to-Purity architects, it might be noted, fastidiously avoid the preferential quirks of the client.

POSTSCRIPT

At best this *Pocket Guide to Architectural Criticism* skims the surface of the tons

(Continued on page 248)

This residence for a young, newly married couple is built on a site 30' x 80'.

OUSE BY KILLINGSWORTH-BRADY-SMITH

PHOTOGRAPHS BY MARVIN RAND

KILLINGSWORTH - BRADY - SMITH

Privacy was the prime consideration of the planning since the small site is dominated by a large old two-story apartment on one side and a story and one-half house on the other. To provide separation from these buildings 18'-0" Redwood walls were set at the 3'-0" side yard lines. Within these walls the block of the house was developed behind a sheltered garden and reflecting pool. The two faces of the house are of glass with one facing the reflecting pool area and the other a glimpse of the bay and an intimate garden.

The living area is two stories in height with the bedrooms enjoying the view through the upper portion without lack of privacy. Kitchen cabinets are designed as furniture and will eventually extend into the living area for storage and T.V. space. The area above the carport and columns at the entrance will be developed in the future as a master suite with access from a stairway located at the platform in the reflecting pool.

The building is of post and beam with shear being taken in moment connections on the all glass walls. Shear panel at the carport supports the two sheltering walls with the beams as struts. Floor is of concrete with perimeter forced air heating system. Colors are keyed to the eucalyptus gold stain of the redwood side walls with dominance of white and tiny accents of brilliant orange and yellow. Area of house—1344 Sq. Ft.

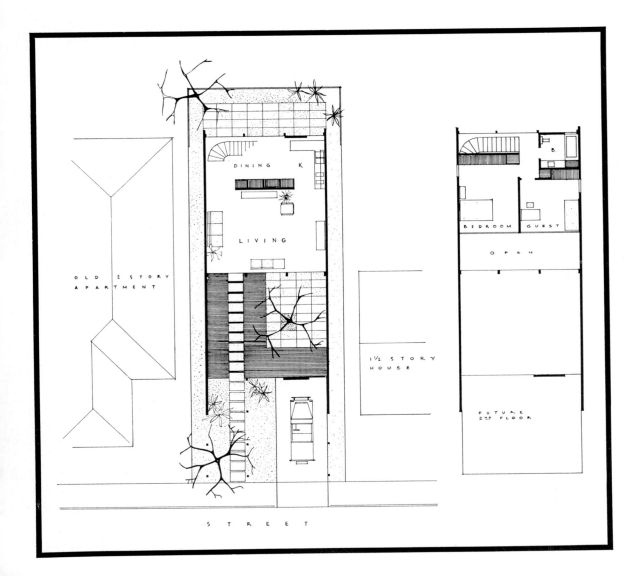

INTERIORS
JOHN NICHOLSON OF FRANK BROS.

ONE OF FIVE HONOR AWARDS IN THE RECENT SOUTHERN CALIFORNIA CHAPTER A.I.A. HONOR AWARDS PROGRAM

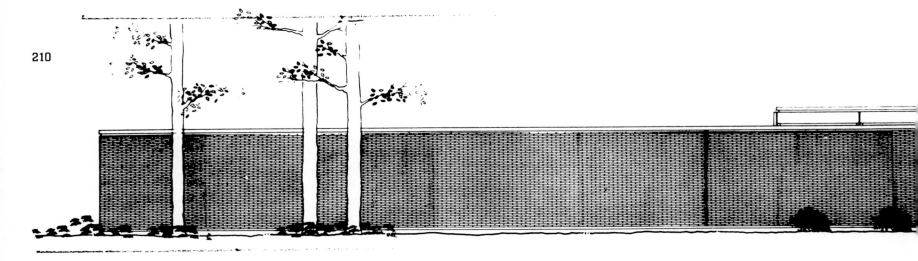

URBAN COURT HOUSE

The plans are for this small house to be situated in Chicago, Illinois on the northwest corner of a quiet residential area. This allows the private bedroom court to have north orientation, a factor that was influenced by the location of the studio. In addition, the living areas, both inside and out have south orientation, screened from the parking space and alley. Main access to the house is from the longitudinal street through the eight-foot high masonry wall into a 7'-0" x 21'-0" entry looking immediately out to a reflecting pool. A storage and plumbing core screens the bedrooms from the pool. The living-dining area is 35'-0" x 21'-0" with access to the living court and in view of the reflecting pool. It is divided by a circular steel stair to the lower level children's play room. The kitchen is the control area having direct access to the dining, service door, and through circulation for outdoor entertaining to either court. It also permits the mistress of the house a direct view to the entry.

The house proper is of steel construction. There are 9 bays 7'-0" x 35'-0" with the spanning

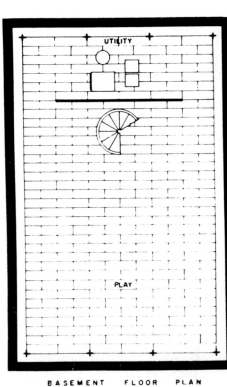

BASEMENT FLOOR PLAN

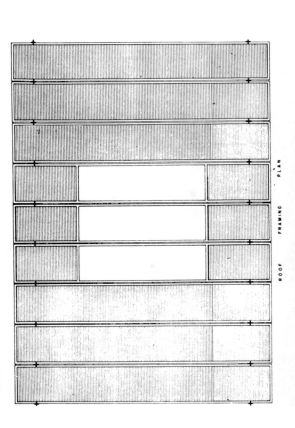

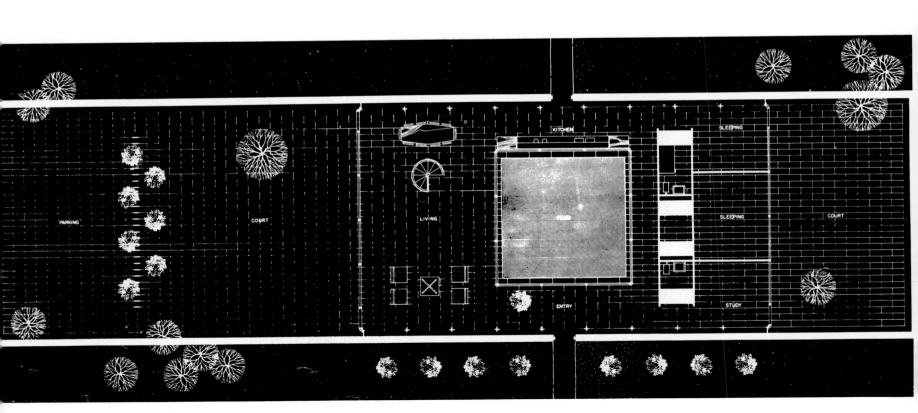

elements overhanging the supports 3'-6" in either direction. Each bay (see roof framing plan) is composed of a shop-welded panel of 12" channels supporting the decking above. These panels are in turn supported by 8" steel cruciform section, the longitudinal webs of which are cut to receive the channels. A rigid frame is thus achieved. The masonry court walls are structurally free from the loads of the house. Glass walls are of shop-welded bar stock construction. The paving (inside and out) is granite in a grid as shown on enclosure. The bedroom plumbing and storage core is paneled with Brazilian rosewood, sections of which act as concealed doors to the toilets and master bedroom.

The enclosed ground floor area consists of 1764 sq. ft. with a basement area of 735 sq. ft. The bedroom court is 735 sq. ft. and the living court 1225 sq. ft. Economy is dictated by the simplicity of construction, combined with many of the structural elements fabricated in the shop, reducing field work to a minimum.

BY STANLEY TIGERMAN, ARCHITECT

Constantino Nivola

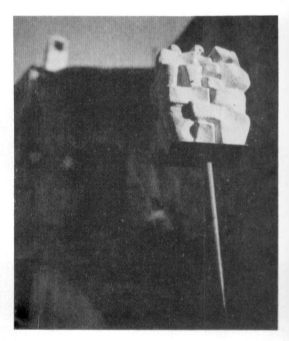

Many sculptors have dreamed of adorning an entire town with the work of their hands, but in recent times very few have realized their dreams.

Constantino Nivola, however, has managed it. A short time ago, Nivola returned to Orani, the small mountain town in Sardinia where he was born, to create a monument for his mother.

In the open, sheltered by the mountains, Nivola built the low-lying concrete sculptures, placing two bronze portraits on poles (as in the ancient Sardinian nuraghe figures) beside them.

e then planted grain seeds which will soon be long, flowing tide nearly concealing the monument. This poetic way of animating his sculpture as inspired by Nivola's memory of his mother. "My mother never accepted being married to an rtisan. She was from farmer stock and she lways wanted a corner to hide things in, like rain for the winter. Here, she gets the grain."

Nivola next got himself assistants—his brothrs who, like him, are trained stone masons—nd decorated the front of the Orani church ith grafitti. Finally, he staged an exhibition of

his sand and concrete sculptures in the streets of Orani. As in the monument, the sculptures were mounted on long poles, like lanterns, and were placed between the cobbles of the streets, standing against the warm, pale walls of the houses like sentinels. His people were puzzled but respectful. They brought wine and made a feast and milled about the streets of Orani examining the "work" of Nivola's hand. A few ventured to ask what the sculptures represented and, Nivola reports, they were satisfied when he asked, in return, if they could explain the mystery of the Trinity.—DORE ASHTON.

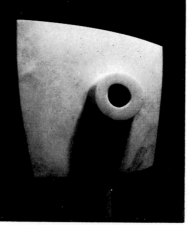

RECURRENT BIRD: GREEK MARBLE

ILLUSTRATIONS FROM A RECENT EXHIBITION AT THE STABLE GALLERY, NEW YORK

CROSS FORM DEVELOPMENT: GREEK MARBLE

BIRD E, SQUARE BIRD: GREEK MARBLE

ISAMU NOGUCHI

WOMAN: IRON

BIRD B, COLLATERAL STUDY OF BIRD ELEMENT FOR LEVER HOUSE: GREEK MARBLE

DORE ASHTON

BELL IMAGE: BELL BRONZE

TETSOBIN: IRON

"Probably Mr. Noguchi's fate will be decided by his sculpture," prophesied critic Henry Mc-Bride twenty-seven years ago. Noguchi's fate, which indeed hung in the balance for many years, and drew him off into an astonishing number of secondary adventures, has at last been decisively revealed. Or so it seemed in a recent exhibition of his sculptures at the Stable Gallery. For, in this show, Noguchi demonstrated that the years of wandering, of divagations, of a search for himself have only served to bring him back to what was his earliest passion: the making of sculpture for its own sake.

Of course, Noguchi still speaks of "integration" and he still seeks to use his sculptural gifts for the creation of overall environment, but his basic strength now appears to have been channeled into the individual work of art. Even a section in the exhibition called "Toward Collaboration" was devoted to marbles that fundamentally stand independent of a controlled, architectural situation.

Fortified by travel, and by varied experiments with paper, wood, terra-cotta, sheet-metal; and by the lessons learned in landscape gardening, set-designing, furniture designing, playground planning; and by his forty years of the working sculptor's life, Noguchi has allowed himself to turn back. Submerged, purist influences from his youth have reappeared.

That is not curious. Noguchi is now in his mid-fifties and it is not rare for a mature artist to gather up his own past in order to arrive at last at a confident style. The early training he received, first as apprentice to Gutzon Borglum, gave him the necessary technical orientation.

By the time Noguchi was twenty-two, he was an accomplished academic sculptor beloved by the National Sculpture Society.

His first esthetic shock occurred around 1925 when he saw an exhibition of Brancusi's sculptures at the Brummer Gallery in New York. As he has said, it was the first time he understood that there was "something else" beside bronze portrait busts in the sculpture universe. One year later he arrived in Paris. His first evening proved the lucky side of his nature. He was found and entertained by the famous courtesan and friend of artists, Kiki. The following day, his luck held out. He made his way to Brancusi's studio, was received cordially and became Brancusi's assistant. He cleaned the studio, polished the sculptures and helped work on the bases for Brancusi's sculpture for two years. That experience above all is what emerges in his newest work. The purity of Brancusi's form is expressly remembered. Variations on Brancusi's Bird and Column, as Noguchi says in his catalogue, are his tribute to the master.

Other tributes in the show are to Greece and Japan. Noguchi has recently worked in both places. Many of the marbles were executed in Greece and all of the bronze castings were made in Japan. Noguchi's deference to ancient Greece also has an early source: his mother was an unorthodox American woman who brought him up on Greek myths. Apollo rather than Christ was the recognized god in the boy's household.

Greece had an extremely salutary effect on Noguchi. In the suave, elegantly rounded pieces based on bird or human shapes, Noguchi has found the equilibrium toward which he has worked for many years. His witty adaptations of his memories both of Brancusi and of ancient Greek marble sculptures have a certainty, a frank simplicity that his earlier work frequently lacked.

I speak particularly of pieces like "Bird E" with its sensitive curving walls, its dramatic circular hole, and its perfectly poised weight. This piece rests on a delicately balanced diagonal axis. It lies on the floor on two crossed wooden bars. The idea of the grounded bird is played against the space which is his natural element by means of the asymmetric hole piercing the marble. "Bird D" again is on a similar motif, only this time, the marble is slender, imperceptibly curved, and the hole is protrusive, funneling space. Here, Noguchi uses a slender, polished pole of wood for support, as he does in many of his sculptures. He always says that he wants to get sculpture away from pedestals, but his most lyrical, most impressive carvings always benefit from their pedestals no matter how unobtrusive the round wood posts are. (Perhaps he doesn't consider them pedestals.)

There are, naturally, a number of pieces that require no separate support and seem to develop directly from foot level. This is the case with some of the bird forms, particularly "Bird B", one of the "collateral studies for Lever House." Here, the stalk supporting the beaked or horned bird-head broadens as it grows up to the head, and relates to the large proboscis (phallic, as are many of Noguchi's allusions).

Noguchi's wit which is sometimes broad and humorous, sometimes subtle and serious, is seen in a superb piece, "Woman and Child." The two figures are girdled by a squared marble form, but they nevertheless swing out into space with tremendous life-lust. Though the forms are tongue-like in their outward curving, the suggestion of the theme is explicit.

Other witty pieces include a take-off on ancient Greek drapery: a fragment of tubular folds cocked slightly to one side; a cast-iron horned pot titled "Who Knows?" since it is a pot without an opening (the horns are a reminder of Noguchi's one-time devotion to surrealism, while the pot itself recalls his attentive study of Haniwa shapes), and a streamlined, square-cut green marble piece called "Man With Seat." There are several angular pieces, by the way, but Noguchi is never entirely comfortable with the severity of the right-angle esthetic and these pieces are not nearly as impressive as those in which he allows his feeling for curving shape to dominate.

Among the metal castings was one outstanding study of a torso called "Woman" in which both the feeling for Greek drapery, with its wetly clinging grace, and the feeling for solid form typical of ancient Japanese sculpture are expressed. This piece is an inspired sculpture by any standards—entirely personal, and expressive to a high degree.

Noguchi has always conceived of sculpture as solid form deploying light. But sometimes he has tried to work with light and shadow literally, as he did when he adjusted lighting within his constructions. This exhibition, with its stress on the solid form modeled and carved to control the light around it, indicates Noguchi's true forte, which is to carve hard materials so that they at once deflect light and absorb it; displace space and absorb it; expand in their sinuous profiles and close in on themselves in their inner structure. He is one of the very few major sculptors we have.

Without question our greatest social disgrace of many years has been the so-called zoot suit riots. Our police department was only exceeded by our press in the shocking competition for first place as principal accessories to the crime. Back of the sanction which they extended to the mobs that roamed our streets lay the emotionally deep-seated sanction of a large proportion of our citizens.

The riots had their origin in many different sources. It is an error of simplification to attempt to assign them to a single cause or even two or three. But they were possible for only one reason, and that is that there is a sanction in public prejudice, however falsely grounded, for this lawless behavior. The power of the law is great enough to prevent such outbreaks. In fact, the physical force of the police is not even necessary in our society in such situations. No mobs form any more unless they feel that they have back of them a justification which is shared by a large part of the community.

The human race in its long, savage history has not lost any of its savage impulses, but it has acquired a system of customs, laws, and standards. This system serves to curb savagery except when the mob can find a means of justifying its unleashed violence in that very ground of established beliefs and customs. What I mean to say is that there are certain beliefs and customs current among us which permitted the savage aggressions of a group of our people to express themselves with the assurance that while they were stripping zoot suiters of their pants and beating them into insensibility they were acting in accordance with certain ideas of the right thing to do. They, in fact, conceived of themselves as nobly preserving certain fundamental principles.

I therefore submit that if we do not wish to see a continuation and an increase of similar riots we must systematically remove the sanctions in our social beliefs upon which these actions depend. It is easier to name these sanctions than it is to correct them, but it is a good first step. They are: first, the myth of racial difference; second, the well-nurtured error of the superiority of some races over others; and third, the common folklore that criminal behavior is an hereditary and racial trait. All three of these are scientific falsehoods.

Biologists have only one specific classification for all mankind, *homo sapiens*. Anthropologists have not been able to find any basis for setting up separate classifications of different peoples based upon physiological measurements or mental tests. Eugenists have not been able to prove the transmissal through physical characteristics of any criminal traits; the latest conclusions are that criminal behavior is social behavior entirely conditioned by the social and economic conditions of the individual.

To disprove these deep-seated myths scientifically is not to eradicate them socially. They have an old, old tradition. They have been common currency for centuries, whereas the scientific truths I have cited are very recent. The job of erasing them is a big one, but not nearly as big as the one of correcting the damage they can cause. They are prevalent not only among the ignorant but are accepted as gospel among our educators, judges, legislators, and police officials. They are the stock in trade of certain editors and they are the very rock upon which our social uppercrust is founded. If these people believe in racial difference, racial superiority, and criminal racial inheritance, why wouldn't our soldiers and sailors? And if the people who make up our mobs march out to batter heads and kill Negroes and Mexicans feel that they are justified by the beliefs of these leading citizens who share them, then zoot suit riots are a wonderful way to satisfy aggressions and uphold a great set of principles at the same time.

Our fundamental problem, then, is to wipe out these underlying premises, to cut the ground of social sanction and justification out from under the feet of those who practice race violence.

It means conducting a systematic campaign of public education in our schools, our press, and our movies. It means lectures and instruction by scientists in the true scientific facts of "race," and it means calling the turn whenever a police inspector reports that the zoot suiters are "of racially criminal inheritance."

It may be hoping for a miracle to expect that our city council and the mayor could achieve such enlightenment, but we should make the effort to bring the facts even to them. Folk beliefs are hard to kill, but we have before us the examples of vaccination, public sanitation, and the syphilis campaigns. It should be possible to achieve as much in the realm of social epidemics.

(July 1943)

September 13, 1944, Arnold Schoenberg will be seventy years old. *Modern Music*, that fitful adolescent whose turns and quirks alarmed the 1910s and the 1920s, is itself respectably forty-four years old. Amateurs of the future, hearing the greater works of Arnold Schoenberg, will turn to us with envy: this is how the men of our time thought in music. It will be accepted as fact the genius of Schoenberg participates and has major importance in the best work of his contemporaries. Their music will not be fully understood without knowledge of his music. The music that will proceed from theirs, the music of the second half of the Twentieth Century, will recognized and accept his inalienable authority.

Schoenberg's genius has been the ability to re-think music within the emotional intensity and philosophic chaos of his own creative lifetime. In the *Harmonybook*, written in 1912, he drew together out of the past a texture of theoretical method which could be used; by 1921 this texture had evolved the first essentially new Twentieth Century strict form. The *Harmonybook* is an assemblage of creative possibilities; the *twelve-tone technic* is a determinative limit and definition of these creative possibilities in terms of usage. These two compensating developments provide the simple framework of his personal growth, the transition, and expansion of his art.

He began as a post-romantic in a dream-world of German neo-impressionism. Values had become indefinite, with psychological evidence replacing form. Instead of the more obvious external representation of events there was a showing forth of the institutional process. Strict form, that positive reaction to prepared intelligence by which intuition, being shaped, produces vital freshness, had been destroyed by the representative habit; it groped for method. There was need of new specifically musical means. In this unreal world appeared the string sextet *Transfigured Night*, now more widely known in arrangement for string orchestra, substituting for the heroic attitude of the larger Germanic music of the Nineteenth Century the fairy-tale pathos of the German song. At the age of 26 Schoenberg had mastered and had begun to outgrow the world of surfaces in which Debussy spent his lifetime. Using the most elaborate contemporary idiom he wrote the symphonic poem *Pelleas and Melisande*, his first work for large orchestra, and with the addition of voice began the giant cycle of the *Gurre Songs*. The evolution of this work over a period of ten years brought him from emotionally decadent exuberance into full maturity, able to control the largest vocal and symphonic combinations of Wagner and Mahler, though not yet upon their level of constructive genius. With this new maturity he began in 1909 the writing of the first *Chambersymphony* and in 1910 the *Second String Quartet*.

The first *Chambersymphony* differs from the earlier large compositions by drastic economy of means, using for example only seventeen instruments. A landmark in music, it marks the turn from Nineteenth Century gigantism to Twentieth Century strictness and internal condensation. Reacting against post-Wagnerian extravagance it confines itself strictly to its own specific musical content. Each instrument serves a constructive purpose and is fully developed within its peculiar limitations; it is never brought in merely to enlarge the tonal means. This music is not neoclassical; in no way does it imitate the idiom of Haydn or of Bach. In comparison with the earlier *First String Quartet* the *Second* asserts the integrative transformation of emotional content into emotional form.

Intense emotion is the dynamic rootwork of Schoenberg's art. The *Harmonybook*, though an invaluable lexicon, is first of all an emotional paean to music as an art. Emotion, which might have been his downfall, he chose instead to set up as a bulwark against philosophic chaos. Emotion being intuitional must be controlled by intelligence before it can become form. Stravinsky, by applying a series of external rhythmic patterns, achieved the first success. The method was external and remained so throughout its many progressively weaker imitations. The result was a return to Eighteenth Century formal patterns and neoclassicism. Schoenberg, avoiding the more obvious appearances of success, thrust his roots still more deeply underground. To support and control the native intensity of his emotion he began the erection of a new method of tight formal counterpoint. With the writing of the *Five Orchestral Pieces* and the *Six Short Piano Pieces* he revolutionized the structural basis of his art. Being implicit in the music this art could no longer be represented apart from the music in any other terms. The art was too vital with emotion to become merely abstract. It depended upon noth-

ing, neither upon the Nineteenth Century heroic attitude nor upon Twentieth Century drive. Its rhythm was not applied; it was endemic. The counterpoint was not of the schools; it had become the necessary organization of the music. Instead of the motif, the contra-puntal germ was continuously varied. The way was clear that would produce the twelve-tone technic.

During the time when Schoenberg was developing the final principles of this technic he composed what had been probably the most debated of his mature masterpieces, the cycle of songs for voice and small chamber group called *Pierrot Lunaire*. The vocal part of this work uses a practice invented by Schoenberg, called in the German *Sprechstimme*, first tried in one section of the *Gurre Songs*. It is a manner of spoken song lacking fixed intervals, the voice following within its speaking range the musical intervals formally indicated by the notes. In *Pierrot Lunaire* the voice, becoming involved with the dynamic and almost hysterical emotional of the words, reaches a pitch of nervous excitement which may embarrass listeners accustomed, in spite of Tchaikovsky, to expecting a certain tactful restraint in formal music. The instruments are driven to an extreme of virtuosity in tone-production. Schoenberg has never gone backward in the demands he customarily makes upon performers.

The twelve-tone technic is not a formula; it is instead a completely self-contained classical system of limitations in the handling of a single theme by every contrapuntal means. In its full development, this technic requires a theme derived out of some melodic arrangement of the octave using the entire twelve tones, no tone being repeated except in direct succession. The time intervals of the thematic melody, as in Bach, set up and counter-point the melodic rhythm. It is not necessary to use all of the twelve tones, but it is necessary that whatever tones are used should be equal in significance without being related to any key-harmonic system. To take the place of key-harmony the twelve-tone technic expects that any significant arrangement of the tones will produce by relationship an individual harmonic system. This audible unity will persist throughout all contrapuntal variants. Those who have learned to hear this music agree that this is fact. Detractors of the twelve-tone technic, as well as many of its earlier

apologists, united in calling it *atonal*. Atonal music does exist, percussion music for instance, as well as a good deal of writing merely experimental in its anti-classical dislike of fixed harmonic relationships. In twelve-tone music by the choice of the original tone-pattern of relationships and by adherence to these relationships the harmony is fixed. Each twelve-tone theme provides its separate and original harmonic basis.

To avoid any audible illusion of key-harmony no tone in any group of twelve may be sounded twice, but any single tone may be indefinitely sustained or repeated. The consequent nervous flickering of repeated tones rapidly sounded on various levels imparts a horizontal impetus unlike anything previously found in European music except the Beethoven *Great Fugue* and the *Fugue…the Diabelli Variations*. Bach and other earlier keyboard composers had experimented with this as genre but had never expanded the use of it to such…. The dynamic effect is to replace the slow underlying impulse customary in European and especially Germanic music with a high-speed pulsation energized and sustained by the use of the repeated tones. Across these horizontal lines of movement leaping thematic figures in wide intervals sharply outline a vertical texture of powerful resistance. Through this vast web of contrasting architectonic energies creep slow chromatic melodies, bursting into arabesques of passionate expressiveness. Using these means in such compositions as the *Third* and *Fourth String Quartets* and the *Suite* for clarinets, string trio, and piano, Schoenberg creates music of a size, integrative complexity, emo-tional force, and architectonic self-sufficiency unmatched since the last quartets of Beethoven.

The first compositions strictly within the contrapuntal limitations of the twelve-tone technic are a *Serenade* for chamber group containing guitar and mandolin and the *Dance Suite* for piano. This was for the composer a period of unusual creative strain in the midst of a world which itself seemed to have lost all fixed relationships. Something of this bitterness entered into Schoenberg's attitude. To clear a way for the understanding of such music and if possible establish a renewed appreciation of esthetic values Schoenberg and his friends founded in November, 1918 in Vienna a *Society for Private Musical Performances*. Newspaper critics were barred from attending; noisy response to the performance was forbidden; and members pledged themselves to give no public report of what happened during the meetings.

In October, 1933, an exile from his own country, Schoenberg came to the United States, settling during 1934 in Hollywood. Despite many problems of readjustment, the change of spiritual climate has been good for him. In Hollywood he wrote first a *Suite* for string orchestra, which Otto Klemperer shortly afterwards conducted in Los Angeles and in New York. This was followed by the mellow richness of his *Fourth String Quartet*, first performed by the Kolisch Quartet as the climax of a cycle during which his four quartets were played in company with the four major Beethoven quartets of the last period. Since then he has been composing with perhaps somewhat more freedom than formerly, using not only the twelve-tone technic but also accepted methods of the past. Some of these works have already been performed, notably the *Second Chamber Symphony*, orchestrated and completed from sketches originally conceived in 1906, the *Violin Concerto* and the recent *Piano Concerto*. Wide hearing of these works presumably must wait the appearance of a new generation of players accustomed to mastering the technical difficulties of this music, unafraid not merely to perform but to love and cherish the tough resistant texture that underlies the intimate emotional cosmos of his art. Such ability and the demand for fresh emotional experience that will awaken such ability must depend upon long knowledge and profoundly personal understanding of what this music as music means to those who have lived with it.

For the last several years Schoenberg has been teaching composition at the University of California in Los Angeles. This year he retired. His classes have had a critical influence upon the writing of American music. His students rapidly become aware that Schoenberg is not pleased by superficial imitation of his style or ignorant attempts to manipulate the twelve-tone technic. His classes are determinedly classical, depending upon thorough harmonic training and detailed analysis. Only advanced students who come to it by artistic necessity may "write like Schoenberg." He has continued composing: among his most recent compositions are *Variations for Organ*, an *Ode to Napoleon* on a text by Byron, and *Theme and Variations for Wind Band*. Some of his earlier pupils have

become world renowned, notably the late Alban Berg, whose last composition, a *Concerto for Violin and Orchestra*, uses the twelve-tone technic in a somewhat more romantic idiom than that of Schoenberg; and Anton von Webern, whose curiously reticent music is almost entirely unknown in this country. Among his more recent private pupils was the beloved American composer George Gershwin. Pursuing their common hobby Gershwin and Schoenberg each painted the other's portrait. In a brief article for a Gershwin memorial volume Schoenberg sets forth his definition of the composer: "Serious or not, he is a composer—that is a man who lives in music and expresses everything, serious or not, sound or superficial, by means of music, because it is his native language…An artist is to me like an apple tree: When his time comes, whether he wants it or not, he bursts into bloom and starts to produce apples. And as an apple tree neither knows nor asks about the value experts of the market will attribute to its product, so a real composer does not ask whether his products will please the experts of serious arts. He only feels he has to say something; and says it."

In honor of Schoenberg's seventieth anniversary Evenings on the Roof will devote a portion of its next chamber music season to the performance of his music.

(August 1944)

CHARLES IVES
Peter Yates

Seventy years ago this month Charles Ives was born in Danbury, Connecticut. His father, a bandmaster and music teacher, like many Americans of his time was also an experimentalist, whose researches into harmony, rhythm, percussion, chord structure, polytonality, atonality, and acoustical perspective transmitted to his son not only the urge but the ability to compose music in non-traditional ways. But the time Charles Ives went to college he had become something more than a well educated young musician. At Yale he absorbed during four years the solid training and massive technique of Horatio Parker, without being diverted from his own creative interests. There was not and has been no greater American teacher of music than Horatio Parker; Ives was

spared the frustration of trying to drive his original ideas through the head of a European pedant or an American academicist. The necessity of going into business did not deter Ives from carrying out his musical purpose. Business offered freedom: in a country not yet ripe for its own art he would not rely for a living on music. As thorough a businessman as a musician, like many successful contemporaries an idealist in a culture that tried to be hardbitten, he grounded his success upon trust in human beings. At the time of his retirement his insurance consulting firm had become the largest of its sort in the United States. Like his great predecessors, Emerson, Melville, and Whitman, he learned to know mankind by dealing with his fellow men on their own terms. Belief in the rightness and divinity of humankind, confirming a simple conviction of the presence of God, is the tap-root of his mind. In a world becoming rapidly cynical because disillusioned he based his strength upon experienced certainties: the spirit of New England hymns, the directness of American speech, the culture of his small-town boyhood, the organic character of the American land. Withdrawing from these into the solitude of his own thought, he produced art in their image, art that was their language.

Music comes back to the people by way of professionals and dilettantes, accustomed to foreign idioms, living in the past, accepting as new images of other days. A nation scarcely aware of Whitman, blind to Melville's genius, could not easily accept the work of Ives. Surprising that Ives himself could find his way in such an environment. He composed in silence, refused to push his work and remained unheard. His many contributions to the support of fellow musicians are well known but unrecorded. Unlike other great radical composers of his time he has never made himself the center of an inspired circle able to procure the necessary performances of his music. Today the first reaction of trained musicians is usually that his music is incorrectly written. With this excuse, supplemented by the forgiving acknowledgement that it might have been better, if Ives could have had the opportunity to hear it played, professional musicians usually drop the subject. The music, when heard, exposes the frailty of such presumptions. Only during the last few years has the greatest music of Beethoven and Bach, the *Great Fugue*, the *Diabelli Variations*, the *Musical Offering*, the *Art of Fugue*, music of Ives' size, been accepted by musicians as suitable for performance.

Ives is not theoretical. The mark of his music is its lack of predetermined attitudes. Like all supremely great artists who spring from a new culture not yet dominated by its own creative past, he is neither classic nor romantic. His roots spring from fresh soil that will not nourish even the most gifted of dilettantes. To the professors of harmonic analysis his compositional technique is enigmatic. His obvious interest in living subject-matter confounds the priests and devotee of abstract music. The sufficiency of the American scene for all his purposes makes him a provincial in the eyes of the expatriates.

Among American artists only the very greatest have dared not to go abroad. The vulgarity, the mass, the confusion of our cities, the unfilled vastness of our land drive the expatriates to seek safety in precise forms and fixed traditions among persons who speak an international language. The technical excesses of Walt Whitman and artistic intransigence of Frank Lloyd Wright, echoing our folk fanatics, our demagogues, our quacks, our revivalists, our small-town editors, our one-track minds, are uncongenial to the expatriates. It is the character of our nationhood the dilettante cannot admit. He is living still in Syracuse, a colony of Greece.

In the first place, for the American mere size is form. It should be useful size: no area, no function should be wasted. Only in museums, memorials, and public buildings, remembering past ties with other lands, does the American accept and monumentalize vast space. In the second place, the great American, slugger, pioneer, technician, remains naive. Right or wrong he believes in being what he is, in saying what he thinks. That is the secret of our national genius, expressed in the violent antagonisms of our successful democratic process. In the third place, because he is naive, the thorough American is an amateur for keeps, untroubled by sophisticated ennui or professional world-weariness. He plays to win; when he is interfered with he fights; to disagree with the umpire is his definition of freedom. In a nation of such individuals the whole country pitches in to straighten out the greatest individualist—*Ahab* against the *Isaiah* of Frank Lloyd Wright. An artist in America must be rugged; he must be large; he expresses himself often with violence; he has the absolute assurance of his personal rightness. Driven in upon himself he is

either frustrated by misunderstanding and opposition or made great by defiance. The enforced solitude in which he must expect to pass the best part of his life cultivates in him an acute sensibility to his environment. He expands not by impressions but with an organic awareness of the significance of real events. Common objects and occurrences, rounded by actuality, are enlarged by the isolated artist's acute perception within continental space.

So in the *Fourth Violin Sonata (Children's Day at the Camp Meeting)*, Ives remembers his childhood, and one hears the plop and echo of a stone flung in the creek. In *Fourth of July* from the *First Set* for orchestra he recalls the parade and how the bands in front and behind played different times. The *Fugue on Greenland's Icy Mountains* from the *Fourth Symphony* contains the baritone who ornamented the congregational hymns with overtones. These by humor convey the enduring present, being included by that necessity, like the country band and birdsongs in Beethoven's *Pastorale Symphony* or *Ach du lieber Augustin!* in Schoenberg's *Second Quartet*. Ives thinks of the loud city and of the sudden end of tiny *Ann Street*; seeing his two nieces in the garden he preserves the experience in *Two Little Flowers* with the naivety of a photograph. Like Joyce he hears the roar of people in the street and calls it God: but it is the striving, determination, and assured rhetoric of *The Masses*. Reading he finds and sets to music in two sentences the meaning of *Tolerance*; hearth and home reverence. For lines from *Paradise Lost* he projects into music the stillness of the Garden (*Evening*). To the drums and syncopated tambourines, the shouted appeals of a Salvation Army band *General William Booth Enters Heaven*; the everlasting march of lost souls following the Evangelist. Sophistication falls away from us, swept with that unwashed parade before the cleansing miracle of Jesus.

These are the songs of Ives, great human utterances, and lighter songs balanced between humor and pathos; a cowboy song, *Charley Rutledge*; a boy's tale of his pa, *The Greatest Man*; songs that participate in motion like *The Swimmers*—Radiana Pazmor said when she sang it that it was the best thing next to swimming—set to words from newspaper articles, casual poems, texts from the classics, Emerson, Keats, Longfellow, Landor, Meredith, texts of his own or written by his friends. Whatever in words

Ives felt most deeply turned into songs. Songs as direct as spirituals or hymns, dictating their own forms, each demanding a peculiar eloquence. Because Ives loved songs he found inspiration in New England hymns, in tunes of the people that are the wordlessness of songs, in forms that progress with the folk simplicity of speech. Since Dowland, Byrd, and Purcell no other composer has so completely and adequately set forth in music the native fall and fluency of English speech.

From the first his songs were his own and independent, with something of convention but no fashion. He knew the literature of the German *lied*; *Ich Grolle Nicht (I'll not complain)*, written in 1899, retains the German poem with the English. At the turn of the century he broke also with convention, reaching the full power of his eloquence between 1910 and 1915 *(General William Booth Enters Heaven, Concord Sonata, Holidays—First Orchestral Set)*. During 1920 and 1921 he revised for piano the accompaniments of many songs originally composed for symphonic orchestra and for a variety of extremely unusual character combinations (two flutes, cornet, violas, and organ; trumpets, clarinet, saxophone, piano, and four violins; four basset horns). Similar extraordinary instrumental combinations fill out his symphonic scores (a solo piano plus a pair of orchestral pianos; a zither; even a Jew's harp). *Hallowe'en* for string quartet completes itself *ad lib.*, the finale being repeated faster and faster with paired combinations of the four instruments. Ives is no stickler for exact performance. When asked how a passage should be played, he answers: play it as you see it.

The *Second Sonata* for piano (*Concord, N.H., 1840-60*) is the largest work of Ives that has reached performance. Even so conservative a critic as the late Lawrence Gilman declared without qualification that this is the most important composition American music has produced—one wonders what would have been his reaction to the symphonies. A performance of *First Set* for orchestra in 1928 won extravagant Sunday morning praise from Olin Downs. What laziness, what evasiveness, what spiritual cowardice have kept this not very difficult work out of the repertoires of our large orchestras! This is our native music; we have every right to demand that it should not be kept from performance. It should be played constantly and at once. End the regular farce of offering as American compositions the lightest, the least characteristic, the safest, the ready-made, the pastiche!

Performances of the *Concord Sonata* by John Kirkpatrick in the East and by Frances Mullen in Los Angeles have brought to many listeners a new understanding of the size and quality of American music. The sonata is in four movements, each characterizing a sage of Concord Village. The first movement (*Emerson*) was begun as a piano concerto. With the economy of structural genius Ives introduces the two main themes of the entire work in the first measures; the third principal theme, expanded out of Beethoven's first theme of the *Fifth Symphony*, immediately follows. In large sections alternately denominated *prose* and *verse*, a manner invented by Couperin for his *Preludes*, the music sets forth an abstract conception of Emerson as mind. The second movement (*Hawthorne*), a scherzo of equal proportions, suggests "wilder, fantastical adventures into the half-childlike, half-fairylike phantasmal realm," haunted by the sense of pervading sin that underlies the Hawthorne tales. One hears the little organ of a parish church, strange variations on well-known American melodies. The third movement is a tone-recreation of the Bronson Alcott household, recalling with love "the little spinet-piano on which Beth played the old Scotch airs, and played at the Fifth Symphony." The final movement, which ends in evening quietness, is a wandering with Thoreau by Walden Lake. "His meditations are interrupted only by the faint sound of the Concord bell—'tis prayer-meeting night in the village. He goes up "the pleasant hillside of pines, hickories," and moonlight to his cabin, 'with a strange liberty in nature a part of herself." I have quoted briefly from the book Ives wrote to accompany and mark the meanings of his *Concord Sonata*, not because the music needs this program, but because it is in words the peculiar idiom of Ives. In words as in music Ives is the brooding transcendental thinker and poet. This language is congenial in his mind because it is the native New England language. But it is not the whole of Ives. He is larger than this language; he broadens to more than American significance.

In successful program devoted entirely to the music of Ives' *Evenings on the Roof* has presented many of his songs, the *Concord Sonata*, and three of the four violin sonatas. The *Second Violin Sonata* and the *First Piano Sonata* are being edited for performance from the manuscripts.

The *Third Violin Sonata*, prepared for publication by Ingolf Dahl, who has played it in many performances with Sol Babitz, violinist, will appear in an early issue of *New Music*. The *Concord Sonata*, musically far in advance of its time, containing many innovations that have since become technically accepted, was composed around 1912. Ives continued composing until some time after 1925. In 1930, a sick man, he retired from business. Sickness has gradually removed him from his friends. His mind continues fiery and active. Admiration of his work has been increasing with the years. Among younger composers he is now acknowledged to be the greatest figure in American music. His wife, Harmony, named as if to express the myth that will some day enshrine his art, during recent years has spoken for Ives in correspondence with the world. A brief note from her that came last Christmas: "This is our little Methodist church where I worship—Mr. Ives would if he could. We hope you are well—thank goodness for children to be happy at Christmas." Enclosed with the note was a photograph of a small white frame New England church.

The seventieth anniversary of Charles Ives should be a national festival. It is a curiosity of our national adolescence that we should have rendered homage instead to the far-off genius of Sibelius. In honor of Ives, *Evenings on the Roof* will devote a portion of the coming season to the performance of his sonatas and his songs. America needs his music and his spirit.

(September 1944)

NOTES IN PASSING

While we are as badly confused as the next one and certainly in possession of no pipeline that leads into the innermost secret heart of the backroom of international politics, we do, within limits understand the meaning of words and we have been known to count up to ten on certain occasions. We know, for instance, that peace does not mean war and we know also that for all practical purposes black does not mean white. Therefore we know as well as we know the nose on our face that world cooperation does not mean the

cooperation of a few of the great in order to manage the rest of the little. We also know that if a peace worth a tinker's damn is to be established, it must not be dependent upon the over-lordship of an international organization which commands nothing but the kind of lip service we have been giving the ten commandments for four thousand years.

The world we are fighting for is not one in which we can any longer maintain a civilization on the basis of anybody's right hand not knowing what somebody else's left hand is doing. This business of the benign pat on the shoulder as we pick the pockets of our fellowmen must be put in the category of dirty pool, if we expect to get anywhere with world organization.

An association of nations if it is to be regarded merely as an international washing machine into which we can thoughtlessly throw our dirty linen will come to the common end of all mechanical contrivances as soon as the first little monkey wrench gets tossed into it. It sounds pretty pompous perhaps to talk about moral forces in the midst of the vast, incredible immoralities of our time, but the only hope of sensible men must be to direct a conviction so certain and so unswerving to the end of a good peace that it cannot be denied. That means that none of us as people or as nations can any longer indulge in the colossal stupidities and hypocrisies that got us into the mess in the first place. We can no longer make the excuse of ignorance—we know what wars are about and we know within reason what makes them come about. But more important, we know now and understand the means by which we can prevent war.

There are no unsurmountable complications, assuming that the majority of human beings have no desire to kill one another. War is a disease, the cure for which we have known for a long time. A large part of that cure must be on the basis of our commitment to the world as fellow members of the great congress of human beings. We can no longer indulge in hysterics when what we think of as our own honor is attacked, if we refuse to regard the honor of others a part of our own. We can no longer think of world affairs as something to be cut up and tailored to the last stitch in order to suit our own very individual tastes. If because we are big and strong we intend to make the world take our kind of medicine and like it then let us at least have the decency to stop pretending about the mantle of nobility under which we intend to cover up such a tattered and tawdry objective and for our own sakes, be prepared to take the consequences.

If, however, we honestly believe in the things for which we are letting our young men die, then there is no time to be lost in resolving the confusions and contra-dictions that now beset us into a solution that is worthy of a worthy objective.

Who among us is not utterly confused by this spectacle of allied men and tanks and guns shooting down a people for whom and with whom we are fighting a war for what we call freedom? No doubt there are a thousand ways in which this incredible situation can be explained. But within the explanation itself lies the inference that in our approach to all the problems of settlement we will bring thinking that has been conditioned by a sense of power and a sense of our own great strength. If our performance and the performance of our allies is to consist in the flexing of our muscles in order to frighten one another, then we are a far way from establishing a world that is based on any of the first principles of decency. Too many of us argue that in a realistic attitude we must be prepared to make concessions and compromises. That is only true when the intention behind those compromises and when the direction of those concessions are demon-stratively good in terms of the welfare of all people. Even then the process is sus-pect and is to be most carefully handled—after all, a hand grenade is sometimes a good and liberating thing—it all depends on where you throw it. At the moment, we are happily bloated with good intentions, but a careful examination of those intentions might be an excellent idea before some of them explode in our face. As the new world is born we must remember that all good people every-where are father to the idea and it is unbecoming of us to assume the attitude of sole parent of a thing which has been the secret wish of all mankind since it first perceived the difference between lightness and darkness.

Eventually the guy who passes around exploding cigars gets one pushed in his own face by mistake, and is sud-denly turned into a revengeful fiend because in his confused knuckle-head he is sure that the world is against him.

The cards are now being dealt for the greatest poker game in history. Let us hope that by the grace of God, and our own good sense, we are playing with an honest deck.

(January 1945)

Now we have decided that we are not to be blown to smithereens simply because there has been no reoccurrence of the catastrophe of Hiroshima. Therefore, we come sneaking out of the caverns of fear, bellowing like bull elephants, and throw ourselves merrily into a mad little game called "kicking the atom around."

The latest but of course inevitable idea is the experiment proposed and being prepared carefully by the United States Navy through which it is hoped to dis-cover the effects of atomic power when used against the battleship as a weapon of war. Personally, we will settle for the fact without the experiment. It is even money that an atomic bomb can be devised which will plain blow the hell out of any battleship or group of battleships that can be assembled anywhere in the world. The only real result can be the possible development of a method or means by which battle-wagons can be deployed in order to run best for their lives, or at least not be destroyed in too great numbers.

The amazing thing about the entire idea is that in order to settle an argument between the pros and cons within a purely military controversy, the atom and every-thing it implies can be used in order that some officers can march up to some other officers and, with the usual smart salutes, say, "I told you so." As laymen we find the whole project incredible though of course we always find the military mind a fear-some thing. It seems that in order to allay the possible suspicion of other great pow-ers, we have hit upon a beautiful solution, reluctantly but with appropriate dignity. It has been decided that representatives of other nations might be permitted to observe the proceedings at reasonably close quarters with, however, the careful provision that they not be close enough to gather any information pertaining to structures and devices, and that they will not be permitted an inkling of the great secret that we have appropriated so evi-dently as our very own.

All this despite the fact that not one major or minor world scientist denies that the only reason we possess a "working" atomic bomb rests simply upon the fact that we were able to appropriate vast amounts of material to its manufacture in an area undisturbed by war-time condi-tions. Otherwise, we are assured Germany, England, Japan, Russia, and God knows who else would have arrived inevitably at a practical solution and

would be at this moment in a position to challenge our atomic-politics with a neat thumb-nosing and a "so's your old man." Furthermore, it is agreed pretty generally that in the next five minutes, forty-eight hours, or a year at the most any one of several dominant nations will suddenly present us with the accomplished fact of their own version of atom splitting in terms of destruction. In the face of all this we continue blithely to offend human decency and provoke perfectly human suspicions, using the prime secret of the universe in an experiment frankly conducted for the purpose of what can be nothing but an implied military threat. And we top it all off with incredible stupidity and smugness, condescendingly inviting the world to watch us flex our muscles.

This is reminiscent of another activity—an echo of another device—more brutally frank perhaps, to invite a world, trembling before the possibility of war, to look at carefully contrived motion pictures of destruction calcu-lated as a warning against the futility of protest in the presence of force.

While such experiments undoubtedly will be of great informative value they should not be conducted solely for the purpose of finding out whether or not a battleship will sink, nor should they be carried out under the exclusive auspices of any purely military establishment anywhere at any time. We can accept only controlled experiments, freely agreed upon by a science bound by a global and not a national responsibility, to bring to mankind whatever good there is to be found in the use of atomic power.

It is just possible that we have not yet devised a political and social climate in which such matters can be resolved with reason and wisdom and honesty. But any-thing else is the crack of doom. We might begin with the simple realization that as a nation we do not *own* the atom by a damn-sight. God help us learn that lesson with-out catastrophe.

(February 1946)

ART IN INDUSTRY, PART I
Laslo Moholy Nagy

To design goods and architecture for mass production calls not only for engineers but also for artists. Art, the sphere of articulated intuition and feelings, is indispensable to a balanced life, indispensable to creative design.

The goal, however, is not to turn artists into designers or designers into artists; rather, to develop all the creative potentialities of the student by producing a rhythm between his individual biological capacities, the requirements of society, and the industrial milieu. We do not believe in trying to graft onto industry a re-created classical craftsman, artist, or artisan, but rather to educate a well-rounded individual who can function as an integrator of art and industry.

Technology is today as much a part of life as is metabolism. Art, science, and technology are merely parts of the sphere of the modern industrial designer, sociological, biological, and psychological elements are equally important factors. Therefore, not the designer-specialist but the man in total, with all his vitality and potentialities, is the desideratum in. Hence, although technological training must never be lost to sight, the modern designer is most successful to the extent that he functions as a healthy individual within the group rather than as a "free" artist. Intellectual integration makes him more than a free artist. He learns, besides the mere esthetic means of expression, that all media must be articulated through a knowledge of relationships between the technology of materials, the tools of production and the proposed function of the article to be designed. He learns about the philosophy of design through analysis of the economics, buying habits, and tastes of different countries. He is aware of the changes shaping the economy of the United States through its greatly increased production capacity. He observes the increasing importance of foreign trade and realizes the need of a re-valuation of the theory of "artificial obsolescence"—the frequent replacement of a product by a new "design" before the product has become technically obsolete—which has been the principal force behind the design and production in recent years. While "arti-ficial obsolescence" may have been justified as an expediency to create prosperity in a self-sufficient country, this policy requires re-examination in relation to the growing competition of other export-conscious nations engaging in mass production.

As mass production increases, the role of the industrial designer becomes more and more important, in so far as he can look at an article dispassionately and be interested only in the optimum solution to the requirements of the problem. His contribution becomes greater in ratio to his ability to take an objective point of view of existing scientific, artistic, and technological processes as well as of the relationship of the product to the market—a point of view usually difficult for either the "pure" artist or the manufacturer.

A properly trained industrial designer, then, serves industry not only as an artist creating an attractive product but also as a specialist in mass production. He is interested in shape and color—the "looks" of the product—not for mere esthetic values but also as they are related to such factors as Function, Lower production costs leading to increased distribution, Greater consumer acceptance of advanced trends. He is concerned, too, beyond mere esthetic values, with such elements as: Form, Assembly, Strength, Size, Weight as these are related to such utilitarian matters as—Packaging, Distribution, Sale, Economy of operation, Long life, Ease of cleaning, Accessibility for service and repairs.

In a word, industrial design is the intelligent, practical and skilled association of art with technology for the benefit of the people.

The functional approach, which has contributed so much to our physical comfort, is today no longer a revolutionary principle but an absolute standard for the modern industrial designer.

This approach is fully achieved only when the designer is trained to think simultaneously in terms of product, manufacturing processes, use, and user.

A visit to a few plants using industrial designers is perhaps as practical a way as any for telling the story of art in industry.

When a product is designed for function by a sensitive artist trained as an industrial designer along the lines described, harmony and proportion, a well-balanced organic appearance, will follow naturally.

In the commercial arts, design for display is a major factor. Planning of exhibitions, expositions, fairs, store displays, and display windows is being increasingly based on the principles of stage design. Here the display is considered as an active principle, where sound, word, color, rhythm and form are supported by motion.

An example is offered in the application to display purposes by the U.S. Gypsum Company of an object which I developed originally as "free" art. The device is a light display machine on which I worked between 1922 and 1930. This kinetic sculpture was constructed for automatic projection of hanging chiaroscuro (light-shadow) and luminous effects. It produces a great range of shadow interpenetrations and simultaneously intercepting patterns in a sequence of slow, flickering rhythm. The reflecting surfaces of the apparatus are discs made of polished metal slotted with regularly spaced perforations, and sheets of glass, celluloid, and screens of different materials. Some fifteen years after its completion, this machine was adapted as the foundation of a display by U.S. Gypsum. Thus is illustrated the thesis that a so-called "abstract" artwork may be first produced as the result of intuitive forces and then adapted to industrial use. Of course there are many more cases in which products must be designed to fit a predetermined need.

The multitudinous needs of industry have indeed created an unprecedented demand for industrial designers. We have compiled a list of some 240 industries at present utilizing such designers, and this list is by no means exhaustive. Products range from airplanes to wallpaper, from fountain pens to exposition architecture, and involve such varied materials as wood, metal, stone, glass, clay, plastics, fabrics, and paper products. Within twenty years all large plants will be doing experimental work in their own design laboratories and no manufacturer will attempt to operate without the services of design consultants. As scientific research has been accepted as an integral part of industry, so will industrial design fight its way to full recognition.

Educational and other cultural institutions like the New York Museum of Modern Art and the Chicago Institute of Design are in the forefront of this task. The Museum with its contemporary exhibitions sensitizes the public to the new expressions, shapes, and forms of the Atomic Age; the Institute continually develops such new forms by devising new uses for old materials and old and new functions for new materials. Stone, glass, and clay on the one hand and plywood and plastics on the other are offering challenging opportunities for the immediate future.

(September 1947)

ART IN INDUSTRY, PART II
Laslo Moholy-Nagy

By seeking the form appropriate to the physical qualities of the material and to the function it is to serve, many of the short-comings of the past can be avoided. In some instances this will be achieved by changing the characteristics of the materials through new combinations or processes, such as electroplating or laminating wood, and cutting and gluing by high-frequency heating.

I believe that just as the revolutionary change in furniture design of the recent past was effected by the introduction of the metal tube, so will the application of plywood offer astonishingly new forms of construction in the near future. Our graduate research workshops can be developed for innumerable tasks of this kind, from the creation of individual useful objects to completely furnished homes.

For example, since the kitchen became modernized in the United States and is shipped as a standardized packaged unit everywhere, it will be possible to design whole units for bedrooms, bathrooms, children's rooms, dining rooms, living rooms, and others. One development will be a grouping of these units with transportable and interchangeable walls and with matching wallpapers or color schemes.

The possibilities of the new plastics too, will stimulate thought in terms of contemporary design.

The all-plastic motor car has been a subject of frequent study by our students. Designs feature invisible bumpers, rubber fenders, pneumatic springs, rear or jet engine, balanced drive, automatically shifting center of gravity, fluid drive, nitrogen-filled doughnut wheels. Plastic walls are stabilized and strengthened through appropriate integral curvature without a skeletal construction.

In textiles, weaving, dyeing, and textures are our concern. The ornament is dead and the investigation of new textures offers much promise. These form a background also for fashion and dress design in which more than mere pattern is involved.

Opportunities also offer for creating from new materials by new techniques completely new textiles of hitherto unknown texture and structure. Small units and individual motifs made over into patterns suitable for continuous mass production offer opportunities for experiment.

In all branches of design experiment color is a most important element. Thus we manipulate color in every possible way, on flat and curved surfaces, incorporating every type of painting, such as easel painting and murals, decoration, frescoes, wallpaper design—executed by hand and by machines. Research in varnish and lacquer techniques, photo mural, and paint spraying is needed not only for the furniture and radio industries but also by many others.

Experiment with color can be both most stimulating to the student and of great practical value to industry.

The modern designer must "know his way around" not only in the use of pigment but also in that of light. He learns to manipulate lenses, cameras, distortions, solarizations, reflections, space, texture, line and tone, in photography, the motion picture, light displays, and related subjects.

Limitations of space prevent extended discussion of one more vital area of industrial design, architecture, in which our students have simultaneous training.

Our period is yet backward in the industrial production of architecture which has formed the apex of every great culture. American industry builds automobiles, tractors, refrigerators, and radios in series, while a house—even a small one—is still a matter of individual planning. The modern manufacturing processes together with the new stimuli coming from the artist, must come to the rescue and bring about a complete change in our architecture in our spatial vision.

No doubt our future town planning will be largely dependent on the realization of this new type of prefabricated house, although at present we still lack adequate cooperation and synthesis of the appropriate sciences and technologies. Much work has yet to be done before we shall be able to formulate a logical and organized building progress, both for domestic and urban architecture.

Design, then, is not a matter of facade, of mere external appearance. Rather, it is the essence of products and institutions. It is indivisible. The internal and external characteristics of a dish, a chair, a table, a machine, or a city are not separable.

Training in design is training in appreciation of the essence of things. It is penetrating and comprehensive. It includes development of various skills in using materials, but goes far beyond that. It involves development of attitudes of flexibility and adaptability to meet all sorts of problems as they arise.

A designer trained to think with both penetration and scope will find solutions, not alone for problems arising in daily routine, or for development of better ways of production, but also for all the problems of living and working together. There is design in family life, in labor relations, in city planning, in living together as civilized human beings. Ultimately all problems of design fuse together into one great problem of "design for living."

If the artist is really to function in the modern world, he must feel himself a part of it, and to have this sense of social integration he must command the instruments and materials of that world. While such integration cannot be achieved solely by intellectual understanding, it certainly cannot be achieved without such understanding. Man is a thinking being whatever else he may be, and no integration is humanly complete which does not include his mind.

Our concern is with the unity of life. It is our belief that all the cultural phalanges at any time move abreast, though often ignorant of their common cultural front. We feel that the integration and interpretation of the characteristic human activities of the artist, scientist, and technologist is a general problem of all education which aims to be of vital contemporary significance, art education included.

A fresh outlook can come only through proper understanding of the machine and its function in relation to our biological needs, and to our instinctive psychological requirements far beyond mere physical contact. Thus the artist must understand himself in relation to other human beings and to the group. All must cooperate—the scientist, the technician, and the artist—in order to find out which direction design should take—how it should be controlled, simplified, or enriched in accordance with the psycho-biological needs of the individual and the group of today and with the needs of future generations.

The designer today has a political and sociological responsibility which is founded in mass-production. What he designs and how he designs it will influence the lives of millions of people. A good designer has to know where he came from historically and where we are going politically. The time of the ignorant specialist are over. It is up to industrial design organizations to stimulate this feeling of enhanced responsibility in a world of pre-fabricated values.

(October 1947)

MOUNTAINHEADS FROM MOLE HILLS
A Review by Victor Gruen

The new Warner Brothers' movie, "The Fountainhead," is remarkable in more than one respect. It has, as its hero, an architect and a contemporary architect at that. It pokes fun at traditional architecture, going so far as to ridicule it by sticking a Greek facade on a model of a modern building. This, coming from our rarely crusading film producers, is final proof that the fight for contemporary architecture has been decided and won, long, long ago. And it is remarkable because, in spite of these laudable facts, it is doing altogether a disservice to architecture generally and to contemporary architecture especially.

At the dramatic high point of the movie, Howard Roarke defends in court his action of blowing up a large housing project, for which he acted as ghost designer, because it was not executed in accordance with his design.

The jury, obviously impressed by his eloquent plea, in which he explains that the design, being the exclusive property of the artist, could be destroyed by him if he so pleases, declares him, after short deliberation, not guilty. In contrast to these jurors and, though believing that the creative artist has definite rights to his design, I find Mr. Howard Roarke, architect, guilty; in fact, very guilty of criminal neglect.

How, otherwise, could we term his action, in going on a long vacation trip on a lovely yacht, unreachable for anybody, just at the time when he is engaged in the execution of the only socially important project he is undertaking during the entire movie, namely a large housing project? If that untimely vacation was more important to him than architectural achievement, he should only blame himself and Warner Brothers for the way the Cortland Housing Project turned out. He could not seriously expect his admittedly untalented and characterless colleague, Peter Keating, to make and supervise working drawings in a sensible manner. He could not reasonably think that same Peter Keating would resist the pressure of miscellaneous interests to make changes on the project as he was completely aware of the fact that Peter didn't have the slightest idea what it was all about. Coming back, he certainly didn't have the right to be outraged and throw a little dynamite into the place which, after all, was only one more bad housing project. (If we would blow up all bad housing projects, where, may I ask you, would we live?)

If I had been on that jury, I would, however, have asked the district attorney to extend the case to include the lady who wrote the book and the screenplay and who neglected, when designing Mr. Roarke, not only proper supervision but the necessary surveys and studies and who did not bother to find out what an architect looks like, lives like, works like; who neglected to acquire the slightest knowledge about the basis of, what we call, contemporary architecture, which she obviously is confusing with contemptuous architecture..

I would propose that she should be charged with negligence, because she did not bother to find out that the very basic content of contemporary architecture is service to society, the fulfillment of the needs of the individual or a group of individuals or a community. Because she didn't find out that the careful analysis of the needs of the project is the basis for any creation of modern architecture and that the problems arising from technical and human difficulties, difficulties inherent to materials, clients, contractors, authorities, are the daily bread of the modern architect and often have the effect, because they form a challenge to the architect, of improving his work.

I would propose to charge her with damaging the reputation and the business of the contemporary architect by implying that only the traditional architect is the one who conforms to wishes and needs of his client and that the contemporary architect, in contrast to him, cares only about monumentality, originality and the cultivation of his ego. If she would have dutifully prepared herself for her task, she would have known that the contrary is the case; namely, that the traditional architect often forces buildings and interiors into the straightjacket of monumental symmetry, traditional shapes and borrowed forms, disregarding human and individual needs.

I would charge her with negligence because she did not bother to find out that the architect can be not only an artist but a responsible professional man and, as such, a servant of his client and of mankind. He cannot afford to create only in his own image any more than an obstetrician can afford to blow up the babies he helps to bring into the world merely because they don't coincide with his esthetic ideals.

I would charge her with misleading the young architect, the architectural student and our youth generally and doing so in a tricky manner. By identifying her hero with qualities and achievements dear to the heart of our youth; by identifying him with a modern architecture independent of its clients, even if they are big corporations; by characterizing him as a non-conformist; by all this camouflage, she may succeed in creating so much admiration for her hero in the hearts of our youth that they may overlook the anti-social, anti-democratic and anti-human message of her novel.

Nonconformism, as such, is not a laudable quality. Roarke's nonconformism is the expression of extreme egotism and is equal to the stubbornness of a naughty child which, if it doesn't get what it wants, breaks its toys. Nonconformism is positive only when its basis is ethical. The truly progressive, truly modern and contemporary architect stands for everything which leads to progress and betterment of the human race. He will not conform with his client or clients if their wishes and aims are in contrast with these aims and artistic and professional honesty. True nonconformity is constructive. Roarke's nonconformity is destructive and anarchistic.

I would charge her, finally, of confusing the public as to what the architectural profession and modern architecture, especially, is about. She is causing distrust of the modern architect by suggesting that he is a man who shoves his ideas down the client's throat, a man who starts to become interested in projects only when they happen to be more than 80 stories high and who goes really all out in his efforts only when he finds a client who signs a contract giving him absolute freedom of action and further obliges him by shooting himself immediately after signing the papers.

Next to the charges against the main defendant, the deeds of her accomplices seem to be only misdemeanors. Extenuating circumstances can definitely be claimed for Warner Brothers who show their disinterest in the author's ideas by presenting a poorly acted, poorly directed show especially in those parts of the movie where architecture is concerned. They find their usual enthusiasm only in those scenes which deal with romance, love and rape.

I would plead for definite clemency for the art director and set designers who made the plans, models and movie sets illustrating the so-called modern architecture, as they should be credited with bringing a little humor into the picture by lending funny touches to their architectural creations, like diving boards on factory buildings and super cantilevers on country homes.

For the main defendant, however, I can't find excuses. It is indicative that she sees, at the high point of her hero's career, the designing and construction of a tremendous building, to be erected for a dead client and a non-existing newspaper enterprise, a multi-million dollar super duper structure with no other visible purpose than to provide, on its 500th floor, a lofty rendezvous for the newly-wedded Roarkes.

On the grounds of the aforesaid, on the grounds of the spirit of the novel and the spirit of the picture, I would propose that the main defendant should be found guilty, guilty of damaging the reputation of the contemporary architect, guilty of misleading our youth and, most of all, guilty of a state of mind which I would call—contempt of mankind.

(May 1949)

NOTES IN PASSING

All right, all right, so maybe we are going to have peace; so maybe we are not going to have peace. It is just that it might be a good idea to test the wind velocities in the twilight zone between two stools if that is where we are going to have to sit until good sense becomes a measure of solution. One fights to find reality in the day-by-day parade of events that make the history of our time, and one knows, as a reasonable being, that nothing need be irrevocable or inevitable. It is only in the complex of events, over which we have so little control, that it is difficult to maintain any kind of ordered thinking this side of the widest generalities. However, that way lies other-worldliness and a kind of personal withdrawal that adds up to the intellectually capon.

It would seem that we now face an adversary that admits no compromise but will, by all and every means, temporize instead at every possible twist and turn of events. It is a little like fighting one's way through a Chinese theater and encountering the same identity behind a lightning change of masks representing innumerable faces to suit any momentary scene. Perhaps we have mistaken the game we are playing. Imagine our surprise to find that it is not chess at all but jack-straws. There is a perilous line between the dream and the nightmare,

and if, indeed we are to continue to dream of hope and peace we cannot go on for too much longer with this business of waking up screaming. Granted that our value system and the manner in which it is to be applied is an invention concocted out of the necessity for some kind of form in human dealing, we must not assume that we are the only reasonable people in the world. But it is, of course, very disturbing to make one's manners and have them shoved down one's throat by someone who obviously has no use for them.

In a world in which we have developed so many pat answers it is very upsetting to find ourselves dealing with people who play the current situation by ear toward a conclusion that so obviously cannot include our way of thinking. To circumvent this horrid thought we go through a kind of self-induced hypnotism within a dream of chicken-every-Sunday as though that happy fact were a part of the cosmic order of things that must happen because we will it so.

At all events, as we recede from reality we must at some point find that everything comes into acute perspective and there, perhaps, we will be able to develop a point of view upon which to base a real policy. Until then we will no doubt continue building walls around ourselves and our possessions and our feelings until we realize that we can make no progress if we are to be imprisoned within our own rigid little moralities. Perhaps that is the nature of the perspective that will free us, and until that moment we will have to suffer the unendurable and dubious pleasures of indefinite postponement.

It would be an immense relief if one could find somewhere between Spengler and Toynbee a pat answer to apply as a vanishing cream to our present world problem. A quiet evening with the political philosophers should, it says here, put one's mind at ease; but ease, like the carriage trade, is evidently becoming a museum piece and only remains to be looked upon as a regrettable apparition from the past.

Of course, it never occurs to us in our vanity that probably the new world calls for an entirely new kind of people. Perish the thought that we could just possibly be obsolete in terms of our own time. It might be that our little rules can make sense only in a kind of tinker-toy world that will not outgrow our peculiar sort of childish play. Maybe in our rather singular conception of life as a game, we can no longer find a valid premise upon which to proceed into the future. Willfulness

however good-hearted may no longer be a means by which any real end can be accomplished.

That, of course, is a sad thought and a very disturbing one.

But while we are in the midst of this project of redesigning a world, it might be that we attack the problem from the wrong end. It might, indeed, be that the only real answer is a redesigning of the human being.

(January 1949)

THE COMPREHENSIVE DESIGNER
R. Buckminster Fuller

The specialist in comprehensive design is an emerging synthesis of artist, inventor, mechanic, objective economist and evolutionary strategist. He bears the same relationship to society in the new interactive continuities of worldwide industrialization that the architect bore to the respective remote independencies of feudal society.

The architect of 400 years ago was the comprehensive harvester of the potentials of the realm. The last 400 years have witnessed the gradual fadeout of feudalism and gradual looming of what will eventually be full world-industrialization—when all people will produce for all people in an infinity of interesting specialized continuities. The more people served by industrialization, the more efficient it becomes. In contrast to the many negative factors inherent in feudalism, such as debt, fear, ignorance and an infinite variety of breakdowns and failures inevitable to dependence on the vagaries of nature, industrialization trends to "accentuate the positive and eliminate the negative" first by measuring nature and converting the principles discovered in the measurements to mastery and anticipation of the vagaries. Day and night, winter and summer, fair weather or bad, time and distance are mastered. Productive continuities may be maintained and forwardly scheduled. There are three fundamental constituents of industry; all are positive.

The first consists of the aspect of energy as mass, inventoried as the 92 primary chemical elements which constitute earth and its enclosing film of ever-alternating liquid-gaseous sequence.

The second fundamental component of industry consists of energy but in a second and two-fold aspect, i.e. (a) energy as radiation and (b) energy as gravitation, of both of which we are in constant receipt from the infinite cosmic fund.

Third and most important component of the industrial equation is the intellect-factor which secretes a continually amplifying advantage in experience-won knowledge.

Complex-component number one cannot wear out. The original chaotic disposition of its 92 chemical elements is gradually being converted by the industrial principle to orderly separation and systematic distribution over the face of earth in structural or mechanical arrangements of active or potential leverage-augmentation.

Component number two, cosmic energy, cannot be lost.

Constituent number three not only improves with use but is interactively self-augmenting.

Summarizing, components #1 and #2 cannot be lost or diminished and #3 increases; net result inherent gain. Inherent gain is realized in physical advantage of forward potential (it cannot be articulated backwards; it is mathematically irreversible). Thus, industrial potential is schematically directional and not "randomly" omni-directional. Thus, the "life" activity as especially demonstrated by man represents an anti-entropic phase of the transformation of non-losable universal energy.

The all-positive principle of industry paradoxically is being assimilated by man only through emergent expedients—adopted—only in emergency because of his preponderant fixation in the direction of tradition. Backing up into his future, man romantically appraises the emergent dorsal sensations in the negatively parroted terms of his ancestors' misadventures.

Essence of the principle of industry is the principle of synergy (Miriam Webster: "Cooperative action of descrete agencies such that the total effect is greater than the sum of two or more effects taken independently"). The principle is manifested both in the inorganic and organic. The alloying of chrome and nickel and steel provides greater tensile strength than that possessed by any of its constituents or by the constituents in proportional addition. Three or more persons by specialized team work can do work far in excess of the work of three independently operating men. Surprisingly, and most contradictory to the concept of feudal ignorance, the industrial chain's strength is not predica-

ted on its weakest link. So strong is the principle that it grows despite a myriad of superficially failing links! In fact there are no continuous "links" in industry or elsewhere in universe because the atomic components are—interiorly, spaciously discontinuous.

The strength of "industry" as with the strength of the "alloy" occurs through the concentric enmeshment of the respective atoms. It is as if two non identical constellations of approximately the same number of stars each were inserted into the same space making approximately twice as many stars, but none touching due to the difference in patterns. The distances between stars would be approximately halved. It is the same with alloyed atoms whose combined energetic cohesion increases as the second power of the relative linear proximities of the component parts. Though the parts do not "touch" their mass cohesive dynamic attraction follows the gravitational law of proportionment to second power of the distance apart of centers. Therefore, alloying strength is not additive arithmetically but is advantaged by gravity which as Newton discovered is inversely proportional to the "square" of the distance apart.

Man has now completed the plumbing and has installed all the valves to turn on infinite cosmic wealth. Looking to the past he wails, "How can I afford to turn on the valve? If I run it on, somebody's going to have to pay for it!" He forgets that the bill has been prepaid by all men through all time, especially by their faithfully productive investments of initiative. The plumbing could not have been realized except through absolute prepayment of intellectually organized physical work, invested in the inherent potentials of nature.

Not only is man continually doing more with less—which is a principle of trend which we will call "ephemeralization"—a corollary of the principle of "synergy"—but he is also demonstrating certain other visible trends of an epochal nature. Not only does he continually increase literacy but he continually affords more years of more advanced study to more people. As man becomes master of the machine and machines are introduced to carry on every kind of physical work with increased precision, effectiveness and velocity, his skilled crafts, formerly intermittently patronized, graduate from labor status to continuity of employment as research and development technicians. As man is progressively disemployed as a

quantity production muscle-and-reflex machine, he becomes progressively reemployed in the rapidly increasing army of research and development—or of production-inaugurating engineering—or of education and recreational extension, as plowed back increment of industrialization.

Product and service production of any one item of industry trends to manipulation by one man for the many through push-button and dial systems. While man trends to increasing specialized function in anticipatory and positive occupations of production, he also trends to comprehensive function as consumer. Because the principle of industry improves as the number of people it serves is increased, it also improves in terms of the increase of the number of functions of the individual to which it is applied and it also improves in terms of its accelerated use.

Throughout the whole history of industrialization to date man has taken with alacrity to the preoccupation of the specialist on the production side of ledger but the amplification of the functions of the individual as comprehensive consumer have been wretched and jerked and suffered into tentative and awkward adoption in the mumbo-jumbo and failure-complex of obsolete feudal economics. Up to yesterday man was unaware of his legacy of infinite cosmic wealth. Somewhere along the line society was convinced that wealth was emanating from especially ordained mortals to whom it should be returned periodically for mystical amplification. Also with feudal fixation man has looked to the leaders of the commercial or political states for their socio-economic readjustments—to the increasing "emergencies."

Throughout these centuries of predominant ignorance and vanity the inherently comprehensive thinking artist has been so competent as to realize that his comprehensive thoughts would only alienate him from the economic patronage of those who successfully exploited each backing up into the future. The exploiters, successively successful, have ever attempted and in vain to anchor or freeze the dynamic expansion at the particular phase of wealth generation which they had come to monopolize.

The fool-hardy inventors and the forthright prospectors in humble trappings of greater potentials have been accounted the notable failures. Every industrial success of man has been built on a foundation of vindictive denouncement of the founders.

Thus the comprehending artist has learned to sublimate his comprehensive proclivities and his heretic forward-looking—toward engagement of the obviously ripening potentials on behalf of the commonwealth. The most successful among the artists are those who have effected their comprehensive ends by indirection and progressive disassociations. So skillful have the artists of the last centuries been that even their aspiring apprentices have been constrained to celebrate only the non-utilitarian aspects of the obvious vehicles adroitly employed by the effective artist to convey their not so obvious but all important burden.

Thus the legend and tradition of a "pure" art or a "pure" science as accredited preoccupation have grown to "generally accepted" proportion. The seemingly irrelevant doings of the pure scientist of recent decades exploded in the face of the tradition of pure mathematical abstraction of Alamagordo. No one could have been more surprised than the rank and file of professional "pure" scientists. The results were implicit in the undertakings of artist-scientists whose names are in the dim forefront or are anonymous in the limbo of real beginnings. How great and exultant their secret conceptioning must have been!

Now the time has arrived for the artist to come out from behind his protective coloring of adopted abstractions and indirections. World society, frustrated in its reliance upon the leaders of might, is ready to be about-faced to step wide-eyed into the obvious advantages of its trending. Ergo—the emergence of comprehensive training for specialists in the husbandry of specialists and the harvesting of the infinite commonwealth.

Will the comprehensive designer, forthrightly emergent, be as forthrightly accepted by the authorities of industrialization and state? If they are accepted, what are the first-things-first to which they must attend?

The answer to the first question is YES. They will be accepted by the industrial authority because the latter has recently shifted from major preoccupation with exploiting original resource to preoccupation with keeping the "wheels" which they manage turning—now that the original inventory of "wheels," i.e. tools in general has been realized from out original resource. Though original resource-exploiters still have great power, that power will diminish* as the mines now existing above grade, in highly concentrated "use" forms

(yet in rapidly obsoleting original design), become the preponderant source of the annual need. Severe acceleration in the trend to increase of performance per pound of invested material now characterizes all world-industry. With no important increase in the rate of annual receipt from original mines, the full array of mechanics and structure requisite amplifying the industrial complex, from its present service to approximately one-third the world's population, may be accomplished by the scrap "mined" from the progressively obsoleting structures and mechanics. World-industrial management will be progressively dependent upon the comprehensive designer to accelerate the turning of his wheels by design acceleration. Each time the wheels go round the infinite energy wealth receptive capacities of the 92 element inventory of earth and those who manage the wheels can make original entry on their books of the new and expanding wealth increments even as the farmer gains cosmic energy wealth in his seasoned cycles.

*See New York Times, June 17, 1949, Page 2

NOTES IN PASSING

Lazlo Moholy-Nagy; born 1895, died 1946. Founder of the Institute of Design.

"The industrial revolution opened up a new dimension—the dimension of a new science and a new technology which could be used for the realization of all-embracing relationships. Contemporary man threw himself into the experience of these new relationships. But saturated with old ideologies, he approached the new dimension with obsolete practices and failed to translate his newly gained experience into emotional language and cultural reality. The result has been and still is misery and conflict, brutality and anguish, unemployment and war."

"We can hope for improvement only after we have surrendered metaphysical interpretations in favor of a scientific analysis of human history. Tradition is man-made and must be constantly re-evaluated."

"The fight for a new social and economic order is a constant process, but it is not the task of schools to make a deci-

sion as to the theories which should be victorious. The duty of the educator is to uncover the forces which form society so that the individual, equipped with the knowledge of the processes, may form his own opinion and make a decision about his position in the world."

"Design has many connotations. It is the organization of materials and processes in the most productive, economic way, in a harmonious balance of all elements necessary for a certain function. It is not a matter of facade, of mere external appearance; rather it is the essence of products and institutions, penetrating and comprehensive. Designing is a complex and intricate task. It is the integration of technological, social and economic requirements, biological necessities, and the psychophysical effects of materials, shape, color, volume, and space: thinking in relationships. The designer must see the periphery as well as the core, the immediate and the ultimate, at least in the biological sense. He must anchor his special job in the complex whole. The designer must be trained not only in the use of materials and various skills, but also in appreciation of organic functions and planning. He must know that design is indivisible, that the internal and external characteristics of a dish, a chair, a table, a machine, painting, sculpture, are not to be separated. The idea of design and the profession of the designer has to be transformed from the notion of a specialist function into a generally valid attitude of resourcefulness and inventiveness which allows projects to be seen not in isolation but in relationship with the needs of the individual and the community."

"The Institute of Design, Chicago, is a laboratory for new education. Founded for the training of artists, industrial designers, photographers and teachers, it embodies the principles and educational methods of the Bauhaus modified in accordance with the circumstances and demands of this country."

"Among the exercises, one of the most important is the re-examination of tools and materials so that a given work can be executed in terms of basic qualities and characteristics. One could call this approach an artless, unprejudiced search which, first on a modest but later on a growing scale, conditions one to creative thinking and acting, to inventiveness and intuitive assurance of judgment. This idea has an affinity with the kindergarten play technique as well as with the apprentice education of the old craftsman. There is, however, a great difference in orientation. The "play" of the grownup, while it offers opportunity for relaxed explorations and collection of data, has implicitly a constructive direction. Through the collaboration of teachers who have the power of discrimination, the significant points are quickly recognized in the experiments and through subtle leadership the "play" is brought to purposeful results. An education in the crafts develops responsibility toward the product as a whole and through this it teaches the student discipline. But the crafts are not emphasized in opposition to machine work. The machine is understood as a very efficient "tool" which—if properly used—will serve the creative intention as well as the traditional handtool. . ."

"The problem of our generation is to bring the intellectual and emotional, the social and technological components into balanced play; to learn to see and feel them in relationship. Without this interrelatedness there remains only the disjunctive technical skill of handling human affairs, a rigidity stifling biological and social impulses; a memorized, not a lived life."

Quotations from L. Moholy-Nagy, "Vision in Motion," Chicago, Paul Theobald, 1947 (I.D. publication)

(July 1952)

THE MATHEMATICAL APPROACH IN CONTEMPORARY ART
Max Bill

By a mathematical approach to art it is hardly necessary to say I do not mean any fanciful ideas for turning out art by some ingenious system of ready reckoning with the aid of mathematical formulas. So far as composition is concerned every former school of art can be said to have had a more or less mathematical basis. There are also many trends in modern art which rely on the same sort of empirical calculations. These, together with the artist's own individual scales of value, are just part of the ordinary elementary principles of design for establishing the proper relationship between component volumes: that is to say for imparting harmony to the whole. Yet it cannot be denied that these same methods have suffered considerable deterioration since the time when mathematics were the foundation of

all forms of artistic expression and the covert link between cult and cosmos. Nor have they seen any progressive development from the days of the ancient Egyptians until quite recently, if we except the discovery of perspective during the Renaissance. This is a system which, by means of pure calculation and artificial reconstruction, enables objects to be reproduced in what is called "true-to-life" facsimile by setting them in an illusory field of space. Perspective certainly presented an entirely new aspect of reality to human consciousness, but one of its consequences was that the artist's primal image was debased into mere naturalistic replica of his subject. Therewith the decadence of painting, both as a symbolic art and an art of free construction, may be said to have begun.

Impressionism, and still more Cubism, brought painting and sculpture much closer to what were the original elements of each: painting as surface design in colors; sculpture as the shaping of bodies to be informed by space. It was probably Kandinsky who gave the immediate impulse towards an entirely fresh conception of art. As early as 1912, in his book on "The Spiritual Harmony in Art," Kandinsky had indicated the possibility of a new direction which, if followed to its logical conclusion, would lead to the substitution of a mathematical approach for improvisations of the artist's imagination. But as he found other ways of liberating painting from romantic and literary associations he did not adapt this particular line in his own work.

If we examine a picture by Klee or one of Brancusi's sculptures we shall soon discover that, though the "subject" may be an indeterminable echo of something or other in the actual world about us, it is an echo which has been transmuted into a form that is original in the sense of being elemental. Kandinsky confronted us with objects and phenomena which have no existence in ordinary life, but which might well have meaning or be portents on some unknown planet; a planet where we should be quite unable to gauge their purpose or relevance. Yet it was undoubtedly Mondrian who went furthest in breaking away from everything that had hitherto been regarded as art. If the technique of structural design may seem to have inspired his rhythms the resemblance is fortuitous and one which was not present in his own intention or consciousness. Although the specific content of his work is constricted with the utmost discipline, the horizontal-vertical emphasis represents a purely emotional factor in

his composition. It is not for any whimsical reason that he called his latest pictures "Broadway Boogie-Woogie" and "Victory Boogie-Woogie," but simply to stress their affinity with jazz rhythms.

If we can agree that Mondrian realized the ultimate possibilities of painting in one direction—that is by his success in eliminating most of the remaining elements which are alien to it—two others still lie open to us: either we can return to traditionalism (in its wider sense), or else we can continue the quest for subjects with a content of a new and altogether different nature.

Let me take this opportunity to explain why it is impossible for many artists to go back to the old type of subjects. In the vast field of pictorial and plastic expression there are a large number of trends and tendencies which have all more or less originated in our own age. Different people look at modern painting and sculpture with different eyes because what they severally recognize as significant of our age is necessarily various. Clergymen have a different idea of art from scientists. Peasants and factory-hands live under radically different conditions. There are inevitable variations in standards of living and levels of culture. Similar differences can be found among artists. They, too, come from different walks of life, and their work reflects different emotional and intellectual undercurrents. There is another attitude to modern art which must not be overlooked as its now numerous followers can always be relied upon to take their stand against every disinterestedly progressive move-ment. I mean the much-boosted school which demands that, since art itself cannot perhaps solve social and political problems, these shall at least be made dramatically "actual" and suitably glorified through its medium. We have good reason to be skeptical about any "Political Art"—regardless of whether it emanates from right or left; especially when, under the cloak of antagonism to the prevailing social order, its aim is to bring about a new but, in all essentials, almost identical structure of society—because this is not art at all but simply propaganda.

After this digression into the potential alternatives which may be said to have existed prior to somewhere about 1910, let me try to make clear why some of us were unable to rest content with what had then been achieved. That would have meant going on marking time over the same ground during the last forty years and painting in one or the other of those manners which may be called "a la Klee," "a la Kandinsky," "a la Picasso," "a la Braque," and "a la Matisse." A great many gifted and intelligent artists are still wearing out their talents in ringing the changes on these modern masters. In fact this sort of painting has now become something in the nature of a substitute for the masters themselves, and "a la" pictures begin to rank as interesting variants of their originals. To acquiesce in this state of stagnation was impossible because we have no right to allow a halt to be called in any genuinely creative field of human activity.

We can safely assume that all the various forms of expression open to painting and sculpture at the present day are now sufficiently known, and that the techniques they postulate have been sufficiently demonstrated and clarified in the work of their respective pioneers (except perhaps for a very few which can be already anticipated, but which have not so far been realized). What, then, it may be asked, are the possibilities of further development? But there are two other important points which must be dealt with before that question can be answered: namely, whether the several idioms just referred to can claim general validity in the plastic arts; and whether there is reason to enlarge the existing limits of their content. Careful study of those forms of expression has led me to the conclusion that all of them were the discoveries of individual artists, either born of their will to overcome particular problems or else expedients called forth by exceptional circumstances; and that therefore they cannot be considered universally applicable or appropriate. As regards content, most of the modern work which is often held to have been largely inspired by mathematical principles cannot, in point of fact, be identified with that entirely new orientation I have called the Mathematical Approach to Art. And as this needs to be more nearly defined, I will now endeavor to elucidate it, and at the same time answer the question I have left in suspense.

I am convinced it is possible to evolve a new form of art in which the artist's work could be founded to quite a substantial degree on a mathematical line of approach to its content. This proposal has, of course, aroused the most vehement opposition. It is objected that art has nothing to do with mathematics; that mathematics, besides being by its very nature as dry as dust and as unemo-tional, is a branch of speculative thought, and as such in direct antithesis to those emotive values inherent in aesthetics; and, finally that anything approaching ratiocination is repugnant, indeed positively injurious to art, which is purely a matter of feeling. Yet art plainly calls for both feeling and reasoning. In support of this assertion the familiar example of Johann Sebastian Bach may be credited; for Bach employed mathematical formulas to fashion the raw material known to us as sound into the exquisite harmonies of his sublime fugues. And it is worth mentioning that, although mathematics had by then fallen into disuse for composition in both his own and the other arts, mathematical and theological books stood side by side on the shelves of his library.

It is mankind's ability to reason which makes it possible to coordinate emotional values in such a way that what we call art ensues. Now in every picture the basis of its composition is geometry or in other words the means of determining the mutual relationship of its component parts either on plane or in space. Thus, just as mathematics provides us with a primary method of cognition, and can therefore enable us to apprehend our physical surroundings, so, too, some of its basic elements will furnish us with laws to appraise the interaction of separate objects, or groups of objects, one to another. And again, since it is mathematics which lends significance to these relationships, it is only a natural step from having perceived them to desiring to portray them. This, in brief, is the genesis of a picture. Pictorial representations of that kind have been known since antiquity, and, like those models at the Musee Poincare in Paris where conceptions of space have been embodied in plastic shapes or made manifest by colored diagrams, they undoubtedly provoke an aesthetic reaction in the beholder. In the search for new formal idioms expressive of the technical sensibilities of our age these borderline exemplars had much the same order of importance as the "discovery" of native West African sculpture by the Cubists; though they were equally inapt for direct assimilation into modern European art. The first result of their influence was the phase known as Constructivism. This, together with the stimulus derived from the use of new materials such as engineering blue prints, aerial photographs, and the like, furnished the necessary incentive for fur-ther developments along mathematical lines. At about the same time mathematics itself had arrived at a stage of evolution in which the proof of many apparently logical deductions ceased to be demonstrable and theorems were presented that the imagination proved incapable of grasping. Though mankind's power of reasoning had not reached the end of its tether, it was clearly beginning to require the assistance of some visualizing agency. Aids of this kind can often be provided by the intervention of art.

As the artist has to forge his concept into unity his vision vouchsafes him a synthesis of what he sees which though essential to his art, may not be necessarily mathematically accurate. This leads to the shifting or blurring of boundaries where clear lines of division would be supposed. Hence abstract conceptions assume concrete and visible shape, and so become perceptible to our emotions. Unknown fields of space, almost unimaginable hypotheses, are boldly bodied forth. We seem to be wandering through a firmament that has had no prior existence; and in the process of attuning ourselves to its strangeness our sensibility is being actively prepared to anticipate still further and, as it were, as yet inconceivable expanses of the infinite.

It must not be supposed that an art based on the principles of mathematics, such as I have just adumbrated, is in any sense the same thing as a plastic or pictorial interpretation of the latter. Indeed, it employs virtually none of the resources implicit in the term Pure Mathematics. The art in question can, perhaps, best be defined as the building up of significant patterns from the everchanging relations, rhythms and proportions of abstract forms, each one of which, having its own causality, is tantamount to a law unto itself. As such, it presents some analogy to mathematics itself where every fresh advance had its immaculate conception in the brain of one or other of the great pioneers. Thus Euclidian geometry no longer possesses more than a limited validity in modern science, and it has an equally restricted utility in modern art. The concept of a Finite Infinity offers yet another parallel. For this essential guide to the speculations of contemporary physicists has likewise become an essential factor in the consciousness of contemporary artists. These, then, are then general lines on which art is daily creating new symbols: symbols that may have their sources in antiquity but which meet the aesthetic emotional needs of our time in a way hardly any other form of expression can hope to realize.

Things having no apparent connection with mankind's daily needs—the mystery enveloping all mathematical problems; the inexplicability of space—space that can stagger us by beginning on one side and ending in a completely changed aspect on the other, which somehow manages to remain that selfsame side; the remoteness or nearness of infinity—infinity which may be found doubling back from the far horizon to present itself to us as immediately at hand; limitations without boundaries; disjunctive and disparate multiplicities constituting coherent and unified entities; identical shapes rendered wholly diverse by the merest inflection; fields of attraction that fluctuate in strength; or, again, the square in all its robust solidity; parallels that intersect; straight lines untroubled by any relativity and ellipses which form straight lines at every point of their curves—can yet be fraught with the greatest moment. For though these evocations might seem only the phantasmagorical figments of the artist's inward vision they are, notwithstanding, the projections of latent forces; forces that may be active or inert, in part revealed, inchoate or still unfathomed, which we are unconsciously at grips with every day of our lives; in fact that music of the spheres which underlies each manmade system and every law of nature it is within our power to discern.

Hence all such visionary elements help to furnish art with a fresh content. Far from creating a new formalism, as it often erroneously asserted, what these can yield us is something far transcending surface values since they not only embody form as beauty, but also form in which intuitions or ideas or conjectures have taken visible substance. The primordial forces contained in those elements call forth intimations of the occult controls which govern the cosmic structure; and these can be made to reflect a semblance of the universe as we have learned to picture it today: an image that is no mere transcript of this invisible world but a systematization of it ideographically conveyed to our senses.

It may, perhaps, be contended that the result of this would be to reduce art to a branch of metaphysical philosophy. But I see no likelihood of that for philosophy is speculative thought of a special kind which can only be made intelligible through the use of words. Mental concepts are not as yet directly communicable to our apprehension without the medium of language; thought they might ultimately become so by the medium of art. Hence I assume that art could be made a unique vehicles for the direct transmission of ideas, because if these were expressed by pictures or plastically there would be no danger of their original meaning being perverted (as happens in literature, for instance, through printer's errors, or thanks to the whim of some prominent executant in music) by whatever fallacious interpretations particular individuals change to put on them. Thus the more succinctly a train of thought was expounded, and the more comprehensive the unity of its basic idea, the closer it would approximate to the prerequisites of the Mathematical Approach to Art. So the nearer we can attain to the first cause or primal core of things by these means, the more universal will the scope of art become—more universal, that is, be being free to express itself directly and without ambivalence; and likewise forthright and immediate in its impact on our sensibility.

To which, no doubt, a further objection will be raised that this is no longer art; though it could equally well be maintained that this alone was art. Such a stricture would be like saying that Euclid's was the only geometry, and that the new conception of geometry associated with the names of Lobaschevsky and Riemann was no geometry at all. One claim would stand against the other and that would be that!

Although this new ideology of art is focused on a spectral field of vision this is one where the mind can still find access. It is a field in which some degree of stability may be found, but in which, too, unknown quantities, indefinable factors will inevitably be encountered. In the ever-shifting frontier zones of this nebular realm new perspectives are continually opening up to invite the artist's creative analysis. The difference between the traditional conception of art and that just defined is much the same as exists between the laws of Archimedes and those we owe to Einstein and other outstanding modern physicists. Archimedes remains our authority in a good many contingencies though no longer in all of them. Phidias, Raphael, and Seurat produced works of art that characterize their several epochs for us because each made full use of such means of expression as his own age afforded him. But since their days the orbit of human vision has widened and art has annexed fresh territories which were formerly denied to it. In one of these recently conquered domains the artist is now free to exploit the untapped resources of that vast new field of inspiration I have described with the means our age vouchsafes him and in a spirit proper to its genius. And despite the fact that the basis of this Mathematical Approach to Art is in reason, its dynamic content is able to launch us on astral flights which soar into unknown and still uncharted regions of the imagination.

(August 1954)

MUSIC COLUMN, Peter Yates
Dylan Thomas and Aaron Copland

In the valley of tract houses he stood up like a mansion, the first poet since Yeats. Opening him was like entering a crowded bus, among his words all sharp-elbowed strangers. Now the best of it goes hiking lonely up mountain ridges among the erect trunks and impeding branches of a direct genius.

He was Dylan Thomas, and I didn't like his poetry or his looks. I was a long time, too, before liking Yeats. In a hazy moral sense I objected to the way these men played the poet. Henry James tells how Tennyson, when urged to recite after supper, put on the seer and the bard. I had the same feeling about Yeats and Thomas. As did many of us.

"The fascination of what's difficult
Has dried the sap out of my veins, and rent
Spontaneous joy and natural content
Out of my heart . . ."

All of us arrived there together with Yeats, sooner or later. The elder poet had learned to sing from his tower war songs of our age fiercer and with more of history in them than survives from the unremembered debris of our front pages. We read the headlines as if these were all that mattered: ground gained or lost, battlefield or gridiron. Thucydides, Julius Caesar, Ibn Khaldun, Ulysses Grant, and Churchill tell of diplomacy and warfare they witnessed and commanded. A thousand or a hundred thousand men die of persecution or in battle and are forgotten, but one poem is not. The enduring war was in Yeats and came out classical or furious.

What afterwards I most admire I come to usually first of all with an objection. Too charged! Too thick! Too dense! I being self constituted a poet am as intolerant of other poets, the best especially, as musicians who amaze me are intolerant of the best music. I must break through my own idiom and then through and into the idiom fresh presented. These objections are finger touches working upon style; and for all the breadth of my taste in music I do not receive style easily. If I may seem overriding after my mind has been made up, take my word for it that I have already, in myself, lazy and unwilling to wrap around into a new shape, overcome the more obvious objections. Though I have hated him before, then I will fight for him.

Take this Dylan Thomas who died unexpectedly in New York on his way out West. He was coming to visit Stravinsky among others, and when before a concert Bob Craft told me he was dead, I could not feel the loss. It wasn't mine yet. But with a sense of guilt in me that I couldn't get rid of, I went back to read the poet.

"After the first death, there is no other," he had written. There were the poems on the shelf, looking as they had. I opened them, and he was

". . . young and easy under the apple boughs

About the lilting house and happy as the grass was green. . And honored among wagons . . ."

I think it was that last image turned me the most. If I could still question whether there are not, after the first death, many others, as I question, "Beauty is truth, truth beauty, these alone . . . ," I could not question the authority of the wagons, among whom a young man, a boy then, he was already honoring with fresh vision, making weighty and massive the fundamentals of his origin. "Inscape," Gerald Manley Hopkins called this inward spiritual vision of the outward object.

Edith Sitwell tells of his voice, seeking poetic symbols of lions and blood to make us hear him read. Mollie Panter-Downes writes in *The New Yorker* of the London evening when, in his memory and to raise money for his wife and children, speeches were offered and sections of his works were recited. At the end, over a bare stage, from a record of his reading his own voice rang.

"And death shall have no dominion . . ."

It is after a poet is dead, then, that we know if death shall have dominion over him. Whether his houseless poems will die or live. Though there may be other deaths, he has survived this one. Then gently, looking for no contradiction, we offer him the word, "Genius."

"Not for the proud man apart
From the raging moon I write…
But for the lovers, their arms
Round the griefs of the ages,
Who pay no praise or wages
Nor heed my craft or art."

Formerly, while he was living, I rejected him; but his art does not reject me. So I learn from his example the love of the creator.

This more than technique, this love makes final judgment among artists. Is it a paradox to insist that the love cannot be without the technique? From Rosamond Tuve I can learn in how many forms the word "manna" appears in medieval and renaissance iconographic imagery and in George Herbert. In Thomas it is "the stars falling cold," "the drifting bread," and becomes "the hand folded air" (how neatly, by the elimination of a hyphen, smoothing the rhythm to enfold sacramental meanings), "the engulfing bride," "White seed," all of these being also images of snow, "the lamb white day." The long line made up of images, deft repetitions, displacements of the vowel, shifting of the consonants, to admit by a swift change of the immediate word more meanings. The syllabic accuracy, always varying the harmony, turning upon rhymes that do not stop but lead. An eye that sees

". . . the drifts of the thickets antlered like deer."

He had an ear out of Joyce and sometimes a little precious with it, but oh, he could sing back to the thing seen, felt, known, the word that in the motion of its meaning will not be forgotten,

"The force that through the green fuse drives the flower . . ."

For me one poet comes alive at one time. I cannot say this of music, except sometimes at the piano or listening. But a poet is my own kin to be argued with, subject to gossip and criticism, like my nearest friends. I cannot read poetry out of a book. I must be the poetry or not, as if I were the writing elbow of the man that made it.

I read of his psychological imagery that it was Freudian. My own reading tells me of his religion, more nearly related to the equations of Einstein than to the ceremony of churches. But his language recalled the ceremonial tradition:

"Nothing I cared, in the lamb white days, that time would take me

Up to the swallow thronged loft by the shadow of my hand. . ."

In a generation of betrayals he betrayed no one, not even himself. If he had temporal, political opinions, he transformed them into ritual. Poetry is a

form of ritual, if one so reads it. It can also, but that is not needed, entertain.

• • •

Aaron Copland has been caught between the poles of technique and entertainment. In his first published composition, *The Cat and the Mouse*, written at the age of nineteen, the two were joined. The musical interest lay in the technique, the audience appeal in the musical characterization of the cat and mouse. For every performance of the Piano Variations, his most concentrated keyboard work, *The Cat and the Mouse* has been played a hundred times.

Copland is, to my knowledge, the solitary American who makes his living by composing serious music. He is not naturally light, as his piano blues testify, and never frivolous. His scores for motion pictures have been consistently as grave as attractive, perfectly resigned, balanced, finished as it were in low relief to maintain their place in the onlooker's attention without distracting him, yet so eloquently chased as to provide full musical enjoyment when relieved from the obligatory restraint of non-distraction. He has set standards of esthetic decency that are still remembered in Hollywood, while giving repeated examples of how the good thing can be done creatively without concessions. Wherever he is and whatever his problems, his influence has been unfailingly benign, outgoing, and magnanimous.

For several months, while discussing other topics, I have been nibbling at the subject of Copland with little remarks that were both complimentary and unfair. The determination to take Copland seriously has had a good effect on the morale of some American composers. He is not too far beyond them in ability or method; they can talk his language. The difficulty has been to praise Copland highly without putting him on the same level, imaginatively, as Stravinsky or in the large frame of reference, conceptually, that is filled out by Schoenberg or by Ives. His admirers are included to set up standards that impose upon Copland, in relation to Stravinsky, a permanent one-two position; and those methods of Copland or Stravinsky which can be thus double-checked are imitated and overpraised. When either composer goes off the road and starts across country in a direction of his own, their mutual admirers emit a mutual gasp. This assumed equivalence not so much of style as of method safeguards the admirers against losing themselves among the nebulae of larger conceptual ideas: design that is too big, subject that is too pervasive; rhetoric too grandiose or too religious; and revolutionary attitudes that dispense with notational and harmonic directness, music that is to say which must be heard before it can be comprehended, then comprehended afresh when it is heard.

Copland's own critical statements on various occasions have tended to follow the same line. He may be, like Hindemith with *Gebrauchsmusik*, the source of the attitude as well as its victim. He admires the conceptual composer and worries about him; he inclines to overvalue the composer who is as methodical as he is inspired, who does not like Schoenberg evolve the method after the inspiration but keeps in mind at all times the need of bridging in his music the gap between art and audience. Copland protests, like Hindemith, that in this regard his terminology has been applied too literally to his own work; that he is not an ambivalent composer; that he does not divide his creative workmanship between two audiences, present and potential, preparing for each a distinct sort of music.

Copland believes in a music which speaks the vernacular of its time and country. With this in mind he has studied and experimented with jazz and made himself a master of the folk-tunes of the larger Americas. The jazz component has become in his use, as it will whenever there is not as in Stravinsky's jazz pieces a feeling of deliberate parody, abstruse and technically assimilated, a classical device, shaping harmony and counterpoint. The folk-tune component has remained romantic, only partially assimilated and for that reason easier to recognize. The two similarly vernacular sources beget unlike conclusions, again emphasizing the apparent ambivalence of his creative mind.

Copland is at his best when he is most direct, when his art speaks immediately to the listener. He can be long but not large. This may be to some extent the result of a natural affinity for those French disciplines, against which such a French composer as Messaien has reacted violently by becoming, like Vincent D'Indy, both too long and too large. When Copland aims at largeness he loses personal force and becomes rhetorical; the vernacular component, though it may be imbedded in the writing, is lost in the technical effort. He has not yet gone the distance of Messaien in trying to justify the rhetoric by supplying it with extra-musical explanations. On the contrary, his best music

does just what it says: *Quiet City, Billy the Kid, Rodeo, El Salon Mexico*: whereas Messaien's, even at its best, is always announcing, like the lesser Mahler, what it wishes to do.

This explanation would be simple enough, and it is sometimes put forward to explain Copland's popularity, but it does not explain his very best music: *Music for the Theatre*, the Piano Variations, the Piano Sonata, the song-cycle for voice and piano on poems by Emily Dickinson, or the settings of Old American Songs, an expert selection which in the handling of another composer would be trite or arty. In these Copland is a composer to be judged not by levels of expertness or even by comparative quality of imagination or conception: the way is his own. You can no more deny its style, its power, its simple complexity, its ability to move a reasonably accepting audience, than you can rate it by comparison. This music has the style that makes style, not only by imitation by robbery.

In *Appalachian Spring* all these strongest elements of Copland's ability come together, though they do not quite fuse, to make a work of art that is at once abstract and self-explanatory, folkish and rhetorically moving, dry, economical, not uninhibited yet fully emotional, deserving the most careful study as a score yet thoroughly satisfying for a popular audience.

Copland has been called a composer of the city, an urban mind that goes out visiting in search of country notions and brings them home to work them up. In fact he is one of the least citified of American composers; except when he is trying to impress the big, formal audience or letting go some trifle for piano, his mind eschews the urban commonplace. He is more American, more continentally American, than Gershwin, almost entirely free of the Jewish European origins of melody that have made Gershwin a sentimental best-seller to the neglect of his most strikingly American quality, his rhythm. Listen to any Gershwin night and observe how every derivative element of Gershwin has been sentimentally exaggerated, how bravura has been substituted for jazz. Listen to the old Gershwin-Whiteman record of *Rhapsody in Blue* and compare it with today's best-selling versions. Gershwin was urban in the same way that our big cities are full of still unassimilated Europe. You don't find this sort of thing in Copland; even the early Piano Trio, *Vitebsk*, is more American than Russian.

When I look at the picture of him at

the front of the new biography by Arthur Berger* and see the long, stooped, ranging, melancholy shape of him I think of America, as I think of it in Abraham Lincoln. Or the lank leading men who ring the bell year after year at the motion picture box office. Berger, by the way, has done a poor job of it, an exterior, critical parsing job, with the wrong sort of praise and the wrong sort of reservations. Lawrence Morton disposed of the book in several pages of *The Music Quarterly*, offering at the same time a few thoughts that said more in understanding and genuine enthusiasm than the whole of Berger's effort. Not that Berger fails entirely: he is too well drilled a critic to miss every point. This sort of book drags along after the composer's reputation, leaving the creative problems unexplained.

Copland himself has done better, in his last book *Music and Imagination*. Why shouldn't a composer be his own best critic? Copland doesn't answer this. In his usual way he rambles along, speaking of one thing and commenting upon another, as if the natural facts of music were everlastingly interesting to look at but writing a book about them, or in this instance a set of Norton lectures for Harvard University,** isn't particularly his job. He starts thinking aloud, covering a wide spread of information, stirs up good and bad personal opinions, lets them go, tries to mention favorably one way or another every composer he has met: but you get no absolute bang of confirmation or disagreement from his gentle flow. One doesn't feel the incisive mind biting gritty reality or find the convinced prejudices, the great style of discourse of Stravinsky's *Musical Poetics*.

As a matter of fact, except the economy and some related attitudes towards high-falutin superlatives of emotion and style, Copland and Stravinsky are utterly unalike. Stravinsky knows to an extraordinary degree exactly what he wants and has an extraordinary capacity for discovering new wants, for exploring new experiences one at a time and to the bottom.*** Copland knows what he likes and likes what he discovers and talks about it or turns it into music in his own agreeable and competent manner.

No one can predict what either of them will do next; each has produced a series of creations that are landmarks, surveyor's stones in contemporary music. Both are optimists, to revive an abused word that is nowadays messed up with wrong connotations; apart from their music, they can lead a crowd by sheer personality. They are distinct personalities: you can't learn much about one from studying the other. The difference is in the vitality and compelling force of the mind when it gets down to creative attention.

Before Copland's mind is always the question, which he has answered variously at different times: "how are we to make contact with this enormously enlarged potential audience, without sacrificing in any way the highest musical standards?" I doubt whether such a question has ever seriously troubled Stravinsky. Both are great showmen, but for Stravinsky the show must follow the latest turning of his art. For Copland there appears to be always the humbling consideration: is he big enough to swing it.

*AARON COPLAND by Arthur Berger; New York; Oxford University Press; 1953
**MUSIC AND IMAGINATION by Aaron Copland; Harvard University Press; Cambridge; 1952.
***More impressive to me than the music of Webern, at the rehearsal for our program of his music last spring, was the experience of watching Stravinsky, with the scores before him, take Webern in. Only once did he break concentration, to come over and ask whether, at the concert, we could not perform each piece twice.

(September 1954)

CITYSCAPE AND LANDSCAPE
Victor Gruen

Excerpts from a speech recently given at the International Conference of Design in Aspen, Colorado.

We are swamped with an avalanche of new inventions, discoveries, machines and gadgets. Our outlook is blurred by daily papers, television, magazines. We are exposed to philosophy, art criticism, analytical psychology, nuclear fission, spiritualism. We are confronted with abstractivism, non-objectivism, new realism, surrealism until we all feel as if we are swimming in the middle of a big pot of "genuine, kosher, Hungarian goulash, dixie style."

If we don't want to get trapped, doubtful and actionless, at the co-merging of the clover leaves, we have to stop looking and listening around and get on the road. Proceeding in accordance with such decision in the field of architecture, one soon finds oneself in the stream of creative action challenged by limitations, restraining discipline and many other problems.

Architecture's most urgent mission today is to convert chaos into order, change mechanization from a tyrant to a slave and thus make place for beauty where there is vulgarity and ugliness. Architecture today cannot concern itself only with that one particular set of structures which happen to stand upright and be hollow "buildings" in the conventional sense. It must concern itself with all man made elements which form our environments, with roads and highways, with signs and posters, with outdoor spaces as created by structures, with cityscape and landscape.

In talking about cityscape and landscape, I would like to define the terms as I use them:

Cityscape obviously is a setting in which manmade structures are predominant.

Landscape is an environment in which nature is predominant.

Just as there are many kinds of landscapes—mountainous areas, tropical settings, desert lands—there are many types of cityscape. Usually we connect with the term in our minds an orderly pattern of substantial buildings, avenues, boulevards, filled with hustling people.

The vast majority of cityscape looks completely different. Let me categorize the various species:

There is *technoscape*—an environment shaped nearly exclusively by the apparatus of technology in its respectable and less reputable forms. It is a cityscape dotted with oil wells, refineries, high voltage lines, derricks, chimneys, conveyors, dump heaps, auto cemeteries.

There is *transportationscape*—featuring the tinny surfaces of miles of cars on the concrete deserts of highways, freeways, expressways, parking lots, cloverleaves, tastefully trimmed with traffic signs, billboards, garlands of power lines and other dangling wire. Transportationscape also includes vast arid lands of airplane runways and railroad yards.

There is *suburbscape*—in all its manifestation from plush settlements of more or less historic mansions to the parade grounds of the anonymous mass housing industry where dingbats are lined up for inspection. Suburbia with phony respectability and genuine boredom effectively isolated from the world of traffic jams.

And there is the *sub-cityscape*—a category covering probably more acreage than all the others combined, a collection of the worst elements of cityscape, technoscape and transportationscape—the "red and green light district" of our major cities—the degrading facade of suburbia, the shameful introduction to our cities, the scourge of the metropolis.

Sub-cityscape consists of elements which cling like leeches to all of our roads, accompanying them far out to where there was, once upon a time, something called *landscape*; sub-cityscape—consisting of gas stations, shacks, shanties, car lots, posters, billboards, dump heaps, roadside stands, rubbish, dirt and trash.

Sub-cityscape fills up the areas between cities and suburbs, between cities and towns, between cities and other cities. Sub-cityscapes spread their tentacles in all directions, overgrow regions, states and country.

Sub-cityscape is the reason why city planning, before it has even had a chance to become effective in our times, is already obsolete and why it has to be replaced with regional planning.

And now let's consider the term LANDSCAPE a little more. There is a difference between it and NATURE as such. Landscape is nature with which man has made intimate contact—nature with human habitations. Landscape is the rolling hills in Pennsylvania with farmhouses. Landscape is the mountain valleys in Tyrol with toy villages strewn about. Landscape is a New England rural area with the slim finger of the church tower pointing up, a rocky coast with a fishing village, an Italian lake with colorful houses clinging to a steep shore.

Landscape is the successful marriage of nature and human endeavor, a surrounding in which man made and nature made elements cooperate to effect highest enjoyment.

The technological age is not favorable for the creation of landscape and, for the time being, I am afraid we have to regard it as a historic relic to be preserved and protected wherever possible.

Once upon a time the world was full of wonderful landscape and beautiful stretches of nature. At that time people complained because it was so hard to get to those places and one had to be satisfied with reading accounts of the courageous adventurers who traveled on foot and on horse and on sailboat.

Today we are nations on wheels. Today we can fly on the "installment plan" anywhere in the world. Improved working conditions allow millions to buy cars. Forty-hour weeks have created the "week-end." Paid vacations seem to many like the fulfillment of their longing for the enjoyment of landscape and nature. But the millions are betrayed and swindled out of their hard-gained advantages.

Hours of their free time are stolen by traffic jams. Their nerves are frayed by traffic risks, and when they finally reach the target of their dreams, the piece of landscape or nature, millions of others have been there first and taken the parking place and, even if one is finally found, the dream looks tainted with beer and trash, studded with the elements of the sub-cityscape.

We have become a nation all "dressed up" with no place to go. What is to be done? A long, hard and stubborn fight is ahead.

The blitzkrieg of technology has taken up by surprise. It has dented our spiritual and physical defenses. There may still be a chance to win if we fight with conviction and perseverance and humility. There may be a chance if the creative people of this age crawl out of their miscellaneous ivory towers and wage battle on the level on which it counts, on the battleground of reality.

We architects experience that the individual structures which we erect cannot obtain their full measure of effectiveness because their settings are unsympathetic. Only in the rarest cases are we lucky enough to find a setting which is in congruity with the structure.

Disturbing, distasteful noises and ugly surroundings are the rule rather than the exception. Smog, poisonous fumes, traffic difficulties add to the discord. Our efforts to create tiny islands of order in the wild sea of anarchy are condemned to failure. Consider, a moment, the pathetically small number of planned cityscapes created in this country in the 20th century.

Rockefeller Center—a few colleges— maybe half a dozen residential projects— a few shopping centers—everything else which was built, good, bad or middling, is threatened with failure, not because of its own inadequacy, but because of the inadequacy of its surroundings.

Before the technological blitzkrieg, cityscape and landscape were neatly and clearly separated. In the middle ages it was most effectively done with fortified walls and moats.

Cityscape has spilled over the walls, has spread out in the form of sub-cityscape and, in the midst of the dirty mire, float suburbia and the landscape waiting to be rescued. Our task today is to bring order on a steadily widening scale. We have to unscramble the melee of flesh and machines, pedestrians and automobiles, junk yards and homes. This is a Herculean task. That it is not quite hopeless I would like to illustrate by the experience of my personal battle against the suburban commercial slum.

Until a few years ago the only form of shopping facilities known in suburbia consisted of long rows of one story structures along the arterials connecting suburbs with the city core. These strip developments still exist and, unfortunately, due to unwise zoning practice, they still grow. The story of their growth sounds like a recipe for building successfully commercial slums.

Their original purpose—to serve suburban customers and to produce profit— is not fulfilled in the long run. Their customers must hunt for parking spaces, cross busy highways repeatedly, walk in dismal surroundings for long stretches. They offer poor shopping conditions and a depressing shopping atmosphere. They do, however, succeed beautifully in the step-by-step deterioration of the surrounding residential areas by their appearance, their noise, their smells, their traffic congestion. Owners and tenants of surrounding residential areas move out, slums develop and, having driven its good customers away, the shopping strip slowly deteriorates, the stores move away, another mile out into the suburb, where they start planfully and effectively to ruin a new environment. Their vacated buildings are taken over by secondhand stores, marginal operators, used car dealers and saloons and the commercial slum is completed.

In these suburban store strips architectural elements, if such ever have existed, are solidly covered by the ugly rash of blatant signs, blinking cascades of neon, paper streamers. The suburban store strip show commercialism at its worst.

Against this sorry backdrop, there appeared a few years ago a new building type—the planned, integrated shopping center. The importance of this event for 20th century architecture can, in my opinion, hardly be exaggerated. It is the first large scale, conscious planning effort made by the forces usually considered as upholders of rugged individualism. The planned shopping center furnishes the proof of the possibilities and of the effectiveness of self-imposed restraint and discipline. How far this self-discipline has been exercised has been illustrated by one little detail of the largest of these planned shopping centers, Northland near Detroit. The huge branch department stores of this center has, as its only identifying sign, 2 1/2 inch high lettering near the entrance doors.

I would like to discuss with you in detail the main principles of shopping center design because I feel that they have significance for other elements of our cityscape including our city cores. Here are the five important ones:

1. Creation of effectively separated spheres of activity:
   The sphere of access
   The sphere of car storage
   The sphere of service activities
   The sphere of selling
   The sphere of walking
   and relaxation
2. Creation of opportunities for social, cultural, civic and recreational activities.
3. Overall architectural planning as related to function, structure and esthetics.
4. Encouragement of individualistic expression of commercial elements but subordinating these expressions to overall discipline by means of architectural coordination, sign control and a code of behavior concerning matters like show window stickers, opening hours, show window lighting, etc.
5. Integration with the surrounding environment in matters of traffic, usage, protection and esthetics.

These principles have been more or less consciously and, with different degrees of success, applied to about a dozen existing regional shopping centers in the nation. They are also used as the basis of about 40 large shopping centers now in the construction or advanced planning stage. The effect of this new phenomenon on the American suburban scene is extremely interesting and gratifying.

Northland near Detroit, which has now been operating for more than a year, has, in the words of many residents, "changed our lives." It has filled that great unanswered need of sprawling suburbia for a crystallization point.

Visited by 50 million people in the first year of its existence, it has already become Detroit's "festival place" where all the important civic events for which there is no place elsewhere, like Army Day, Fourth of July, Christmas and Easter and many others are celebrated. On such days, there is in the landscaped courts and malls the atmosphere of a gay fiesta. But all through the year, week days and holidays, thousands promenade, amble, gossip, sit around on garden benches, study outdoor exhibits which at different times feature giant bombers, fashion shows, garden furniture, new car models and art. They participate in the events in the two auditoriums, in the community center and in Kiddyland; they lunch or dine in one of the dozen eating places; they have made it their club, their public park, the center of their social activities.

The residents of surrounding areas are well satisfied too. Instead of the feared deterioration usually connected with the appearance of commercial facilities, they experienced a pleasant surprise. None of the traffic spilled into the residential streets, there are no evil sights, no evil noises, no evil smells. Neither did they mind that, because of the vicinity of so many desirable facilities, the demand for residential sites in the neighborhood grew and the value of their property rose considerably.

The 50 million people who came to Northland did one other thing also. They shopped—they did it with so much joy, intensity and gusto that the sales figures per one square foot of store area reached amounts unprecedented in suburban shopping facilities to date.

The basic principles of Northland are applied to a number of other shopping centers but also, and maybe this is more significant, to other types of projects.

In two suburban areas we are planning at present the construction of Recreational Health Centers. Their concept is to combine, in one indigenous environment, related facilities like hospitals, clinics, laboratories, medical and dental offices, nurses' homes, hotel accommodations for visitors, and the related commercial services like restaurants, lunch rooms, cafeterias, pharmacists medical supply stores. Following the shopping center pattern, we create on the one hand separation between various usages and, on the other hand, combine the functions of all buildings of the same denomination, thus creating a common access road system, common parking areas, common heating and air conditioning services and common loading, deliveries, repair and maintenance areas. In the midst of the various buildings there will be, reserved for pedestrians, outdoor spaces richly landscaped, offering restfulness and creating another segment of 20th century cityscape.

For two other cities we are planning suburban Regional Office Centers. We are employing for them the same principles as for the shopping and health centers.

We are working on the extension of this principle of creating integrated nuclei for other clearly defined usages. We are planning home buildings and furnishing centers, research and laboratory centers, light industry centers.

And, as we proceed with these various plans for many cities of the nation, it seems to us that here might be a weapon for a successful counter-attack in the technological blitzkrieg. If we use the weapon and if we can create large numbers of these cluster-like centers, we will be able to raze the tenantless string of shanty towns along our roads and when the rubble is cleared away, we will plant trees and shrubs and grass and flowers where the suburban slums stood. We will gain space to widen strangled thoroughfares, space for picnic grounds, playgrounds, parks; we will get rid of wide stretches of sub-cityscape.

And we are trying another move. We are trying to apply this process of making order by departmentalization and integrated planning to our existing city cores. We are working on a number of replanning projects for downtown areas of smaller cities and on one project for the rehabilitation of the downtown area of a city of 600 thousand.

The mainspring of our design intention is the wish to create undisturbed and beautiful areas in which one can walk. The size of these areas is determined by human scale, by manageable walking distances; each such walking area, with its building, forms one super block. They serve various purposes, sometimes more than one. There will be a block for shopping, a block for offices and shopping, a block for civic activities, a block for hotels and offices. The blocks are interconnected by a spine-like promenade which, besides pleasant walkways, features some auxiliary means of motion such as moving sidewalks and small exhibition-type electric buses.

The blocks are surrounded by a car storage area which, depending on varying conditions, will take the form of garages, multiple deck parking, underground parking or surface parking. All service traffic moves on underground roads. The car storage areas are looped by traffic access and circulatory roads from which branch off feeder roads toward the spine promenade between the individual blocks. Some of these feeder roads interconnect by dipping under the promenade.

The traffic access and circulatory road system is integrated and connected with the roads of the outlying city portions and with the existing and projected expressway system.

The measures for curing the ills of the business area would not be complete and effective without the rehabilitation of downtown residential areas. They have to be made desirable again for the millions of Americans who today are involuntary suburbanites, for all those people who hate gardening and commuting, for all those people who would like to be near their offices and near the theaters and museums and libraries, but who cannot do so because living near downtown has become synonymous with living in slums.

Slum clearance is not good enough if it results in the replacement of old slums by brand new ones with better plumbing. We have to create new urban neighborhoods offering a variety of living unit types for all tastes and all pocketbooks from low cost housing to luxury apartments.

Once the slums which choke the heart of our cities are removed and replaced with highly desirable living environments, new life blood will flow into the rebuilt city core, and with freeways and rapid transit transportation interconnecting the rejuvenated downtown area with healthy satellite towns, a new age of enjoyment of urban life may be born.

You realize, of course, that these are big and costly plans, but there is in this country today an atmosphere extremely favorable to their implementation. These plans are practical because they are firmly founded on our existing economic system. The suburban centers—shopping centers, health centers, office building centers, etc.—are profitable ventures and downtown rehabilitation is profitable too in the sense of saving tremendous real estate values from deterioration, in the sense of being the only means of staving off accelerated downfall and disaster.

I am encouraged by the fact that during the last years architects and planners in many cities have actually received commissions for downtown master planning projects. I am encouraged by the fact that rehabilitation has moved into the public limelight. I am encouraged by my personal experience in the work with my friends and associates, Yamasaki and Stonorov, in connection with the downtown rehabilitation project in Detroit. Here, a citizens' committee composed of bankers, merchants, automobile industry executives, union leaders, minority representatives, have not only put an amazing amount of work and energy but also a large amount of dollars into the venture of taking measures to save downtown.

For success on a grand scale, we will need more than plans and energy and even money. We will need the legal weapons to fight the battle, we need more effective legislation for condemnation proceedings, we need new zoning laws, and we may need federal funds at least as a guarantee for loans for urban and suburban rehabilitation. We need educational programs for our architectural schools in which integrated planning is stressed, and we need the active help and cooperation of artists, designers and creative men in all fields in order to win in the blitzkrieg of technology.

(September 1955)

MUSIC COLUMN, Peter Yates
Pierre Boulez

"He is erudite an arid, challenging and not very competent." That was my judgement of Pierre Boulez, in the February issue of this magazine. I was speaking with some experience.

Several years ago a young fellow announced himself on the phone as David Tudor; John Cage had directed him to call on us. We begged him to come over in the evening. When he arrived there was some embarrassment about the large suitcase he was carrying, which he insisted on carrying right upstairs into the studio. At last we were given an explanation: it had his music in it. Try as I may, I can't recall how he looked. His conversation was eager and impenetrable. He was talking about new music in terms we did not understand. After a few minutes he took the scores to the piano.

Since then David Tudor has made a reputation. At the time I knew nothing about him. His peculiar skill represents a new era in musical thinking, post World War 2. John Cage is its direct precursor. Its musical thinking begins in the music it invents: it rejects tradition. It is fiercely, mystically convinced of its purpose, to reject tradition, to make new.

So in David Tudor's playing there were only three shades, no colors: loud, louder, soft. In the rare passages of sentiment he could do nothing but play on the tops of the keys. For these limits he had good reason. The music he played is structurally discontinuous. The piece by John Cage had been put together according to a system related to the Chinese game *I-ching*, the choice of notes determined by successive throws of dice. I hesitate always to speak for John Cage, he speaks so much more relevantly for himself. The purpose of this composition by chance is to get rid of everything having to do with the determinants of Western European music, its traditions, forms, systems. In his enthusiasm John Cage had not got rid of the piano nor of musical notation, and this in spite of his earlier successful experiments with electronic noise-makers and combinations of home-made percussion instruments. David Tudor was trying to produce as sound from a piano notation having no actual relevance to the sound of a piano or to the means by which such sound is produced. Disembodied clusters resembling chords and haphazard successions of odd notes flew about like spilled shot. What dynamic effects could there be except loud, louder, and soft?

Then a piece by a young member of the Cage group, whose name I have lost. This composer has reduced the problems of composition to black squares on a stave with three spaces. A square in the top space means, play any combination of notes you wish in the upper third of the piano; a square in the middle space does the same for the middle third, one in the lower space for the lower third. David Tudor did not play us this piece, he showed it to us. When I asked for a demonstration, he was cautious. To play it, you have to know what sort of sound the composer wishes you to choose. This was a new piece, and he hadn't worked it up.

Please don't believe I am making fun of David Tudor or this music. As memory permits, I am relating facts, seriously offered and seriously, if skeptically received. As far as I am concerned, composers by the thousands may go to anonymity down the traditional grooves, never having made the effort to think their way from one groove beyond the next. A young man who has the guts to cut himself off arbitrarily and go blind into a creative alley, blind alley though it may be, of his own choosing will always have my sympathetic interest. I may disagree; I may dislike what he does; I may find no sense or art in it. That is to no purpose. I respect whatever it may be in his private cosmos that impels him to go it alone, outside the esthetic community. Of course he may be wrong; he usually is. Faith, conviction, an exclusive breaking away, however negatively based, is the distinctive power of the human spirit, beyond the common gift of thought. Every time we meet such a one we are forced to reconsider the works of culture, the origins of human experience. The revolutionary individual, the radical, I do not mean the member of a revolutionary party, carries forward the work of the spirit at a depth never to be reached by corporate or institutional effort.

The third piece David Tudor offered was a set of variations on a system of tone-rows, put together according to some intellectual process. The music proceeded with regard for the scale and the piano. Passages plainly showed the influence of Brahms. Like any listener who for a brief period has encountered the esthetic unknown, I was relieved by the familiar, indeed rather contemptuously enjoyed it.

The last piece of the evening was the *Second Sonata*, subtitled *The Battle*, by Pierre Boulez. Three of the five movements were played. I have never watched a pianist go through such contortions, nor suffered such a continuum of musical violence bringing forth less discriminable sound. The piano and the scale were disregarded. At the mid-point in the performance my wife, who has played what was until recently the most demanding music of the future, became so upset she was forced to leave the room. How much of this effect was inherent in the music, which was of unrelieved violence, and how much the result of the pianist's incapacity to perform it beyond the sheer virtuosity of leaping from one notational impasse to the next, I have no way to determine. The Sonata has been publicly performed, and I am assured that Mr. Boulez himself can manage two of the five movements.

I ended the evening with a thorough respect for David Tudor's gifts as a keyboard gymnast and for his musical convictions. If I had been able to afford inviting Mr. Tudor to return from New York to perform for Evenings on the Roof, I would unhesitatingly have done so. Nothing is better for an audience than to have its musical complacency, its belief in its ability to hear, completely shaken up. Such esthetic earthquakes, though we read about them, occur so seldom in the normal experience that we should be devoutly grateful to any creative or performing artist who can set the world shaking even a few minutes. David Tudor did it for me, and I have not ceased to be grateful.

In a later season Robert Craft managed to achieve for us a performance of the Boulez *Polyphony X* for 18 solo instruments. During rehearsals he went through some three teams of musicians before he was able to bring together one that would stay the course. I have never watched a group of musicians go on the stage so much like a team expecting to be badly beaten and come off so much as if they were carrying the goalposts. Some said they played twice as well as at the dress rehearsal. One has been quoted to me as remarking: "We got off at the start, and we never got back." I take the latter for pure cynicism, because I was able to follow clearly from beginning to end. A listener should not ask new music to explain itself; he should simply listen to it. The plan of the composition is not difficult, whatever its notational organization: the difficulty is in the manner of playing. Rather simple figurations, sometimes alone, sometimes counterpointed, are passed among the 18 instruments, usually a note to an instrument, in any brevity of time-division, so that the relationship of entry to beat must be achieved by intricate counting. The figurations are relatively discontinuous, like flowers on wallpaper, but they are not unlike in duration and are varied in such manner that several having been heard the remainder can be accepted. I thought at the time that the result was somewhat like a ballet by Delibes, a sequence of figures, each as acceptable as the next, which adds up to nothing more than a series of events. Let us say that from such a ballet the harmonic stuffing has been left out, and the melodic patterns reassigned so that each note is played by a different instrument, but each pattern recomposed in such a way that all alike are determined by a preconceived plan of pitches, dynamics, and so on, the former right notes becoming harmonically wrong but "right," since each can be explained by its derivation from a note in the begetting design: thus Delibes becomes Boulez. In spite of the new intricate notation and the loss of harmonic guidance, the essential content (or audible contour) of the music has not changed. Beethoven in the *Diabelli Variations* and Gertrude Stein in many writings follow the same mode. We are concerned with what happens to a series of consequences in relation to their origins within a determining event. The maker does not aim at "meaning" or to please. Does the unreadable philosopher condemn his purpose?

Then this season we had the Sonatina for Flute and Piano. I have already committed myself to an opinion about it. It is an early work, crudely written for the piano and incapable of finding an end. I heard it again at the University of California at Los Angeles, in Schoenberg Hall, after a lecture by Pierre Boulez.

Mr. Boulez is music-director for the Jean-Louis Barrault theatrical company in Paris, one of the most respected theatrical repertory groups presently in existence. In a loft above the theatre Mr. Boulez every year offers a series of four to six programs, each performed twice. The room seats about two hundred. These are, I am assured, the only programs of radically contemporary music which may be heard in Paris. One program this season, shifted to a larger auditorium, drew a thousand attendance.

Because the Barrault company was appearing in New York, it was possible for Mr. Boulez to visit us for this lecture. And by a fortunate chance the Monday Evening Concerts was able to invite him to conduct a performance of his composition in nine parts, *Le Marteau sans Maitre*, already in rehearsal under Robert Craft.

First the lecture, the Sonatina, and the ensuing panel discussion. The lecturer was in a tough spot. Stravinsky and Mrs. Schoenberg were in the audience. He was aware that, as possible never before in his career, the past sat in judgment on him. He must be tactful, lest the past misinterpret. For the audience that past was its present, won to after a long climb against cultural resistance as steep as any mountainside. Many indeed were still climbing to reach that past. He began therefore as a spokesman of a present trying to be present, a challenger of that past, which the audience, whatever it might feel about the past still present, would defend as sanity against him. Try as we might, we could not be otherwise.

He had assets: an unpretentious, alert, dark, roguish presence, very French; was witty; handles English ably, knew exactly what he meant to say; spoke with an unfailing conviction, which carried conviction; brilliant mental footwork, the ability to take whatever was thrown at him and give it back with force. Most of us spent the evening hoping he would be upset and knowing he would not.

He took for subject *The Evolution of Style and Meaning Among the Young Composers*. Opening he paid respect to the composers, his predecessors, from whom proceeds all that he will now accept as style and meaning in contemporary music, Stravinsky, Bartok, and the Viennese composers, Schoenberg, Berg, Webern. He identified the contemporary composers who are of his own mind, Stockhausen in Germany, Nono in Italy, Leibowitz in France, giving as their common origin the work of Stravinsky and Webern. He did not mention his teacher and occasional collaborator, Messiaen. He made clear his method, criticism, the negative, of which the positive is the new-created work. The criticism he directed primarily at Schoenberg.

In a caustic article, *Schoenberg Is Dead*, Boulez had welcomed the death of this composer as a liberation of his disciples from the pressure of a great master who had falsified his own tradition: the later work of Schoenberg had prejudiced the achievement of the tone-row by reintroducing tonality. Boulez holds against Schoenberg what most of us might consider his admirable virtue, that having defined new potentialities of musical technique by an exclusive device, he could then modify the device to readmit what had been excluded, thus reintegrating the new method with its past. The contrary method, however significant, is confined by its exclusions. During the evening Boulez offered no criticism of Stravinsky, whose recent row compositions begin at this point of reintegration.

Musical criticism, positive or negative, crawls forward on legs of identification. Against the great trunk of Schoenberg's career negative critics have thrown up, over a long period, Stravinsky, and in shorter bursts such composers as Sibelius, Prokofief, Hindemith, and Berg, more recently Webern. These have been the main contenders. Advocates of Sibelius, Prokofief, Hindemith, and until lately Stravinsky, consider the work of Schoenberg a technical or emotional aberration. Advocates of Berg accept the Expressionist period of Schoenberg, until *Die Glueckliche Hand*, plus a qualified tolerance of the tone-row method. Advocates of Webern—among them Boulez—accept as in the right direction only those works of the atonal and early twelve-tone period, composed between 1910 and 1925 (*Pierrot Lunaire* to Wind Quintet). Lately Stravinsky has embraced the tone-row, qualifying it by an unyielding retention of tonality. At the present time the chief synthetic opponent of Schoenberg is Webern, a position I doubt that composer, if he were living, would tolerate.

Late Webern is imitable; late Schoenberg is not: no composer, at least, has yet managed it. The long progress of Schoenberg's evolution at no point denied the past, most nearly so during the period when he worked to exclude the traditional pull of tonality. The shorter career of Webern recognized almost no influence by that of the Schoenberg at this atonal period. Thorough digestion of Webern will stimulate an appetite for the later works by Schoenberg. I look for this as the next stage of musical development. In the same way, thorough digestion of Satie will stimulate a fresh appetite for those late works by Debussy, *Jeux*, the Etudes, the last three sonatas, in which, as Boulez told us, Debussy cut himself off from the past. Webern's compositions, short, exact, translucent, free of Schoenberg's larger conceptions, his immense forms, his classically derived movements, appeal to the young composer who values technique and denies "inspiration." To the end of his life Schoenberg never ceased to attribute the working of his art to a power, an inspiration, beyond himself.

Boulez began composing during the German occupation of France. The violence of his earlier music may reflect the spirit of resistance let loose during that time. Since then he has lived at the center of a culture, the one-city intellectual culture of Paris, which has transformed the spirit of resistance into a philosophy. I do not say Boulez has been influenced by Existentialism. He did not mention it. His conception of art expresses a like discipline: a man is responsible in detail for what he does—in music, for every note he makes. He can expect no other salvation. He does not aim to please, to be popular, but to live, to be noticed. Since he can depend only on himself, his art must begin in his technique. As Boulez explains it, the older composer began with the *essence*, the tradition in being, of which he made the composition; the new composer begins with his technique, of which he makes the work of art, the unique realization, the *essence*. The new composer accepts the destruction of traditional music as having been accomplished by his predecessors, an accomplishment I doubt that Stravinsky, for example, would willingly admit. The new composer dispenses with the tradition, what Boulez calls the "background," and concentrates on his technique, which is at present only and inescapably the *row* or *serial principle*. Indeed, Boulez favors eliminating "row" or "serial" and using the word "principle," alone to signify the independence of his theory.

Schoenberg began with the tone-row, usually of twelve tones, or "six-plus-six," as he slyly told me one of the last times I talked with him. (The number 12 is unnecessary; any number may be used. Stravinsky has used more than twelve.)

Schoenberg limited the constructive possibilities of his composition by his insistence on preserving the identifiable row, in whatever position. Thus he was able to work with *pitch* or *interval* (the whole row as a unit) but not freely with *dynamic* or *timbre*, which refer to the individual note. Webern emancipated *dynamic* and *timbre*, that is to say, the individual note, from the over-all authority of the row. (There is a like distinction between Bach and Beethoven). These are, according to Boulez, the four elements of music, which are guided not by the whole row as a unit but by the *principle* of the row. A row can be any length, include any extremes of dynamic contrast. If *pitch* and *interval* remain the prime elements, *dynamic* and *timbre* take on a far greater influence, affording fresh means of identification, enabling the composer to set up fresh signals of motivic recognition apart from the succession of the row.

As I have said, the works by Boulez are not so much complex as damnably difficult to perform. I cannot escape the suspicion that his music must be made difficult, because if it were not it would be reduced to its elements, and these, without the elaboration of his technique, are bodiless. Like a number of startling composers of the past, like Webern to a degree, his art is cerebral but insubstantial. One evidence is lack of economy, the all too evident fault of the Sonatina for Flute and Piano which was played after the lecture ended.

In his discussion of technique Boulez was very precise, as far as he went, but he did not go far enough to satisfy Mrs. Schoenberg, who was sitting beside me. She wished him to tell exactly how he goes about making a composition, not an unfair question, if it be simply a matter of applying a technique. (One might expect that a composer so armed would give off compositions as rapidly as Sebastian Bach or Mozart; Boulez has been anything but prolific, 15 compositions. The questions rises: what does it take to set him off, since he has only to put down a few notes in series, define their principle and entrust the outcome to his technique? I am not inferring a reductio *ad absurdum*. This is precisely the method, based on improvisation, used by Bach and Mozart. The answer to this question may bring us near the blind spot in the Boulez argument. During a short conversation alone with Mr. Boulez before a rehearsal, I put the question to him. His answer, after two false starts and some mutual clarification, amounts to this: Bach and Mozart composed with familiar materials,

the scale and so on, and made music easily. Beethoven exploited less familiar situations, making less music with more difficulty. Debussy composed still less with less reliance on the past, the technical background. Yes, yes, children, I see you all raising your hands, your shouting faces!).

At the end of his lecture Boulez told us he would be back to answer questions and hear arguments, and he would "argue with us all the evening." I cannot praise him enough as the spokesman for a point of view; the force of his mind and culture showed to full advantage in the panel discussion.

He had for opponents the composers Lukas Foss and Paul Des Marais, and to assist him, when the questions went beyond his limited English, Robert Craft. It was the heathen attacking the true believer, who never qualified or wavered in the exposition of his faith. To the chief question of the evening, thrown at him in several versions, whether it is possible now to compose by other means apart from the row-principle, he replied with a soft "No." When the question was repeated in more complex language, Craft answered for him, a soft "No" again. One word never more decisively cut off two young composers from the future. To other questions, from stage and audience, Boulez reaffirmed his undeviating attitude, always with humor and a charm that, as much as his personal authority, disarmed the questioners of antagonism. Technically, philosophically, from a background of culture as substantial as his music may not be, he dealt with each problem amply, in a minimum of verbiage. Whether or not he is a great composer, he is an admirable intelligence. Such a mind, though it may not itself come to glory in music, charges the creative atmosphere with ideas.

When we talked together I asked him about two other radicals, Harry Partch, whose work he does not know, and John Cage. Of Cage's several disjunct types of composition he prefers those for *prepared piano*. the later "works by chance" he does not approve. He believes in what he calls "the musical continuum," which I take to mean the ordering of sound by controllable means. "This I do not care for" he told me, tapping the wood under the piano keyboard. Though he admires Cage's earlier percussion pieces, he says they are not in his direction.

The concert promised *The Lamentations of Jeremiah* by Thomas Tallis and *Le Marteau sans Maitre* by

Boulez. We were given as bonus a composition on electronic tape by Stockhausen, *Song of the Adolescents* which Boulez had brought with him. It is one of four such compositions on tape Stockhausen has prepared. The medium consists of electronic sound-producing equipment, a boy's voice, and the sorcery of tape, cut, rerecorded, distorted, altered in pitch. The boy's voice became a chorus, called to itself simultaneously out of many perspectives, spoke abruptly in startling nearness. The electronic sound came in several packages: a crescendo or decrescendo of bubblings in which the boy at first seemed to drown; a whisk-like scratching of metal; a golden clangor like a spilled pocketful of gold change; various resonances of more or less indefinite duration, pitch, and audibility, often emphasizing extreme overtones. The combinations, sometimes very beautiful, sometimes drawn apart in schizophrenic nightmare, were part montage, part a sort of sound-landscape of fantastic dimensions, par the familiar grotesquerie of Germanic expressionism, characteristic of German painting and sculpture in many periods. The fault of the composition is its length; it will not leave off when all possibilities seem to have been exploited.

A few listeners fled during the first minutes, a few more at the end; others sat it out stoically, or with plugged ears or witty comments. At times it was like sitting under Niagara Falls with your head in a bucket, at times a physically felt nightmare that would not cease. Yet there were passages, moments, of an extraordinary richness. We are only at the beginning of such music. Boulez tells us, he believes the future of poetry lies in such means. I am not sure I follow him. I felt the text was lost in the distractions.

It was possible to admire and to dislike this composition more intensely than the *Contrapunkte No. 1* for 10 instruments by Stockhausen, which Robert Craft conducted for these same concerts last season. That was a thin piece, its design unpredictable but unconvincing when presented. Stockhausen appears to lack the instrumental resources of Boulez.

Even Robert Craft had reached an impasse in rehearsing *Le Marteau sans Maitre* when he turned it over to Boulez. The musicians had nearly given up hope of mastering their parts. But Boulez, who has prepared some thirty different performances of the work, drew everything together, rehearsing the musicians in groups and separately, revealing himself a master in every aspect of his art. He won the devotion of his players, so thoroughly that after the performance they presented him with a set of gold cufflinks engraved with his initials.

Let me pay my respects to the players, Catherine Gayer, voice, Arthur Gleghorn, alto flute, Milton Thomas, viola, Theodore Norman, guitar, William Kraft, vibraphone, Dorothy Remsen, xylorimba, and Lester Remsen, percussion.

I am told that Robert Craft had subdivided the measures to facilitate the counting. Boulez proceeded by the opposite method. He spread the passages in long lines, punctuated by accents, conducting, unlike most radical composers, with graceful curving motions, articulated in such manner as to bring out the contours of the long melodies. Everything he wished to emphasize was brought out visibly, allowing rather free disposition of the smaller details. Even for the listener his manner of conducting conveyed the flowing he desired.

The text consists of three short poems by Rene Char. The work is developed in three series of interlocked movements, numbers 1, 3, and 7, numbers 2, 4, 6, and 8, and numbers 5 and 9, each series related to one of the poems. In his lecture Boulez told us that the listener should find his way into and through the music by identifying the distinctive characteristics or "signals" of these interrelated sections. He was frank to admit that many hearings might be necessary to accomplish this. Since we were hearing the first American performance and had no prospect of a second, the preface was not encouraging. The future of such music would seem to be in recording, to permit unlimited rehearings. And there is no reason why music of such complexity should not satisfy an audience already at the point of exhausting the resources of the classics. It will certainly attract the lovers of hi-fi. I am told that Boulez has recorded it for *Vega* in Europe.

The music moves entirely in the upper registers of rather sweet sound, the basses being principally non-tonal percussion. By eliminating identifiable bass tones—Lawrence Morton pointed this out to me—the composer frees his long melodies from false harmonic reference. The percussion sounds are so placed as to reflect, almost like metal mirrors, the colors of the instruments. The melodies are not passed so continuously note by note among the instruments as in *Polyphony X*. The movements proceed rather by instrumental groupings, with long solos for each instrument. Such a combination of registers, if not expertly controlled, could degenerate into sentimental bleatings. No one, listening to the resulting music, could doubt the composer's expertness. Here was not any, as in the other compositions, any failure in the long design, no question of the placing of accents, no hesitation as to the rightness of the constant interruptions by silence, no struggle for an ending. If the music was spread thin, it was spread evenly; whatever its points might signify, it made them. The verbal inflections and distortions did not disguise the color of the voice. Whether any part of it was "beautiful" I did not stop to question. The "beautiful" did not separate itself from the ongoing context, as in the Stockhausen tape. Whatever it may not have been, it was, undeniably, music. Researching his medium, exploiting his technique, Boulez has come a long way from the earlier pieces.

Whether such an achievement represents an ultimate sophistication, whether it is really a new music or only the working out of an aberration, I hesitate to say. Boulez accepts the decision of the future, and for that we must wait.

My own opinion is that in *Le Marteau* Boulez resumes composition at the point near chaos (lack of classical reference) Schoenberg had reached in *Pierrot Lunaire*. The two works have many aspects of similarity. If the Boulez work reaches farther into the unknown, it does so with less certainty of detailed relationship between the unit and the whole. His *principle*, though a technique and logical, will not of itself make music. He admits that it will not make simple or easy music. He is not yet the composer Schoenberg was at the same period, though he lacks nothing by comparison in mastery of the means. Like Schoenberg he is deeply learned in music of all periods. He may distort the history of music to support his practice; he does not deny that history or its influence.

Boulez deserves the respect he won from all who met him during his visit here. His art bears watching. He is a master of the unknown. Yet I believe his direction lies, in spite of whatever personal resistance, in the same way as the later Schoenberg, back into rather than out of deeply formal music.

I hope to talk with him again. Having met him, listened to him and watched him work, I have quite revised my former judgment.

(July 1957)

(Continued from page 20, Spaulding)

none of us be shocked at such liberties as were taken. They show a trend, yes—but give only a feeble hint of what is in store for us when synthetic dirt, air conditioning eliminates conventional openings and bed blankets, and clothing of synthetic materials will be so cheap that laundries will not be needed.

(Continued from page 22, Neutra)

implied by his design will always be but limited and in need of practical check and re-check.

Apart from this portion of the entries, there are several other categories of fabrication ideas which strive to retain a flexibility of the product. It all is intensely interesting and gratifying to me, since in so many past years I have myself hopefully worked on everything from panels to prefab utility units, and to houses consisting of individual portions that could be added up, one plus one plus one, carefully fitting all onto a desirable site plan. Here now in this present contest of design contributions, the main shoot exfoliates into three branches (with all designers carefully guarding themselves against the reproach of advocating a fabricated straightjacket!)

Number one branch is predicated on the decision to divide the structure into a part that is shop manufactured and another part which is flexibly, sometimes very flexibly, constructed right on the premises. The shop finished item is usually a unit in which all now complicated plumbing: bath, laundry, kitchen is pre-assembled. But sometimes, like in the first award, it contains even one or two bedrooms, leaving, however the living room to a more elastic dimensioning and shaping, as individual taste may prefer to indulge in.

In the second award, such integral shop manufactured standard units are put on top of each other to fit a two-story layout. In some cases they appear as exterior appendages to a field assembled house, in others they form the innermost core, around which that field built structure is erected.

There appeared also a second line of thought where the house is again divided in two or more portions, but this time all units are completed in advance. In this case the designer endeavored to show how pleasing and desirable elasticity and variety could be obtained in just the relative positioning of a living and social unit on one hand and the private sleeping quarters on the other. One contestant placed these units in angled variations; further, he handled them overlapping each other in one and finally in two stories; another arranged them around a semi-open porch-like atrium; one clustered his barrel-shaped unit cells in one or two planes, with some incidental connective tissue between them.

The projects premiated with the third award also represents a third school of thought. Here the dwelling, by carefully conceived parallel cuts, is divided into slices of typical dimensions, each slice representing a prefabricated unit and at the same time a fairly differentiated functional parcel; I mean a portion that as such serves the occupant when such extension in the future should become a requirement. The growing house idea is preserved in this scheme, and although in need of further sound elaboration, initial structural details accompanied the design.

Generally, in viewing the vast material submitted, it became clear that in a competition like this the slightest attempt of structural of fabricational inventiveness would multiply with a big factor both the work and risk of the contestant and may expose him easily to criticism and that irony which seems the God-given fate to be lived down by all inventors. And of course, truly full grown, promising and defensibly detailed inventions are rather submitted to the U.S. Commissioner of Patents, then to a jury that can grant no protection.

Legal and economic protection granted and safeguarded would undoubtedly elicit more well-worked-out inventive schemes. However, more moral protection of recognized first authorship might help and produce also in our profession that gratification which stimulates astronomers, physiologists, surgeons and other professionals to present their findings to co-professionals and the world. Reading not scientific fiction but unmitigated professional accounts of today, be it on electronics or on brain histology, the layman may be sometimes annoyed by stumbling from one quotation to the other, wherein multitudes of papers are cited that were delivered at such and such scientific conferences of the last ten years all over the world. However right, there is the second secure

and systematic basis for truly contemporary and cosmopolitan progress. Something similar to it in the field of tomorrow's design and professional treatment of human dwellings would safeguard the postwar consumer against dependence on the crossfire barrages of sales effort. Improved professional standards, acknowledgment of loans and sources strengthen and civilize the design profession by a basic sincerity of performance and service.

(Continued from page 31, Minorities and the Screen)

But one looks in vain for dramatic material which presents such Negro types as Brigadier General Benjamin O. Davis, Sr., who rose from the rank of private; or Captain Hugh Mulzac, skipper of the Liberty Ship *Booker T. Washington*; or Dean Dixon, the youngest man ever to conduct the NBC Symphony, and the first of his race to conduct the New York Philharmonic; or Richard Barthe, the sculptor; or Paul Williams, the architect, or William Grant Still, the composer; or Katherine Dunham, the dancer; or the late George Washington Carver, or any of hundreds of other distinguished Negroes.

But you may object, these are exceptional and unusual people, and no true representatives of the group as a whole. And I might counter with the observation that so are Scarlett O'Hara and Rhett Butler and ex-Ambassador Davies and the Invisible Man exceptional and unusual people, and no true representatives of the group as a whole.

Time Magazine recently declared it an open question whether the Negro is the white man's equal as a soldier. As writers, we might dispel such doubts by pointing to the record of the Negro in all the wars of the American Republic. We might dramatize the Negroes with Perry on Lake Erie, with Jackson at New Orleans, with Roosevelt at San Juan Hill. Half of Hobson's men were Negroes when he sailed into Santiago Harbor, and it was John Jordan, Negro, who fired the first shot from Dewey's flagship in Manila Bay.

We might dramatize the record of the 369th Volunteer Negro Infantry from New York City, a regiment which was under fire for 191 days with casualties of 1500 killed or wounded, yet yielded not one prisoner or one foot of earth to the enemy. The 369th's regimental colors were decorated with the Croix de Guerre, while two of its officers received the Congressional Medal of Honor, nine the Legion d'Honneur, ten the Distinguished Service Cross, sixty-one the Croix de Guerre and eight the American Citation for Gallantry.

But, you may object, these are individual heroes and exceptional regiments. And I might counter with the observation that so was Sergeant York an individual hero, and so was the Fighting Sixty-Ninth an exceptional regiment—and from the same city as the 369th to boot!

Not a single picture which I have seen deals with Negroes in the war effort—a job in which they are heavily active, as witness the fifty per cent drop in Detroit production following the recent insurrection in that city. Long shots of assembly lines consistently fail to include Negroes in our factories. It would seem reasonable, and certainly truthful, to place Negroes in such scenes, not necessarily to build parts around them, but to lend authenticity to the script and to remind the audience that the Negro people are playing an important part in every aspect of the war effort, from the skies above Sicily to the assembly lines of Willow Run. We should, of course, avoid the self-conscious use of Negroes; but we might well profit from the French example in "Grand Illusion," where we caught glimpses of a Negro officer in the prison camp. He had nothing to say; he was not emphasized; but he was there, a living part of the whole canvas; his existence as a fellow sharer of war's vicissitudes was admitted.

But if we shy from Negro themes, we also shy from Negro writers. A shocking and, to us, most pertinent example of the race myth in operation may be found in Hollywood's failure to tap the great reservoir of creative Negro talent. To my knowledge, only Langston Hughes and Clarence Muse have been employed as screen writers, and then but briefly. Richard Wright, certainly one of the major writing talents of our time, has heard no studios clamoring at his door. And there are innumerable others—J. Saunders Redding, Roi Ottley, Margaret Walker, Carl Ruthaven Offord, Sterling Brown, Countee Cullen, Claude McKay, W.E.B. DuBois, Walter White, James Weldon Johnson, Zora Neale Hurston, Henrietta Buckmaster to mention only a few—none of whom has had the opportunity to devote his gifts to the widest and most influential medium of our age in its period of most desperate need.

And what are we to do about it? Are we to accept the racial stereotypes exposed by Mr. Hoijer and support the patterns of racial discrimination revealed by Mr. White? Are we to continue to act as literary typhoid Marys, consciously or unconsciously purveying Fascist poison? Or are we simply to swear an oath never again to permit ourselves to be beguiled into ridiculing and insulting racial minorities? Here, to be sure, is progress of a kind, for to write nothing is better by far than to write viciously. But simply to foreswear evil is a peculiarly supine and negative contribution to human progress, which leads in the end to writing nothing about any controversial subject, Fascism included.

No, there is a more positive course of action. It is logical to believe that a war against Facism, a war for the Four Freedoms, a war for the People's Revolution, a war for the Century of the Common Man must affect writers, must galvanize them, precisely a it affects and galvanizes all other professions and classes. Traditionally we are the bearers of ideas and in performing this task many of us risk becoming writers who are, as Petronius Arbiter discovered long ago, "of the kind that rich men hate." But if we aspire to continue our traditional function we must necessarily resume our honorable and ancient marching position in the vanguard of human thought moving toward a better world for all the people who inhabit it.

We have, therefore, no other course but to act positively, to write positively, to abandon neutrality, to forsake negation. In any positive decision for action we may take as a result of this Writers' Congress, we shall not be acting alone. There is no occasion for dashing about like ink-stained Don Quixotes individually assaulting the bastions of persecution and injustice. For we are at war, and war requires organization. Fortunately we have at hand, in the many writers' organizations represented here, the instrumentalities with which to fortify ourselves. We can, under their sponsorship, form an army with an invincible singleness of purpose and an opportunity for all the rich diversity of attack of which our individual soldiers are capable. For only by such mobilization can we constructively assist in winning the war, in winning the peace, and, quite incidentally, in winning our self-respect as writers who truly believe that we are recording, at this time, "the history of the world."

This article is one of a hundred papers which will appear in the Complete Proceedings of the Writers Congress soon to be published by the University of California Press.

(Continued from page 50, Surrealist Art)

mark of contemporary culture, is the fabulous progenitor of other equally astonishing phenomena; mass travel, mass spectator participation, mass entertainment, mass play. The patent medicine myth of modern advertising articulated through loudspeakers on the radio and in the movies, selling coming attractions, leisure and pleasure, spreads the dreams of insomnia over everyday life.

These and a hundred other aspects of daily experience accepted in the natural course of things by masses who are swayed by the spell of contemporary trends, are surrealist in essence. For all that, surrealist art in America is comparatively young. Yet its infectious gaiety and sardonic seriousness, its lush though dark beauty, have rapidly gained for it a place in the sun. In contrast with the severe intellectuality and almost puritanical restraint of much abstraction which many temperaments find too constricting, it has a wide and instantaneous appeal.

This quick acceptance has occurred without benefit of the organized group concentration that launched surrealist activity in Paris, London and other international centers. In New York, and dispersed throughout the country, an increasing number of practicing artists including many new young painters make up its voluntary rank and file. While in their earlier phases the work of some of them introduced fragmentary surrealist elements, time, experience and the presence here of artists in exile, among them leaders of the movement, have brought about a clearer comprehension of the expansive nature of surrealist method and the implications of the "marvellous" that constitute the surrealist point of view.

• • •

By their authority, the artists in exile, many of whom have worked in their respective idioms for a generation or more, have produced that heightened activity which comes from personal contact, besides nurturing in Americans—painters and public alike—a reassuring sense of the permanency of our common culture. Because of this common culture the merging of artists in exile with our painters is a natural consequence of their being here together. This indicates once more the international character of the art of our time, the esthetics of a science- and machine-minded age, a time of dynamic expansion in all fields of endeavor. As there emerges an ever-wider understanding of the importance of basic scientific principles, appreciation for abstract and surrealist art, which may be regarded as the esthetic counterpart of modern science, is being raised to its proper level. Man, manipulating the lever of contemporary culture upon the fulcrum of science, attains the vital balance for 20th century art.

(Continued from page 53, Audio-Visual-Music)

A second factor of limitation is the persistence of vision and certain inherent natural differences in response to rhythm of the eye and ear. Particularly with regard to rapid rhythmic alterations, effects actually painful to the eyes are encountered.

Finally a third difference between image time and sound time is the significance of the relation of graphic space to time. Space-time considerations are brought into striking pre-eminence. No movement within the screen area can be thought of oblivious of time. No shape, no space eludes movement consideration void of the time factor. Space and time are here inseparable in a very real, practical sense. A tiny animated shape creating a rhythmic movement in a given screen space may produce on effect. The same animation magnified many times so as to fill the entire screen area produces a radically different temporal experience, though the time of each may be exactly the same. The change is qualitative to such a degree that variation upon a thematic idea by magnification or reduction in size is generally not clear or recognizable as a variation.

Sufficient experiment has indicated rather conclusively the minor extent to which full screen passages of mere color sequences void of graphic form can be used to carry a rhythmic idea. Unless supported by a strong musical reinforcement, the effect is surprisingly ambiguous. Such sequences introduced as thematic ideas to be later subjected to variation and development are even more generally foredoomed to meaninglessness. These observation reflect the apparent failure of all color-music experiments which treated color as an independent visual entity. The established doctrine that color and graphic form (line mass and texture) exist inseparably in experience is here only reaffirmed with perhaps new dynamic significance. Analysis would reveal that whereas variety in color may be achieved by virtue of some temperal patter it is overburdened with an obviously monotonous graphic form structure: the static screen.

What then, can be the role of color in audio-visual-music? It is still the most vital element of the total sensory experience. Color structure united with a graphic-time structure is comparable to the relationship between orchestration and theme structure of a music composition, the two being a unified whole. Just as orchestration provides the composer with a large textural vocabulary with which he may freely build as richly or as thinly as is his structural need, so with the use of color there must be this same liberty. Color will probably never for long be restricted to a theoretical key of relationships. Though theoretical systems or keys will often account for the special unity of one composition or the works of one composer.

Audio-visual relationships offer promise of profoundly unique experience; witness Alexander Nevsky, Memphis Bell and White Floor. This type of relationship is the primary attribute of audio-visual-music. One may expect the broadcast variety of relationships possible, covering a gamut from the freest interplay of sound and image through counterplay to the strict temporal correlation.

The fallacy of mechanically translating previously composed music into some visual equivalent, having been established repeatedly enough in critical writings on the subject, a freer less encumbered approach is possible today. Even so-called interpretation of existing music graphically is at best an exceedingly difficult technical achievement and practically barren of reward to the artist seeking creative expression. The truly creative possibilities remain where the image structure dictates or inspires sound structure and visa versa or both are reached simultaneously. This obviously can be realized best when both parts have common creative origins. This is becoming possible today even for the amateur as soundtrack writing or synthesizing devices, manageable by one person appear on the horizon along with simplified animation techniques. The generally accepted assumption that the cinema must by nature be an industrial, cooperative art, is least likely to be so with audio-visual-music. Amateur cine equipment compares well in quality today with that of the industry. There already exist small enterprises prepared to supply special processing, sound recording and duplicating services to small scale limited budget film makers. The remaining technological problem of the independent artist is to somehow assure final perfection of these new means.

The role that television can play in the development of audio-visual-music probably cannot be underestimated. Undoubtedly the most striking quality of the television program is its intense realism; the realism of spot news and spontaneous programs of all sorts. But this very spontaneity has as by-product a degree of disorganization which will have to be dealt with in much the same manner that radio finds a compensation of contrast in the use of music. The so-called music bridge or incidental music of radio serves this specific purpose. The relatively unorganized spontaneous portions of the radio program are carefully sandwiched between periods of music.

This radio has found a real organic need for specially composed music. Even though it had the enormous accumulation of western civilization's music to draw from, radio found it necessary recently to begin employing composers to supply these specific needs. It is fairly safe to assume that television will discover an equally organic need for an audio-visual equivalent to radio's music-bridge, and it is also safe to judge that the discovery will institute a search beyond current solution which are usually motivated by economic expediency. The artist with a sense of the deeper meaning of organic structure alone can make the distinction between the "current solution" and an organic solution. Technological trinkets in the form of Kaleidescopes and other mechanical devices which fill the television screen with arbitrary patter and are related to music mechanically if at all are certainly not the organic solution. Television insofar as it functions fully, an integral part of the new time and society, will not only employ audio-visual-music organically within its regular programs but will perform individual works of the contemporary composers.

(Continued from page 57, Russia)

film visitors to Hollywood: Leonid Antanov, Serge Irski, Mikhail Kalatozov, Nicholas Napoli, representing Amkino. Their visits had two chief purposes: first to buy American films for Russian distribution; and second to buy American film producing and projection equipment for Russian theaters and mobile field units for the Soviet Army and for workers.

"We are conducting negotiations," Kalatozov said during his trip last year, "upon an agreement which envisages the broadening of mutual cinematographic services—wider distribution of American films in the Soviet Union, and of Soviet pictures in the United States."

Kalatozov also pointed out that it was the hope of the Russian film industry to arrange for the interchange of directors and technicians on both Russian and American pictures. There was no need, he pointed out, to fear propaganda. "I think," he said, "all objective people will agree with me that we do not need to propagandize our people—the people who have proved to be so united, so monolithic in their views and their convictions, who now are striking mortal blows against the greatest evil—Fascism. If we want you to see our pictures it is only for one reason—so that you may learn who the Soviet people are."

Nor has the Soviet Union any reason to be concerned with the American pictures they show inside Russia. Several years ago a film festival was held in Moscow in which tribute was paid by Soviet film industry leaders to American picture-makers. Bolshkov, Chairman of the Committee on Cinematography of the Council of the People's Commissars of the USSR paid direct tribute to Hollywood's influence on Russian films, and singled out John Ford, Charlie Chaplin, Walt Disney, and Frank Capra for honors.

Eisenstein at this important meeting spoke of the American film industry as "one huge epic poem, no smaller in significance than the Odyssey or the Iliad, an art that is of the people, by the people, and for the people."

"There is" (Eisenstein continued) "warm lyricism, the love for family,

the ideas of the people who know their power and strength and aren't afraid to laugh at their weaknesses."

"Here we see the anger and despair of those who have to struggle for their existence; here is the joy of life of the young and healthy, of the gay children of the skyscrapers. We have the fantasy of fairyland side by side with the realism and the sweeping comedy of the Marx Brothers. Sometimes this epic of America goes back to the past, and then it becomes the poetry of the covered wagon and later the story of the two boys who grew up in 'Old Chicago.'"

"The history of the American people is linked with Abraham Lincoln," Eisenstein continued, "and this is reflected in the film about the youth of Lincoln. Henry Fonda makes Lincoln human, democratic, irresistible. In the great, gaunt figure, we see, best of the democratic ideas of the American people, that people which has now been driven to join in the just fight again fascism."

"We love and value our friends in America," Eisenstein said, "their talent, their ability to produce. Now when they have become our comrades-in-arms, it is especially great joy to greet them in the name of our peoples."

"Through the smoke and fire of this war, we can see the bright gleam of the future, and this gleam is the friendship between our country, the USA and England."

Russian film makers have become increasingly aware of the need for entertainment in their films. They have had twenty-two years in which to make pictures that teach and inform. In this summer conference of 1942 new trends in Russian film production were indicated and promised. As one English journal summed up the program: "For many years the Russian cinema has had to teach, and it is reasonable to suppose that the new generation accepts most of those teachings as part of their lives, and now demand films which will entertain in a more direct way."

Motion pictures will be all-important in the post-war world. Hollywood film makers have seen with their own eyes the important results achieved through training and indoctrination films made with industry help for all branches of the Service. And Hollywood feels that if it can make films for war, it can also make them for peace. Part of that policy will be closer relations between American and Russian studios.

And the hope for this postwar planning is best expressed by Pudovkin when he said, "the cinematographic art has a much more powerful effect on the people than any other. Accordingly, I was considering it during the war and immediately after it, as being particularly great. I think we need strong and bold films that will lead the people of the United Nations towards three principal lines: the first is—to bring to speedy annihilation the fascist brigant army by the concerted efforts of the nations. Justice demands that. The second is—the utter disqualification of the present fascist theories, for that will help to rid the world of slavery and make for liberty. The third is—show all that was best and more virile in the past, all that is best and most virile in the present. That will serve to prevent a recrudescence of the despicable fascist propaganda and make for lasting peace and cultural progress. Liberty, justice and culture—these are the three ideals which the Powers are called upon to serve."

(Continued from page 59, Henry Moore)

pastel drawings done in the air-raid shelters of London. Here men and women returned like larvae under the surface of the earth. Last withdrawal. Life reduced to the roots, to fear, to love. And reduced to the simplest of forms, to spindles in tubes, to the crouched, the twisted, to the barest. Nearly to stone. But color sweated out from stone, moss color, lichen color. Life presses from inward outward, surface and substance are one.

Many of Moore's drawings and sculptures deal with sleep, with reclining forms, the mystery is greater near the source: awakening, sleep, death, where does life begin?

Henry Moore's sculpture reaches up to higher awareness: mother and child, the most animate symbol of the mold, form in the form, child in the womb, child in the mother's lap, two in one. And highest symbol of it, the Madonna. "I began thinking of the Madonna and child by considering in what ways a Madonna and child differs from a carving of just a mother and child—that is, by considering how in my opinion religious art differs from secular art." (Statement by the artist to Iris Conley, art critic of the Catholic Herald.) The solution is given by the monumental statue for the church of St. Matthews. "The infant is the center of the work and yet the subject speaks of the incarnation, the fact that Christ was born of a human mother—and so the statue is conceived as any small child would in essence think of his mother, not as small and frail, but as the one large, secure and solid background to life." (Statement by the artist in Magazine of Art.) Still the religious symbol of Christian tradition is connected to the basic concept of the sculptor. Not only "background of life" but shelter of life—form, mold of life. Yet ordinarily Moore avoids specifications: specifications of culture, religion, nationality. He avoids even human features, except in the crudest, because he is not dealing with the awakened, the self-aware, the individual. He is not creating humans, but symbols of humans in stone.

Meaning and form penetrate into each other, we cannot separate them. Each of these enigmas is, as far as its form goes, a solution. The hidden lives in the revealed. If the form is not distinct, definite and organized, it is not a good work of art. Therefore, another aliveness of the art work: the fusion between the dimness of meaning and the clarity of form. Who can explain a sculpture by Moore like a mathematical formula? The inexplainable in Moore as in contemporary art in general is many things in one: Its creative fluctuation, its truthfulness, and perhaps its imperfection. The formal problems of Henry Moore are those of a true sculptor of the modern age. They belong to him, but also to his older contemporaries, especially to Brancusi and to Picasso. They develop an aesthetic for which our language is still short of words because there are no similar sensations within the experience of sound. They deal with the relation of solid bodies to hollowed out parts, with holes in matter, with matter around holes. The safety pin represents this problem in its most abstract form: elastic extension protruding from a solid and bridging a larger unit with a smaller, a void between. Here is everything: motion arrested but flexible, function but design, function and design depending on the air space in between just as much as on solid mass. Unlimited tasks for the contemporary sculptor. But Moore is not doing paraphrases of safety pins. Since this is the magic of art that reclining figures are both, reclining and safety pin forms. If you deduct the one from the other, it becomes either literature or abstract formalism.

How did Henry Moore become what he is today? One of the most original sculptors of our century, a fascinating draughtsman. Nobody in the 20th century, if he wants to, can escape contact with the universal aspects of art in time and space. Museums, reproductions, books: Moore, the son of a coal miner from Leeds in England could see all that he needed for his art in Leeds: mothers and children, shafts, mines, tubes, stone, coal, moss. But also the collection of Michael Sadler visited by him as a student with its Gauguins, its contemporary art. In the library he read with due impression Roger Fry's *Vision and Design* which has directed the minds and eyes of many to an understanding of the primitive and the basic in art. In Italy he admired most Massaccio. Classical sculpture "builds up" the form, modeling in clay it cuts away matter, but it also affixes lumps of matter, it adds features which are not contained in the material on which he works. Contemporary sculpture and Moore derive part of their inspiration directly from the material on which they work and they take away until enough of the image appears, which they have seen enclosed in the bloc. Such procedure Moore could find in the stones of Stonehenge and in the phantasies of Picasso's. Picasso who was one of the first to take take the human form as a point of departure, but not as its aim. Figures possible, but not real, surreal like the inventions of Franz Kafka. Listen to the description of Odradek as Kafka gives it: "at the first sight it looks like a flat, star shaped spindle of thread, and, indeed, it seems to be covered with thread although these could be only torn, old, knotted together but also confusedly intertwined pieces of thread of the most varied type and color. But it is not only a coil but from the center of the star emerges a small diagonal rod and added to it on a right angle is still another one. With the help of the latter little rod on the one side and one of the radiating forms of the star on the other side the whole thing can stand upright as if on two legs." (The drawing Spring and Wood from 1938, represented in Geoffrey Grigson Henry Moore, Penguin Books, ed. Kenneth Clark (London, 1943, plate 20) recalls Kafka's creation.)

This was published in 1919, earliest expression of a newly discovered world in art. Art deals with what is possible, not with what is real.

Yet it has to make the possible real, otherwise it is not art. This Henry Moore could discover in William Blake's water colors of whom his own sometimes remind. He could find it in Negro fetishes, in Brancusi, in Arp, in Picasso—in Kafka. None of them is a surrealist in the present sense of the word because they do not connect already existing objects in a nonexisting way, but they are makers of new objects. Dali's limp watches, presuppose the knowledge of watches, but Odradek presupposes nothing. Just, therefore, it has haunting reality. Moore in recent years under the impact of a common human destiny has become simpler, less playful, less formalistic and more concerned with the human aspects. Such humanization shows the feeling of responsibility of the artist. Otherwise the monument for St. Matthews in Northhampton would have been impossible.

This is the first important sculptor England has produced. The monuments in St. Paul's as well as medieval tombstones bespeak of the art of the masses and volumina. The English, not by chance, preferred the water color more than another other nation. Something atmospheric, lyrical, and literary prevails. Henry Moore has given a sturdiness, an element of the primitive and the essential to English art which it has not had before. Should this be a parallel to D.H. Lawrence in literature? Lawrence too was a son of a coal miner. But Henry Moore not only belongs to England, but to all the people who are awake in 1945.

(Continued from page 61, What is Landscape Architecture)

Having enclosed such a space we have next to determine its surfacing, its furnishing, its shading by tree or arbor, and perhaps its enrichment with flowers, specimen plants, or sculpture.

Did you say that this sounds too formal? I don't like formal gardens either, if by that you mean all the obvious arbitrary dull axial garden vista "compositions" with which we have been plagued so long. But every garden has to have some sort of form—the choice is between good and bad form, not between formal and informal. A building is a formal geometric man-made element, no matter how rustic, and its site or lot is an informal irregular piece of nature, no matter how flat and bare. Our problem is to add these two things together so thoroughly and completely that they become one thing, one continuous pattern of indoor-outdoor living space. We can't possibly accomplish this by carrying on the traditional mock tournament between arbitrarily defined "formal" and "informal," man and nature, axes and wiggles. There is no real argument between these kinds of things. We need the broadest possible vocabulary to carry on our job of integrating building and site, man and nature, refined structural materials and unrefined natural ones. Gardens have to be both formal and informal at once in order to do their job. The integrating factor for buildings and grounds is the concept of space given positive symphonic form and continuity, rather than any arbitrary patchwork of axes, terminal features and naturalistic glades. (-istic usually seems to denote a weak imitation of the real thing.) The characteristic of man is clear geometric organization; the characteristic of nature is free growth and development; put these together and we will produce a landscape tradition and expression that will carry on where Vignola, Le Notre, Repton, and the Oriental masters left off.

Man doesn't automatically deface the landscape. Some men deface it through a substandard marginal struggle for bare subsistence; more do it through uncontrolled speculative commercial profit-taking activities. A glance at the wastes produced by the greed of lumber and hydraulic mining interests is proof enough of this—or again the slightly different structural wastes along most major thoroughfares in most urban centers, produced by unrestrained poorly conceived commercial enterprises.

To sum up we might say that landscaping is the organization of outdoor space for people to use and enjoy; that it is so inextricably connected with the problems of structurally enclosed indoor space that the two problems can only satisfactorily be solved in one joint operation; and finally that materials, particularly plants, must be used in an integral structural way that combines common sense and imagination, in order to get the most from them.

(Continued from page 63, Alexander Calder)

color as an element of composition, Calder is approaching nature from a dynamic and variable point of reference to time and space, giving his sculpture extra power through plastic relationships which evolve in space. His sculptures are as at home in the fields of Connecticut as the barn-top weathervanes made by earlier American craftsmen out of iron and wood and set up to whirl about in the wind. Both are spontaneous and unselfconscious, stripped of non-essentials.

Calder's new gouache paintings appeal to the child in us. They have a stark simplicity, a directness of line and color. They are bright, gay, and full of characteristic humor. Behind the delightful fantasy of these works is a strong fibre of the essential, based on contrasts of primary colors, textures, and simple rhythms, and a sensitivity to the rhythm of the world in which he lives.

(Continued from page 65, Notes in Passing)

circumstances and built on the lives and the hopes of our fellowman everywhere. We must accept our world responsibilities with a little less of the noble self-satisfaction and pious graciousness of the Lady Bountiful. We must accept these things because we have to and because as our vision becomes clearer and our knowledge greater and our wisdom deeper we can no longer force ourselves to believe in the validity of our own special excellence in this world of people.

These are large times—large and wide as the world is large and wide. And if, for the moment, we hold the instruments of power it would be a greater tribute to our Yankee shrewdness that we not use that power for temporary national victories but turn the weapon of our own strength as it should be turned—to the service of an eventual victory for mankind.

(Continued from page 74, Construction)

construction. First is an eye and pin connection by which eight-foot lengths of tubular metal can be joined in almost any desired combination. The second is a self-supported and self-propelled wall unit which can be rolled away and removed completely from the building.

The eight-foot tube which becomes the standard part in the structure itself has a double eye welded to each end. The eye consists of one heavy plate, a space of the same thickness, and a light piece. Inside face of the heavier plate is on the precise diameter of the tube. When two tubes are to be connected, therefore, the four plates splice together with two heavy pieces on the inside. A pin slips through the eye and is held in place by a screw cap at each end. The load is directly along the axis of the tube.

Load requirement will determine the thickness of the tube walls for specific structures, but the outside diameter will be made in only one or two sizes. Parallel pieces can be used where the load is to be heavy. Standard length and identical eyes and pins make it possible to fit even a complex structure together like a child's Erector set.

The Mobilar wall unit is an eight-foot-wide panel supported by two sets of nine-inch wheels. The wheels retract two inches when the unit is in place as a wall. At the top of each unit are two spring plungers that latch into a channel on the underside of the roof, securing the wall to the structure. Metal channels running horizontally along the unit link it to the next one at two places while still allowing it to move up beside it. When a series of units forms a wall, there is a wind-proof seal of flexible rubber gasket at each juncture.

With this arrangement, one panel, a whole wall, or all walls can be opened. If a wall were to be removed a relay would start with a unit at one end. Wheels would be lowered by air pressure stored in the tubular framing, jacking the unit up into mobile position. A third-horsepower electric motor would roll it beside the next unit which also would jack up. The two would roll beside the next in the series and the action would be repeated until all the units were in a horizontal stack at one end of the building. Power could then be disconnected and the stack towed away and stored. Light-weight property of Mobilar construction, simple support well inside the building, and complete independence of walls make it idea for any type of structure in which large unobstructed areas are needed. First example built was an airplane hanger, but it is adaptable also to recreation halls, railroad stations, factories, and warehouses.

Despite the obvious advantages of Mobilar Structures over standard type buildings in all these categories, engineers who developed the system report construction costs will be no more—and possibly less—than the costs of present methods. Licensee of Mobilar Structures is the Atlas Aircraft Products Company of New York.

(Continued from page 77, Gyorgy Kepes)

nature of things. With painstaking efforts toward objectivity, precision, and mechanical perfection, he documented the physical and social world. He surveyed his world as if surveying a volcano with a microscope. Amassing detail after detail, he never achieved the whole, because the unifying force—man himself—was relegated to the position of only one more object among objects.

But man is not an object, and his eye is not the lens of a camera. Human vision is not merely a mirroring of external reality; a simultaneous emotional response inheres in every act of perception. This response is determined not only by the things which are represented but also by the visual qualities which are the vehicles of this representation. The structure of brightness values in a photographic image evokes not only the percept and the affective tone of the things it makes visible but also an innate feeling-quality in its sensuous assimilation.

Vision thus has always a double component: the perspective of the objective world, or life as it is; and the perspective of the beholder with his aspirations, dreams, and passions, or life as he would like to see it. The true vision of reality lies in the congruence of these two; it is life seen not only through the eye and intellect but also through the heart. Photography short-circuited this wholeness of vision. For it to achieve its full potentialities and to become more than a recording instrument, it must synchronize with its precision a flexibility, intimacy, and spontaneity embodied in the sensuous structure of light relationships.

Camera-less photography, unchained from the compulsion to optical truth, helped to explore this poetry of light. Insofar as it escapes becoming a means of playing with forms or a highly personal language, it has an important function in fermenting the visual arts based upon photographic techniques.

The creative use of plastic structure, the rhythm of modulated light, is today only an accidental element of photography, motion picture, and television. Its introduction into them as an important component is a point of leverage on which photographic expression can be raised above its present limitations.

(Continued from page 85, Jewelry by Margaret DePatta)

thereby causing the design to become so familiar to all people that the stimulating interest in it is lost. This is a very controversial point and one on which I take a definite stand.

There are those who maintain that an article well designed, having within itself essentials of contemporary expression and genuine quality does not lose these qualities by being endlessly produced. Is it not possible to become insensitive to a musical composition, no matter how fine, if it is heard every fifteen minutes over the radio? Jewelry functions in the realm of aesthetic perceptions of human beings, a consideration that cannot be overlooked.

The choice of a piece of jewelry reveals much of the character and personality and the understandings of the individual. A piece of jewelry well designed should be the embodiment of the trends of our times—these new types of structures, clean line, elimination of decoration, new spatial concepts, new use of transparencies, and a fresh appreciation and use of organic form—recognition of the true essence of these is growing, consciously or unconsciously, in an ever increasing minority.

(Continued from page 97, Design and the Machine)

from these clear lines, from these pure curves, clarifies one's thinking and transmits itself inevitably to the problems of the drafting table.

Such explorations are invaluable to the industrial designer from a practical point of view. When he is designing an item to be made on a machine the first important thing is to know what that machine can do. If he is assigning more to the machine than lies within the orbit of its possibilities the engineering staff must reject the design. If, on the other hand, he does not utilize the potentialities of the machine completely, he is designing for yesterday. When he lets the machine make a contribution to the character of the design and proves that it can be made before it is put on paper, he is assured of a product that properly fuses function and production.

We are now organizing such studies of various machines, including wood-working, metal, and plastics machines, to make them generally available. An ideal arrangement would be to have a permanent collection of these studies...a library of techniques...from which artists, architects, and designers can draw when they are searching for a certain construction, textural effect, or spatial solution that can be achieved on the machine in the simplest possible manner. Engineers and chemists would add their valuable contributions to such a project. If all the various forces of sincere exploration could pool the facts they discover the result would be a treasury of ideas which might become an important factor in developing a rich vocabulary for this age of the machine.

(Continued from page 127, Idea and Pure Form)

say, "magical" reunion with the outer world. It was a re-identification of the ego with the objective image, not in an interpretive function, but on a higher plane of the ideological transfiguration of matter. A new representational art is in the making that incarnates the idea into painterly form. The interpretation of these forms in terms of known objects is relevant only as the statement of a new faith. Through the image, emerging from the mastered visual element, a new contact has been established with the phenomenal world. (Fig. 9) The creative ego need no longer shrink from the definitive form. Deprived of its dependence on literary concepts on the one hand, and of the anarchic chaos of the retreat from the model on the other, art can affirm its identity with BEING. Imagination has overcome the arbitrariness of life with a new sense of duration, because expression and communication are again one. Like the Chippewa Indians, the new painters transform thought into image and image into universally valid statement. The guided eye learns to have faith in the inexhaustible richness and honesty of fundamental vision, born with every child. There, the painter knows, is the common substance from which the adult shapes the structural reality of the three-dimensional world as well as the visual reality of the inner image. The motive power of both is a striving for order—for the orderly equilibrium of mechanical forces in the realm of matter, and for the spiritual order of the creative substance in art, transfiguring the idea into pure form.

(Continued from page 142, O'Gorman)

with a better adaptation to climate, to customs and to site. It should be planned for its regional use and not as a universal utility. It should appeal to the people's taste and not to the elite of academic abstractionists.

"We must also consider an architect that responds to the need for decoration, recognizing that architecture is the environment of the human being and not only the housing of machinery. Therefore it is important to have sculpture, murals of stone or glass, etc., and to integrate these into the architecture to such a degree that it will not be possible to say where the architecture ends and the murals or the sculpture begins.

"We need for Mexico a Mexican architecture that uses functionalism for its real value, which is efficiency and comfort, and not for the purpose of producing in a roundabout and infantile way a supposed mechanical beauty."

(Continued from page 143, Architecture in Mexico)

couple of boulders, placed not as a guard but to form a pleasant composition. In the same room is a playful circular stairway to a low balcony. Stairways in Mexico are delightful, the curve being the personal expression of the designer rather than a manufacturer's product. The early houses of Juan O'Gorman used beautiful exterior curving stairs that appear to lead his rational houses into the realm of fantasy. The new airport building at Guadalajara, an uninspired edifice, has an impressive stairway with a bold curve. It has a metal guard rail, often omitted. The factor of safety is not always the first consideration in Mexican design. Everywhere are unrailed stairways, cantilevered stairways, fireman's pole stairways. In Luis Barragan's house is an unrailed stairway from library to mezzanine-study with wood risers and treads anchored into a masonry wall.

The imagination shown in the details of the most everyday commercial building in Mexico is astonishing. One never gets the impression, as in the United States, that each part was selected from a catalog. It may not always work, but it is thoughtful and it is fresh. It is this freshness that makes a visit to Mexico memorable. This is not to suggest in any way that Mexicans are children—delightful, impractical, incapable of learning to use a machine. They are not deficient mechanically. They drive automobile very well, and if the tempo is fast it is because they have not yet developed a traffic system or thoroughfares designed to carry heavy traffic. As industries grow in Mexico, facility in the use of the machine has grown.

Mexico has long been a borrower of architectural styles from Europe, but today she turns seriously to her own past for her inspiration. The architects have shown a willingness to revalue their own culture and to learn a lesson in design and construction from indigenous building.

Mexico, for the first time, faces itself.

(Continued from page 149, Motherwell)

their previous appreciation of the various modes of realism in painting, I cannot persuade them to return—though they always are at liberty to—to the live model They say that it gets in the way of their real conceptions. As indeed I believe it does. Some of my academic colleagues tend to be shocked at my students' works, as though I were destroying the students' respect for the past and its traditions! But I think that the students know that their work has so "modern" an aspect in part at least because it has so broader a background of traditional culture, that past can only be recovered genuinely through the needs of the present. Otherwise it remains a series of alien monuments to be forgotten as soon as they walk out into the street. But Piero della Francesca and Uccello are real to them in a sense that they were not to 19th century students; and these modern students realize that what happened was that modern art intervened, that Seurat, Cezanne and the cubist collage helped us recover Piero and Uccello. In this sense, modern art is universalizing and humanizing.

There is a danger to this great augmentation of our plastic repertoire, the danger of a sort of universal electicism. To be cultivated and to be creative are not the same thing; though each vivifies the other. But the answer has already been implied. The recovery of the past through present needs teaches us what is relevant. That is, the immediate demands of one's subject-matter determine what is living in past cultures. But the subject-matter of modern art is another topic.

The emphasis here is that much of the seeming radicality of the appearance of modern art derives from its greatly enlarged frame of reference, a frame still missing from the minds of most observors.—ROBERT MOTHERWELL

(Continued from page 158, The Bread of Architecture)

pulpit. The Bible is noncommittal as to whether Adam built a house, or, even a well. To judge from his better know circumstances, this is not likely. True, Adam was able to converse with the Lord. But nothing points to his having had creative ability. In the light of psychological evidence, we may assume that, to erect a well,—moreover to build the original wall, so to speak—a man must possess Spieltrieb, the instinct for play. Or, perhaps, we ought to say that, like any good architect, he must be possessed by that instinct.

Play is the glorious substance of childhood. The passion for play arises early in the very small child. But, for all we know, Adam is the only man who had no childhood—not even an unhappy one. We imagine him a rather glum character; his early, paradisiac surroundings lacked any incitement to travail and were unconducive to action. The initiative was with his wife.

. . .

The more sensitive souls among the readers are perhaps aware that a wall has, apart from its utilitarian and esthetic virtues, a unique quality which radiates comfort far beyond and above bodily comfort. (It is somehow understood that a wall be made of stone or baked earth; a wooden wall may serve some purpose but it is of an ephemeral quality. All the wooden buildings of time are but a memory.) Within the last thirty years or so, we have seen, at least in pictures, houses so transparent, so airy, so weightless in appearance, that they seemed to be poised on taking off at any moment, like a magic carpet. This impression vanished when the architects of the ethereal fraternity began to introduce into the general frailty of the construction a rustic wall. Thus, the seemingly weightless glassy or wooden houses, received at least one wall of unhewn stone, as ballast and anchor. Grave discussions ensued, and many explanations were volunteered for this paradoxical novelty. There was much talk about texture and contrast and color, but it seems that a genuine wall needs no apology.

There is no counterpart in modern architecture of the multitude of plastic elements which are at the border line of indoors and outdoors, and are lumped together, not always convincingly, as "garden architecture." This sort of architecture reached perfection in the gardens of the Baroque, in the Moorish gardens of Spain, and in the house gardens of antiquity. It is worth noting that its elements were not of a vegetable sort, but rather built solidly in stone. Where trees and shrubs had been included in the design, these had shed all their individuality and had been trained to imitate architecture.

The contemporary house garden is purely a gardener's idea. Like the parlor of our grandmothers, it is the object of infinite care, but it is of a poor living quality.

Here is an unconventional garden without gardening. The meager vegetation was left untouched. A few walls, posts, screens and pavements were carefully placed to set off the individuality, the "calligraphic subtleties" of some old apple trees, pines and bushes of beach plum.

Sacheverell Sitwell (Arch. Review, March '44) compared my Brazilian house gardens to the classical gardens of Japan. However, I believe that what I had in mind—in Brazil as well as here, in Long Island—is a kind of fragmentary architecture. I have always been fascinated by ruins. Not by the ivy-covered, romantic sort, but by the intimate, classical kind: the roofless houses of antiquity.

Walls. A free-standing wall, plain and simple, with no special task assigned, today is unheard of. In a garden, such a wall assumes the character of sculpture. Moreover, if it is of utmost precision and of a brilliant whiteness, it clashes—as it should—with the natural forms of the vegetation an engenders a gratuitous and continuously changing spectacle of shadows and reflections. And aside from serving as the projection screen for the surrounding plants, the wall creates a sense of order. Three abstract murals compete with the umbrageous phantasmagories.

Plants. An old apple tree pierces one of the walls, lending it (methinks) a peculiar monumental quality. The pergola is reduced to almost linear design and does not intend to be more than abciss and coordinate. A wisteria has taken possession of it in the space of a few months; bamboo shades are hung from it in summer. The wiry appearance of the poles is accentuated by bright colors.

The solarium is an ample room with immaculately white walls, a floor of red bricks, set in sand, and a diminutive lawn. Wall openings were omitted to avoid drafts; the solarium is accessible by stairs only.

This room has become the favorite abode of the family. To the architect who has experimented with walled outdoor rooms in three continents, it seems incomprehensible why the sunbath is not as common as the sauna is in northern countries, or why it should not become a regular adjunct to the bathroom. In any case, it would compensate for the unattractiveness of the climate.

(Continued from page 168, Courtyard Apartment)

Glide-All. Fluorescent tubes over the wardrobes light the cabinet interiors, as well as provide general room illumination. Generous bathroom storage is provided with the wall-to-wall pullman unit and the wall-hung cabinet over the water closet. The oversize shower is Mosaic ceramic tile; the high curb allows it to be used for bathing.

Except for the masonry, all construction is dry wall: wood siding is 1" x 6" T&G Douglas fir; the walls of kitchens and baths are 1/8" Armstrong's cork tile over 3/8" Douglas fir Plypanel. First story floor construction is concrete slab; second floor, 5/8" Douglas fir Plyscord. Finish flooring throughout is Matico gray asphalt tile.

The steel frames are exposed to become the basic element of the architectural expression. Panels between the truss members are 1/4" Transite outside and 1/4" vertical grain Douglas fir plywood inside. Additional features include vent fans in bathrooms, mercury switches, courtyard storage units for garden furniture, tools, etc., built-in TV and telephone provisions, two Utility wall heaters in each unit, chromed metal extrusions on stair nosing and outside corners of cork walls, Formica counter tops, storage closets on stair landings.

(Continued from page 176, Schindler)

For Schindler's flair for mechanical invention was a minor expression of his creativity in pure design. He sometimes talked about "space design." The words have little meaning until one has moved through and walked around one of his buildings. The movement of the observer is an important element in the understanding and enjoyment of his work. For this reason, photographs and drawings fail to reveal the essential character and the uniqueness of his contribution to architecture. Schindler aspired to and achieved more than fine relationships of forms. He composed sequences of forms, patterns of changing relationships in which time and movement were a part. Trite as it may sound, his work had the character of music. He really added a dimension to our concept of space.

It is strange that Schindler had so little recognition here during his lifetime. The lack of recognition was no tragedy to him, but greater renown could have brought him more important commissions. When

he died, a few months ago, in his middle sixties, he was still a young man. His extraordinary zest for living and his capacity for work were unmatched in people half his age in years.

Talbot Hamlin:

Mr. Schindler was the least understood and the least appreciated of all the American pioneers of modern architecture. He was imaginative—creating houses distinguished by remarkable and significant shapes, admirably adapted to their sites; he was an important theoretician and idealist, writing inspiringly on architecture. His indomitable faith in the dynamism and creative force of modern architecture brought cheer and hope to many architects and designers in the depression period. In future years his imaginative cubism, his daring creation of dynamic architectural forms, and his many writings will, I believe, be more and more seen as the truly important contributions of the 20th century architecture that they are.

Richard Neutra:

A creative thinker and prolific pioneering practitioner in architectural space play, R.M. Schindler was equally prominent in the ingenuity of conceiving structure or selecting material and bending it to ever new uses.

William Wilson Wurster:

R.M. Schindler was a creative artist. I only had the pleasure of meeting him once, but I've never forgotten his friendliness. Mr. Schindler's contribution I have always felt was in the imaginative use of common materials in an uncommon way. Thus one had the feeling of the honest approach of a peasant, but at no time naive. His things have an esthetic sturdiness and pleasure never depended upon their brittleness of over-neat workmanship. The depth of his influence, one could say in praise, exceeded any series of architectural jobs.

Harwell Hamilton Harris:

To R.M. Schindler each design was an exercise in the development of an idea. The idea might be a system of construction, the shape of a space, or a way of living. Its expression was unexpected because it was logical. The unexpected—the surprise—was one of the delights of his work. He loved to use common materials and methods for uncommon ends. Logic became the tool of a sense of humor as well as a remarkable architectural imagination. The result was a delightful architectural play. For me he was the first to point out in the connection of a frame, or a method of flashing, a theme sufficient to regulate an entire composition. It led me to look to each new job as a new set of circumstances, and to expect new forms to emerge naturally from it.

Philip C. Johnson:

R.M. Schindler was among the great pioneers of modern architecture in this country. His work was not only great in itself but had a lasting influence for the good in later modern development. His single minded devotion to the main principles of architecture was extraordinary and should serve as an example to the younger architects of our time.

Juan O'Gorman:

Mr. R.M. Schindler stands out among the European architects who brought modern architecture to America. Today few know the excellent work of R.M. Schindler, who was a modest man and one of the most distinguished and outstanding architects of our time. His great interest and his most important achievements were the planning and building of small houses at a minimum cost, but nevertheless beautiful in their proportions and use of materials, a great quality within the turmoil of commercial competition of our "marvelous civilization."

Let America be proud to honor him for the service he did for our culture and for the people he worked for.

Let us hope that the posthumous exhibition of his work will give him the fame that he merited during his lifetime, if only the people of the U.S.A. were more sensitive to architecture.

Carol Aronovici:

Rudolph M. Schindler's work has the great merit of embracing instead of enclosing space. The inner part of the enclosure always remained a part of and in harmony with the outer space. Nothing that was within the reach of vision, from the outer lawn to the distant mountains was left out of the concept and rhythm of his buildings. He never succumbed to the platitudes of internationalism and functionalism, but was content to interpret his vision of the new humanism in its proper perspective in relation to the nature of the site, the economy of materials, the personalities of the occupants and the grace of living. As an artist he molded mass and space to the nuances of individualism rather than attempt to mold and stifle individuality for the sake of some fashionable shibboleth. He was one of the few architects of our day who recognized and lived up to the idea that a home is a dwelling place for both body and the soul.

Arthur B. Gallion:

R.M. Schindler worked with an uncommon seriousness and diligence as a creative architect in our time. And his work is more than a memorial; it is a tribute to an architectural genius, encouraging to all who assume responsibility for work of creative significance in our age.

John Rex:

Michael Schindler's great vision, imagination and creative ability made him an outstanding pioneer in contemporary architecture. Breaking with tradition he had the determination and integrity never to vary from his belief and philosophy of planning. Michael Schindler's great talent and insight coupled with his own gentle, patient and warm-hearted knowledge of men enabled him to design some of the first buildings and homes that were truly sympathetic to modern man's needs.

We have followed the trail blazed by Schindler and from this journey can truly appreciate and pay tribute to an artist so far advanced in his own lifetime.

Wayne R. Williams:

If the building concepts of the majority of architects are broader today, it is the result of a few architects who have practiced with imagination and virility. R.M. Schindler was one of the more forceful. His influence will be felt by many who do not even know his name.

Whitney R. Smith:

Few architects combined ingenuity of construction and creative space design as well as R.M. Schindler. The Packard house excels all others of its type.

William S. Beckett:

R.M. Schindler's significance to me is as an architect who practiced his architecture in its complete potential. By virtue of the date of his work alone it has significance. This may only be said of a very few architects practicing today.

His was a full creativity: his work demonstrates his exploration of structure as a basic component of design, his brave experimentation, his all-encompassing attention to detail, and his unfaltering respect for the totality of a building. Each structure evidences conception as organic rather than resolved. This was a sensitive man and architect.

Ultimately and as basis for any final critique, he was a modern architect whose work was his own individual expression. His personal signature is on all his work.

William G. Purcell:

Rudolph Schindler was certainly well focused on functional forms, but his forms were the shape of events acting between man and his implements. Schindler's forms were not the assemblements themselves, as static objects nor were they patterns and contours of self-conscious and self important "design." He kept the "tool-for-living" idea very firmly in hand to provide owners with effective economic and mechanical facilities. He did not demand that the client offer his body and soul for the benefit of experimental shelter-machines and the resulting abstractionist negations. How to help the human being up and out of his domestic and business gadgets, where current esthetic fancies were pleased to let him struggle, was solved by Schindler with characteristic genial wit. He never let his customers get into the trick traps of the push button world in the first place. This keen sense of humor never failed him and his analyses of fashionable esthetics and neo-bozart slicks were offered with good natured cynicism which was both entertaining and irrefutable.

(Continued from page 187, Rico LeBrun)

that, once creatively vital, are accepted unquestioningly as immutable canons. It is Lebrun's hope that architecture, having at its fingertips twentieth century techniques and materials, is ready to accept the challenge of investing buildings with symbols of the spirit. To accomplish this investiture of meaningful symbols in buildings requires painting and sculpture that do more than endorse the structure. The work of art that seeks to go beyond the immediate domain of the building's "function" must involve the spectator profoundly, must surround and contain him. Thus Lebrun's recent pictures oppose linear regularity, staccato rhythms shak-

ing up forms instead of merging imperceptibly into their projected architectural setting. In effect what Lebrun aims to do would be comparable to a Tiepolo bursting the enclosing structure, making the ceiling, for example, open to the sky.

We are at the threshold of a new age in which Man grasps insights and power of transcendental scope. Has not the time come for the sister arts of painting and architecture to provide us with new dimensions in building and visual imagery in keeping with this extraordinary epoch?

(Continued from page 191, Pinwheel House)

each side of the house.

If the day is sunny and warm, the 18' wall slides over to the right, or on two, three, or all four sides, which creates a shady pavilion, with views all around, and a steady breeze. To close the house up for the evening, the 18' wall slides back again, leaving only the 6' wide glass panel in each corner exposed, giving plenty of light, almost 200 sq. ft. of glass area for a 580 sq. ft. room.

The two-story plan was dictated by the obvious economies inherent in a smaller roof area and the space gained between foundation walls. On the lower floor, the house has two very compact bedrooms, utilities, storage room, four closets, a full bath.

It was found that the house was very simple to build and very simple to prefabricate in part. The sliding walls were assembled in a local mill and trucked to the site and hung. Screens were replaced by curtains of nylon mosquito netting, although the house is detailed to receive sliding screens as well. Light steel I-beams for the 12 columns that hold up the house were used in order to brace the sliding walls against the wind when they are in their extended position. Although the walls will not generally be open, or fully open, in any severe storm, it was decided to design the structure to resist wind velocities of considerable strength. The steel columns are 15' long. The section is a 4" by 8" I weighing only 10 lbs. per foot. Some shop fabrication was necessary to prepare the columns to receive wood beams at floor and roof. Each column is set into a 24" diam. steel drum filled with concrete. This footing is 4' deep, so that only 11' of each column appear above grade. The steel was given a rust-preventive shop-coat and then painted black with a metal paint. The solid, plywood-faced panels that are fixed in each wall were designed for lateral bracing of the structure. Plywood was also used in the sub floor and the roof deck. The rigidity of the house under extremely high wind pressures is due to a large extent to the structural qualities of the plywood.

Because the house can be adjusted to any orientation and any view or combination of views, it is a universal vacation house for almost any site.

(Continued from page 201, Felix Candela)

form had yet to be exploited.

Candela educated his senses in direct observation and reasoning, and his writings are filled with references to the superiority of the intuitive approach over handbook engineering methods. "What we need is a structure, not an analysis," he quotes from H. Cross. An observation of the Spanish philosopher, Ortega y Gasset, served as a guiding principle. "Science likes abstractions, and abstractions are always clear. The essential confusion is the concrete vital reality, which is always unique."

In 1939 Candela, a supporter of the Republican Government in Spain, and an architect serving with its army, found it necessary to leave his country, and he went to Mexico to live. There, he says, he threw aside his scruples and made a start building some catenary-shaped cylindrical vaults.

"A picture of the reinforcement of Maillart's shell at the Zurich Exposition gave me a hint of the real behavior of such vaults," he reports.

He executed three shells before the important Cosmic Ray Pavilion, and since then he has designed and built all the various types. His preference for hyperbolic paraboloids is based on their superior economy, but he has executed folded slabs, undulating shells, short and long cylindrical shells, revolution and elliptical domes, and conoids.

Experience has strengthened his belief that the difficult analytical calculations which are still considered necessary to the design of the shell are a myth, born of a blind faith in mathematics.

In the practical world of building the mathematician's truth has proved to be a fallacy. Too many factors are not taken into account; he cites as some the contractions of concrete during curing, temperature differences between points on the structure, and the uneven settling of the foundations due to the fact that construction crews cannot work to a close tolerance. Since extensive analyses can yield only approximate information, and add considerably to the cost, he looks upon them as economically unjustified.

The Iglesia de la Virgen Milagrosa was designed in one week, and an analysis conducted later only as a check.

Had not the art of building made a good account of itself in earlier eras? "The imposing stone vaults of the Gothic cathedrals, and the daring domes of the Renaissance were built without the help of differential calculus but, instead, with a great sense of equilibrium and sound judgment of the play of forces, qualities more necessary indeed to the real builder than full knowledge of mathematical intricacies."

Candela builds no models of his work simply because it is practically impossible to reproduce the real conditions. His models are all carried out life-size.

The Iglesia de la Virgen Milagrosa was the first structure in which Candela had an opportunity to fuse his talents as architect and engineer. An authentic architecture, it blooms out of its own internal order, revealing the mysterious connection between the laws of physics and our esthetic sensibility.

Structurally, it is a series of hyperbolic paraboloidical shells of two heights. Visually it is sculpture of a rich complexity. It has the fancifulness of a flock of Japanese paper birds, but the poetry of its form was conceived as structure not as sculpture.

The logic of the plan is responsible for the lower shells which roof the chapel, at the right of the entrance to the nave. But by introducing smaller forms he has scaled down a portion to the size of man, and the effect is one of measuring his everyday height against his aspirations.

The spirit of the Gothic, which has eluded architects who set out to copy its outwardness, appeared magically for Candela, whose purpose was not to create a style face but to make use of his experiments in shell forms in terms of traditional ecclesiastical architecture. The commission was awarded him in the first place because he builds more economically than any other architect in Mexico today.

In all of Candela's work design and construction are one and the same. It is in the separation of these two that we have sacrificed, he believes, "an intimate combination between structure and expression," which was present in the building of the Middle Ages.

"The professions of architect and engineer were one and the same long ago, and then the title of 'Master Builder' had real significance, but since then their interests have become separate, and in the past century the breach has widened to create a no-man's land on which few dared to walk with assurance. However, on a few occasions someone with sufficient talent and decision has taken his stand there with authority—Maillart and Nervi from one field, and Nowicki and at times Wright from another—and the results have been so extraordinary that one is led seriously to believe that there, finally, lies the looked-for solution to the fundamental problems of our age."

Of this we can be certain: Felix Candela has narrowed that field, to give us some of the most imaginative work of our day, shells of concrete so thin that they appear to have their origin not in engineering but in nature.

Man is capable of many kinds of bravery: the least noted of these are the new structures he builds.

Esther McCoy

(Continued from page 206, Pocket Guide to Architectural Criticism)
of verbiage that has poured forth on the subject of architecture in the last fifty years. No guide, no set of structures can substitute for perceptive reading between the lines. The *Guide* will have served its purpose if it alerts the intelligent layman to the fact that Modern Architecture, like other facets of modern life, is subject to rhetorical special pleading.

Modern Architecture suffers from the absence of cool, tough-minded, discerning, independent criticism. The interested layman must, therefore, be equipped with a more than ordinary semantic sophistication.

P. P. S. Just in case it may have occurred to the reader that no space is given in this *Guide* to "traditionalist critics," the writer felt there was no point in beating a dead dog. The Caretakers of the Royal Mausoleum, as the traditionalists might be called, are there embalmed.

JOHN DYMOCK ENTENZA
1903-1984

Education
Stanford University, Tulane University, University of Virginia

Work History
Preparatory training for the diplomatic service, office of Secretary of Labor, James J. Davis in Washington D.C.
MGM experimental film production unit, under Paul Bern and Irving Pitchel.
Editor and publisher *Arts & Architecture* magazine, 1938 through 1962.
Manager and later President of Plyformed Wood Company under contract to the United States Navy and the Air Corps.
Director, Graham Foundation for Advanced Studies in the Fine Arts, 1960 through 1971.

Boards and Honors
Member, Governor's Council on Regional Planning
Member, Board of Telises (Regional Planning)
Member, California Housing Council for Migratory Workers
Member, Board of the Mental Health Association
Member, Board of the Tamarind Foundation.
Consultant, General Panel Corporation (Konrad Wachsmann, Walter Gropius)
American Editor, Zodiac magazine.
American Delegate, International Art Critics Congress, Brazil, 1959.
Honorary Member, American Institute of Architects, National
Honorary Member, American Institute of Architects, Los Angeles and Chicago Chapters
Distinguished Service Citation, American Institute of Architects 1959 Pacific Rim Convention
Member, later Vice President, Board of Directors, International Design Conference, Aspen, Colorado
Member, Governor's Committee, Illinois Visual Research Projects
Consultant, Board of Reclamation, Department of the Interior
Trustee, Museum of Contemporary Art, Chicago
Trustee, Amon Carter Museum of Western Art, Fort Worth, Texas
Trustee, National Citizens Committee for Broadcasting, New York, New York
1966 Medalist, Yale University School of Architecture
1968, Honorary Doctorate of Laws, Illinois Institute of Technology
Commission Member, Chicago Historical and Architectural Landmark
Executive Committee, Humanities and Arts, Illinois Board of Higher Education.